ENCHANTED
EVENINGS

ENCHANTED EVENINGS

The Broadway Musical from
Show Boat to Sondheim
and Lloyd Webber

SECOND EDITION

Geoffrey Block

OXFORD
UNIVERSITY PRESS
2009

OXFORD
UNIVERSITY PRESS

Oxford University Press, Inc., publishes works that further
Oxford University's objective of excellence
in research, scholarship, and education.

Oxford   New York
Auckland   Cape Town   Dar es Salaam   Hong Kong   Karachi
Kuala Lumpur   Madrid   Melbourne   Mexico City   Nairobi
New Delhi   Shanghai   Taipei   Toronto

With offices in
Argentina   Austria   Brazil   Chile   Czech Republic   France   Greece
Guatemala   Hungary   Italy   Japan   Poland   Portugal   Singapore
South Korea   Switzerland   Thailand   Turkey   Ukraine   Vietnam

Library of Congress Cataloging-in-Publication Data
Block, Geoffrey Holden, 1948–
Enchanted evenings: the Broadway musical from Show Boat
to Sondheim and Lloyd Webber / Geoffrey Block.—2nd ed.
p.   cm.
Includes bibliographical references and index.
ISBN 978-0-19-538400-0 (pbk.)
1. Musicals—New York (State)—New York—History and criticism.   I. Title.
ML1711.8.N3B56 2009
782.1'4097471—dc22   2009003980

 Visit the companion website at: www.oup.com/us/enchantedevenings

1 3 5 7 9 8 6 4 2
Printed in the United States of America
on acid-free paper

First Edition

To the beloved memory of

JOHN EASTBURN BOSWELL ("JEB"), 1947–1994

Best friend, best man,

Godfather to Jessamyn and (in spirit) to Eliza

Second Edition

To the memory of my beloved parents

RUTH BLOCK (1913–2007) AND

STANLEY BLOCK (1906–2008)

Devoted wife and husband to each other, in-laws to Jacqueline,

and grandparents to Jessamyn and Eliza

CONTENTS

PREFACE TO THE
FIRST EDITION

In many ways the preparation of this book brings me back to my child-hood, where Rodgers and Hammerstein as well as Bach and Beethoven were frequent and compatible visitors. I cannot remember a time when my father, a professional jazz violinist and part-time lawyer (before he meta-morphosed into a full-time attorney and part-time classical violinist), was not playing Cole Porter's "Anything Goes" on the piano, invariably in the key of E♭. Like many Americans in the 1950s, our family record library included the heavy shellac 78 R.P.M. boxed album of *South Pacific* with Mary Martin and Ezio Pinza and the lighter 33 R.P.M. cast album of *Carousel* with Jan Clayton and John Raitt. A major event was the arrival of Rodgers and Ham-merstein's *Oklahoma!* and *South Pacific* in their newly released film versions. Keeping in tune with Rodgers and Hammerstein mania, I played every note and memorized many words of the songs contained in *The Rodgers and Ham-merstein Song Book* and read Hammerstein's librettos in the (then) readily obtainable Modern Library edition of *Six Plays by Rodgers & Hammerstein*.[1]

My family was one of the eighteen million to purchase the cast album of *My Fair Lady*, and my sister quickly mastered the dialect and memorized the lyrics for all the roles. With the dawn of the stereo era in the late 1950s, we purchased *The Music Man* to test out our new portable KLH record player.[2] My parents, transplanted New Yorkers who settled near San Francisco, would see the traveling versions of Broadway shows, and by the early 1960s they began to take their offspring along.

Musicals created before the era of Rodgers and Hammerstein and Lerner and Loewe were less known. Only Gilbert and Sullivan and the occasional 1920s operetta were presented as dramatic entities. The songs, however, of many musicals from the 1920s and '30s were heard and played regularly in our community as well as in our home, especially those from *Porgy and Bess*. A memorable event occurred in the sixth grade when a dear family friend from Boston came to visit, sang and played Kern and Hammerstein's "Make Believe," and assisted me in my efforts to compose a small musical of three songs as a creative arts project. Earlier that year I had written a short term paper, "Rodgers and Hammerstein II with Lorenz Hart."

By the time I entered high school I had churlishly abandoned Broadway in favor of Bach, Beethoven, and Ives. As a sophomore I somewhat grudgingly served as rehearsal pianist for *South Pacific* and the following year still more grudgingly played the saxophone and clarinet in the *Guys and Dolls* pit band. Soon even Gershwin was suspect. I had not yet read the philosopher and sociologist Theodor Adorno and the highly acclaimed but decidedly unpopular composer Arnold Schoenberg, both of whom vigorously championed and successfully promoted the view that great art was rightfully destined to be unpopular. Only in retrospect did I realize that an ideological and elitist component was somehow connected to my genuine love of classical or "serious" music. Disdain for the music of the masses followed, including hit Broadway musicals, until and unless this repertory could earn endorsements from respectable sources, such as when Leonard Bernstein compared the Beatles' "She's Leaving Home" from *Sergeant Pepper's Lonely Hearts Club Band* favorably with Schubert.

In the early 1970s graduate students in historical musicology in many programs were strongly discouraged from studying American music of any kind. Instead, my colleagues and I at Harvard dutifully learned to decipher medieval notation and researched such topics as the life and works of King Henry VIII's Flemish-born court composer Philip van Wilder, Haydn's *opera seria*, and what really happened at the first performance of *Rite of Spring*. A research paper on the chronology and compositional process of Beethoven's piano concertos evolved into a dissertation and inaugurated my lifetime desire to understand how compositions of all types initially take shape and the practical as well as artistic reasons behind their revision.

These activities did not prevent me from stumbling on a free ticket to *Kiss Me, Kate*, which to my surprise I enjoyed immensely, despite a negative predisposition. My dormant love for Broadway musicals would receive additional rekindling when, several years later, I found myself the musical director in a private secondary school in Ojai, California, selecting a musical to produce and choosing *Kiss Me, Kate* to everyone's enjoyment and delight, including mine. In my second year at The Thacher School I anticipated *Crazy for You*, the 1992 musical based on *Girl Crazy*, with my own assemblage of freely interpolated Gershwin songs mixed with songs from the "dated" 1930 show—a triumph of accessibility over authenticity. By the end of that year I completed my doctorate, a milestone that somehow liberated me to explore American popular music of all types.

By then I had witnessed a broadcast in which Stephen Sondheim and conductor André Previn conversed with extraordinary articulateness about what a musical can accomplish.[3] Increasingly, stage and film musicals of both recent and ancient vintage occupied a major and passionate role in my life. After teaching a sequence of one-month "winterim" courses on American musical theater at the University of Puget Sound, including one in which students collaborated to create an original musical, I began to teach a Survey of American Musical Theater course first during alternate years and later annually. When faced with the dearth of usable textbooks, I began writing one of my own in the late 1980s. The book would, of course, correspond to what I had been teaching, a musical-by-musical study beginning with *Show Boat* that focused on the so-called Golden Era from the 1930s to the late 1950s, with a survey of Sondheim to round out the semester. You are now holding this book.

Before the 1990s, books on Broadway musicals were almost without exception written by theater historians and critics. For the most part these journalistic accounts typically covered a large number of musicals somewhat briefly and offered a useful and entertaining mixture of facts, gossip, and criticism. What they did not try to do is address what happens *musically* or how songs interact with lyrics within a dramatic context.[4]

Most books on the Broadway musical provided biographical profiles of principal composers and lyricists and plot summaries of popular musicals or those judged artistically significant. Some authors went considerably beyond these parameters, for example, Gerald Bordman by his comprehensiveness and Lehman Engel by focusing more selectively on critical topics and other issues such as adaptation of literary sources.[5] Two of the musicals surveyed in the present volume, *Show Boat* and *Porgy and Bess*, have inspired book-length monographs, and several musicals and their creators have received rigorously thoughtful scholarly, bibliographic, and critical attention. The fruits of this activity will be duly acknowledged in what follows.[6]

With few exceptions the musicological community studiously ignored the Broadway terrain. In the 1990s two important books emphasized (or "privileged") music for the first time: Joseph P. Swain's *The Broadway Musical: A Critical and Musical Survey* (1990), a study of selected musicals from *Show Boat* to *Sweeney Todd*, and Stephen Banfield's more specialized study,

Sondheim's Broadway Musicals (1993).[7] Swain's valuable survey contains a great deal of perceptive musical and dramatic criticism and analysis. Nevertheless, Swain only rarely tries to place the discussion in a historical, social, or political context, he presents virtually no documentary history of a musical, and he does not address the questions of how and why musicals evolved as they did, either before opening night or in revival. Most general readers will also find Swain's analysis, which deals primarily with harmony, too technical to be easily understood. In contrast to Swain, Banfield, who focuses on a body of work by one significant composer-lyricist, does address compositional history and offers a multivalent and less autonomous approach; additionally, his sophisticated and frequently dense musical and dramatic analysis successfully incorporates techniques borrowed from literary criticism. Building on the solid edifices constructed by Swain and Banfield, the present book attempts to offer a musical and dramatic discussion more accessible to readers unfamiliar with analytical terminology.

Two important books on European opera have influenced the ensuing discussion of American musicals and merit special mention and gratitude here: Joseph Kerman's *Opera as Drama* and Paul Robinson's *Opera & Ideas*.[8] Kerman's unflinching insistence on music's primary role in defining character, generating action, and establishing atmosphere results in a somewhat sparse assemblage of canonic masterpieces. However, his brilliant overview of opera with its powerful guiding principle, "the dramatist is the composer," can be fruitfully applied to Broadway, even to those works that resolutely reject Kerman's model of a major operatic musical masterpiece. Robinson's accessible yet subtle survey of six operas (one each by Mozart, Rossini, Berlioz, Verdi, Wagner, and Strauss) and of dramatic meaning in the two Schubert song cycles offers imaginative and convincing insights on the power of texted music to express emotional and intellectual nuance. Both studies display a standard of excellence that might serve and inspire nearly any serious study of dramatic music, including the Broadway musical.

A third book on opera, Peter Kivy's *Osmin's Rage*, supplies valuable philosophical underpinning for a discussion on music and text.[9] Kivy's distinctions between the opposite principles of "textual realism" (music that "sets meanings, not words") and "opulent adornment" (music that "sets words, not meanings") are particularly helpful. The tensions between these two principles are embodied in the "song and dance" musicals (composed mainly but by no means exclusively in the 1920s and '30s) that feature "opulent adornment," and the so-called integrated musicals, the Rodgers and Hammerstein models of "textual realism" that gained commercial success, critical stature, and cultural hegemony beginning in the 1940s.

In the recent past intense ideological differences have been solidified. In one camp are those who argue that musicals are at their best when fully integrated and aspiring toward nineteenth-century European tragic opera; in another are those who relish nonintegrated and nonoperatic musical comedies. The contrasting perspectives of Swain and Banfield offer strong advocates for each side. Swain, who claims to disparage the taxonomic differences between opera and Broadway shows, nonetheless invariably places the latter, especially musicals that eschew their tragic potential, on a lower echelon. Thus for Swain, "though a number of its best plots have offered opportunities for tragic composition," the Broadway musical provides a litany of "missed chances and unanswered challenges."[10] Even *West Side Story*, the only musical that Swain unhesitatingly designates a masterpiece (in part because a central character achieves the heights of tragedy when he dies singing), falls short of operatic tragedy when Maria speaks rather than sings her response to the death of her beloved Tony.

Banfield, sympathetic to a subject (Sondheim) who is rarely "trying to challenge opera on its own territory," argues that in musicals, in contrast to operas that are through-sung, music "can often not just move in and out of the drama but in and out of itself, and is more dramatically agile...than in most opera."[11] For Banfield, *West Side Story* keeps faith with Bernstein's desire to avoid "falling into the 'operatic trap,'" and Maria's final speech works perfectly.[12]

Among other juicy bones of contention are the conflicts between popularity and critical acclaim, authenticity and accessibility, opulent adornment and textual realism, artistic autonomy and social and political contextuality, and nonintegrated versus integrated musical ideals. This preface has introduced some of these issues and critical quagmires that will be reintroduced in chapter 1 and developed in subsequent chapters. Neutrality is neither always possible nor always desirable to achieve, especially on the subject of critical relationships between music and text and music and drama. My general intent, however, is to articulate the merits as well as the flaws of opposing arguments. In the court of free intellectual inquiry, more frequently than not, at least two sides are competent to withstand scrutiny and trial.

Tacoma, Wash.   G. B.
January 1997

A NEW PREFACE

Broadway's "Golden Age"

Still popular with audiences young and old, the musicals explored in *Enchanted Evenings* have not vanished from our stages or our consciousness. In fact, the situation is just the reverse. Judging by the frequency and perennial popularity of revivals (the practice of restaging favorite musicals from the past) and the competitiveness of the revival category at the annual Tony Awards (Broadway's Oscars), the Broadway musical has evolved into one of America's greatest and most distinctive cultural institutions as well as an opportunity for new work. Increasingly, classic musicals have received serious critical scrutiny by directors with wide-ranging visions, and audiences from all over the world flock to see and experience this unique American (and sometimes British) contribution to popular culture. If there is a Broadway Museum, and I think there is, the musicals you will read about in *Enchanted Evenings* occupy a major wing. In fact, in the years immediately prior to, during, and since the period I wrote *Enchanted Evenings* all of the shows I discussed continued to receive attention in high-profile revivals, the vast majority on Broadway as well as elsewhere. In addition, revival recordings and reissues with new and original casts or other recordings in meticulous scholarly reconstructions for some of the older models were also made for most of these shows.

Here are some highlights of the stage resurrections since 1980 of shows featured in the first edition of *Enchanted Evenings* arranged chronologically by show. No show from this edition is absent from the list.[1]

- *Show Boat*: The acclaimed (and controversial) Broadway revival staged by Harold Prince (1994)

- *Anything Goes*: Broadway revival at the Vivian Beaumont (1987); London revival (1989); Royal National Theatre revival in London (2003); London revival (2005)

- *Porgy and Bess*: Glyndebourne Opera staged by Trevor Nunn (1986); New York City Opera (2000 and 2002); Los Angeles Opera (2007)

- *The Cradle Will Rock*: Off-Broadway production directed by John Houseman and starring Patti Lupone (1983); feature film about the making of the show against the backdrop of other turbulent events in art and politics in the 1930s, directed by Tim Robbins (1999)

- *On Your Toes*: Broadway revival directed by George Abbott (1983)

- *Pal Joey*: New York City Center's *Encores! Great American Musicals in Concert* (1995); Broadway run at Studio 54, with a rewritten book and added songs from other Rodgers and Hart shows (2008)

- *Lady in the Dark*: New York City Center's *Encores!* (1994); London premiere (1997) followed by major performances in Japan and Philadelphia

- *One Touch of Venus*: Goodspeed Opera House (1987); New York City Center's *Encores!* (1995); three productions mounted by Discovering Lost Musicals Charitable Trust (1992–2000); BBC broadcast (1995); London premiere at The King's Head Theatre in 2001 (a production that failed to go beyond the workshop stage for a New York performance two weeks after September 11); Opera North in Leeds (2004); 42nd Street Moon staging in San Francisco (2007)

- *Kiss Me, Kate*: Broadway revival directed by Michael Blakemore (881 performances) (1999–2003); London revival (2001); Italian version in Bologna (2007)

- *Carousel*: Directed for London and Broadway by Nicholas Hytner (1994); London revival (2008)

- *Guys and Dolls*: Long-running Broadway revival (1,143 performances) starring Nathan Lane, not coincidentally named for its star comic Nathan Detroit (1992–94); long-running London revival (2005–07); Broadway revival (2009)

- *The Most Happy Fella*: Broadway revival (1992); New York City Opera (2006)

- *My Fair Lady*: Broadway revival (1981); Broadway revival (1993); London revival (2001)

- *West Side Story*: Broadway revival (1980); London revival (1998); Hong Kong production (with lyrics in Cantonese) (2000); Bregenz Festival, Austria (in German) (2003 and 2004); London revival (2008); Montreal revival (in French) (2008); Philippine production (2008); Broadway revival directed by Arthur Laurents which includes significant dialogue and singing in Spanish (2009)

Today the American musical also thrives as a burgeoning subdiscipline in musicology and a significant topic of study across disciplinary boundaries. This is a relatively new phenomenon. When I embarked on *Enchanted Evenings* in the early 1990s, historical musicology had not yet found the Broadway musical a fertile grazing land. Musical theater historians Gerald Bordman (in a series of Oxford volumes), and the conductor and influential musical theater workshop director Lehman Engel wrote knowledgeably and engagingly about musicals, although neither seriously engaged their *musical* component.[2] In *The American Musical Theater*, first published in 1967, Engel also offered a paradigm of "workable principles" that reveal what made certain shows "models of excellence."[3] In Engel's view, nearly all great musicals were a product of a "Golden Age" that started with *Pal Joey* (1940) and ended with *Fiddler on the Roof* (1964). For the 1975 second edition, Engel found two worthy Sondheim shows to add to the list, *Company* (1970) and *A Little Night Music* (1973). Although *Cabaret* (1966) did not make the cut, Engel singled out this work for distinction as his sole "strong runner-up to the list of 'best' shows."[4]

The booming cultural canon wars of the 1990s brought about the breakdown of classical canons in literature and the arts. It also led to the formation of new ones, albeit under various pseudonyms and disguises. Despite the increasing postmodern discontent among scholars and even some musical-theater lovers with the idea of a prescribed list of canonic "masterpieces," Broadway surveys, including scholarly ones such as Joseph P. Swain's *The Broadway Musical: A Critical and Musical Survey* (Oxford, 1990), generally followed Engel and without apparent collusion favored the same small group of shows.[5] Whatever its intentions, the overlapping between one list and another gave the appearance that a Broadway canon had emerged, despite protestations to the contrary and however unwelcome. *Enchanted Evenings* focused on a representative few of the usual canonic suspects, starting with *Show Boat* (outside Engel's list but the starting point for many others) and ending with *West Side Story*. As an epilogue, I added one post–*West Side Story* chapter, a survey of Sondheim that touched on *Follies* and *Sunday in the Park with George*.

New Broadway Scholarship

Aside from correcting some errors—such as the perpetuation of the unfounded rumor that *Carousel*'s "A Real Nice Clambake" was derived from an unused *Oklahoma!* song "A Real Nice Hayride"—and other minor updating and clarifications, I have left chapters 1–12 of the first edition largely unchanged. Were I writing these chapters for the first time, no doubt I would do some things differently. For example, the controversy over the two Kurt Weills, the German Weill versus the American Weill, of pressing concern in the early 1990s and a division partially reconciled in the first edition, is now a nonissue. Just as Germany gradually became unified in the 1990s, so did Weill. On the other hand, the notion of the "integrated" musical has become so questionable and contentious that the new protocol is to problematize the term or at least to place it in quotation marks (what Richard Taruskin calls scare quotes) to mark the increasing discomfort with the term. Since I did already problematize the idea of the integrated musical to some extent in the first edition and since I later addressed the issue in a separate essay, I decided not to dig up these bones of contention further.[6] By letting these now wide-awake dogs lie in the first edition chapters, I am acknowledging that in these instances musical theater historians, like the musicals they study, reflect their own time in their efforts to serve our understanding of the past.

In the two new chapters on film adaptation (chapters 8 and 14) and the Epilogue chapters (chapter 15 and 16), however, I have called attention to some of the exciting new scholarship that has appeared since the mid-1990s. In the Epilogue, for example, I revisit the notion of the integrated musical as it evolves into what has become known as the concept musical (another controversial notion also commonly placed in quotation marks) and the still-more problematic, but less discussed, "totally integrated" approach common to the megamusical. Since the quality and quantity of bibliographic, scholarly, and critical material on the Broadway musical has grown impressively, even exponentially, over the last decade, I was not able to take full advantage of the new research and thinking on the musicals discussed in the first edition. The expanded Bibliography, which includes some of this unincorporated literature, will point the way to new directions and possibilities.

As in the past, much of this new work emphasizes biography, social history, and the librettos of musicals without addressing how the *music* works with words and stories. I have addressed some of the negative ramifications of this trend in a review essay published in 2004.[7] In contrast to the isolated exceptions that precede the first edition of *Enchanted Evenings*, however, many studies do now seriously engage with music and music's interaction with lyrics and narratives.[8]

Another noticeable trend among the many books that have appeared since the mid-1990s is the relative absence of attention, or sympathy, to musicals that arrived after the end of the so-called Golden Age in the mid-1960s. In an "Omnibus Review" of five significant books in the field published between 2003 and 2005, for example, Charles Hamm notes "an almost complete absence in these books of meaningful commentary on American musicals of the past three decades."[9] When books do not ignore the musicals of the last generation (other than Sondheim), the tone frequently changes from respect to disdain, with special xenophobic antipathy reserved for the imported megamusicals of Andrew Lloyd Webber (*Cats, Phantom*), the team of Alain Boublil and Claude-Michel Schönberg (*Les Misérables* and *Miss Saigon*), and the Godfather who produced this quartet of box office juggernauts, Cameron Macintosh.[10] Another assumption governing many Broadway surveys and other recent scholarship is that anything backed by Disney cannot be good, despite the fact that *Beauty and the Beast* (1994) and the still-running *The Lion King* (1997), directed and designed by Julie Taymor, currently stand as the fifth and eighth most popular Broadway musicals of all time.

Among the many new books in the field published during the past decade or so, major work has been published on several of the musicals featured in the first edition of *Enchanted Evenings*. Biographies, autobiographies, critical studies, publications of letters and lyrics, and other important books and essays have appeared to inform and enlighten the life and work of many major figures and shows and offer new information and ideas to those introduced in acts I and II.[11] Here are a few samples:

- *Show Boat*: Stephen Banfield includes an important analytical and critical study of *Show Boat* in his book, *Jerome Kern*, and Todd Decker has begun to publish the fruits of his archival work on *Show Boat*.[12]

- *Porgy and Bess*: Howard Pollack's monumental life and works study of *George Gershwin* devotes nearly one hundred pages to multiple aspects of this important work from its genesis and production history to revivals, recordings, and films. I have also had the privilege of reading Larry Starr's insightful chapter on this work that will soon be readily available.[13]

- *Lady in the Dark* and *Oklahoma!*: In 2007, Oxford University Press published bruce d. mcclung's award-winning "biography" of *Lady in the Dark*, published by Oxford University Press, a study that expands and offers new insights on the research of earlier articles I was able to use in the first edition. Although I have chosen to focus on *Carousel* rather than *Oklahoma!*, I would be remiss if I did not single out Tim Carter's exceptionally well-researched archival study of *Oklahoma!* published by Yale University Press, also in 2007.[14] Both books are models for future studies of individual musicals.

- Thomas L. Riis has added considerably to our knowledge of *Guys and Dolls* and *The Most Happy Fella* in his recent book on Frank Loesser.[15]

- Scott Miller's three volumes containing thirty-four essays on musicals (1996–2001), Raymond Knapp's two-volume collection of essays on thirty-eight individual stage musicals, ten musical films, and one television musical (2005–2006), and Joseph P. Swain's 1990 survey of sixteen musicals (which includes a new chapter on *Les Misérables* and a new concluding essay in its second edition published in 2002) also complement and expand on many of the shows discussed in the two editions of *Enchanted Evenings* among other shows.[16]

Stage versus Screen

For good or ill, many first experience Broadway musicals through film adaptations, which, no matter how faithful to their stage sources (not always a plus), remain distinct and even contradictory entities. The congruities and distinctions between stage and screen versions of the shows we love merit close study. In the first edition of *Enchanted Evenings*, however, I did not devote much attention to these film adaptations. I have tried to fill in this lacuna in the second edition with two new chapters on the film adaptations of musicals featured in act I and act II, a discussion of the 2007 Tim Burton *Sweeney Todd* with Johnny Depp in the greatly expanded Sondheim chapter, and a discussion of Joel Schumacher's *Phantom of the Opera* film adaptation in 2004 in the newly written chapter on Lloyd Webber. Like Tolstoy's unhappy families, nearly all the stage musicals featured in the first edition have suffered (and occasionally enjoyed) a musical film adaptation, and in these new film chapters and portions of other chapters I write about most of them. Existing material on these films tend to focus on behind-the-scene stories and casting gossip rather than on how these adaptations altered or added to the stage shows. These surveys also rarely discuss how the nature of film media—and surrounding ideologies—moved directors and producers to treat the stage originals in some cases as expendable and in others as sacrosanct. The second edition of *Enchanted Evenings* will engage these neglected issues.

Some of the film adaptations discussed in chapter 8 are difficult to obtain. One of these is the 1936 film version of *Anything Goes* with rising film star Bing Crosby and its already risen stage star, Ethel Merman. Another is Samuel Goldwyn's unfairly maligned eightieth and final film of 1959, *Porgy and Bess*, directed by Otto Preminger and starring Sidney Poitier and Dorothy Dandridge in the title roles. Despite numerous infelicities and distortions, both films are well worth the effort it might take to locate them. In contrast, some of the film adaptations discussed in chapter 14 are probably better known than their stage versions. Prime specimens in this category include the Academy Award–winning musical film adaptations of *My Fair Lady* with Audrey Hepburn as Eliza Doolittle and Broadway's original Henry Higgins, Rex Harrison, and *West Side Story*, a frequent visitor to high schools all over America to complement the study of *Romeo and Juliet*. What are we seeing (and hearing) when we see these films? What are we missing?

The film chapters and remarks on the *Sweeney Todd* and *The Phantom of the Opera* film adaptations will address these and other questions, including how the plots, scripts, songs, and Broadway casts have been altered, what was cut, what was retained, and why. Some of the films explored, while not without controversy, were financially and critically successful in their own day and remain well known and loved in ours. Until the 1950s, the producers who controlled the studios and their contracted stars and songwriters preferred infidelity over allegiance to Broadway stage sources. From the 1930s through the 1950s all films were also subject to the Hays Production Code, which enforced a stricter view than Broadway censors of what was proper for a song lyric or a plot. This alternative universe explains the expurgations of Cole Porter's famously adult lyrics in the film adaptations of both *Anything Goes* and *Kiss Me, Kate* and the disposal of Vera Simpson's husband from the plot so that her affair with Pal Joey would not be an adulterous one. Nearly twenty years earlier Broadway audiences were already free to experience and relish this unsavory material. Before the 1960s had ended, Hollywood had achieved parity with Broadway on the degree of unsavoriness permitted.

Despite the liberties they often take with their stage sources (Kim Kowalke refers to most film adaptations as "generic deformation"), the films do not invariably suffer by comparison.[17] Take the 1936 *Show Boat*, in which, unusually, the authors were able to exert some creative control, including the use of a screenplay by Hammerstein. Here, the new songs were all by Hammerstein and Kern and the creators of these songs were the same people who helped make the thoughtful and imaginative changes necessary to adhere to the unofficial but binding "two hour" rule operative from the 1930s through the 1950s. Arriving a few years after the 1932 New York revival, the film featured timeless performances by Charles Winninger and Helen Morgan, reprising their stage roles of Cap'n Andy and Julie LaVerne, and Paul Robeson, the actor originally intended to play Joe. The result was a film that inspired Kern scholar Stephen Banfield to make the case that the film's dramatic structure constitutes an *improvement* of the problematic original Broadway second act.[18]

The 1936 *Anything Goes* adaptation may have cut or mutilated much of Porter, but it does give audiences a chance to see the original Ethel Merman in her prime and fine film portrayals of Billy Crocker by the young Bing Crosby, and the character of Moon by Charlie Ruggles. It also delivers a surprising amount of the original Broadway libretto, which is much funnier than later revisionists give it credit for. Most of the films that adapted Broadway shows did *something* right, and we will gain a better understanding about the films, their sources, and ourselves from watching them—as long as we do not rest our evaluation solely on their fidelity to the stage works we hold dear.

Film adaptations of the Golden Age musicals, most of which were released about a decade after their Broadway debuts, tend to be more faithful to their original plots, scripts, and songs, and despite some deleted and rearranged dialogue and song cuts, the new songs (e.g., in the *Kiss Me, Kate* and *Guys and Dolls* adaptations) are almost invariably those of the Broadway songwriters. In addition to discussing their relative fidelity and completeness, the film chapters will address the practice of voice dubbing and various less noticeable technological changes that manipulate and transform live theater into the deceptively more realistic film medium. Some of these films have exerted a profound effect on how audiences have come to appreciate the stage originals, and these chapters will address this historical legacy as well.

Sources on *West Side Story* (to conclude with a particularly well-known example) seldom neglect to mention that it was the film version rather than the stage version that catapulted this show into universal popular consciousness. Indeed, the 1961 film, co-directed by Robert Wise and Jerome Robbins, came within one award of a clean Academy Awards sweep, winning ten out of a possible eleven awards. Despite a few conspicuous changes in the song order, all the original *West Side Story* songs are present and accounted for (unlike virtually every preceding film adaptation of a musical). Also in marked contrast to most Hollywood film adaptations of Broadway from the 1930s to the 1950s, no songs were added, either by studio composers on contract or by Leonard Bernstein, the composer. Although Robbins, the original director and choreographer of the stage version, was fired from the film after directing the Prologue for his inability to maintain a financially sound production schedule, most of the choreography that appears on screen is faithful to Robbins's vision and that of original and film co-choreographer Peter Gennaro.

The love versus hate theme of Romeo and Juliet carries over into the contrasting reactions this (and other) film adaptations inspire. Some film critics loved the Robbins-Wise translation from stage to screen. Arthur Knight, in the *Saturday Review*, considered it "a triumphant work of art"; Stanley Kauffmann went even further when he proclaimed the adaptation "the best film musical ever made."[19] On the other hand, an uncharacteristically grumpy Pauline Kael did not even like the dancing and asked, "How can so many critics have fallen for all this frenzied hokum."[20] Love it or hate it, the film remains one of the most memorable film adaptations of a Broadway show.

Enchanted Evenings: *A Textbook Example?*

In the Preface to the First Edition I relate what brought me to write *Enchanted Evenings*. I described the role musicals played in my childhood and adolescence, my rejection of musicals as unworthy of my love, and my return to the fold after completing a dissertation on the genesis and compositional process of Beethoven's early piano concertos. I also explain how this book was the first to combine traditional musicological practices, such as the study of primary manuscripts, with a serious discussion of how musicals took shape in the minds of their creators and how the music in musicals dramatically enhances words and stories. My goal was to write a book that I wanted to write and at the same time a book that corresponded to what I wanted to teach in my course, The Broadway Musical. Although most of the musicals I chose to write about would generally be classified among the usual suspects, others (e.g., *The Cradle Will Rock, One Touch of Venus,* and *The Most Happy Fella*) might be considered idiosyncratic. Even when dealing with such an essential component as Rodgers and Hammerstein, I felt free to include Rodgers's personal favorite, simply because it also interested and moved me more than, say, *Oklahoma!* The book was my party, and I could cry over *Carousel* if I wanted to.

Increasingly, however, the first edition seemed in need of some updating to better serve a general audience. It also constituted an incomplete reflection of what I covered in my course in a given semester. Long before Johnny Depp came along, a Broadway course without *Sweeney Todd* seemed unthinkable. For years I have also spent a week on *The Phantom of the Opera,* now included prominently in the second edition. Although I rarely fail to single out Engel's runner-up *Cabaret* in my course, unfortunately space did not permit me to give this show or the important career of John Kander and Fred Ebb (almost, but not quite brought to a halt by the death of Ebb in 2004) the attention they merit.[21]

In preparing a second edition, I soon realized I would need to neglect other major shows by those who followed the composers and lyricists who starred in the first edition, Jerome Kern, Cole Porter, Richard Rodgers and Lorenz Hart, Marc Blitzstein, Kurt Weill, Rodgers and Oscar Hammerstein, Frank Loesser, Alan Jay Lerner and Frederic Loewe, and Leonard Bernstein, and in the process featured roles by major directors and choreographers, including George Abbott, George Balanchine, Agnes de Mille, Moss Hart, George S. Kaufman, Rouben Mamoulian, and Jerome Robbins. Nearly fifty years have gone by since the Rodgers and Hammerstein generation passed the torch to a new generation starting in the late 1950s with Jerry Bock and Sheldon Harnick and then moving into the early 1960s with Cy Coleman, Jerry Herman, John Kander and Fred Ebb, Stephen Sondheim, and Charles Strouse; the 1970s with Marvin Hamlisch, Andrew Lloyd Webber, and Stephen Schwartz; the 1980s with Alain Boublil and Claude-Michel Schönberg, William Finn, Alan Menken and Howard Ashman, and Maury Yeston; the 1990s and 2000s with Jason Robert Brown, Stephen Flaherty and Lynn Ahrens, Adam Guettel, Michael John LaChuisa, Jonathan Larson, and Jeanine Tesori. The above list is by no means exhaustive.

With the exception of the Sondheim–Lloyd Webber Epilogue and some attention to Hal Prince (who as the director of both *Sweeney Todd* and *The Phantom of the Opera* successfully bridged the divide between these central musical figures) and James Lapine, the second edition leaves most of the lacunae unfilled. Nevertheless, my intention and hope is that this new edition will serve readers at least a little more adequately and usefully. For those who arrived on Broadway through Hollywood (and for those who want to know thine enemy), the two new chapters on film adaptations and the discussions of the *Sweeney Todd* and *Phantom of the Opera* films in the greatly expanded Sondheim and entirely new Lloyd Webber chapters could perhaps provide a point of access and lead to greater understanding and appreciation of both stage and screen musicals.

When *Enchanted Evenings* appeared in 1997, Lloyd Webber's *Cats*, directed by Trevor Nunn, was on the verge of surpassing Michael Bennett and Marvin Hamlisch's *A Chorus Line* as Broadway's longest running show, and *Phantom* stood in fourth place behind the then still running *Les Misérables, Cats*, and *A Chorus Line* on the all-time Broadway Hit Parade. Other shows by the popular French and British invaders, *Les Misérables* and *Miss Saigon* (lyrics by Boublil, music by Schönberg, and produced by Cameron Mackintosh), *Phantom* (Lloyd Webber, also produced by Mackintosh), and *Sunset Boulevard* (Lloyd Webber, directed by Nunn) were in the process of extending their runs, in some cases for more than a decade.

As I write this new preface, *Phantom* stands alone as the reigning champion, followed by *Cats*, "*Les Miz*," *Chorus Line*, and two shows new to the Broadway scene twelve years ago, the *Chicago* revival and *The Lion King*. Musicals that arrived about the time of *Enchanted Evening*'s first edition or since have both begun and ended some of the longest runs in Broadway history (see "The Top Forty Greatest Hit Musicals from 1920 to 2008 in the online website www.oup .com/us/enchantedevenings—the numbers in parentheses refer to their current place in this list): *Beauty and the Beast* (5), *Rent* (6), *Hairspray* (16), *The Producers* (17), *Cabaret* (Revival) (18), *Smokey Joe's Café* (24), *Aida* (28), *Monty Python's Spamalot* (35), *Jekyll & Hyde* (37), and *42nd Street* (Revival) (38). Another trio of megahit shows that opened after *Enchanted Evenings* are still running, one or more of which may reach the Top Broadway 10 by the time they eventually close their curtains: *Mamma Mia!* (13), *Avenue Q* (22), and *Wicked* (23).

While these shows have attracted large audiences, Sondheim's shows continued to enjoy greater critical prestige. In 1993, Sondheim became the subject of the first major musicological study of a Broadway composer, Stephen Banfield's *Sondheim's Broadway Musicals*. Five years later the American Musicological Society national meeting in Boston devoted a special evening session to Sondheim. Lloyd Webber's musicals have gradually attracted theater scholars and musicologists as well, albeit far fewer than the legions of literary and dramatic critics, cultural historians, and sociologists in addition to the many musicologists attracted to the work of Sondheim. The chapters on Sondheim and Lloyd Webber will try to shed light on why there exists such a deep chasm between the ways audiences, critics, and theater historians have assessed these two major contributors to the American musical.

Audiences did not know it at the time but by 1997 both Sondheim and Lloyd Webber had completed most of their Broadway work.[22] Their most recent New York successes, Sondheim and Lapine's *Passion* and Lloyd Webber's *Sunset Boulevard*, both arriving in 1994, had also recently closed. It turns out that the years since the first edition of *Enchanted Evenings* marked the beginning of the Post-Sondheim and Post–Lloyd Webber Era, a subject for future books by future authors. Meanwhile, the contrasting achievements and reputations of Sondheim and Lloyd Webber and the issues these important Broadway figures raise (e.g., tradition vs. modernity and popularity vs. critical acclaim) will serve in this second edition of *Enchanted Evenings* as worthy representatives of the Broadway story beyond *West Side Story*.

To quote Cinderella's opening and closing lines in *Into the Woods*, "I wish."

Tacoma, Wash.   G. B.
January 2009

ACKNOWLEDGMENTS

Without more than a little help from parents, family, friends, teachers and professors, colleagues, students, readers and editors, librarians and archivists and the collections they serve, and copyright owners and their assistants and lawyers, this book could not have been written. I am glad for this opportunity to thank some of the institutions and people that contributed to this collaborative process.

Collections in the New York Public Library (Loesser), Yale University (Porter, Weill), the State Historical Society of Wisconsin (Blitzstein, Moss Hart, Sondheim), the Kurt Weill Foundation (Weill), and the Library of Congress (Gershwin, Kern, Loewe, Porter, Rodgers, and Weill) were indispensable in my research. Of the many who facilitated my use of these priceless holdings I would like to thank individually Harold L. Miller of the State Historical Society of Wisconsin, David Farneth and Joanna C. Lee of The Kurt Weill Foundation, Victor Cardell and Kendall Crilly of Yale University, and especially Raymond A. White of the Library of Congress, for sharing his time and knowledge so generously.

For special kindnesses I would like to identify and thank the following: Louis H. Aborn, President, Tams-Witmark; Tom Briggs, Director, The Rodgers and Hammerstein Theatre Library; Tom Creamer, Dramaturg, The Goodman Theater; Marty Jacobs and Marguerite Lavin of the Museum of the City of New York; David Leopold, Al Hirschfeld's representative at the Margo Feiden Galleries; and Roberta Staats and Robert H. Montgomery of the Cole Porter Musical and Literary Property Trusts. A grant from the National Endowment for the Humanities in 1990 enabled me to research and draft several chapters, and the University of Puget Sound provided generous financial and other assistance at several stages over the past decade. I am also grateful for the expertise and helpfulness of Oxford University Press, especially my editor, Maribeth Payne, her assistant, Soo Mee Kwon, production editor Joellyn M. Ausanka, and copy editor Paul Schlotthauer.

Jacqueline Block, Andrew Buchman, and Richard Lewis read portions of various early drafts, offered useful advice and encouragement, and helped me to consolidate central ideas as well as many details. In later stages several reviewers offered valuable suggestions both large and small that I was able to incorporate into the final draft. Throughout I was guided by the wise counsel of my friend, colleague, and "ideal reader" (i.e., intelligent, curious, and challenging, but not necessarily a musician), Michael Veseth, Professor of Economics.

The following people also provided much-needed information, services, or support: Marcie Bates, Ronald L. Blanc, Abba Bogin, John E. Boswell, J. Peter Burkholder, Theodore S. Chapin, Tara Corcoran, Christopher Davis, Lee Davis, Denise Dumke, Sarah Dunlop, Arthur Elias, Hugh Fordin, April Franks, Peter P. Mc.N. Gates, Rosemarie Gawelko, Peter Greenfield, David Grossberg, John L Hughes, Judy Hulbert, Autumn Inglin, Caroline Kane, Andrew King, Al Kohn, Frank Korach, Deann Kreutzer, Arthur Laurents, Florence Leeds, bruce d. mcclung, Anne McCormick, Judith McCulloh, Kathy McCullough, Paul McKibbins, Zoraya Mendez, Betty Kern Miller, Jeremy Nussbaum, Leonard Pailet, Harriet F. Pilpel, Mitchell Salem, Evelyn Sasko, Joan Schulman, Larry Starr, Jo Sullivan, Hope H. Taylor, Andrea N. Van Kampen, and Robin Walton.

Finally, I would like to thank my family and friends. My parents and my sister, Norma, introduced me to the joy of musicals when I was a child, and the senior Blocks have unceasingly nurtured my intellectual and aesthetic growth ever since. My friends shared and profoundly enriched my processes of discovery. My wife, Jacqueline, was my friendliest and most helpful critic. My daughters, Jessamyn and Eliza, not only inspired me to organize my time more efficiently but gave perspective and meaning to this and all my other work.

The second edition of *Enchanted Evenings* was born and nurtured from inception to fruition through the generosity and wisdom of my editor at Oxford University Press, Norm Hirschy. Throughout every stage of the process, including an insightful reading of the new chapters, Norm offered the full range of his punctual, thoughtful, nuanced, and always kind and enthusiastic editorial expertise, guidance, and support. I can't thank him enough. Thanks also to Oxford's Senior Production Editor Joellyn Ausanka for honoring me by requesting this book and then ably guiding it through the production process as she did with the first edition and with *The Richard Rodgers Reader*. I would also like to thank Patterson Lamb for her unobtrusive and helpful copy editing and Katharine Boone and Madelyn Sutton for their administrative assistance.

For this, as with every project I have undertaken, the library and music office staff at the University of Puget Sound was invariably friendly and helpful. In addition, Media Consultant Stephen Philbrook and his student assistant Kyle Cramer provided indispensable assistance through the complicated task of locating and processing the new film photos. I am also grateful to my students for keeping me in touch with what is happening on Broadway (and in general for that matter) and for sharing their perceptive thoughts, observations, and reactions.

Michael Veseth, the "ideal reader" of the first edition, was always available to demonstrate his problem-solving acumen and to help me figure out what I was trying to accomplish. Andrew Buchman offered thorough, knowledgeable, and helpful comments on the expanded Sondheim chapter and the three new chapters and provided an invaluable sounding board and an endless source of enthusiasm and encouragement at every stage.

As with the first edition, my wife, Jacqueline, and daughters, Jessamyn and Eliza, provided a family ambiance of love and encouragement, blessings that were deeply appreciated and especially meaningful at a time of loss and mourning. My mother died in August 2007, not long after Norm first proposed my doing an expanded second edition of *Enchanted Evenings*, and my dad died while I was writing the new chapters last October. I dedicate this second edition to their inspiring example and beloved memory.

USING THE ENCHANTED
EVENINGS *WEBSITE*

Oxford has created a companion website, [www] www.oup.com/us/
enchantedevenings, to accompany *Enchanted Evenings: The Broadway Musical from* Show Boat *to Sondheim and Lloyd Webber*, and the
reader is encouraged to take full advantage of it. Among its contents, the
website offers plot synopses, a discography and filmography, appendices
of Sources, Published Librettos, and Vocal Scores, Long Runs: Decade by
Decade 1920s–2000s, The Forty Longest-Running Musicals on Broadway
1920–1959 and 1920–2008, and additional useful and extensive appendices listing scenes and songs for the opening night Broadway versions of all
of the principal shows discussed in the main text. In addition, the website
offers outlines of scenes and songs from pre-Broadway tryouts, Broadway
revivals, and other source material to assist the reader's understanding and
comprehension of the discussions. The phrase "online website" will appear
at the mention of these appendices in the main text.

OVERTURE

CHAPTER ONE

INTRODUCTION

Setting the Stage

The central subjects in acts I and II of this book are fourteen "book" musicals that premiered on Broadway between the late 1920s and the late 1950s, beginning with *Show Boat* (1927) and ending with *West Side Story* (1957).[1] All of these shows, and the Sondheim and Lloyd Webber shows discussed in the Epilogue—most for several generations—have demonstrated a measure of popularity and critical approbation. They also offer an array of fascinating critical, analytical, social, and historical issues. Perhaps more important, the musicals surveyed here continue to move us to applaud and cheer (and sometimes hiss), to sing their songs, follow their stories, and make us laugh and cry. In short, they entertain us. Forty, fifty, sixty, even eighty years later we eagerly revisit these shows, not only on Broadway, but in high school and college productions and amateur and professional regional theaters of all shapes and sizes, artistic aims, audiences, and budgets.

In this selective (and to some degree idiosyncratic) survey I do not presume to develop a theory of permanent or ephemeral values or to unravel the mysteries of either artistic merit or popular success. I do, however, attempt to establish a critical and analytical framework that might contribute to an understanding, appreciation, and enjoyment of the selected musicals. The purpose of this introduction is to present recurring topics and issues, to encapsulate the approach to the subject this book will take, and to explain—and sometimes defend—the choices.

3

Why start with *Show Boat*? Certainly, other American musicals that premiered before December 27, 1927, are still successfully revived. Nevertheless, although the choice of where to begin a survey of Broadway is by nature somewhat arbitrary and destined to generate controversy, Broadway historians and critics with surprising unanimity subscribe to the view espoused by the admittedly biased judgment of *Show Boat* enthusiast Miles Kreuger: "The history of the American Musical Theatre, quite simply, is divided into two eras—everything before *Show Boat* and everything after *Show Boat*."[2] *Show Boat* not only opened up a world of possibilities for what an ambitious American musical on an American theme could accomplish; it remains firmly anchored as the first made-in-America musical to achieve a secure place in the core repertory of Broadway musicals.

Before *Show Boat* the Broadway shows that created their greatest initial and most lasting imprints were often British and Viennese imports such as William S. Gilbert and Arthur Sullivan's *H.M.S. Pinafore* (1879) and Franz Lehár's *The Merry Widow* (1907), respectively. Earlier shows that displayed unequivocally American themes—for example, the so-called Mulligan shows of Edward Harrigan and Tony Hart between 1879 and 1883, Percy Gaunt and Charles H. Hoyt's phenomenally successful *A Trip to Chinatown* in 1891 (657 performances), and George M. Cohan's *Little Johnny Jones* in 1904—are today remembered for their songs.[3] The latter show is perhaps best known from its partly staged reincarnation in film (the 1942 classic film biography of Cohan, *Yankee Doodle Dandy*, starring James Cagney) or the musical biography *George M!* (1968), which features a potpourri of memorable Cohan songs. Victor Herbert's *Naughty Marietta* (1910), Jerome Kern's so-called Princess Theatre Shows (1915–1918) with books and lyrics by P. G. Wodehouse and Guy Bolton (especially *Very Good Eddie* and *Leave It to Jane*), Harry Tierney and Joseph McCarthy's *Irene* (1919), Sigmund Romberg's *The Student Prince in Heidelberg* (1924), Vincent Youmans's and Irving Caesar's *No, No, Nanette* (1925), and *The Desert Song* (1926) (music by Romberg, lyrics by Otto Harbach and Oscar Hammerstein 2nd) are occasionally revived and singled out as outstanding exponents of the American musical before *Show Boat*.[4] But unlike Gilbert and Sullivan and Lehár's imported classics, these stageworthy as well as melodious operettas and musical comedies are not widely known, and the Herbert and Romberg operettas are mainly familiar to the Broadway-attending public primarily in greatly altered MGM film versions.[5] The unfairly neglected musicals before *Show Boat* certainly merit a book of their own.

By 1927, the early masters of the American Broadway musical, Herbert, Cohan, Romberg, and Rudolf Friml, either had completed or were nearing the end of their numerous, lucrative, and—for their era—long-lived Broadway runs. Joining Kern, a new generation of Broadway composers and lyricists—Irving Berlin, Cole Porter, Oscar Hammerstein, George and Ira Gershwin, Richard Rodgers, Lorenz Hart, and, in Germany, Kurt Weill—all but Hammerstein and Weill are featured in Al Hirschfeld's drawing "American Popular Song: Great American Songwriters"—had already launched their Broadway careers by 1927.[6]

But despite their auspicious opening salvos, the greatest triumphs for this illustrious list, with the exception of Kern's, would arrive after *Show Boat* in the 1930s and 1940s.

"American Popular Song: Great American Songwriters" (clockwise from left): Richard Rodgers, Lorenz Hart, Cole Porter, Harold Arlen, Dorothy Fields, Jerome Kern, Johnny Mercer, Ira Gershwin, Irving Berlin, Hoagy Carmichael, George Gershwin, and Duke Ellington. 1983. © AL HIRSCHFELD. Reproduced by arrangement with Hirschfeld's exclusive representative, the MARGO FEIDEN GALLERIES LTD., NEW YORK. WWW. ALHIRSCHFELD.COM

Critical Issues

Although the present survey will offer biographical profiles of the composers, lyricists, librettists, and other key players in order to place their careers
in the context of a particular musical, critical and analytical concerns will
receive primary attention. In fact, each of the fourteen musicals explored
in the main body of the text and the Stephen Sondheim and Andrew Lloyd
Webber musicals in chapters 15 and 16 demonstrate critical issues of enduring interest. Two issues in particular emerge as central themes and will
occur repeatedly throughout this survey: the tension between two ideological approaches—song and dance versus integrated—to the Broadway musical, and the alleged conflict between temporal popularity and lasting value
and the selling out, again alleged, not of tickets but of artistic integrity.

Acute manifestations of the latter conflict have been attributed to the
careers of Gershwin, Rodgers, Weill, Frank Loesser, Leonard Bernstein, and
Sondheim. The former issue is embodied in (but by no means confined to) the
differences between the Rodgers and Hart and the Rodgers and Hammerstein
shows; the career of Porter, who, after a string of hits (and then some flops)
in musicals modeled after *Anything Goes*, responded in *Kiss Me, Kate* to the
"anxiety of influence" generated by Rodgers and Hammerstein; and the controversial but frequently alleged schism between the European and the
American musicals of Weill.[7] At the risk of giving away the plot, the view
espoused here is that the song and dance musical comedies that prevailed in
the 1920s and '30s and the integrated musicals that became more influential
in the 1940s and '50s both allow a meaningful dramatic relationship between
songs and their shows. A subtext of the ensuing discussion is that selling
tickets does not necessarily mean selling out artistic integrity.

In each chapter readers will hear again from opening-night theater (and
occasionally music) critics. These critics were usually the first to offer pro-
phetic pontifications for Broadway audiences eager to discover whether or
not they should feel smug or inadequate in their appreciation or rejection
of a show. The critics (again, mostly theater critics) can be reviled but they
cannot be ignored, especially since, despite their lack of specialized musical training, they have consistently demonstrated remarkable precognition
(or inspired self-fulfilling prophecies) regarding the critical as well as the
popular fate of Broadway shows. Although they must produce their work
under enormous pressure and seemingly against all odds, receiving little
sympathy in the process, opening-night critics frequently call attention to
issues that will reappear to haunt a show. Such early perceived problems
and issues as *Show Boat*'s second act or the jarring stylistic heterogeneity of

Porgy and Bess or *The Most Happy Fella* do not go away but remain to be reassessed and reinterpreted by future generations.

The degree to which the stage works we love should be performed in authentic versions—to the often questionable extent this is possible—has been a source of debate in America for more than two centuries. Writing about nineteenth-century American approaches to European opera, Richard Crawford defines accessibility as "the tailoring of the music to suit particular audiences and circumstances" and authenticity "as an ideal countering the marketplace's devotion to accessibility."[8] According to Crawford, accessibility "privileges occasions over works" and "*invests ultimate authority in the present-day audiences.*" "Authenticity privileges works over occasions" and "*invests ultimate authority in works and the traditions within which they are composed.*" The desirability of—or resistance to—establishing an authentic musical and literary text for a show and the struggle between authenticity and accessibility will loom as a major issue in several chapters of this survey, in particular those on *Show Boat, Anything Goes, On Your Toes, Porgy and Bess,* and the James Goldman-Stephen Sondheim-Hal Prince-Michael Bennett *Follies.*[9] Kern and Hammerstein, the principal creators of *Show Boat,* themselves produced a second "authentic" version that would be more "accessible" to audiences desiring the newer Rodgers and Hammerstein model. *Anything Goes* revivals in 1962 and 1987 would be equipped with a new book and many songs interpolated from other Porter shows. The 1983 *On Your Toes* would match a new book with the original score (albeit somewhat rearranged).

The original "operatic" sung form (emphasizing authenticity) of *Porgy and Bess* has clearly prevailed in recent years over its "Broadway" form with spoken dialogue (emphasizing accessibility). Nevertheless, considerable debate continues to rage over what constitutes an authentic text for this work. Charles Hamm has argued that the cuts made by the creators in its original Theatre Guild production are justifiable for artistic as well as for commercial reasons and that the current urge to restore these cuts creates a historically and aesthetically untenable reconstruction.[10] With the purpose of shedding some light on this heated subject, the chapter on *Porgy and Bess* will treat at length the historical background and aesthetic problems posed by one such cut, the "Buzzard Song."

The starting point for contemplating the "text" of a musical is almost invariably a vocal score rather than a full orchestral score, and later—after the release of *Oklahoma!* in 1943—the cast recording in various states of completion. It is therefore not surprising that Broadway musicals as a genre have been unusually susceptible to identity crises. Although some musicals after *Oklahoma!* were considerably reworked in future productions, musicals prior to this landmark show typically have been treated as less fixed and therefore more subject to revision and interpolation. The first part of this survey will trace how several shows have evolved in response to the competing interests of accessibility or authenticity and what these responses tell us about changing social and aesthetic tastes and values.

Analytical Issues

The principal analytical question raised in this survey is how music and lyrics serve, ignore, or contradict dramatic themes and ideas, both in specific scenes and in the shows as a whole. Although this study will only infrequently treat music autonomously, a major factor behind the selection of the shows surveyed is the widely appreciated musical richness and enduring appeal of their scores. In contrast to most previous surveys, in which music is neglected beyond unhelpful generalities about its power to convey mood, music in this study will emerge as an equal (and occasionally more than equal) partner to the other components of a show, including lyrics, librettos, choreography, and stage direction.

Even when a musical is seemingly distinguished more by self-contained rather than integrated songs, the relationship of music and lyrics and music's power to express dramatic themes will be a central aesthetic issue for each musical. While some admiration will be reserved for those musicals that approximate Joseph Kerman's criteria for European operatic excellence, using music to define character and generate action as espoused in his *Opera as Drama*, other musicals considered with equal favor here do not accomplish this at all.[11]

The philosophical distinctions regarding text setting expressed by Peter Kivy apply also to the disparate approaches of Broadway musicals. As noted in the Preface to the First Edition, Kivy contrasts "the *principle of textual realism*," in which the meanings of words are "interpreted" musically, "with another approach to the setting of texts...the *principle of opulent adornment*," in which texts are set like precious jewels "hindered neither by the meaning nor the intelligibility of what he [the composer] 'sets.'"[12] The contrasting careers of Rodgers and Hart and Rodgers and Hammerstein represent these different approaches. Comparisons might suggest that something was lost as well as gained by the abandonment of cleverness, wit, and autonomous memorable tunes (Kivy's "opulent adornment" of words) in favor of integrated and more operatically constructed musicals filled with such techniques such as leitmotivs, foreshadowing, thematic transformation, and classical borrowings, however convincingly employed for various dramatic purposes (Kivy's "textual realism").

The language of the analysis is intended to be accessible to readers unversed in musical vocabulary. For this reason harmonic details will receive less emphasis than melodic and rhythmic aspects. Some of the shows discussed here adopt techniques analogous to those practiced in the operas of Mozart, Verdi, and Wagner, and the book is based on the premises that for some musicals, melodic and rhythmic connections and imaginative use of classical borrowings (for striking examples of the latter see *West Side Story*) audibly enrich the dramatic fabric, and that some knowledge of these connections might contribute to the appreciation and enjoyment of these works.

For readers who neither read music nor profess any musical discernment beyond knowledge of what they like, the intent here is that the lyrics that accompany most of the musical examples will provide an aid in figuring out the point and purpose of the analytical discussion without undue discomfort. Since for many, negotiating musical terminology of any kind is an ordeal, occasionally even rudimentary concepts, including intervals, rhythmic note values, and the idea of central and hierarchical key relationships, will need to be explained. Although the attempt to create a text suitable for a "Broadway audience" unaccustomed to musical terminology may inevitably lead to some oversimplification from the perspective of theorists and musicologists, it is nevertheless the goal that something meaningful and new can be gained for this audience as well. In nearly all cases the focus will be on those musical features that can actually be heard, and on the musical expression of dramatic meanings and dramatic context.

The Making of a Musical, Adaptation, and Social Issues

How is a musical created and how does knowledge of compositional process, including the revisions made during out-of-town tryouts, lead to a better understanding and appreciation of the works we see and hear today? How were the composers, lyricists, and librettists, our principal subjects, influenced by directors, choreographers, producers, and audiences? How did the creators of these shows achieve a balance between artistic and commercial control of their work?

Although a knowledge of a musical's compositional process can provide partial answers to these questions, the study of how a musical evolves from pre-compositional discussions, early sketches, and drafts to opening night and subsequent revivals has not been widely explored in the literature on Broadway.[13] In fact, this book is the first to do so over a broad spectrum of the field. Sometimes the creative problems posed by musicals seem to find solutions by opening night or shortly thereafter; other problems remain for the life (and afterlife) of the show. When source materials permit this type of an inquiry—and some musicals were selected for this survey in part because they left conspicuous paper trails—the present study will examine how unpublished compositional materials (such as early libretto and lyric drafts, musical sketches, and letters) support or contradict more widely available published memoirs, interviews, and retrospective panels of creative participants.

One common denominator that links most of the musicals discussed in this survey is the practice, ubiquitous after *Oklahoma!*, of adapting a literary source for the musical stage (see "Sources, Published Librettos, and Vocal Scores" in the online website). Three adaptations that contend with formidable antecedents are explored at some length. The chapters on these shows will examine how and why these famous plays were adapted for new audiences in a new medium and how they preserved (*Kiss Me, Kate* and *West Side Story*) or distorted (*My Fair Lady*) the fundamental dramatic meanings of their sources in their musical reincarnations. The two new chapters that conclude acts I and II (chapters 8 and 14) and the expanded Sondheim and new Lloyd Webber chapters (chapters 15 and 16) will also examine what happened in the next step of the adaptation process experienced by most Broadway musicals, the conversion to film, and how partisans of stage performances might handle the realities of an interloping medium.

When comparing stage musicals with their literary origins, the chapter on *Kiss Me, Kate* (chapter 10) will discuss how Sam and Bella Spewack's original libretto differs from the final Broadway version as well as with Shakespeare's *The Taming of the Shrew*, and in the process suggest that Porter may have learned as much from his own *Anything Goes* as he did from Rodgers and Hammerstein about how to relate music to character. In *My Fair Lady* (chapter 12) Alan Jay Lerner and Frederick Loewe departed significantly from Shaw's ending to *Pygmalion*. After giving the mean-spirited Professor Henry Higgins a more humane face (intentionally denied by Shaw) by the end of act I, the Broadway team, in their second act, made explicit, mainly through the songs, what Shaw implies or omits. Ironically, although they romanticized—and thereby misrepresented—Shaw's intentions, Lerner and Loewe managed to convey Eliza Doolittle's metamorphosis as Higgins's equal, through both Lerner's lyrics and Loewe's reversal of their musical roles, more clearly than either Shaw's play or director Gabriel Pascal's 1938 film, upon which *My Fair Lady* was based.

When discussing *West Side Story* (chapter 13) the point argued is not simply that the Broadway collaboration more closely approximates the spirit of Shakespeare's *Romeo and Juliet* than earlier operatic adaptations (or some films) that retain the Bard's namesakes and setting, but that Bernstein—with considerable help from Sondheim (lyrics), Arthur Laurents (libretto), and Jerome Robbins (choreography and conception)—found a musical solution to convey the dramatic meaning of Shakespeare through the use of leit-motivs and their transformations in combination with a jazz and Hispanic American vernacular.

The present survey will only occasionally emphasize social history. That is another book that very much needs to be written. Nevertheless, the study of a musical most often leads to political and cultural issues, even if it was the expressed intent of its creators to escape from meaning. For many of the musicals discussed in act I especially, the changes that went into their revivals over the decades offer a valuable tool to measure changing social as well as artistic concerns. Some musicals, such as *Show Boat, Porgy and Bess*, and *West Side Story* are overtly concerned with racial conflicts; others, such as *Anything Goes, On Your Toes, One Touch of Venus*, and *My Fair Lady*, explore class differences. All musicals discussed here either directly or inad-vertently make powerful statements about what James Thurber called The War between Men and Women.[14]

The Cradle Will Rock serves as a worthy representative to show both the wisdom and futility of the didactic political musical. Two songs from this "avant-garde" musical will be discussed from this perspective. The first is "Croon–Spoon," which satirizes the vapidity of ephemeral popular music, and the second is "Art for Art's Sake," which from Marc Blitzstein's perspec-tive indicts the equally vapid messages of so-called high art, the purposes to which art is used, and the blatant hypocrisy of some artists.

Not surprisingly, few musicals measure up to evolving sensibilities. The disparity between these shows and feminist values will be given special attention in interpreting *Anything Goes, Lady in the Dark, One Touch of Venus, Carousel, Kiss Me, Kate, Guys and Dolls*, and *My Fair Lady*, all of which pro-vide gender issues of unusual interest. Some musicals fare better than others from the vantage point of the future, but no musical surveyed here can fully escape the assumptions and collective values of their era.

Why These Musicals?

The present selection makes an effort to include representative musicals from *Show Boat* to *The Phantom of the Opera* that pose intriguing critical, analytical, aesthetic, and political issues as well as musicals that engage the enthusi-asm of the selector. No attempt was made either to be comprehensive or to discuss only the very most popular musicals of the era, but the lists of "Long Runs" and "The Forty Longest Running Musicals on Broadway" in the online website will provide useful reference points for measuring and interpreting the degree of popularity these musicals enjoyed. Despite the above disclaimer, a few words should be said about the degree to which popularity governed the present selections.

Ten of the fourteen Broadway musicals receiving top billing here (not including those by Sondheim and Andrew Lloyd Webber) were also among the most popular of their respective decades. *Show Boat* was the third longest running musical of the 1920s, *Anything Goes* and *On Your Toes* ranked second and eighth, respectively, among book shows in the 1930s—the two longest running 1930s shows, *Hellzapoppin'* and *Pins and Needles* were revues—and in the 1940s and '50s *Kiss Me, Kate, Carousel, One Touch of Venus, My Fair Lady, Guys and Dolls, West Side Story*, and *The Most Happy Fella* all fall within the top fifteen longest runs. Eight of these musicals are among the top thirty-eight musicals spanning these four decades; three rank among the top nine book shows.[15]

While one measure of a show's popularity and its even more important correlate, commercial success, is the length of its initial run, the revivability of a show arguably constitutes a more compelling measure of its success. Many musicals, even blockbusters of their day, never manage to regain their hit status and acquire a place in the Broadway repertory despite rigorous marketing or a lustrous star. For example, despite its many merits, *Of Thee I Sing* (1931), the longest running book musical of the 1930s and the recipient of the first Pulitzer Prize for drama, has disappeared as a staged work on Broadway after its disappointing seventy-two performance revival in 1952. Two of the musicals under scrutiny here, *Lady in the Dark* (1941) and *One Touch of Venus* (1943), both enormous hits in their time, still await a fully staged New York revival. The chapter devoted to these last mentioned shows (chapter 7) will offer the view that the absence of *One Touch of Venus* is especially lamentable.

The remaining twelve musicals have resurfaced in at least one popular Broadway, Off-Broadway, or other prominent New York revival from 1980 to the present (if the prestigious New City Center's *Encores!* counts as a prominent performance, all fourteen shows would be accounted for).[16] By 1960, New York audiences had had the opportunity to see *Show Boat* 1,344 times, a total that more than doubled its original run and was surpassed only by five continuously running book musicals in the top forty before 1960 ("The Forty Longest Running Musicals on Broadway 1920–1959" in the online website). *The Cradle Will Rock*, something of a cult musical, admittedly remains an idiosyncratic choice for a selective survey. Nevertheless, this controversial and sometimes alienating show has been revived in New York City no less than four times since its original short but historic runs in 1937 and 1938. Although these *Cradle* revivals may have been generated out of political sympathy, the present study will make a case for the work's still unacknowledged and unappreciated artistic merits.

If popularity in absolute numbers is the ticket for admittance, what then are *Pal Joey* (1940), *Lady in the Dark* (1941), and *Porgy and Bess* (1935), three shows that were neither in the top forty nor among the top ten or fifteen musicals of their decades, doing in a survey of popular Broadway musicals? To answer this question, it might be helpful to consider a musical's popularity by the standards of its immediate predecessors. Although it may not have enjoyed a major New York revival in more than sixty years, at 467 performances *Lady in the Dark* would surpass even the longest running book musical of the 1930s, *Of Thee I Sing*.[17] *Pal Joey* (374 performances) would rank as the fifth longest running book show of the 1930s had it premiered one year earlier.[18] More significantly, in contrast to nearly every other musical *comedy* before *Guys and Dolls*, including *Anything Goes* and *On Your Toes*, revivals of *Pal Joey* for the most part retain the original book without fear of ridicule or loss of accessibility.

The inclusion of *Porgy and Bess* on popular grounds requires some spin control. Because it lost money, it is fair to judge its initial total of 124 performances as a relatively poor showing—even in a decade when two hundred performances could constitute a hit. As a musical in the commercial marketplace, *Porgy and Bess* failed; as an opera, arguably a more accurate taxonomic classification, it can be interpreted as a phenomenal success. No other American opera of its (or any) generation comes close.[19] Of course it helps that it is also an acknowledged American classic.

In contrast to his musical comedies and operettas, Gershwin's only Broadway opera returned a few years later in 1942, albeit more like a conventional musical with spoken dialogue replacing sung recitative—favoring accessibility over authenticity—and became a modest commercial success at 286 performances. Within seven years New York audiences thus were able to see Gershwin's opera (or a reasonable facsimile) 410 times before the arrival of *Oklahoma!*, thirty performances fewer than *Of Thee I Sing*, the biggest hit of the 1930s and of Gershwin's career. And in contrast to Gershwin shows that, in revival, have been transformed into barely recognizable but highly accessible and commercially successful adaptations (*My One and Only* [1983], *Oh, Kay!* [1990], and *Crazy for You* [1992]), revivals of *Porgy and Bess*, at least since the mid-1970s, often go to great lengths to restore Gershwin's opera to prevailing notions of authenticity.

The willingness to eschew comprehensiveness leads to inevitable omissions. In addition to Jule Styne's four top forty musicals, the most conspicuous absentees are Berlin, whose *Annie Get Your Gun* (ranked eighth among book shows) has for many years earned an enduring place in the core repertory (and major New York revivals in 1966 and 1999), and the team of Richard Adler and Jerry Ross, the composer-lyricists who in 1954 and 1955 produced two of the most successful book musicals before 1960, *Pajama Game* (tenth) and *Damn Yankees* (eleventh), before Ross's premature death in 1955 at the age of twenty-nine. Some readers may lament the absence of lyricist E. Y. ("Yip") Harburg's collaborations with composers Harold Arlen and Burton Lane, or of composer-lyricists Harold Rome and Robert Wright and George Forrest.[20]

Despite these omissions, the present representative survey includes at least one musical selected from the work of those composers, lyricists, and librettists responsible for many of the top forty musicals shown in the online website ("The Forty Longest…1920–1959"). The most popular creators of each decade are also well represented. In the 1920s, six of the eleven longest runs had either a score by Kern or lyrics or a libretto by Hammerstein. In the 1930s, only two book musicals of the twelve longest runs did not feature a score by Rodgers and Hart, Kern, Porter, or the Gershwins (who provided four, three, two, and one, respectively), and one of these consisted of recycled music by Johann Strauss Jr. By the 1940s and '50s, Rodgers, now teamed with Hammerstein, dominated the musical marketplace with no less than five of the ten longest runs of those years.[21]

Coda

In *The American Musical Theater* noted Broadway conductor and educator Lehman Engel offered the following list of fifteen Broadway "models of excellence" that "represent that theater in its most complete and mature state": *Pal Joey; Oklahoma!; Carousel; Annie Get Your Gun; Brigadoon; Kiss Me, Kate; South Pacific; Guys and Dolls; The King and I; My Fair Lady; West Side Story; Gypsy; Fiddler on the Roof; Company*; and *A Little Night Music*.[22] The first twelve of Engel's list fall within the central focus period of this study (acts I and II), and six of these will be explored. In his pioneering volume Engel is primarily concerned with the "working principles" that govern "excellent" musicals. In another chapter he singles out four "Broadway operas" that also embody these principles—*Porgy and Bess, The Cradle Will Rock, The Consul* (Gian-Carlo Menotti), and *The Most Happy Fella*. Three of these will be featured in the present volume.

All the musicals in Engel's list of fifteen turned a profit and nearly all had long runs, including seven of the ten longest runs between *Oklahoma!* and

The Sound of Music. Engel's most conspicuous omission is without a doubt *Show Boat*, a musical almost invariably honored by subsequent list-makers and Broadway historians and critics as the first major musical on a uniquely American theme, one of the first to thoroughly integrate music and drama, and the first American musical to firmly enter the Broadway repertory. Although subsequent lists added a few scattered musical comedies from the 1930s and the musicals of Weill, all of which Engel excludes, the spirit of Engel's list is echoed in nearly all those that followed.[23] With virtually no exceptions the musicals on these lists enjoyed long initial runs and critical acclaim and usually received one or more major New York revivals.[24]

Within a few years after *West Side Story*, the age of Porter, Lerner and Loewe, Loesser, Bernstein, Blitzstein, Berlin, and Rodgers and Hammerstein was over. These classical Broadway masters of the 1930s, '40s, and '50s had generally enjoyed a combination of popularity and critical acclaim analogous to that of their nineteenth-century operatic and instrumental predecessors in Europe. After 1970, irreconcilable differences between this incompatible pair of attributes began to surface, exemplified by the contrasting trajecto- ries of Sondheim and Lloyd Webber, and few musicals by either of these two emblematic artists would readily receive the combination of love and respect enjoyed by the most popular and critically acclaimed musicals of the 1940s and '50s.

The penultimate chapter of this survey will take a look at the career of Sondheim, the lyricist-composer generally recognized as a central artistic figure on Broadway after 1960. The position taken here is that Sondheim's modernism and postmodernism can be viewed as an extension and reinter- pretation of the Rodgers and Hammerstein model rather than a rebellion from it. It will also be argued that although Sondheim has vigorously denied autobiographical elements in his shows, the pressure to compromise faced by his characters is markedly similar to that faced by Sondheim himself as he creates their songs and faces the demands of commercial theater.

After exploring the issue on an impersonal fictive level, Sondheim, in his first two shows of the 1980s, *Merrily We Roll Along* and *Sunday in the Park with George*, directly confronted the issue of artistic compromise in his own work. Such conflicts had been faced more obliquely by several of his spiri- tual Broadway ancestors surveyed here who experienced similar creative crises in their effort to simultaneously transcend the conventions of their genre and retain their audiences. The Sondheim chapter will acknowledge his attempt to move beyond the integrated action model to the concept (or thematic) musical and his ability to convey the nuances of his increasingly complex characters and musically capture the meaning of his dramatic subjects. It will additionally emphasize how Sondheim's musicals can be viewed as the proud inheritance of the great traditional musicals from *Show Boat* to *West Side Story*.

As revivals continue to demonstrate, many musicals between *Show Boat* and *Gypsy* (1927–1959), as well as another group created in the 1960s by several relatively new Broadway artists (perhaps most notably Jerry Bock and Sheldon Harnick's *Fiddler on the Roof* [1964] and John Kander and Fred Ebb's *Cabaret* [1966]), have not simply disappeared. Although the verdict for these more recent musicals is still inconclusive, it is not too soon to notice the spectacularly long runs and endless tours of Lloyd Webber musicals and the revivals of Sondheim's earlier shows in the 1970s, '80s, and '90s. Even if one hesitates to speak openly of a Broadway canon, few would deny the presence of a core repertory of Broadway musicals for the period of this study and considerably beyond. While the term "core repertory" avoids cultural bias and has the benefit of inclusiveness—in the core repertory there is a place somewhere for both Sondheim and Lloyd Webber (the subject of a new final chapter in this second edition)—the idea of a canon, a nucleus of works within a genre perceived as models of excellence or, more simply, the musicals audiences want to see over and over again, remains a useful if somewhat unpalatable construct. In any event, it is ironic that the deconstruction and even demolition of canons, including the venerable and unassailable eighteenth- and nineteenth-century European classical repertory, has become fashionable just as a firm foundation for canonization has begun to emerge in the genre of Broadway musicals.

While it is still permissible to say that some musicals are more popular than others, most critics and historians are loath to argue that some are actually more worthy of canonical status.[25] Northrop Frye, perhaps wisely (or least safely), chastised advocates of both "popular" and "art for art's sake" camps when he wrote in his *Anatomy of Criticism* that "the fallacy common to both attitudes is that a rough correlation between the merit of art and the degree of public response to it, though the correlation assumed is direct in one case and inverse in the other."[26]

The stance of the present volume is that "popularity" and "art for art's sake" are not mutually exclusive values, that writing for a commercial market can lead to inspiration as well as compromise. Perhaps we cannot explain or tell why this is so, but we can nonetheless revel in the many enchanted evenings (and some matinees) that these musicals continue to provide.

· ACT I ·

Before Rodgers and Hammerstein

CHAPTER TWO

SHOW BOAT

In the Beginning

The *New Grove Dictionary of Music and Musicians* informed its readers in 1980 without exaggeration or understatement that *Show Boat* is "perhaps the most successful and influential Broadway musical play ever written."[1] For the authors of *New Grove*, the impact of *Show Boat* has been "inestimable, particularly in that it impelled composers of Broadway musicals to concern themselves with the whole production as opposed to writing Tin Pan Alley songs for interpolation."[2] For the many who judge a show by how many songs they can hum or whistle when they leave (or enter) the theater, *Show Boat* offered "at least" an unprecedented six song hits for the ages; moreover, nearly all of these songs, according to *Grove*, "are integral to the characterization and story." And the many who place opera on a more elevated plane than Broadway musicals could be impressed by the knowledge that *Show Boat*, when it entered the repertory of the New York City Opera in 1954, was the first Broadway show to attain operatic stature.[3] By virtually any criteria, *Show Boat* marks a major milestone in the history of the American musical and has long since become the first Broadway show to be enshrined in the musical theater museum.

Show Boat gained recognition in the scholarly world too when in 1977 it became the first Broadway musical to receive book-length attention in Miles Kreuger's thorough and authoritative *"Show Boat": The Story of a Classic American Musical*.[4] Five years later, manuscript material for the musical numbers discarded during the tryout months prior to the December 1927 premiere was discovered in the Warner Brothers Warehouse in Secaucus, New Jersey.[5] By April 1983 the Houston Opera Company—which had in the late 1970s presented and recorded a *Porgy and Bess* that restored material cut from its pre-Broadway tryouts—arrived in New York with a version of *Show Boat* that used Robert Russell Bennett's original orchestrations (rediscovered in 1978) and most of the previously discarded tryout material.

In 1988 John McGlinn (1953–2009), who had served as a music editor for the Houston Opera, conducted a recording of *Show Boat* on EMI/Angel that incorporated Bennett's 1927 orchestrations and restored tryout material. McGlinn's recording offered a significant amount of dialogue with musical underscoring. It even included an appendix containing longer versions of several scenes (shortened for the New York opening) and songs that Kern composed for the 1928 London engagement, the 1936 Universal film (with a screenplay by Hammerstein and new songs by Kern), and the New York revival in 1946.[6]

Critics who attended the opening night on December 27, 1927, at the Ziegfeld sensed that *Show Boat* was not only a hit but a show of originality and significance. Robert Coleman, for example, described *Show Boat* in the *Daily Mirror* as "a work of genius" and a show which demonstrated the sad fact that "managers have not until now realized the tremendous possibilities of the musical comedy as an art form."[7] Coleman's review is also representative in its praise of the original run's exceptional production values, including "fourteen glorious settings" and a superb cast. Although *Show Boat*, in contrast to other Ziegfeld productions, did not open with a lineup of scantily clad chorus girls, Coleman thought he saw "a chorus of 150 of the most beautiful girls ever glorified by Mr. Ziegfeld."[8]

Within a few days after its opening Percy Hammond wrote that *Show Boat* was "the most distinguished light opera of its generation," and Brooks Atkinson described it as "one of those epochal works about which garrulous old men gabble for twenty-five years after the scenery has rattled off to the storehouse."[9] Nearly every critic described Kern's score either as his best or at least his recent best. Surveys of the American musical as far back as Cecil Smith's *Musical Comedy in America* (1950) support these original assessments and single out *Show Boat* as the only musical of its time "to achieve a dramatic verisimilitude that seemed comparable to that of the speaking stage."[10] Beginning in the late 1960s historians would almost invariably emphasize *Show Boat*'s unprecedented integration of music and drama, its three-dimensional characters, and its bold and serious subject matter, including miscegenation and unhappy marriages.

Although critics for the most part found silver linings nearly everywhere, they also freely voiced their discontent with one aspect of the work:

the libretto. *Show Boat* might give the highly respected (albeit somewhat curmudgeonly) critic George Jean Nathan "a welcome holiday from the usual grumbling," but most critics felt that the libretto, while vastly superior to other books of the time, did not demonstrate the same perfection as Jerome Kern's music and Florenz Ziegfeld's production.[11] In particular, critics voiced their displeasure with the final scene. Robert Garland, who described *Show Boat* as "an American masterpiece," noted some "faltering, like many another offering, only when it approaches the end," and Alexander Woollcott wrote that "until the last scene, when it all goes gaudy and empty and routine, it is a fine and distinguished achievement."[12]

More recent historians continued to view *Show Boat* as a refreshing but flawed departure from other shows of its day. Richard Traubner, for example, who praised *Show Boat* as "the greatest of all American operettas," attributed this greatness to its triumph over "libretto problems."[13] Even *Show Boat* aficionado Kreuger corroborates the verdict of earlier complaints: "As a concession to theatrical conventions of the time, Hammerstein kept everyone alive to the end and even arranged a happy reunion for the long-parted lovers, decisions, he revealed to this writer, that he came to regret."[14]

Despite these reservations, only Lehman Engel, the distinguished Broadway conductor and the first writer to establish canonical criteria for the American musical (see the "Coda" to chapter 1), would banish *Show Boat* from this elite group. Although Engel acknowledges that *Show Boat*'s "score and lyrics are among the best ever written in our theater," he tempers this praise by his assessment of "serious weaknesses."[15] For Engel, *Show Boat*'s "characters are two-dimensional, its proportions are outrageous, its plot development predictable and corny, and its ending unbearably sweet."[16] Engel is particularly perturbed by six "not only silly but sloppy" coincidences that take place in Chicago within a three-week period in 1904 (significantly all in the second act), coincidences that are comically improbable, even in a city with half its present population.[17]

Of the two principal collaborators, Hammerstein (1895–1960) had far more experience with operetta-type musicals as well as recent successes. *Wildflower* (1923), created with co-librettist Otto Harbach and composers Herbert Stothart and Vincent Youmans, launched a phenomenally successful decade for Hammerstein as librettist, lyricist, and director for many of Broadway's most popular operettas and musical comedies: *Rose-Marie* (1924) and *The Wild Rose* (1926) with Rudolf Friml and Stothart; *Song of the Flame* (1925) with George Gershwin and Stothart; and the still-revived *The Desert Song* (1926) with Sigmund Romberg. Two years before *Show Boat* Hammerstein had also collaborated with Harbach and Kern on the latter's most recent success, *Sunny*.

Kern (1885–1945), whose mother was a musician, "had some European training in a small town outside of Heidelberg" when he was seventeen and studied piano, counterpoint, harmony, and composition the following year at the New York College of Music.[18] Ten years before *Show Boat*, Kern stated in interviews that "songs must be suited to the action and the mood of the play."[19] At the same time he also considered devoting his full attention to composing symphonies.

Although there is no reason to doubt Kern's aspiration "to apply modern art to light music as Debussy and those men have done to more serious work,"[20] it was not until *Show Boat* that Kern was able to fully realize these goals. Kern had, of course, previously created complete scores for an impressive series of precocious integrated musicals during the Princess Theatre years (1915–1918), at least two of which, *Very Good Eddie* and *Leave It to Jane*, have been successfully revived in recent decades. For the earlier years of his career, however, Kern had been confined mainly to composing interpolated songs to augment the music of others. Two of these, "How'd You Like to Spoon with Me?" interpolated into *The Earl and the Girl* (1905), and "They Didn't Believe Me" from *The Girl from Utah* (1914), remain among his best known. Similarly, *Sally* (1920) and *Sunny* (1925), two vehicles for the superstar Marilyn Miller and his most popular shows composed during the years between the intimate Princess Theatre productions and the grandiose *Show Boat*, are remembered primarily for their respective songs "Look for the Silver Lining" and "Who?" and have not fared well in staged revivals.

Before 1924, Edna Ferber had never even heard of the once-popular traveling river productions that made their home on show boats. By the following summer she had begun the novel *Show Boat*, which was published serially in *Woman's Home Companion* between April and September 1926 and in its entirety in August by Doubleday. Early in October, Kern, who had read half of Ferber's new book, phoned Woollcott to ask for a letter of introduction to its author and met her at a performance of Kern's latest musical, *Criss Cross*, that same evening. Even before Ferber had signed a contract on November 17 giving Kern and Hammerstein "dramatico-musical" rights to her hot property, the co-conspirators had already completed enough material to impress *Follies* impresario Ziegfeld nine days later.[21] On December 11 Kern and Hammerstein signed their contracts, according to which a script was to be delivered by January 1 and the play was to appear "on or before the first day of April 1927."[22]

By 1927, Kern had long since earned the mantle allegedly bestowed on him by Victor Herbert (1859–1924), the composer of *Naughty Marietta* (1910) and dozens of other Broadway shows, as the most distinguished American-born theater composer. For more than a decade Kern had been the model and envy of Porter, Gershwin, and Rodgers, who were embarking on their careers during the Princess Theatre years. But it was not until *Show Boat* that Kern had the opportunity to create a more ambitious species of Broadway musical. The care which he lavished on the score is conspicuously evident from the numerous extant pre-tryout drafts on deposit at the Library of Congress (see "Manuscript Sources for Ravenal's Entrance and Meeting with Magnolia" no. 1 in the online website) and by an unprecedentedly long gestation period from November 1926 to November 1927 that included numerous and lengthy discussions with librettist and lyricist Hammerstein. Many other changes were made during the out-of-town tryouts.

Reconstructing Show Boat *(1927–1994)*

In order to provide a framework for discussing *Show Boat* it will be useful to distinguish among its various stage and film versions. Although the vocal score of the 1927 production, published by T. B. Harms in April 1928, has been out of print for decades, much of this original Broadway version was retained in the still-available London vocal score published by Chappell & Co. (also 1928). It is also fortunate that much of the Convent Scene and two brief passages absent from the Chappell score—the parade music in act I, scene 1, and the "Happy New Year" music ("Hot Time in the Old Town Tonight") in act II, scene 6—can be found in a third vocal score, published by the Welk Music Group, that also corresponds reasonably well to the 1946 touring production.[23]

McGlinn's 1988 recording is an indispensable starting point for anyone interested in exploring a compendium of the versions produced between 1927 and 1946 (as well as the 1936 film).[24] All of these versions incorporate new ideas and usually new songs by the original creators. Even if one does not agree with all of McGlinn's artistic and editorial decisions, especially his decision to include in the main body of the recording (rather than in the appendix) material that Kern and Hammerstein had agreed to cut from the production during tryouts, the performances are impressive and the notes by Kreuger and McGlinn carefully researched.

In the introduction to his monograph Kreuger notes that "one fascinating aspect of *Show Boat* is that, unlike most major musicals, it has never had an official script or score."[25] The lack of the former did not pose a problem to Kreuger, who had obtained the 1927 libretto directly from Hammerstein himself a few days before his death in August 1960.[26] Its absence has proven, however, to be an enormous headache for historians and, conversely, a source of opportunity for some directors (for example, Hal Prince), who have been given a free hand to decipher and interpret the complicated evolution and varied documentary legacy of this musical according to their personal visions.

One extended number published by Harms, "Mis'ry's Comin' Aroun,'" had been dropped from the production in Washington, D.C., as early as November 15 after the very first evening of the tryouts. Because Kern "insisted that the number be published in the complete vocal score," McGlinn argued, not without justification, that Kern "hoped the sequence would have an afterlife in a more enlightened theatrical world."[27] For this reason McGlinn includes "Mis'ry" into the body of his recording rather than in an appendix.

McGlinn's other "restorations and re-evaluations" are less convincing on historical grounds. Dropped from both the Harms score and the 1927 production were two numbers, "I Would Like to Play a Lover's Part" (originally placed at the beginning of act I, scene 5) and "It's Getting Hotter in the North" (act II, scene 9). The latter song was replaced by a reprise of "Why Do I Love You?" called "Kim's Imitations," performed by the original Magnolia, Norma Terris, who was made up to look like her daughter Kim and performed impressions of famous vaudeville stars. Since Kern did not wish to include this discarded material in the vocal score (and it was in response to Kern's wishes that McGlinn reinserted "Mis'ry"), its presence in the body of McGlinn's recording is questionable. One other number deleted before the December premiere, "Trocadero Opening Chorus" (at one time in act II, scene 6), was placed in the main portion of McGlinn's recording for "technical reasons."[28]

For the first London production in 1928—which premiered after the New York version had been playing for a little more than four months—Kern and Hammerstein wrote "Dance Away the Night" (replacing Kim's reprise of "Why Do I Love You?," itself a replacement of "Kim's Imitations"). Also in this production Kern's 1905 London hit, "How'd You Like to Spoon with Me?" replaced the non-Kern interpolation, "Good-bye, Ma Lady Love." Two scenes were entirely omitted, the Convent Scene (act II, scene 4) and the scene in the Sherman Hotel Lobby (act II, scene 5), along with the song, "Hey, Feller!" (act II, scene 7). Another song, "Me and My Boss," composed especially for Paul Robeson, who sang the role of Joe, was not used and is presumed lost.[29]

After returning to Broadway in 1932 for 181 performances (with several members of the 1927 cast and Robeson), the next major Broadway revival, with extensive changes by Kern and Hammerstein, arrived on January 5, 1946.[30] Even the overture was new, a more traditional medley-type version to replace the "Mis'ry"-dominated overture of the 1927 production. The first word heard in the original 1927 New York production, "niggers," had

"*Show Boat,* the marriage of Magnolia and Ravenal at the end of act I (1946)."
Photograph: Graphic House. Museum of the City of New York. Theater
Collection. For a film still of this scene see p. 159.

already been replaced by "coloured folks" in the 1928 London production.
For the 1946 revival Hammerstein removed other references to this offensive
word and rewrote a quatrain in the opening chorus in which "Coal Black
Rose or High Brown Sal" was replaced by the less racially tinted phrase in
dialect, "Y'work all day, y'git no fun."

Other changes in 1946 included a new emphasis on dance numbers, the
composition of yet another song for Kim in the final scene, "Nobody Else but
Me" (Kern's final song before he died on November 11, 1945, during auditions),
three major deletions ("Till Good Luck Comes My Way," "I Might Fall Back on
You," and "Hey, Feller!" [dropped in London 1928]), an abbreviation ("C'Mon
Folks"), a repositioning ("Life upon the Wicked Stage"), the deletion of two
scenes (act I, scene 3, and act II, scene 5), and the rewriting of a third (act II,
scene 7).[31] Kreuger, who briefly discusses these changes, does not mention the
elimination of local color (including banjos and tubas) and comedic elements
such as Cap'n Andy Hawks's introduction of Rubber-Face Smith in the opening scene. Although Kreuger regretted the absence of style in the stage performances, he unhesitatingly supported these revisions as improvements.[32]

Theater historian and critic Ethan Mordden in a *New Yorker* essay on *Show Boat* published one year after the McGlinn reconstruction assesses the 1946 version far less favorably. Although, like Kreuger, Mordden recognizes the incalculable influence of *Oklahoma!* and *Carousel*, he regrets the alterations that "homogenized a timeless, diverse piece into a document of a specific place and time: Broadway mid-nineteen-forties."[33] Mordden continues:

> In 1927, "Ol' Man River" and the miscegenation scene and "Bill" derived their power partly from a comparison with the musical-comedy elements dancing around them. Take the fun away, the apparently aimless vitality, and "Show Boat" loses its transcendence. The 1946 "Show Boat" is dated now, too consistent, too much of its day. The 1927 "Show Boat" is eclectic, of many days. Nevertheless, the revisions were locked in. American "Show Boat" revivals honored the 1946 version without question, and it became standard.[34]

In contrast to most of the musicals discussed in subsequent chapters, *Show Boat* directors and their public can choose among two authentic stageworthy versions and one film version (considerably fewer, for instance, than the possibilities extant for Handel's *Messiah*). More commonly, they have chosen to assemble a version of their own. Just as conductors have for two hundred years created their own *Messiah* hybrids, the 1971 London and 1994 Broadway revivals presented provocative conflations of several staged versions of *Show Boat* as well as the 1936 film.[35] For example, two songs from the 1971 London revival that were part of the 1928 London version did not appear in the original 1927 New York production.[36] Kern's swan song and last attempt at a final song for the show, "Nobody Else but Me," introduced in the 1946 New York revival (but not in the touring production), also appears, albeit sung out of context in 1971 by superstar Cleo Laine, who refused the role of Julie unless she was assigned a third song. From the 1936 Universal film the 1971 London revival recycled two of its three new songs, "Ah Still Suits Me" (for Paul Robeson's Joe) and "I Have the Room above Her" (for Allan Jones's Ravenal), sung by their rightful characters but in newly conceived dramatic contexts.[37] Although critical assessments may vary, the 1971 London production provides an unmistakable example of the triumph of accessibility over authenticity.

In director Hal Prince's revival of *Show Boat* in 1994 (the first Broadway production to take full advantage of McGlinn's research), "brothers" and later "coloreds" "all work on the Mississippi" and racial prejudice is acknowledged onstage throughout the evening.[38] Blacks move scenery and pick up messes left by whites, whites steal the Charleston dance steps from black originators, and an endlessly reprised "Ol' Man River" sung by Michel

Bell looms larger than ever. In scenes depicting 1927 as well as the late 1880s, audiences could see conspicuous signs over drinking fountains and elsewhere marked "White Only" and "Colored Only."[39]

Prince and production designer Eugene Lee employed modern stagecraft "to create montages which integrate a leap of years, restore serious incidents and clarify plot and character motivations."[40] From the 1928 London version Prince borrowed "Dance Away the Night" when he needed some music for the radio. From the 1936 film he used Ravenal's suggestive song, "I Have the Room above Her" and, more pervasively, "motion picture techniques such as cross-fades, dissolves and even close-ups."[41] As in the 1946 Broadway production, Frank and Ellie's "I Might Fall Back on You" was dropped (although used as underscoring) and dance assumed a still more important role, especially in the montages staged by choreographer Susan Stroman.[42] The powerful "Mis'ry's Comin' Aroun,'" restored for the Houston Opera production on Broadway in 1983, was again featured.

In earlier productions act II opened with a crowd scene at the 1893 World's Fair in Chicago. Prince drops this scene along with its two songs ("At the Fair" and "In Dahomey") and takes the duet between Magnolia and Ravenal, "Why Do I Love You?," which was sandwiched between these songs, and gives it to the otherwise songless Parthy (Elaine Stritch) to sing to her granddaughter. Perhaps inspired by the 1936 film, which, unlike the stage version, shows the birth of Kim and Parthy rocking her, the effect of this change is enormous. With this one gesture, the shrewish, bigoted, and largely unsympathetic Parthy gains a humanity denied in all previous staged versions.

Musical Symbolism and Dramatic Meaning

In an article that appeared in *Modern Music* during *Show Boat*'s initial New York run, Robert Simon, a staff writer for the *New Yorker* and an opera librettist, wrote about what he perceived as Kern's operatic predilections:

> In *Show Boat*, Kern has an opportunity to make much of his dramatic gift. The action is accompanied by a great deal of incidental music—although "incidental" is a misleading trade term, for Kern's music heightens immeasurably the emotional value of the situation.... Themes are quoted and even developed in almost Wagnerian fashion.[43]

Without further elaboration Simon suggests that Kern, like Wagner and several of the Broadway theater composers considered in this study, embraces his principal dramatic themes within a family of leitmotivs.[44] All of these motives in Kern and Hammerstein's "leit-opera" (a term perhaps coined by Simon) can be seen against the backdrop of the Mississippi, arguably the principal protagonist of the drama, much as the "folk" form the heart and center of Musorgsky's *Boris Godunov* and Gershwin's *Porgy and Bess*.

In its purest form, closest to nature, like Mahler's cuckoos in his First Symphony (1888), Kern has chosen to represent the river by the interval of a perfect fourth (the same interval that begins "Taps" and "Reveille"). As shown in Example 2.1a, "Fish got to swim [B♭-E♭], and birds got to fly" [E♭-B♭]), Kern uses this perfect fourth to connect the force of the natural world with the central human theme of the work embodied in "Can't Help Lovin' Dat Man": a woman in love is destined to love her man forever, even when he abandons her. The theme first appears early in the work as underscoring for the dialogue in which the unrequited lover Pete questions Queenie about how she acquired the brooch he had given Julie. Since audiences have not yet heard the words to this song, its meaning cannot be fully grasped during the exchange between Pete and Queenie that interrupts choruses of "Cotton Blossom." But with Example 2.1a, the lyrical version of Julie's song that whites would not know (it was sung by her African-American mother when Julie was a child), Kern and Hammerstein have successfully connected Queenie and Julie from the outset of the show. Julie's identity as a mulatto otherwise remains undisclosed until two scenes later, when the meaning and impact of her association with Queenie's race will be clarified.

Significantly, the five three-note *Show Boat* themes shown in Example 2.2 are sung by and to people—or in one case to an anthromorphized boat—who are part of the river and close to nature.[45] The largest group of these "river" motives, nearly all introduced in *Show Boat*'s opening scene, consist of short

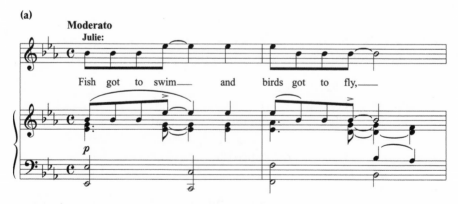

Example 2.1. "Can't Help Lovin' Dat Man"
(a) original form
(b) transformation into a rag

(b)

Magnolia tries and fails to sing in this tempo
Allegro

Example 2.1. Continued

musical figures, in which Kern fills in the perfect fourth of "Can't Help Lovin' Dat Man" with a single additional note. The four notes of the "Cotton Blossom" (Example 2.2a) when reversed provide the opening musical material for the main chorus of Joe's "Ol' Man River" (Example 2.2b) and, when reshuffled, Cap'n Andy's theme (Example 2.2c).[46] Additional transformations of these three notes encompassed within a perfect fourth can be found in the opening of "Queenie's Ballyhoo" (Example 2.2d) and in a prominent segment of "Mis'ry's Comin' Aroun'" (Example 2.2e), included in all three published vocal scores. Although Kern never acknowledged a source, all of these themes might be traced, appropriately enough, to Dvořák's contemporaneously composed "New World" Symphony (1893) (Example 2.2f).[47]

Parthy and Sheriff Vallon also lead their lives along the river. In contrast to the characters who are in sympathy with this life force, however (Cap'n Andy and his *Cotton Blossom*, Joe, Queenie, the black laborers, and the women of any race who can't help loving their men), Parthy and Vallon demonstrate their intrinsic antipathy to the river with subtle alterations that intrude on the simplicity and perfection of the perfect fourth. Audiences first meet Parthy and her

(a)

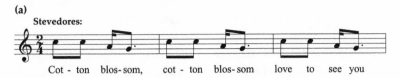

Stevedores:

Cot - ton blos - som, cot - ton blos - som love to see you

Example 2.2. "River Family" of motives (transposed to the key of C Major)
(a) "Cotton Blossom"
(b) "Ol' Man River"
(c) Cap'n Andy's theme
(d) "Queenie's Ballyhoo"
(e) "Mis'ry" theme
(f) from Dvořák's "New World" Symphony

Example 2.2. (Continued)

theme (Example 2.3) after the climax of the song "Cotton Blossom" as underscoring to her yelling "Andy!!!! Drat that man, he's never around!" moments before we hear Magnolia's piano theme (Example 2.4).

The first two notes of Parthy's theme are a descending perfect fourth (D-A). But although Parthy may lead a life along the river, Cap'n Andy cannot and Kern will not make her drink in its physical beauty and spiritual richness. Consequently, after this perfect fourth, Kern has Parthy introduce a Bb, only a half-step up from the A but a giant step removed from the natural world of the river. The Bb and its following note G combine with the still-held D above to produce a G-minor triad, significantly the same chord that generates and supports Magnolia's inhibition and lament later in the scene in section 4 of "Make Believe" ("Though the cold and brutal

Example 2.3. Parthy's theme

fact is"). By the second measure of her theme Parthy has moved below the descending fourth of the "Cotton Blossom" (to an F♯). In the third and fourth measures—a repetition of the first two but transposed up a sinister augmented fourth or tritone (D to G♯), the tense and dissonant interval that will figure so prominently in the music of Sporting Life (*Porgy and Bess*) and the Jets (*West Side Story*)—Parthy's theme has moved radically from G minor to C♯ minor (also a tritone) where it will remain for the duration of its remaining four measures. Perhaps in her musical resistance to the river Parthy is expressing a longing for her home state of Massachusetts, where "no decent body'd touch this show boat riffraff with a ten foot pole."[48]

Once he has established musical equivalents for his characters and their world, Kern transforms and links these themes melodically and rhythmically to make his (and Hammerstein's) dramatic points, as, for example, the transformation of Cap'n Andy's theme into a wedding march at the end of act I and then into a processional and hymn in Kim's convent school.[49] Perhaps the clearest example of this technique can be observed in the evolution of "Can't Help Lovin' Dat Man." In the late 1880s the song is introduced in its lyrical form by Julie (Example 2.1a) followed immediately by an accelerated version sung by Queenie, Joe, the black chorus, and Magnolia (act I, scene 2); in the second act (scene 4) the song undergoes further transformation into a rag tune in 1904, when the Trocadero pianist Jake encourages Magnolia to sing a more animated modern version in order to get her act into the Trocadero production (Example 2.1b).

Example 2.4. Magnolia's piano theme and "Where's the Mate for Me?"
  (a) Magnolia's piano theme
  (b) "Where's the Mate for Me?" (B section, or release)

Magnolia's piano theme (Example 2.4), one of the most ubiquitous themes of the show, will also undergo various transformations after its introduction in the opening scene. These include a reharmonized statement that underscores Cap'n Andy's announcement of Magnolia's wedding to Ravenal near the end of act I and a jazzy version, "It's Getting Hotter in the North" (the original finale dropped after the Washington, D.C., tryouts), sung by Magnolia's daughter, Kim, in 1927. It is also possible that Kern intended audiences to hear a musical connection between Magnolia's piano theme and the opening fragment of the verse to "Ol' Man River"—a verse that not incidentally also begins the show opener, "Cotton Blossom"—when he decided to adopt it almost unchanged from *The Beauty Prize* (1923).[50] In any event, Kern's decision to join the second measure of Magnolia's theme with the central theme of the all-knowing and timeless river is more than a detail. Not only does this touch provide another dramatically strong musical linkage, but it also bonds Ravenal to his future bride and all she represents. Her theme immediately enters his consciousness (even before they meet) and takes over the B section of his song, "Where's the Mate for Me?"[51]

The vast network of thematic foreshadowings and reminiscences introduced here rarely fail to credibly unite the present with the past. One such example of Kern's ability to make a dramatic point through a musical reference is his use of the "Mis'ry" theme (from the discarded song), which underscores Julie's lecture to Magnolia about men, immediately after the impressionable younger woman has met Ravenal (at which point such a lecture is, of course, already too late). The presence of "Mis'ry'" here anticipates Julie's misery two scenes later, when her partially black heritage is exposed and she and her blood partner Steve are exiled from the *Cotton Blossom*. It also prepares listeners for Julie's and Magnolia's eventual misery in act II when both will lose the men they love.[52] A rhythmic connection that might also suggest a dramatic interpretation is the similarity between the prevalent long-short-short rhythm of this "Mis'ry" theme and the opening two measures of Ravenal's "Where's the Mate for Me?" (Example 2.5).[53] In any event Ravenal's musical remembrance of the waltz portion (section 2) of "Make Believe," when he sings "I let fate decide if I walk or ride" in "Till Good Luck Comes My Way" (the latter unfortunately dropped from the 1946 revival), reveals more clearly than anything he could say or do that Ravenal's own destiny is to love Magnolia even as he will one day abandon her.[54]

Ravenal's Entrance and Meeting with Magnolia

An exceptionally powerful example of what Kern and Hammerstein were able to achieve with their second collaboration can be found in *Show Boat*'s expansive, intricate, and brilliantly conceived opening scene (act I, scene 1). After the opening chorus, "Cotton Blossom," and Cap'n Andy's "Bal-lyhoo," we meet the river gambler Gaylord Ravenal, he meets his future bride Magnolia Hawks (Andy's daughter), and the two fall in love at first sight. In addition to its classic status as the quintessential Broadway "boy meets girl" scene, Ravenal's entrance and meeting with Magnolia offers two major songs, "Where's the Mate for Me?" and "Make Believe," as well as a continuous scene in which all actions and dialogue are underscored.

Ravenal's meeting with Magnolia also provides an example of how per-ceptively Kern and Hammerstein understood the dramatic potential of Ferber's narrative. In the novel Ravenal notices Magnolia on the deck of the *Cotton Blossom* at the same moment Cap'n Andy offers him the leading romantic role in their troupe. When Ravenal finds out that she will be his dramatic counterpart, he unhesitatingly accepts the challenge even though he has no experience (but of course he will not actually need to act). Ferber then tells her readers of Ravenal's and Magnolia's destiny, an "inevitable" and "cosmic course."[55] After describing this silent meeting, Ferber conspires with her character Parthy and does not allow the future lovers to speak to one another again for another twelve pages—and then not alone. Although Kern and Hammerstein made many revisions in this portion of scene 1 dur-ing the 1927 tryouts, only relatively minor changes differentiate the original New York and London books from the 1946 revival and the three published scores for this scene.[56]

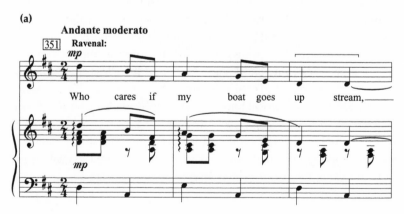

Example 2.5. "Where's the Mate for Me?" (opening and "fancy" harmonizations)
   (a) "Who cares if my boat goes up stream?"
   (b) "I drift along with my fancy"
   (c) "I drift along with my fancy"

Example 2.5. Continued

From the moment audiences first glimpse the future hero, Kern establishes the connection between Ravenal and his theme, capturing his aimlessness with a harmonically ambiguous accompaniment that refuses to find a tonal harbor. The theme continues to underscore Ellie May Chipley, the leading female comic with the *Show Boat* troupe, in her endeavor to attract Ravenal's attention. Ellie drops her handkerchief, Ravenal picks it up—but not her cue—"hands it to her with courtesy," and graciously acknowledges her gratitude before leaving the embarrassed comedian to fall back on her stage partner, Frank Schultz. After Sheriff Vallon's appearance interrupts what would have been a harmonic resting point on D major, Kern foreshadows Ravenal's song from scene 3, "Till Good Luck Comes My Way," to underscore the remaining dialogue in which Vallon and Ravenal reflect on the drifter's bachelorhood.

In the thrice-repeated opening phrase of "Where's the Mate for Me?" the first shown in Example 2.5a ("Who cares if my boat goes up stream?" and two statements of "I drift along with my fancy"), Kern ingeniously varies the harmony of the final melodic note D (Example 2.5b and c). Its first appearance on the words "up stream" (the third measure) is paradoxically and perhaps unintentionally the *lowest* note of the phrase—after all, the point is that Ravenal does not care whether he is going upstream or downstream. Here Kern harmonizes the tonic or central key, D, with a conventional tonic D-major triad. Although Kern's music initially *preceded* Hammerstein's lyrics here and elsewhere in *Show Boat*, one nonetheless suspects that Kern may have occasionally altered his harmonies to correspond to the musical potential of Hammerstein's lyrics. A major candidate for this creative scenario occurs in the third measure of the opening phrase of "Where's the Mate?" (Example 2.5b), where Kern sets the word "fancy" with a fancy (and deceptive) resolution to a minor triad on the sixth degree of the scale.[57] On the final statement of this phrase (Example 2.5c), moments before Ravenal hears Magnolia's piano theme, Kern displays his fanciest chord, again on the word "fancy."[58] Ravenal is now as far adrift as Broadway harmony can take him.

To depict his speechlessness (or songlessness) upon seeing Magnolia, Ravenal stops abruptly before the music moves toward a conclusion on the expected tonal center. But "Where's the Mate for Me?," in contrast to most Broadway songs, remains incomplete. Instead, Ravenal's unasked final musical question is answered by the mere presence of Magnolia. For such a special occasion Kern and Hammerstein were willing to deprive audiences of the opportunity to disturb dramatic continuity with applause. Even before Magnolia's physical presence interrupts the final statement of the A section, however, Ravenal had already become subliminally aware of the answer to his question "Where's the mate?" In what is clearly a case of love at first sound as well as first sight, Magnolia's music (her piano theme shown in Example 2.4) becomes immediately and completely absorbed into the B section of Ravenal's song.

In "Make Believe," the ensuing duet between Magnolia and Ravenal (thankfully, in contrast to the Ferber novel they are allowed to speak and sing), Kern connects no less than four individual melodies and distinguishes each by metrical or key changes. As in Ravenal's "Where's the Mate for Me?" Kern's purpose here is to provide a musical narrative that accurately reflects the psychological progression of a budding romance. By the end of the first section Ravenal has already admitted that his love for Magnolia is not a pretense ("For, to tell the truth, I do"). On the word "do" the music responds by becoming a waltz, which as far back as Franz Lehár's *The Merry Widow* and Johann Strauss Jr.'s *Die Fledermaus* had come to represent the language of love for American as well as European audiences.[59] Ravenal apologizes for "the words that betray my heart," but Magnolia, who has in fact betrayed her heart by joining Ravenal's waltz, is not quite ready to abandon the "game of just supposing" when she sings, "we only pretend." Although Magnolia wants to pretend that Ravenal is only "playing a lover's part," Kern's music belies Hammerstein's words.

The third section of "Make Believe" leaves the tonic D major and modulates four notes above to the subdominant (G major) with another metrical change, this time from triple (waltz time) back to duple meter. Now Magnolia plays her game with a new level of flirtation accompanied by appropriate melodic playfulness ("The game of just supposing"). Following Ravenal's reply to this flirtation, Magnolia introduces a fourth section in the parallel minor mode (G minor, foreshadowed in Parthy's theme), a response to her sobering realization that "the cold and brutal fact is" they have never met before. But the pessimism of the minor mode disappears after only four measures when Magnolia states her rationale: since they are only playing a lover's part, they "need not mind convention's P's and Q's." Clearly, imagination that "can banish all regret" can also banish minor modes.[60]

Magnolia, a bystander in the first section and half of the second, has now dominated all but eight measures since she first pointed out to Ravenal that they are only pretending, after all. Most significantly, Magnolia introduces the return of the central "Make Believe" melody more intensely than Ravenal's opening gambit, and to match this intensity the music escalates a half-step higher (E♭ major) from the original tonic D. When Ravenal joins her on the words "others find peace of mind in pretending," it is by now unequivocally clear that Ravenal and Magnolia are not like these others. Their love is real.

The distribution between Magnolia and Ravenal during this return of the main tune underwent several changes between the tryouts and the New York premiere, and there remains some lingering ambiguity about who should sing what after the first two lines (invariably given to Magnolia). For example, according to the libretto typescript in the Library of Congress's Jerome Kern Collection (see "Manuscript Sources" no. 1 in the online website), Kern and Hammerstein had once indicated that Magnolia alone should sing the next lines ("Others find peace of mind in pretending—/ Couldn't you, / Couldn't I? / Couldn't we?") before they conclude their duet. The evolution of the final line is especially intricate.

Hammerstein remained unsatisfied by his decision to have both principals sing the last line ("For, to tell the truth,—I do"). Was Magnolia ready to admit the truth of her love to Ravenal? In a penciled change Hammerstein has Ravenal sing the "I do" without Magnolia. In the New York Public Library libretto typescript (see "Manuscript Sources" no. 2 in the online website) the entire last line is given to Ravenal alone but placed in brackets. In the New York production libretto published with the McGlinn recording (no. 3) Ravenal sings the final line (without brackets), and this version is preserved in the published London libretto of 1934 (no. 4), the 1936 screen-play (no. 5), and the 1946 New York revival (no. 6).[61] Further contributing to the ambiguity and confusion is the lack of correspondence between these text versions and the piano-vocal drafts and published scores, none of which specifies that Ravenal profess his love alone until the Welk score (which cor-responds to the 1946 production), where Magnolia's "For, to tell the truth,— I do" is placed in brackets.[62]

Perhaps most revelatory about these manuscripts are Kern and Hammer-stein's gradual realization that this portion of the scene needed to focus more exclusively on Ravenal and Magnolia. The New York Public Library and Library of Congress typescripts, for example, present two versions of a con-versation between Ellie and Frank that would be discarded by the December premiere.[63] Hammerstein eventually concluded that this exchange slowed down the action and distracted audiences from their focus on Ravenal.[64]

A second interruption, also eventually discarded, occurred after the B section of Ravenal's song "Where's the Mate for Me?" (based on Magnolia's piano theme, Example 2.4). Both the Library of Congress and New York Public Library typescripts present some dialogue and stage action during the twenty-six measures of underscoring that have survived in Draft 2: Parthy's theme (Example 2.3), Cap'n Andy's theme minus its six opening measures (Example 2.2c), and Ravenal's theme (Example 2.5).[65] Moments later Parthy intrudes once again, shouting "Nola!," and Hammerstein provides the following comment: "Magnolia looks down on this splendid fellow, Ravenal. Her maidenly heart flutters. She really should go in and answer mother—but she stays."[66]

Like the brief dialogue between Ellie and Frank that intrudes on this moment in the 1936 film, the appearance of Parthy here and after the B section of "Where's the Mate for Me?" interrupts the focus on the soon-to-be-lovers. Parthy, while always unwelcome, is also unnecessary dur-ing this portion of the scene, particularly since she had made a prominent exit shortly before we met Ravenal. Wisely, Kern and Hammerstein in 1927 allowed Parthy's music to prompt Magnolia to tell Ravenal she "must go now" and avoided the reality of Parthy's intrusion on the young couple's private moment before "Make Believe."[67]

After *Show Boat* Kern and Hammerstein would collaborate on three of the composer's remaining five Broadway shows, two with respectable runs, *Sweet Adeline* (1929) and *Music in the Air* (1932), and a disappointing *Very Warm for May* (1939). Despite their considerable merits, none of these shows have entered the repertory (although *Music in the Air* was chosen for New York City Center's *Encores! Great American Musicals in Concert* in the 2008–09 season). Less than a year after *Show Boat* Hammerstein collaborated with Romberg on *The New Moon*, a show that went on for an impressive 509 performances. Then, despite the success of individual songs, including "All the Things You Are" from his final collaboration with Kern, Hammerstein's series of unwise choices (both in dramatic material and collaborators) and hurried work resulted in eleven years of Broadway failures before he rose from the ashes with *Oklahoma!*

Similarly, Hammerstein's Hollywood years in the 1930s and early 1940s yielded no original musical films of lasting acclaim, although here, too, a considerable number of songs with Hammerstein lyrics have become standards.[68] Hammerstein also adapted the screenplay for the penultimate Fred Astaire and Ginger Rogers film, *The Story of Vernon and Irene Castle* (1939).[69] In the next decade Hammerstein began his historic collaboration with Rodgers, and by the time *Show Boat* was revived in 1946, they had already written two of their five major hit musicals, *Oklahoma!* and *Carousel* (the latter the subject of chapter 9).[70]

In addition to his subsequent work with Hammerstein, Kern created two successful musicals with Harbach, the unfortunately overlooked *The Cat and the Fiddle* (1931) and *Roberta* (1933), the latter best known in its greatly altered 1935 film version. In fact, most of Kern's career after *Show Boat* was occupied with the creation of twenty-two full or partial film scores— thirteen original and nine adapted from Broadway—including several with lyrics by Hammerstein and the Astaire and Rogers classic *Swing Time* (1936), with lyrics by Dorothy Fields. Unfortunately, Kern never had the opportunity even to begin a new musical in the Rodgers and Hammerstein era, since he died shortly after Rodgers, who was producing a musical based on the life of Annie Oakley, had asked him to write the music.[71]

Kern and Hammerstein's inability to produce another *Show Boat* in the 1930s enhances the significance of their earlier achievement. Although its ending did not embrace Ferber's darker version, *Show Boat*, "the first truly, totally American operetta" had dared to present an American epic with a credible story, three-dimensional characters, a convincing use of American vernacular appropriate to the changing world (including the African-Americanization of culture) from the late 1880s to 1927, and a sensitive portrayal of race relations that ranged from the plight of the black underclass to miscegenation.[72] As the first Broadway musical to keep rolling along in the repertory from its time to ours, while at the same time enjoying the critical respect of musical-theater historians for more than seventy years, *Show Boat*, the musical "that demanded a new maturity from musical theatre and from its audience,"[73] has long since earned its coveted historical position as the foundation of the modern American musical.

CHAPTER THREE

ANYTHING GOES

Songs Ten, Book Three

B efore the curtain rose on the 1987 revival of *Anything Goes* at Lincoln Center's Vivian Beaumont Theater, audiences heard the strains of Cole Porter's own rendition of the title song recorded in 1934. At the conclusion of this critically well-received and popularly successful show a large silkscreen photograph of Porter (1891–1964) appeared behind a scrim to cast a literal as well as metaphoric shadow over the cast. More than fifty years after its premiere the message was clear: the real star of *Anything Goes* was its composer-lyricist, the creator of such timeless song classics as "I Get a Kick Out of You," "You're the Top," "Blow, Gabriel, Blow," "All Through the Night," "Easy to Love," "Friendship," "It's De-Lovely," and the title song. Readers familiar with *Anything Goes* from various amateur and semi-professional productions over the past thirty years may scarcely notice that the last three songs named were taken from other Porter shows.

Anything Goes, after the Gershwins' Pulitzer Prize–winning *Of Thee I Sing* the longest running book musical of the 1930s and almost certainly the most frequently revived musical of its time (in one form or another), was Porter's first major hit. Otherwise virtually forgotten, each of Porter's five musicals preceding *Anything Goes* introduced at least one song that would rank a ten in almost anyone's book: "What Is This Thing Called Love?" in *Wake Up and Dream* (1929), "You Do Something to Me" in *Fifty Million Frenchmen* (1929), "Love for Sale" in *The New Yorkers* (1930), and "Night and Day" in *Gay Divorce* (1932). The Porter shows that debuted in the years between *Anything*

Anything Goes, act II, finale (1987). Photograph: Brigitte Lacombe.

Goes and *Kiss Me, Kate* (1948) are similarly remembered mainly because they contain one or more hit songs.

In the unlikely Midwestern town of Peru, Indiana, Porter's mother, appropriately named Kate, arranged to have Cole's first song published at her own expense in 1902 (he was eleven at the time). Three years later Porter entered the exclusive Worcester Academy in Massachusetts. Upon his graduation from Yale in 1913, where he had delighted his fellow students with fraternity shows and football songs, Porter endured an unhappy year at Harvard Law School. Against his grandfather's wishes and in spite of financial threats, Porter enrolled in Harvard's music department for the 1914–1915 academic year. In 1917 he furthered his musical training with private studies in New

York City with Pietro Yon, the musical director and organist at Saint Patrick's Cathedral; in 1919–1920 the future Broadway composer continued his studies in composition, counterpoint, harmony, and orchestration with Vincent D'Indy at the Schola Cantorum in Paris.

Although his first success, *Paris*, would not arrive for another twelve years, Porter had already produced a musical on Broadway, *See America First* (1916), before Gershwin or Rodgers had begun their Broadway careers and only one year after Kern had inaugurated his series of distinctive musicals at the Princess Theatre. The years between the failure of his Broadway debut after fifteen performances (inspiring the famous quip from *Variety*, "*See America First* last!") and the success of Irene Bordoni's singing "Let's Do It" in *Paris* were largely dormant ones for Porter. In fact, the sum total of his Broadway work other than *See America First* was one song interpolation for Kern's *Miss Information* in 1915 and approximately ten songs each in *Hitchy-Koo of 1919* and the *Greenwich Village Follies* in 1924. During these years the already wealthy Porter—despite his profligacy an heir to his grandfather's fortune—grew still wealthier when he married the socialite and famous beauty Linda Lee Thomas in 1919. In 1924 the Porters moved to Italy where they would soon launch three years of lavish party-throwing and party-going in their Venetian palazzos. On numerous such occasions the expatriate songwriter would entertain his friends with his witty lyrics and melodies. Near the end of this partying, Porter in 1927 auditioned unsuccessfully for Vinton Freedley and Alex Aarons, the producers of several Gershwin hit musicals and the future producers of four Porter shows starting with *Anything Goes*. When the following year Rodgers and Hart were preoccupied with *A Connecticut Yankee*, Porter was easily persuaded to leave Europe and bring *Paris* to New York. *Anything Goes* would arrive six years and many perennial song favorites later.

The Changing Times of Anything Goes

Most accounts of the genesis of *Anything Goes* attribute the disastrous fire that took between 125 and 180 passengers' lives on the pleasure ship *Morro Castle* off the coast at Asbury Park, New Jersey, on September 8, 1934, as the catalyst that led to the revised book by Howard Lindsay and Russel Crouse. According to conventional wisdom, the earlier libretto about a shipwreck could not be used any more than Porter could use his line about Mrs. Lindbergh in "I Get a Kick Out of You" after the kidnapping and murder of the Lindbergh baby.[1] But at least two sources, George Eells's biography of Porter and Miles Kreuger's introductory notes to conductor John McGlinn's reconstructed recording, report that producer Freedley was dissatisfied by the Guy Bolton–P. G. Wodehouse book when he received it on August 15 and that the *Morro* disaster served mainly as a convenient explanation.

According to Eells, Freedley thought there was "a tastelessness about this piece of work that no amount of rewriting would eradicate," a view echoed by both Kreuger and Bolton-Wodehouse biographer Lee Davis. Kreuger writes, "Freedley was fearful that the rather derisive attitude toward Hollywood might ruin chances of a film sale." Davis goes further: "The first script was rejected by Freedley for its Hollywood treatment, not its similarity to the tragic fire at sea of the liner *Morro Castle*, as has been historically accepted. Nor would he blanch at the second version because of its continued treatment of a catastrophe at sea. It would be because the second version was a hopeless mess."[2]

In an interview with Richard Hubler published in 1965, one year after Porter's death, the composer-lyricist anticipated the future conclusions of Eells, Kreuger, and Davis. Porter recalled that the *Morro Castle* tragedy provided an excuse to scrap a Wodehouse-Bolton book whose quality was "so bad that it was obvious that the work was completely inadequate."[3] The synopsis included in this book is of course based on the revised *Anything Goes* book by Lindsay and Crouse, based in part on the rejected and now presumed lost second draft by Bolton and Wodehouse and Bolton's original scenario from early 1934, currently housed at the State Historical Society of Wisconsin (which includes some dialogue for "Gaxton" and "Ethel" and "Moore").

Since it is possible that Lindsay and Crouse retained relatively little of the Bolton-Wodehouse second draft—although the new book may have contained more than an alleged five lines—it is not surprising that the inexperienced collaborators would be able to complete only a few scenes from act I and nothing of act II before rehearsals began on October 8. In contrast to the painstaking work and lengthy gestation period of most of the musicals surveyed in this volume, *Anything Goes* was hastily, perhaps even frantically, put together.

But Freedley, Lindsay, Crouse, and Porter had other objectives than to create an epic book musical along the lines of *Show Boat*. Their central concern was to produce a comic hit and to provide dramatic and musical opportunities to suit their outstanding preassembled cast. In particular, they needed a vehicle to display William Gaxton's (Billy) proven flair for multifarious disguises and to exploit the inspired silliness of comedian Victor Moore's incongruous casting as a notorious gangster (Moon). The result was enough to prompt Brooks Atkinson to exclaim that "comedy is the most satisfying invention of the human race."[4] Atkinson could not ask anything more of a show that exuded such refreshing topicality and personality, a show for the moment, if not for the ages. If one or two songs stuck around for awhile, so much the better.

Although John McGlinn later proclaimed the 1934 *Anything Goes* as "one of the most perfect farces ever written," most producers and directors for the past forty years have been trying to solve the perceived disparity in quality between the book and the songs by altering the former and interpolating more of the latter.[5] The 1987 revival at the Vivian Beaumont was not the first time audiences found themselves leaving a production of *Anything Goes* humming or whistling songs from other Porter shows. In the 1962 revival, the only version distributed by Tams-Witmark for the next twenty-five years, still other songs from other Porter shows had been interpolated. The lyricist-composer's own reputed cavalier attitude toward his books and song interpolations prompted Broadway and Hollywood historian Gerald Mast to state erroneously that Porter's last will and testament "granted explicit permission to take any Porter song from any Porter show and use it in any other."[6] Unfortunately, the relative commercial success of McGlinn's recorded enterprise has not encouraged most producers and directors to revive the 1934 *Anything Goes*.

The online website presents an outline of the scenes and songs of the *Anything Goes* that audiences would have heard during most of the initial run of the show that opened on November 21, 1934 (as well the scenes and songs seen and heard in the Off-Broadway Revival of 1962 and the Vivian Beaumont Revival of 1987). As in the case of most musicals from any period (and many eighteenth-century operas), additional songs were tried and then discarded during tryouts or during the early weeks of the first New York run. In act I, scene 2, "Bon Voyage" was originally juxtaposed, then ingeniously combined, with another song, "There's No Cure like Travel," a song that interestingly contains the main musical material of "Bon Voyage."[7] Just as Mozart composed the easier-to-sing aria "Dalla sua pace" to accommodate the Viennese singer in *Don Giovanni* who was unable to negotiate the demands of the aria from the original Prague production ("Il mio tesoro"), Porter composed "All through the Night" in this scene for Gaxton (Billy Crocker) to replace the difficult-to-sing "Easy to Love."

Another song intended for this scene, "Kate the Great," was, according to the recollection of *Anything Goes* orchestrator Hans Spialek, rejected by Ethel Merman who "vouldn't sing it" because it was a "*durr-ty* song!"[8] A song planned as a tongue-in-cheek romantic duet in act I, scene 6, between Hope and Billy, "Waltz down the Aisle" (which bears striking melodic and rhythmic similarities as well as a similar dramatic purpose to "Wunderbar" from Porter's *Kiss Me, Kate*) was also dropped from *Anything Goes*. A song for

Hope in act II, scene 1, "What a Joy to Be Young," was deleted before the Broadway premiere.[9]

One song in the beginning of the Broadway run, "Buddie, Beware," was replaced by a reprise of "I Get a Kick Out of You" within a few weeks. In order to understand the artistic implications of this change it is necessary to recall Porter's original motivation. Composers of musicals before (or after) the Rodgers and Hammerstein era could not, of course, always predict which song would become a hit. Nevertheless, they almost invariably tried to place their best bets *after* an opening number, usually for chorus. In *Anything Goes* Porter tried something more unusual. Instead of opening with a chorus, Porter decided to begin less conventionally with a potential hit song for Ethel Merman five minutes into the show, "I Get a Kick Out of You."

Porter's reasons for beginning with what he felt would be the hit of the show may have been somewhat perverse. According to Kreuger, Porter's "society friends thought it was amusing to drift into the theatre fifteen or twenty minutes after the curtain had gone up, so that all their friends could observe what they were wearing."[10] Porter therefore "warned his friends for weeks before the opening that they had better arrive on time or they would miss the big song."[11] There is no record that Merman objected to "Buddie, Beware" in act II, scene 2, for the same reason she objected to a song about the sexual exploits of Catherine (Kate) the Great. Her objections in this case were practical rather than moral: the show needed a reprise of "I Get a Kick Out of You" "for the benefit of those who had arrived late!"[12] If this undocumented anecdote is to be believed, Porter, who had earlier agreed to cut "Kate the Great," was again willing to accommodate his star and cut "Buddie, Beware."[13]

The history of *Anything Goes* after its premiere in 1934 differs markedly from the fate of *Show Boat* discussed in the previous chapter. The original 1927 Broadway version of *Show Boat* was superseded by Kern and Hammerstein's own rethinking of the work in the 1946 revival that included a reworked book, several deleted songs and a brand new one, and new orchestrations. As we have seen, after Hammerstein's death in 1960, the 1971 London and 1994 Broadway *Show Boat* revivals presented conflated versions of the musical that included songs from various earlier stage productions (New York, 1927; London, 1928; New York, 1946) and also songs from the 1936 film classic. Some of the original as well as interpolated songs were also either placed in different contexts or distributed to different characters.

Despite these liberties, both the 1971 London and 1994 Broadway revivals contained interpolated songs that had been associated with one version or another of this musical ("How'd You Like to Spoon with Me?" from the

1971 London production is an isolated exception). In contrast, the *Anything Goes* revival in 1962, the version distributed to prospective producers until replaced by the 1987 revival, incorporated no less than six songs out of a total of fourteen from *other* Porter shows ("It's De-Lovely," "Heaven Hop," "Friendship," "Let's Step Out," "Let's Misbehave," and "Take Me Back to Manhattan"). Also, in 1962 the order of several songs was rearranged and, ironically, a thoroughly revised book was written by Guy Bolton, who had prepared the original scenario early in 1934 and with P. G. Wodehouse had submitted the rejected 1934 book.

The 1987 revival contained yet another new book, this time by Russel Crouse's son Timothy and John Weidman.[14] This book retained two of the interpolations from 1962 ("It's De-Lovely" and "Friendship"), and added two other Porter tunes from shows that had not even appeared on Broadway, "Goodbye, Little Dream, Goodbye" from *O Mistress Mine*, a 1936 musical produced in London, and "I Want to Row on the Crew," from the Yale fraternity show *Paranoia* of 1914. The 1987 production also rearranged the order and dramatic context of several other songs from the original 1934 Broadway run. Most strikingly, the 1987 revision resurrected three songs that had appeared at various phases of the 1934 tryouts and initial run: "There's No Cure like Travel," "Easy to Love," and "Buddie, Beware" (see the online Appendix for the sources of all the interpolated songs).

One year before criticizing the undramatic use of recitative in the Theatre Guild production of *Porgy and Bess*, Brooks Atkinson reviewed the Broadway premiere of *Anything Goes*. The review is an unequivocal rave of "a thundering good musical show" with "a rag, tag and bobtail of comic situations and of music sung in the spots when it is most exhilarating."[15] Most surprisingly from a modern perspective is the fact that Atkinson praises the book, not as a work of art, perhaps, but as a well-crafted vehicle to set off William Gaxton's talent for wearing disguises and the comic characterization of Victor Moore's Moon, "the quintessence of musical comedy humor." Atkinson does not feel the need to consider *Anything Goes* as anything other than the "thundering good song-and-dance show" it purports to be.[16] Another reviewer, Franklin P. Adams, lambasted the *songs* from *Anything Goes* (because they were difficult to remember or whistle), but offered no negative remarks about the book.[17]

Like Atkinson's newfound distaste for *On Your Toes* upon its ill-fated 1954 revival (discussed in chapter 5), the *New York Times* review of the 1962 Off-Broadway revival, twenty-eight years after *Anything Goes* made its debut, demonstrates that a new standard for musical theater had evolved during the intervening years. In contrast to Atkinson's appreciation of the original book, Lewis Funke wrote that "if you can get by the deserts that lurk in the libretto, knowing that there always will be that oasis of a Cole Porter tune waiting at the end of each rugged journey, you may find yourself enjoying the revival of *Anything Goes*."[18] In Funke's account, "only some of the lines retain their mirth" and the encapsulated plot summary that he offers serves merely to remind sophisticated 1960s audiences that "those were simple days in musical comedy."[19] What Funke neglects to report is that the book he is criticizing is *not* the 1934 book by Lindsay and Crouse but a version rewritten in 1962 by Bolton.

In his autobiography, director and librettist George Abbott (1887–1995), who authored or co-authored books for an impressive array of musicals, including *On Your Toes, The Boys from Syracuse, Where's Charley?, A Tree Grows in Brooklyn, The Pajama Game, Damn Yankees*, and *Fiorello!*, discusses a review of a 1963 Off-Broadway revival directed by Richard York of the 1938 Rodgers and Hart classic *The Boys from Syracuse*:

> I was delighted to read of its outstanding success, and distressed that some of the reviewers referred to the old-fashioned jokes in the book. But I was puzzled when one of the reviewers cited one of these jokes, a corny pun: "Dozens of men are at my feet." "Yes, I know, chiropodists." This kind of humor is so alien to me that I knew I could never have written it; and when I got back to New York I found that the "old jokes" in the revival were new jokes inserted by Mr. [Richard] York to "modernize" the script. I took out some of these gags, but because the production as a whole was so delightful, I couldn't get very angry.[20]

It has become a commonplace almost universally shared by writers on Broadway musicals—along with directors and producers—that weak books are the main reason for the neglect of most musicals before *Oklahoma!* and *Carousel*. For this reason, after Rodgers and Hammerstein began an irreversible vogue for integrated book musicals, revivals of musicals were almost invariably accompanied by a team of doctors performing major surgery that included the reordering of songs and interpolations from other musicals of the same composer.

This type of surgical procedure begs several questions that merit further exploration. Is the idea of the so-called integrated musical heralded by Rodgers and Hammerstein in the 1940s intrinsically superior to a musical with an anachronistic book and timeless songs? Are the books of the 1930s as weak as later critics make them out to be? Can some of the alleged weaknesses be attributed to the modernized books rather than to the originals? If the books of 1930s musicals are weak, why are they weak, and can they be salvaged by revisions and interpolations? Is it really a good idea to strip the original books down to their underwear and then dress them up again with as many songs as possible from other shows? Or can reasonable men and women provide an acceptable modern alternative? Are modern actors unable to successfully recapture and convey an older brand of comedy? Might the problem with *Anything Goes* stem more from an incongruity between music and text than from a diseased book?

Part of the answer to these questions might be traced to evolving social concerns rather than aesthetic considerations. Our current sensitivities and our understanding of topical issues are no longer what they were in 1934. As Porter would say, "times have changed." The following chapter will suggest that much of the criticism of *Porgy and Bess*, which followed the Porter hit one year later, was due (especially after the civil rights movement of the 1950s and '60s) less to its artistic qualities than to its perceived perpetuation of negative black stereotypes and Heyward's and Gershwin's presumption to speak for blacks. In *Show Boat*, changing sensitivities made it necessary for Hammerstein to alter offending references, and later versions, especially the 1951 MGM film and the 1966 Lincoln Center production, tried to deflect criticism by minimizing the miscegenation scene and the role of blacks in general. Most musicals suffer, some irreparably, when their depiction of women is judged by feminist standards that emerged in the 1970s (see the discussion of *Kiss Me, Kate* in chapter 10).

Although increasing sensitivity to ethnic minority groups or to women is probably not the major obstacle to the revivability of *Anything Goes*, the stereotypic depiction of Reverend Dobson's Chinese converts to Christianity, Ching and Ling (and the pidgin English adopted by Billy and Reno when they put on Ching's and Ling's costumes), were subsequently considered to be racially insensitive. In act I, scene 6, of the 1934 libretto, Moon refers to the converts as "Chinamen"; in the analogous place in 1962 he refers to them as Chinese.[21] In 1987 Reverend Dobson was still accompanied by two Chinese converts, but their names have been changed to the more biblical John and Luke. The new authors also took care "to give them independent comic personas and not base the humor on the fact that they're Chinese."[22]

In response to dated slang, Crouse (the younger) and Weidman removed some "terrible words in the language like, 'wacky' and 'zany'" and other topical words and phrases that required a 1930s cultural literacy alien to later audiences.[23] But since the lyrics to the musical numbers were considered untouchable onstage, if not the screen (see the discussion of the *Anything Goes* and *Kiss Me, Kate* film adaptations in chapters 8 and 14, respectively), the removal of "wacky" and "zany" do not fully solve the problems of topicality. In the preface to his essay "The Annotated 'Anything Goes'" that accompanies McGlinn's reconstructed recording, Kreuger describes the audiences for this and other 1930s shows as a "constricted group of *cognoscenti*, who went to the same night spots, read the same newspaper columns, and spent weekends at the same estates," and were therefore "swift to pick up even the most obscure references in all the lyrics."[24] Kreuger goes on to explain the meaning of seven references in the title song and no less than thirty-eight topical references in "You're the Top."[25]

Although this level of topicality is problematic to modern audiences who have neither lived through the 1930s nor had the opportunity to study Kreuger's annotated guide, it might also be said that Porter's lyrics presented problems to his British neighbors in his own time. In fact, in preparing for the London opening of June 14, 1935, Porter was asked by producer C. B. Cochran to remove several incomprehensible Americanisms when he took his show across the Atlantic. Eells mentions a few of these changes: "Cole agreed and set about converting the Bendel bonnet into an Ascot bonnet; a dress by Saks into one by Patous; and the eyes of Irene Bordoni into those of Tallulah Bankhead."[26] Nevertheless, in contrast to audiences who attended the 1962 and 1987 productions, most 1930s audiences, both in New York and London, would have recognized the parodistic parallels between Reno Sweeney, the evangelist who became a singer, and the then-famous evangelist Aimée Semple McPherson.[27] What about audiences in 1962 or 1987 and beyond? And does it matter?

In a *New York Times* interview that appeared shortly before the 1987 revival, the younger Crouse and Weidman admit to adding even more "swashbuckling slapstick gags" to their updated version, although they quickly add that none of these new gags were "gratuitous" and that they are "all closely tied to the plot."[28] Crouse and Weidman also express their intention to take their characters "more seriously" and to make them three-dimensional (or "maybe two and two-thirds").[29] In a feature story on *Anything Goes* that also appeared several days before the premiere of the 1987 revival, director, editor, and dramaturge Jerry Zaks discusses his search for a theme ("people dealing with the ramifications of trying to fall in love") and explains his intention "to ground everything in a recognizable reality," that is, to remake the book in a post–Rodgers and Hammerstein image. He continues with a telling example: "In previous versions of the show, Lord Evelyn Oakleigh, with whom Reno Sweeney falls in love, is someone so totally foppish and out of touch with his sexuality that she ends up looking stupid for having fallen for him. Both in the book and the casting we tried to suggest the potential for a real relationship between them."[30]

Zaks makes a good point. When Sir Evelyn is introduced in 1934 (scene 2) his masculine identity is immediately called into question:

> REPORTER: Sir Oakleigh, you and Miss Harcourt. Right here, please.
> (SIR EVELYN OAKLEIGH *and* HOPE HARCOURT *are pushed into focus*) Society stuff.
> CAMERA MAN: What are their names? Who are they?
> REPORTER: Sir—what's your first name?

OAKLEIGH: Evelyn.

1ST CAMERA MAN: Not her first name—your first name!

When in act II, scene 1, Sir Evelyn relates that he "had an unpremeditated roll in the rice and enjoyed it very much" with a Chinese maiden named Plum Blossom, his admission may be taken more as a boast of his full-blooded heterosexuality than the confession of a sin. And Reno, who has experienced chagrin that Evelyn has been treating her every inch a lady and is much relieved by this welcome revelation, immediately responds accordingly: "Brother, I've been worried about you but I feel better now."[31] Reno will repeat this sentiment in both 1962 and 1987.

The main reason that the generally stiff and staid Sir Evelyn provides a less-than-perfect match for the exuberant Reno in the original *Anything Goes* is more substantive than his androgynous first name and questionable heterosexuality: the Englishman is never allowed to sing. Although his sexual identity is eventually resolved to the satisfaction of a 1930s audience, his non-singing status significantly reduces his dramatic identity. In a musical (or opera) a character who does not sing—for example, Parthy before the 1994 *Show Boat* revival (discussed in chapter 2)—proceeds at his or her own peril.

Apparently, future book doctors saw this as an illness that needed a cure. Thus in the 1962 revival Bolton celebrates Sir Evelyn's emergence as a regular fellow in act II, scene 1, by letting him sing an innocuously risqué interpolated duet with Reno, "Let's Misbehave." In 1987 Sir Evelyn remains musically silent in his stateroom scene with Reno but eventually emerges in act II, scene 3, with his own song for the first time, "The Gypsy in Me," a song that Hope sang in the 1934 original and no one sang in 1962.[32]

Extending the premise that a musical comedy character will be denied three-dimensionality or identity if he or she is not allowed to sing, even Billy's boss, Elisha J. Whitney, is given a brief interpolated song to open act I, scene 4, in 1987. On this occasion he sings "I Want to Row on the Crew," borrowed not from Broadway but from one of Porter's fraternity shows at Yale. The ship's deck becomes even more crowded when Moon's female accomplice, Bonnie, is given two interpolated numbers in 1962 ("Heaven Hop" in act I and "Let's Step Out" in act II). In 1987 Crouse and Weidman discard these interpolations and in act II give Bonnie (now named Erma) "Buddie, Beware," the tune sung briefly by Ethel Merman as Reno in the original Broadway production before she persuaded Porter to give his late-arriving friends an opportunity to hear a reprise of "I Get a Kick Out of You."

In the 1987 revival words such as "wacky" and "zany" had been replaced, offending ethnic stereotypes were removed, and all the important characters were dramatically enhanced and, more important, allowed to sing. But do these changes make the 1987 *Anything Goes* superior to the original? Is it any funnier to hear a new set of topical jibes at Yale, Porter's alma mater, in a libretto created by two former Harvard roommates? Is it an improvement that Reno in 1934 is asked by Billy to seduce Sir Evelyn while in 1987 Reno meets and falls in love with the Englishman on her own?

What is lost and gained by this book surgery? Gone from latter-day versions of *Anything Goes*, for example, is much of the Marx Brothers humor built on puns and misunderstandings. Note the following exchange between Mrs. Wentworth (a humorless society matron not unlike Groucho's Margaret Dumont) and Moon, an exchange missing from the 1962 and 1987 revivals. Are modern audiences better or worse off for its absence?

MRS. WENTWORTH: We have a great deal to talk about. You see, I'm honorary president of the Texas Epworth League.

MOON: Oh, the Texas League—you must know the Dean Boys.

MRS. WENTWORTH: The Dean boys?

MOON: Yes, Dizzy and Daffy.

MRS. WENTWORTH: No, I don't remember them—

MOON: Well, you ask the Detroit Tigers about them. They remember them.

MRS. WENTWORTH: The Detroit Tigers? I know a family in Detroit named Lyons.

MOON: Lyons? Well, I know Maxie Baer [the boxing champion], but he's from San Francisco.

MRS. WENTWORTH: Ah, San Francisco. Have you ever been there?

MOON: I summered a few years at San Quentin.

MRS. WENTWORTH: San Quentin...Is that near Santa Clara?

MOON: Clara wasn't there when I was there. I wonder what ever became of Clara?

MRS. WENTWORTH: I'm not sure I understood what you just said.

MOON: Well, I wasn't listening.[33]

Some things about the evolving *Anything Goes* books stay the same the more they change. In 1987 Billy still has the opportunity to reply when asked his nationality that he is Pomeranian—the beard he is wearing was taken from a dog of that breed—even though Reno no longer notices that Billy is "putting on the dog."[34] Although many of the original puns and gags had disappeared by 1987, one 1934 line, "calling all pants," remained a part of *Anything Goes* scripture because it always got a laugh, even though no one involved in the production was able to explain why it was so funny or even precisely what it meant (the discussion of the 1936 film adaptation of *Anything Goes* in chapter 8 should hopefully clear up this mystery).

This survey of the reworked books for *Anything Goes* in 1962 and 1987 evokes a paradox: comedy seems especially susceptible to becoming dated, yet many of the plays that have survived from the 1930s are comedies rather than serious dramas. Revivals of George S. Kaufman's and Moss Hart's comedies *You Can't Take It with You* (1936) and *The Man Who Came to Dinner* (1939) or Noël Coward's British import *Private Lives* (1930) are frequent guests on modern stages, yet audiences may have to wait a lifetime before getting an opportunity to see Clifford Odets's *Waiting for Lefty* (1935). Theater historian Gerald Bordman, who plays an active role in the resurrection of unjustifiably forgotten musicals, concedes "that some older musicals seem old-fashioned," but is quick to point out that "so are gingerbread houses, Charles Dickens, and Mozart symphonies."[35]

Dramatic and Musical Meaning

Is it fair to ask of *Anything Goes* what we ask of some of the other musicals featured in this volume? What dramatic meaning does the work possess, and how is this meaning conveyed through Porter's music? What, if anything, goes? In fact, *Anything Goes* is about many things, including the wrong-headedness of disguises and pretenses of various kinds and the unthinking attraction that common folk have for celebrities, even celebrity criminals.

Perhaps the central dramatic moral of *Anything Goes* is that sexual attraction and the desire for wealth exert a power superior to friendship and camaraderie in determining long-term partnerships. A few minutes into the play, for example, we learn that Reno has a romantic interest—or, as Sir Evelyn will later declare in his typical malapropian American English, "hot pants"—for Billy that has gone unreciprocated for years. In any event, although Billy thinks Reno is the "top" as well, he nevertheless enlists her help to wean Sir Evelyn from Hope, Evelyn's fiancée at the beginning of the musical.

The final pairing of Hope with Billy and Reno with Sir Evelyn has some satisfying aspects to it. Billy brings out the "gypsy" in Hope and, because he stays on board the ship, he is eventually able to extricate Hope and her family from a bad marriage and financial ruin. For her part, Hope proves a positive influence in Billy's life when she persuades him to drop his pretenses and confess that he is not the celebrity criminal Snake Eyes Johnson, even though he will be penalized by the rest of the ship, even temporarily imprisoned, for his newfound integrity. Reno rekindles Sir Evelyn's dormant masculinity; Sir Evelyn will continue to entertain his future bride by his quaint Britishisms and distortions of American vernacular and, not incidentally, make an excellent provider for the lifestyle to which Reno would like to become accustomed.

But there is a darker side to the happily-ever-after denouement in this rags-to-riches Depression fantasy. Even though Hope appreciates Billy's persistence and joie de vivre, she berates him for being a clown and will not speak to him until he confesses (at her insistence) that he is not Snake Eyes Johnson. More significantly, the main reason Reno rather than Hope remains "the top" is because Porter's music for Reno is the top. For all his wealth, the non-singing Sir Evelyn might be considered the consolation prize.

Porter certainly cannot be faulted for giving nearly all his best songs in the show—"I Get a Kick Out of You," "You're the Top," "Anything Goes," and "Blow, Gabriel, Blow"—to Reno as played by Merman, a singer-actress of true star quality. As the curtain opens, Reno sings the first two of these songs to Billy, the man she supposedly loves, before he asks her to seduce Sir Evelyn so that Billy can successfully woo Hope. The degree to which Reno expresses her admiration for Billy in "I Get a Kick Out of You" and the mutual admiration expressed between Billy and Reno in "You're the Top" might prompt some in the audience to ask why the creators of *Anything Goes* could not bring themselves to "make two lovers of friends."[36]

In *Anything Goes* Porter does not attempt the variety of musical and dramatic connections that will mark his relatively more integrated classic fourteen years later, *Kiss Me, Kate* (discussed in chapter 10). But Porter does pay attention to nuances in characterization and to the symbiotic relationship between music and words. To cite three examples, the sailor song, "There'll Always Be a Lady Fair," sounds appropriately like a sea chantey, the chorus of "Public Enemy No. 1" is a parodistic hymn of praise, and Moon's song, "Be Like the Bluebird," makes a credible pseudo-Australian folk song (at least for those unfamiliar with "authentic" Australian folk songs).

More significantly, Reno's music, as befitting her persona, is rhythmically intricate, ubiquitously syncopated, and harmonically straightforward. It is also equally meaningful that in "You're the Top" Billy adopts Reno's musical language as his own but changes his tune and his personality when he sings the more lugubrious "All through the Night" with Hope. But even this song, dominated by descending half steps and long held notes, exhibits Reno's influence with the syncopations on alternate measures in the A section of the chorus and especially in the release when Billy laments the daylight reality (Hope does not sing this portion). Billy's syncopated reality partially supplants the long held notes: "When dawn comes to waken me, / You're never there at all. / I know you've forsaken me / Till the shadows fall."

Although rarely faithfully executed in performance, Porter's score also gives Reno an idiosyncratic and persistent rhythmic figure in "I Get a Kick

Out of You," quarter-note triplets in the verse ("sad to *be*" and "leaves me total*ly*") and half-note triplets in the chorus ("kick from cham-[pagne]," "[alco]-*hol* doesn't thrill me at [*all*]," and "tell me why should it be"), the latter group shown in Example 3.1a. Because they occupy more than one beat, quarter-note and half-note triplets are generally perceived as more rhythmically disruptive than eighth-note triplets.[37] Consequently, Reno's half-note triplets shown in Example 3.1a, like the quarter-note triplets that open the main chorus of Tony's "Maria" ("I just met a girl named Maria" [Example 13.2b, p. 283]), are experienced as rhythmically out of phase with the prevailing duple framework. A good Broadway example of the conventional and nondisruptive eighth-note triplet rhythm (one beat for each triplet) can be observed at the beginning of every phrase in Laurey's "Many a New Day" from *Oklahoma!* (Example 3.1b). Broadway composers have never to my knowledge articulated the intentionality or metaphoric meaning behind this practice. Nevertheless, with striking consistency, more than a few songs featured in this survey employ quarter-note and half-note triplets in duple meter (where triplets stretch in syncopated fashion over three beats instead of two) to musically depict characters who are temporarily or permanently removed from conventional social norms and expectations: Venus in *One Touch of Venus*, Julie Jordan in *Carousel*, Tony in *West Side Story*.[38] In *Guys and Dolls*, rhythms are employed or avoided to distinguish one character type from another. The tinhorn gamblers and Adelaide frequently use quarter-note triplets, while Sarah Brown and her Salvation Army cohorts do not.

Porter's use of Reno's rhythm in the chorus of "I Get a Kick Out of You" constitutes perhaps his most consistent attempt to create meaning from his

Example 3.1. Triplet rhythms

  (a) "I Get a Kick Out of You" (*Anything Goes*)

  (b) "Many a New Day" (*Oklahoma!*)

  (c) "Gypsy in Me" (*Anything Goes*)

(b)

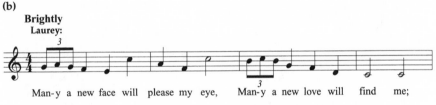

(c)

Example 3.1. Continued

musical language. Half-note triplets dominate Reno's explication of all the things in life that do not give her a kick; they disappear when (with continued syncopation, however) she informs Billy that she does get a kick out of him. Reno will also sing her quarter-note triplets briefly in the release of "Blow, Gabriel, Blow" (not shown), when she is ready to fly higher and higher.[39] By the time Hope loses some of her inhibitions and finds the gypsy in herself ("Gypsy in Me") in act II, she too will adopt this rhythmic figure on "hiding a-[way]," "never been," and "waiting its" (Example 3.1c). By usurping Reno's rhythm, Hope will become more like the former evangelist and, ironically, a more suitable partner for Billy.[40]

The verse of the title song shown in Example 3.2 offers a striking example of Porter's "word painting," Kivy's "textual realism" introduced in chapter 1. Even if a listener remains unconvinced that the gradually rising half-steps in the bass line between measures 3 and 7 (C-Db-D) depict the winding and consequently faster ticking of a clock, Porter unmistakably captures the changing times in his title song. He does this by contrasting the descending C-minor arpeggiated triad (C-G-Eb-C) that opens the song on the words "Times have changed" with a descending C-major arpeggiated triad (C-G-E-C) on the words "If today."[41] The topsy-turvy Depression-tinted world of 1934 is indeed different from the world of our Puritan ancestors. Porter makes this change known to us musically as well as in his text.

Example 3.2. "Anything Goes" (verse, mm. 1-10)

In the chorus of "Anything Goes" Porter abandons "textual realism" in favor of a jazzy "opulent adornment" and does not attempt to convey nuances and distinctions between "olden days," a time when "a glimpse of stocking was looked on as something shocking," and the present day when "anything goes." Much has changed between 1934 and today and the chorus of "Anything Goes" remains one of the most memorable of its time or ours. Nevertheless, it is difficult to argue that this central portion of the song possesses (or attempts to convey) a dramatic equivalence with its text, even if it brilliantly captures an accepting attitude to a syncopated world "gone mad." Similarly, in "You're the Top" Porter does not capitalize on the text's potential for realism and opts for inspired opulent adornment instead. Thus, although the "I" always appears in the bottom throughout most of the song, the "you" blithely moves back and forth from top to bottom."[42] The upward leaping orchestral figure anticipates the word, "top," but the sung line does not, and at the punch line, "But if Baby I'm the bottom, / You're the top," both Billy and Reno ("I'm" and "You're") share a melodic line at the top of their respective ranges.[43]

In the end a search for an underlying theme in *Anything Goes* yields more fun than profundity. An Englishman is good-naturedly spoofed for speaking a quaint "foreign" language and for his slowness in understanding American vernacular, and the celebrity status of religious entertainers like Aimée Semple McPherson and public criminals like Baby Face Nelson are caricatured by evangelist-singer Reno Sweeney and Public Enemy No. 1 (Moon Face). On a somewhat deeper level, the music suggests that the friendship between Reno and Billy has more vitality and perhaps greater substance than the eventual romantic pairings of Billy and Hope and Reno and Sir Evelyn. Not only does Porter demonstrate their compatibility by having Billy and Reno share quarter- and half-note triplet rhythms, but he shows his affection for them by giving them his most memorable songs. By the end of *Anything Goes* some may wonder how a person who cannot even sing could deserve a gem like Reno who sings nothing but hits.

Anything Goes does not conform to the organic "Wagnerian" model of some pre- and post-Rodgers and Hammerstein musicals beginning with *Show Boat*. Instead it presents a striking parallel with the generally less ostentatiously organic world of Baroque opera, in which great stars and show-stopping arias can ensure at least short-term success (which is all that is required). In any of its forms, including the 1962 *Anything Goes* that held the stage for almost three decades and the 1987 reincarnation with its new book and numerous interpolated songs (today's default rental version), *Anything Goes* still works. And even if the book that changes with the times falls short of the integrated ideal, it continues to provide marvelous vehicles to drive and showcase a parade of timeless hit songs. Times have changed, but *Anything Goes* is apparently here to stay.

CHAPTER FOUR

PORGY AND BESS

Broadway Opera

orgy and Bess, described by its composer George Gershwin (1898–1937) as "a serious attempt to put in operatic form a purely American theme" and "a new form, which combines opera with theatre," began its public life in 1935 before a Broadway audience.[1] While the possibilities of a Metropolitan Opera production had been explored, a Theatre Guild production offered a more extended rehearsal schedule (six weeks), many more performances, and fewer logistical problems in assembling a large cast of operatically trained African-American singers.[2] Six years earlier the Met had signed a contract with Gershwin to produce an opera based on Sholem Ansky's version of the Jewish folktale "The Dybbuk" but abandoned the project after Gershwin was denied musical rights to this property.[3]

After a disappointing initial Broadway run of 124 performances, *Porgy and Bess* achieved a wider audience seven years later in the most successful Broadway revival up to that time. But in contrast to the 1935 operatic form, the 1942 revival presented a Broadway opera shorn of its operatic accoutrements, that is, without recitatives (sung dialogue). Although some spoken dialogue replaced Gershwin's recitative, in the 1950s *Porgy and Bess* regained more of its operatic form as it toured opera houses all over the world (including La Scala).

In 1976 the work gained additional acceptance as an authentic as well as an accessible operatic classic when the Houston Opera performed the first largely uncut stage version since the Boston tryouts in 1935. By 1980 two competing unexpurgated recordings, one by the Houston Opera and another by the Cleveland Orchestra and Chorus, had appeared. Then, after fifty years of negotiations, *Porgy and Bess* appeared at the Met in 1985.[4] Nevertheless, despite its newfound popularity and acclaim among opera audiences, *Porgy and Bess* remains best known to the general public today as a collection of Broadway show tunes including "Summertime," "I Got Plenty o' Nuttin,'" and "Bess, You Is My Woman Now," sung, played, and recorded by jazz and popular artists as diverse as Ella Fitzgerald and Louis Armstrong, Sammy Davis Jr. and Diahann Carroll, Harry Belafonte and Lena Horne, Mel Tormé and Frances Faye, and Miles Davis.

Gershwin's exposure to the European classical tradition began two years after he started to play the piano at the relatively late age of twelve in 1910, when his teacher Charles Hambitzer introduced him to the music of Debussy and Ravel. Following his apprenticeship as a popular song "plugger" for the publishing house Remick & Company and some modest success in his own right as a songwriter for various revues between 1919 and 1921, Gershwin studied theory, composition, and orchestration with Edward Kilenyi. For more than a decade before completing *Porgy and Bess* Gershwin had composed a small body of jazz-influenced classical instrumental works including *Rhapsody in Blue* (1924), *Concerto in F* (1925), and *An American in Paris* (1928) that earned the respect, or at least the attention, of composers as diverse as Ravel, Prokofiev, and Berg. Between 1932 and 1936, partly in preparation for his first opera, Gershwin continued his studies in composition with Joseph Schillinger, a theorist who had developed a teachable system of melodic composition (including some techniques that Gershwin was able to incorporate in *Porgy and Bess*).

For the revue, *George White Scandals of 1922*, Gershwin created an unusual work that revealed an interest in opera parallel to his interest in instrumental music, a work that similarly combined the cultivated European tradition with the American vernacular. This modest first effort, *Blue Monday*, a one-act verismo opera about blacks in Harlem, was dropped after opening night. For the next thirteen years Gershwin would undergo a rigorous Broadway apprenticeship that eventually gave him the technique and the experience he needed to attempt a full-length opera in the European tradition, again using the black experience for subject matter.

By 1924, with *Lady, Be Good!*, George had found a first-rate lyricist in his brother Ira (1896–1983), and over the next decade the Gershwins produced mostly successful musical comedies filled with great songs and great stars such as *Tip-Toes* (1925) with Queenie Smith, *Oh, Kay!* (1926) with Gertrude

George and Ira Gershwin. © AL HIRSCHFELD. Reproduced by arrangement with Hirschfeld's exclusive representative, the MARGO FEIDEN GALLERIES LTD., NEW YORK. WWW. ALHIRSCHFELD.COM

Lawrence, *Funny Face* (1927) with *Lady, Be Good!* leads Fred and Adele Astaire, and *Girl Crazy* (1930) with new stars Ethel Merman and Ginger Rogers. All of these shows were produced by Alex Aarons (who had independently presented George's first book musical *La La Lucille* in 1919) and Vinton Freedley.[5] From 1930 to 1933 the Gershwins created a trilogy of musicals that satirized contemporary politics: *Strike Up the Band* (1930), *Of Thee I Sing* (1931), and *Let 'Em Eat Cake* (1933). In addition to the opportunities they provided for musical humor and wit, these political musicals allowed Gershwin to continue the practice he started in *Oh, Kay!*, in which extended ensemble finales are presented continuously with a minimum of intervening dialogue.

The act I Finale to *Of Thee I Sing* also displays a substantial passage of accompanied recitative or arioso (a singing style between recitative and aria). This passage is sung by Diana Devereaux, the character who, by winning first prize in a national beauty contest, was entitled to become the First Lady but was passed over in favor of Mary Turner because the latter could make irresistible corn muffins. When instead of muffins Diana serves President Wintergreen a summons for breach of promise, Gershwin gives the jilted Southerner a blues-inflected musical line in recitative that would not be out of place in *Porgy and Bess*.

When Gershwin finished reading the novel *Porgy* (1925) by DuBose Heyward (1885–1940) after a sleepless night in October 1926, he wrote a letter to the author, a leading Southern novelist and poet, informing him that he wanted to use the novel as the basis for an opera. Nine years later *Porgy and Bess* appeared on Broadway, a delay that can be contributed both to the successful run of the Theatre Guild production of the play *Porgy* in 1927 and to Gershwin's many commitments and excuses and his sense that he needed more experience before tackling a full-scale opera.

Since several Gershwin biographies offer detailed surveys of *Porgy and Bess*'s pre-history, the events leading to the premiere need only be encapsulated here.[6] The summer after he had first written Heyward, Gershwin met the author for the first time, and they agreed to collaborate on an opera based on *Porgy*. DuBose's wife, Dorothy, who had co-authored the play, recalled years later that Gershwin informed her husband that he "wanted to spend years in study before composing his opera."[7] Although by March 1932 he wrote Heyward to express a continued interest in composing the opera, two months later Gershwin hedged again when he informed DuBose that "there is no possibility of the operatic version's being written before January 1933."[8] The two men met in New York City even as plans were brewing for a *Porgy* that would feature the popular entertainer Al Jolson in blackface with lyrics and music by *Show Boat* collaborators Hammerstein and Kern. The Jolson project was not abandoned until September 1934, long after Gershwin and Heyward had begun their version.

By November 1933, Gershwin had experienced two successive Broadway flops, *Pardon My English* and *Let 'Em Eat Cake*, the latter a bitter sequel to the less acerbic Pulitzer Prize–winning *Of Thee I Sing*. Despite these setbacks, the Theatre Guild, which had produced the popular play *Porgy* six years earlier, announced that Gershwin and Heyward had signed a contract to produce a musical version. On November 12, Heyward sent Gershwin a typescript of the first scene, and in December and again the following January the composer visited the librettist in Charleston, South Carolina.

On February 6, 1934, Heyward mailed Gershwin a typescript of act II, scenes 1 and 2. Several weeks later (February 26) Gershwin informed Heyward that he had begun to compose the music for the first act and expressed his relief that their work would not suffer in comparison with the all-black opera by Virgil Thomson and Gertrude Stein, *Four Saints in Three Acts*, that had recently premiered on Broadway (February 20). On March 2 Heyward sent the composer a typescript of act II, scene 3, and six days later Gershwin wrote that Ira was working on lyrics for the opening of the opera.[9] By the end of March, Heyward had sent act II, scene 4, and completed a draft for act III. In April Heyward traveled to New York to meet with the Gershwins and together they created "I Got Plenty o' Nuttin,'" one of the few numbers in the opera in which the music preceded the lyrics.

Gershwin completed the music for act I, scene 1, before the end of May. In the summer he worked on the opera in Charleston (June 16 to July 21). In a letter to Heyward dated November 5, Gershwin announced he had completed act II and begun act III, scene 2. On December 17 he reported to Heyward that he had heard a singer, Todd Duncan, who would make "a superb Crown and, I think, just as good a Porgy," and several weeks later he wrote to Duncan (who would in fact be cast as Porgy) that he had just completed the trio in act III, scene 3 ("Oh, Bess, Oh Where's My Bess"), and was about to orchestrate his opera. The arduous task of orchestration occupied Gershwin until three days before rehearsals began August 26.[10] The Boston tryouts began on September 30 and the Broadway premiere took place October 10 at the Alvin Theatre.

Questions of Genre, Authenticity, and Race

Genre

Prior to its eventual acceptance into the operatic community, reviewers and historians alike were uncertain how to classify *Porgy and Bess*. At its premiere the *New York Times* did not know whether to approach the work as a dramatic event or a musical event, and assigned first-string reviewers in both camps, drama critic Brooks Atkinson and music critic Olin Downes, to review the work in adjacent columns.[11] Most subsequent accounts of these reviews conclude that Atkinson, who praised Gershwin for establishing "a personal voice that was inarticulate in the original play," appreciated the work more fully than Downes.[12] It is true that Downes, in contrast to Atkinson, expressed reservations about the stylistic disparities in the work when he wrote that Gershwin "has not completely formed his style as an opera composer" and that "the style is at one moment of opera and another of operetta or sheer Broadway entertainment."[13] Nevertheless, Downes found much to praise in Gershwin's melody, harmony, vocal writing, and the "elements of a more organic kind," especially the "flashes of real contrapuntal ingenuity."

Atkinson, who had nothing but praise for *Anything Goes* the previous year, put his cards on the table when he now wrote that "what a theatre critic probably wants is a musical show with songs that evoke the emotion of situations and make no further pretensions."[14] It is not surprising then that he expressed such distaste for the convention of recitative, which he, like Gershwin, designated as "operatic form." Atkinson also questioned "why commonplace remarks that carry no emotion have to be made in a chanting monotone."[15] Playing from the same deck, Downes lamented that a composer like Gershwin, "with a true lyrical gift and with original and racy things to say, has turned with his score of 'Porgy and Bess' to the more pretentious ways of musical theatre."[16] For Downes as well as for Atkinson, a composer who can "go upstairs and write a Gershwin tune" but whose "treatment of passages of recitative is seldom significant," should know his place and stick to writing great but unpretentious tunes.[17]

The question of genre and "operatic form" raised by Atkinson and Downes can be traced to the earliest stages in the collaboration of Gershwin and Heyward. In fact, the issue of recitatives was their principal source of artistic disagreement. As early as November 12, 1933, when he sent the first scene, Heyward offered the following suggestion: "I feel more and more that all dialogue should be spoken. It is fast moving, and we will cut it to the bone, but this will give the opera speed and tempo."[18] Gershwin differed strongly and overruled his librettist.

For the first decades of its history a critical consensus supported Heyward's original conviction. In his review of the Theatre Guild production in 1935 Virgil Thomson writes critically of Gershwin's recitative as "vocally uneasy and dramatically cumbersome" and concludes that "it would have been better if he had stuck to [spoken dialogue]...all the time."[19] Part of Thomson's subsequent praise in 1941 for the Cheryl Crawford revival in Maplewood, New Jersey, can be attributed to her practice "of eliminating, where possible, the embarrassment due to Gershwin's incredibly amateurish way of writing recitative."[20]

Vernon Duke—like Gershwin a hybrid classical-popular composer but unlike Gershwin a man sharply divided between his two artistic personalities, Duke and Dukelsky—was similarly critical. In their pre-compositional discussions about *Porgy and Bess* he recalled that "George was still under the sway of the Wagnerian formula," which Duke believed to be "anti-theatrical," and wrote somewhat smugly that "it is generally acknowledged that the separate numbers are superior to the somewhat amorphous stretches of music that hold them together," that is, the recitatives.[21] Less surprisingly, Richard Rodgers, who rarely abandoned the Broadway convention of spoken dialogue, also believed that Gershwin had made "a mistake in writing *Porgy and Bess* as an opera."[22] According to Rodgers, "the *recitative* device was an unfamiliar and difficult one for Broadway audiences, and it didn't sustain the story." Consequently, it was only "when Cheryl Crawford revived it later as a musical play that it gained such overwhelming success and universal acceptance."[23] More recently, Gershwin biographer Charles Schwartz concurred with the above-mentioned composers that the Crawford revival "vindicated" Heyward's original conception of the work, "for as he had argued, Gershwin's recitatives impeded the pacing of the original production."[24]

In addition to his controversial decision to give his work operatic form by connecting his musical numbers with recitatives, the composer had the audacity to load his score with hit songs, which makes the distinction between aria and recitative more glaring than in most hitless operatic works (see the list of scenes and songs in the online website). Clearly this issue was a sensitive one for Gershwin, who felt the need to publicly defend the presence of songs in *Porgy and Bess*:

> It is true that I have written songs for "Porgy and Bess." I am not ashamed of writing songs at any time so long as they are good songs. In "Porgy and Bess" I realized I was writing an opera for the theatre and without songs it could be neither of the theatre nor entertaining from my viewpoint. But songs are entirely within the operatic tradition. Many of the most successful operas of the past have had songs. Nearly all of Verdi's operas contain what are known as "song hits." "Carmen" [then performed with Ernest Guiraud's added recitatives] is almost a collection of song hits.[25]

In his overview of Gershwin's posthumous reputation Richard Crawford offers an insightful summary of several seemingly insurmountable criticisms that made Gershwin so defensive about inserting popular songs in a serious work that in the composer's words "used sustained symphonic music to unify entire scenes."[26] Crawford writes:

> We see Gershwin as a great natural talent, to be sure, but technically suspect, and working in a commercial realm quite separate from the neighborhood in which true art is created. So there sits Gershwin, as Virgil Thomson once wrote, "between two stools," vastly appealing to the mass audience and hence a bit raffish, not quite deserving of serious academic scrutiny: a man without a category.[27]

Authenticity

Somewhat related to the problems of genre definition is another controversy surrounding *Porgy and Bess*: how to determine an authentic performing version. To place this debate in perspective it may be helpful to recall the difficulties in establishing a text for *Show Boat* (discussed in chapter 2). Since Kern and Hammerstein themselves revised their work nineteen years after its original Broadway run for the 1946 Broadway revival, it is arguable that this later version represents the final intentions of the creators. Despite its claim to legitimacy, however, revisionists such as John McGlinn rejected the 1946 version as an impure mutation of original authorial intent. Further, the Houston Opera (1983), McGlinn (1988), and Prince (for the 1994 Broadway revival) restored material that had been discarded—presumably with the consent of the Kern and Hammerstein estates—in the pre-Broadway tryouts. The appearance of the dropped "Mis'ry's Comin' Aroun'" in the first published vocal score provides fuel for the idea that Kern really wanted this music in the show but capitulated to external pressures. Other reinsertions were not supported by equally compelling evidence.

The authenticity problems associated with *Porgy and Bess* (and many European operas in the core repertory) differ from those posed by the performance history of *Show Boat*. For example, in contrast to the *Show Boat* score, which was published four months into the original Broadway run, by which time the cuts had been stabilized, the *Porgy and Bess* vocal score was published as a rehearsal score prior to the Boston tryouts on September 30, 1935, and therefore includes most of the music that was later cut in the Boston tryouts. Thus the Gershwin score, unlike the first published *Show Boat* score (with the exception of "Mis'ry's Comin' Aroun'"), is not a score that accurately represents what New York audiences actually heard on opening night ten days later. Thanks to the work of Charles Hamm it is now possible to reconstruct what audiences did hear on the opening night of *Porgy and Bess* (October 10, 1935) down to the last measure.[28] But the question remains: Were these cuts made for artistic or for practical or commercial considerations?

Hamm argues that "most cuts made for apparently practical reasons were of passages already questioned on artistic grounds," and that "the composer's mastery of technique, his critical judgment, his imagination, and his taste come as much in play in the process of final revisions as in the first stages of composition." In addition to the relatively modest "cuts to tighten dialogue or action," "cuts of repeated material mostly made before the opening in Boston," and "cuts to shorten the opera," the openings of three scenes were greatly reduced. By the time *Porgy and Bess* reached New York, only twenty measures of Jazzbo Brown's music remained before "Summertime" (and even these were eliminated a few days later), and the "six prayers" that opened act II, scene 4 were removed (though a far shorter reprise could still be heard at the end of the scene). More than two hundred measures from act III, scene 3, had also been discarded, including much of the trio portion of "Oh, Bess, Oh Where's My Bess."

An examination of one deleted portion, Porgy's "Buzzard Song" from act II, scene 1, might help to shed light on the complex issues of "authenticity" and the relative virtues of "absolute completeness."[29] As in the play *Porgy* by Dorothy and DuBose Heyward, upon which the opera libretto is based (rather than on the novel *Porgy*), the libretto draft that DuBose sent to George on February 6, 1934, concludes this scene with the appearance of a buzzard.[30] In the play, the fact that the buzzard lights over Porgy's door represents the end of the protagonist's newly acquired happiness and peace of mind with Bess and prompts the final stage direction of the scene, "Porgy sits looking up at the bird with an expression of hopelessness as the curtain falls."[31]

The text of the "Buzzard Song" in the libretto shows Porgy's superstitious response to and fear of the buzzard, but in keeping with his attempt to be more upbeat in his adaptation from play to opera, Heyward presents a triumphant protagonist who reminds the buzzard that a former Porgy, decaying with loneliness, "don't live here no mo.'"[32] Because he is no longer lonely, the Porgy in the first draft of Heyward's libretto revels in his victory over superstition and loneliness: "There's two folks livin' in dis shelter / Eatin,' sleepin,' singin,' prayin.' / Ain't no such thing as loneliness, / An' Porgy's young again."[33]

Several pages earlier in the libretto manuscript George wrote the words "Buzzard Song." The song cue appears shortly after the arrival of the bird in the scene and Porgy's observation that "once de buzzard fold his wing an' light over yo' house, all yo' happiness done dead."[34] By placing the "Buzzard Song" earlier in the scene, Gershwin paved the way for the following duet between Porgy and Bess, "Bess, You Is My Woman Now," a subsequent addition.

Shortly before *Porgy and Bess* premiered in New York, the "Buzzard Song" was among the deletions agreed to by Gershwin and director Rouben Mamoulian. There is general agreement among various first- and second-hand explanations for this cut. Mamoulian, in his 1938 tribute to Gershwin, wrote that "no matter how well he loved a musical passage or an aria (like the Buzzard Song in *Porgy and Bess* for instance), he would cut it out without hesitation if that improved the performance as a whole."[35] According to Edith Garson's completion of Isaac Goldberg's 1931 Gershwin biography, the composer agreed to this particular cut for practical reasons: "In fact, during the Boston run, it was George who insisted on cutting fifteen minutes from one section, saying to Ira, 'You won't have a Porgy by the time we reach New York. No one can sing that much, eight performances a week.' "[36] David Ewen writes that "Porgy's effective 'Buzzard Song' and other of his passages were removed at George's suggestion."[37] Edward Jablonski explains, "Unlike recent productions of Porgy and Bess, the 1935 production had but one Porgy. So 'Buzzard Song' was among the first cut, in order to provide [Todd] Duncan with a chance to breathe between songs."[38]

There is little doubt that Heyward and the brothers Gershwin (mainly, of course, George) agreed to relocate the buzzard number prior to the composition of the short score that served as the foundation of the published piano-vocal version used in rehearsal. It can also be determined that those most involved in the production, particularly the composer and the director, agreed to cut the "Buzzard Song," perhaps on the eve of the New York premiere. Presumably the cut was made primarily for the practical reason that the opera was forty-five minutes too long and that Porgy already had two big numbers in this scene.

But the buzzard would light again with remarkable tenacity. Even during the initial run of the Broadway *Porgy and Bess*, the discarded "Buzzard Song" would appear among the first recorded excerpts from the opera. It was ironic that the singer on the recording—Lawrence Tibbett—was white. According to Gershwin, Tibbett was the likely candidate for a Metropolitan Opera production rather than the original Porgy, Todd Duncan.[39] Duncan himself sang the "Buzzard Song" along with "I Got Plenty o' Nuttin'" and "Bess, You Is My Woman Now" (with Marguerite Chapman) in the Los Angeles Philharmonic concerts organized by Merle Armitage in February 1937, and he included it along with other excerpts for a recording released in 1942.[40]

The "Buzzard Song" was also one of the few items cut from the Boston tryouts to resurface on the first nearly complete *Porgy* recording (and first published libretto in English) in 1951 produced by Goddard Lieberson and conducted by Lehman Engel, with Lawrence Winters and Camilla Williams singing the title roles.[41] And the song was among those portions reinstated for the Blevins Davis-Robert Breen revival that premiered in Dallas in 1952 and toured Europe later that year.[42] But in 1952 the buzzard did not appear until the final scene of the opera, perhaps to symbolize Porgy's bad luck in losing Bess.[43]

Does the "Buzzard Song" belong in future productions of *Porgy and Bess*? The central practical issue that led to its original omission was not really its length (less than four minutes, including the recitative with the lawyer Archdale) but the strain on Porgy's voice. Does this mean that if several Porgys had been available or if the Broadway equivalent of Lauritz Melchior had surfaced, the composer might have fought for its inclusion? Not necessarily.

The artistic aspects are naturally more problematic than the practical ones. Can we interpret Gershwin's remarks in 1935—"The reason I did not submit this work to the usual sponsors of opera in America was that I hoped to have developed something in American music that would appeal to the many rather than to the cultured few"—to justify the removal of forty-five expendable minutes?[44] What are present-day audiences to make of Gershwin's contemporaries, many directly involved in the first production, who without exception concluded that *Porgy and Bess* was better off with the cuts, including that of the "Buzzard Song"?

Clearly, even if Gershwin strove to approximate the "beauty of *Meister-singer*," he did not want to approximate its length, at least not on Broadway.[45] But opera epicureans used to *Die Meistersinger* and desirous of savoring every possible morsel of a work might eagerly welcome back the deleted forty-five minutes and perhaps endorse portions of the opera that never made it even to Boston, for example, the reconciliation duet between Bess and Serena in act III, scene 1.[46] The Houston Opera producers, who felt no remorse at dividing the work into two long acts rather than the specified three in order to save overtime labor costs, perhaps did not even consider the option of cutting the "Buzzard Song."

Several years before the Cleveland and Houston recordings were issued, Wayne Shirley, an authority on the opera and a persuasive advocate for a score that represents the composer's intentions, wrote that the "Buzzard Song" "is always cut, since Porgy has two other strenuous numbers in the scene, and the work flows better for the cut."[47] And although he does not offer an artistic justification for deleting this particular song, Hamm, who contends, as we have seen, that "most cuts made for apparently practical reasons were of passages already questioned on artistic grounds," would presumably support Fred Graham, who introduces *Kiss Me, Kate* with the line, "Yes, the cut's good, leave it in."[48] In contrast to Shirley and Hamm, Wilfrid Mellers has argued that the "Buzzard Song" constitutes "the turning-point of the opera, for it forces him [Porgy] to face up to reality and suffering.... The appearance of the buzzard marks Porgy's realization of the significance of his love."[49]

Some might argue for the retention of the "Buzzard Song" on musical grounds; others might conclude with equal justification that the song creates a dramatic intrusion. Certainly the "Buzzard Song" undermines the effect of a scene that otherwise successfully shows Porgy and Bess as fully accepted members of the Catfish Row community and, of course, illustrates their genuine and optimistic love. Because Porgy's superstitious nature had been de-emphasized in the adaptation of play to opera, its sudden appearance in this scene, despite Porgy's ultimate ability to conquer his fear, creates an ominous tone that the love duet "Bess, You Is My Woman Now" cannot overcome. Porgy's extraordinary fear in act III, scene 2, when he learns that he must look on Crown's face or serve time in jail, is generated by his sense of guilt at having murdered Crown rather than by irrational superstition. (For this reason, its placement in act III of the Davis-Breen libretto makes artistic sense despite the absence of historical justification.) To historians troubled by the dramatic effect of the song, it comes as a relief to learn that the composer had agreed to and perhaps even suggested its deletion.

Since the late 1970s the prevailing view holds that an uncut version of Gershwin's rehearsal vocal score best represents the composer's final intentions for the work. The more complete, the more authentic. For this reason few of the cuts noted by Hamm are in fact observed in current productions (although interestingly the video directed by Trevor Nunn in 1993 omitted the "Buzzard Song"); virtually none are observed in the three recordings of the work.[50] The merits of the cuts can and should be argued on aesthetic as well as historical grounds, and perhaps *Porgy*'s cuts should be disregarded, especially on recordings, which are less beholden to the time constraints of a Broadway production. But any careful consideration must acknowledge that the published score does not represent what Theatre Guild audiences heard during the initial run and may be alien to Gershwin's considered thoughts on the work.

Race

The criticism leveled at Gershwin for making his Broadway opera through-composed and for straddling two worlds with his concoction of sung speech and hit songs has somewhat abated in recent years. More persistently controversial is Gershwin's claim that his "folk opera" expressed the African-American experience. Criticisms of Gershwin's racial presumptions appeared as early as the 1935 Broadway premiere, but in contrast to the gradual tolerance and eventual appreciation of his musical ambitions and the work's length, the hubris of Gershwin's depiction of black culture has not diminished over time despite the proliferation of performances throughout the world.[51] In fact, the growing "classic" stature of *Porgy and Bess* may actually have fueled racial controversies in recent years to a point that the problems brought about by what is perceived as cultural colonization and exploitation seems destined to remain central to the work in the minds of many for some time to come.[52]

In chapter 2 it was noted that the creators and future producers of *Show Boat* made some revisions in response to evolving racial sensibilities. Hammerstein replaced the word "niggers" with "coloured folks" as early as the 1928 London production ("colored" in 1946) as the first words of the show. For his screenplay to the 1936 film Hammerstein substituted "Darkies all work on de Mississippi," and in the 1946 film biography of Kern audiences heard "Here we all work on de Mississippi." Miles Kreuger wrote that in a 1966 Lincoln Center revival, "Nobody works on the Mississippi, because the Negro chorus was omitted altogether from the opening number."[53] In the 1994 Broadway revival directed by Hal Prince, "Brothers all work on the Mississippi."

Accounts of the genesis of McGlinn's recording of the "authentic" *Show Boat* of 1927 report that the contracted African-American chorus refused to sing the offending word "niggers" and therefore was replaced by the Ambrosian Chorus, who had been contracted to sing the white choral parts. To show his solidarity with the black chorus, Willard White, the Joe for this recording, resigned, and only after consultation with Eartha Kitt, a black performer and an articulate and influential opponent of racial indignities, did Bruce Hubbard consent to sing the role of Joe and the word "niggers." Earlier, Etta Moten Barnett, who sang Bess in the popular 1942 revival of *Porgy and Bess*, recalled that the cast "refused to used the word 'nigger,' and it was removed from all of the lines except those spoken by white characters."[54] Some stage productions (and the 1951 film) of *Show Boat* circumvented the issue by minimizing the role of blacks, but this type of evasive action was, of course, impossible to accomplish with *Porgy and Bess*, Thus, from his time to ours, Gershwin's opera has been chastised for its composer's presumption to speak for another race.

Thomson in his 1935 review takes Gershwin to task for attempting a folk subject: "Folklore subjects recounted by an outsider are only valid as long as the folk in question is unable to speak for itself, which is certainly not true of the American Negro in 1935."[55] A more detailed and closely reasoned critique of what Thomson termed "fake folk-lore" can be found in a review of the opera by Hall Johnson that appeared in the African-American journal *Opportunity* a few months after the Theatre Guild premiere.[56] As the composer of *The Green Pastures* (1930) and *Run, Little Chillun!* (1933), two undisputed examples of authentic black folklore, Johnson's credentials were impeccable for this task.

Although Johnson, like Downes and Thomson, criticizes Gershwin's craftsmanship, again mainly in the recitatives, most of his remarks focus on Gershwin's misunderstanding of the African-American character and experience.[57] According to Johnson, the first of Gershwin's many inauthentic elements is his failure to capture "Negro simplicity." For Johnson, Gershwin's music "suggests sophisticated intricacies of attitude which could not possibly be native to the minds of the people who make up his story."[58] What makes the work "genuine" are the performances, particularly that of John W. Bubbles, of the vaudeville team Buck and Bubbles, who as Sporting Life played the central non-operatic character among the leading players. But despite Bubbles's genuineness, Johnson viewed "It Ain't Necessarily So" as "so un-Negroid, in thought and in structure that even Bubbles cannot save it."[59] On the other hand, perhaps because its derivations were more urban than folk, Johnson praises the authenticity of Sporting Life's "There's a Boat Dat's Leavin' Soon for New York" as a "real Negro gem."[60]

Criticism of *Porgy and Bess* on racial grounds reached a new level of intensity in the 1950s and 1960s, the era of *Brown v. Board of Education* and the civil rights struggles for equality. Many blacks resented the fact that the State Department, in sponsoring a global tour in 1952, was propagating negative stereotypes. On a televised broadcast playwright Lorraine Hansberry, author of *Raisin in the Sun*, criticized Otto Preminger, director of the 1959 film version of the opera, for "portraying Negroes at their worst."[61] A. S. "Doc" Young wrote in the *Los Angeles Sentinel* that *Porgy and Bess* "is completely out of context with modern times…it perpetuates old stereotypes that right-thinking people have buried long ago."[62]

Social historian Harold Cruse takes Hansberry to task for focusing on content in her criticism of *Porgy and Bess*.[63] Cruse instead sees the work "as the most perfect symbol of the Negro creative artist's cultural denial, degradation, exclusion, exploitation and acceptance of white paternalism."[64] He deeply resents the fact that blacks themselves did not produce their own authentic folk opera. He also considers it as indisputable that even if blacks had written such a work, it "would never have been supported, glorified and acclaimed, as *Porgy* has, by the white cultural elite of America."[65]

In Gershwin's time knowledgeable black critics responded negatively to the composer's attempt to come "as close to the Negro inflection in speech as possible" in his recitatives.[66] Even the normally circumspect and polite Duke Ellington was reported to have said that *Porgy and Bess* "does not use the Negro musical idiom" and that "it was not the music of Catfish Row or any other kind of Negroes."[67] Others found the idea of whites speaking for blacks and the subject matter itself rather than the final product the principal source of consternation.

Even those who for the most part reject Gershwin's "fake folk-lore" might find something to appreciate in Gershwin's assimilation of black culture inspired by his month at Folly Beach in 1934. Although simplistic by the standards of a master drummer, the polyrhythmic drumming that precedes

"I Ain't Got No Shame" in act II, scene 2, comes closer to black African drumming style than most jazz drumming (by drummers of any race) before the 1950s. Similarly, Gershwin's attempt to capture the effect he and Heyward heard while listening outside a Pentecostal church in the opening and closing of act II, scene 4, "Oh, Doctor Jesus," in which six prayers are presented in a six-part texture (unfortunately mostly cut in Boston and New York), is a dazzling translation of the black experience.[68] Certainly, these two examples possess a "fake authenticity" analogous to nineteenth-century slave narratives written by whites or Forrest Carter's best-selling bogus biography of the Cherokee Indian, *The Education of Little Tree*.[69] If we use Henry Louis Gates Jr.'s "blindfold test" (in which an expert usually failed to determine the race of various jazz trumpeters without previous knowledge) to judge a work's authenticity, Gershwin's evocation of African-American drumming and prayer meetings might be heard more charitably.[70]

For the sake of musical homogeneity, Gershwin in most instances purposefully created his own idiosyncratic pseudo-spirituals rather than copy those he had heard. He also preferred to freely adapt his own Russian-Jewish ethnicity into a personal interpretation of the African-American experience rather than slavishly imitate it. The strong kinship between these musically compatible traditions is evident in Sporting Life's theme, which might be interpreted as a chromatic transformation of the Jewish blessing that precedes and follows the reading of the Torah (Example 4.2b).[71]

How do we judge *Porgy and Bess* today, an opera that plays on black stereotypes and has served as a negative symbol of black exploitation? Is it enough to counter that the "civilized" and, moreover, non-singing whites in the drama "are also more unemotional, drab and dull" and, as Edith Garson says in her completion of Goldberg's biography, "cruel and foolish"?[72] In the 1980s, Lawrence Starr attempted to defuse the passions of this debate: "To insist on viewing *Porgy and Bess* as a racial document is to apply criteria which lie wholly outside the tradition to which this work relates, with the consequent risk of blinding oneself to the virtues it possesses."[73] Unfortunately, when considering the escalating tensions between Jews and African Americans after 1935, it seems less likely in the 1990s that the universal values of Gershwin's opera espoused by Starr will soon transcend artistically as well as politically divisive racial issues.

Establishing and Transforming Musical Character

It was previously observed when discussing *Show Boat* that Kern chose musical themes in part for their symbolic possibilities and reworked these themes in order to reveal dramatic connections and oppositions (see the "River Family" of motives, Example 2.2, pp. 29–30). Kern also transformed two themes, Cap'n Andy's musical signature and Magnolia's piano music, to convey the continuity that underlies changing dramatic situations. Gershwin's treatment of the first technique is similar to that of Kern, since Gershwin assigns specific themes to important characters (or to a thing like "happy dust") and allows his listeners actively or subliminally the possibility of attributing dramatic significance to these themes.

But Gershwin went beyond Kern in discovering varied and ingenious new ways to transform his melodies (even his hit tunes) for credible dramatic purposes. In altering Cap'n Andy's theme and Magnolia's piano theme, Kern altered tempo and character—and presumably asked Robert Russell Bennett to orchestrate these transformations—but he did not change the pitch content of either theme. When Gershwin musically responds to the ever-changing dramatic circumstances of his characters and their relationships, he frequently alters the pitches of the initial melodies by using a technique known as paraphrase. As his characters evolve, Gershwin adds and subtracts pitches and alters rhythms to create new melodies. In most cases these new melodies retain the identity inherent in their fundamental melodic contours. Some of Gershwin's melodic transformations are difficult to perceive and are consequently meaningless to most listeners. Other transformations are questionably related to the central themes. The remarks that follow will focus on the most audible and dramatically meaningful of Gershwin's melodic manipulations, a union of craft and art.

Musicals, operatic and otherwise, thrive when they show two people in love that audiences can care about. The opera *Porgy and Bess*, like all the adaptations treated in this book, similarly places its greatest dramatic emphasis on the love-story component of its literary source. A related theme is the attempt of the principal characters to overcome their physical and emotional handicaps and dependencies, their loneliness and poor self-esteem, and to establish themselves as fully accepted members within a loving community. Act II, scenes 1 and 3, provide a good introduction to how Gershwin created a symbolic musical language to express these great dramatic themes.

At the musical heart of the opera stands (or kneels, depending on the production) Porgy, not only because Gershwin gives him several themes but because these themes relate so closely to the Catfish Row community.[74] Porgy may not feel as though he is a "complete" man (until ironically he gains his manhood and loses his humanity by killing Crown and then gloating over it), but from the outset of the drama he is definitely, unlike Bess, part of the community. It is fitting, then, that his main theme, shown in Example

Porgy and Bess, act II, scene 1. Todd Duncan in window at right (1935).
Museum of the City of New York. Theater Collection.

4.1a, introduced by the orchestra rather than by Porgy himself, emphasizes a pure (or perfect) fifth and a minor (or blue) third, intervals that reasonably (if somewhat inexplicably) represent both the solidity and folk-like nature Porgy shares with Catfish Row as well as his sadness before he met Bess.[75] Soon after his introduction in act I Porgy sings the first of two loneliness themes, "They pass by singin'" (Example 4.1b), a theme that melodically consists entirely of minor thirds and a theme that will retain its strong rhythmic profile in many future contexts.[76]

Moments later in this same monologue Gershwin has Porgy introduce a second loneliness theme (Example 4.1c), a melody that emphasizes a major second on "night time, day time" and "lonesome road" and a prominent syncopated rhythm (♪♩.) derived from the last two notes of Porgy's central theme (Example 4.1a) and the rhythm of "singin'" (Example 4.1b).[77] Having introduced these three rhythmically connected Porgy themes in the opening scene, Gershwin will, in act II, scene 1, establish connections between Porgy and his community to reveal how Bess and Catfish Row work together to eliminate Porgy's loneliness.

Example 4.1. Porgy's themes
- (a) Porgy's central theme
- (b) Loneliness theme
- (c) Loneliness theme
- (d) Loneliness theme in "Buzzard Song"
- (e) Loneliness theme in "Bess, You Is My Woman Now"

Porgy's loneliness themes will undergo further audible transformations in the "Buzzard Song." Throughout much of the "Buzzard Song" Gershwin emphasizes the minor thirds that were so prominent in Porgy's central theme (e.g., "Don' you let dat buzzard keep you hangin' 'round my do'"), and he also retains the syncopations of the loneliness theme. But as seen in Example 4.1d, Gershwin intensifies Porgy's loneliness by contracting his major second a half step in the song's principal melodic motive to create a still-harsher minor second. Even if one questions the dramatic effect of the "Buzzard Song" on this scene and the drama as a whole and embraces the decision to remove it, its omnipresent syncopations and dissonant minor seconds certainly provide a fitting musical counterpart to Porgy's sudden apprehension upon seeing a buzzard.

The original form of Porgy's loneliness theme returns in act II, scene 1, to introduce the duet between Porgy and Bess, "Bess, You Is My Woman Now." The dramatic point of this duet, that Bess's love can eliminate Porgy's loneliness, soon becomes apparent when we hear Bess sing the second loneliness theme, "I ain' goin'! / You hear me *sayin*,' / if you ain' goin',' / wid you I'm *stayin*'" (Example 4.1e). Significantly, Porgy does not sing about his loneliness with Bess, and when Bess returns to it later in the song, Porgy sings a different counter line. In their fleeting, almost magical, moment of happiness, Bess has thus absorbed Porgy's loneliness while at the same time relieving her own. Act II, scene 1, is thus the only scene in which Porgy and Bess express their love with uninhibited optimism for their future together. Musically, "Bess, You Is My Woman Now," as Starr has noted, marks a special and ephemeral moment of F-sharp major, a distant key heard nowhere else in the opera.[78]

The final transformation of Porgy's loneliness in act II, scene 1, occurs in the pseudo-spiritual "Oh, I Can't Sit Down!" that immediately follows Porgy and Bess's love duet, a spiritual that could, without stretching things too much, be interpreted as a melodic transformation of "It Take a Long Pull to Get There" (with a switch of mode from minor to major) and especially "I Got Plenty o' Nuttin.'" In any event, all of these melodies display the short-long syncopated loneliness rhythm (in most cases the short note receives an accent) prominently at the ends of many phrases.[79] In the main portion of this final chorus Gershwin not only preserves the G major tonality of Porgy's earlier tune, he creates another melody that manages to sound new while operating completely within Porgy's perfect fifth. More strikingly, Gershwin in "Oh, I Can't Sit Down" maintains the melodic connection with Porgy's central theme (the prominent minor thirds in the opening musical line that correspond to the song title) and the rhythmic connection (the characteristic syncopation on "happy *feelin*,'" "no con*cealin*,'" and many other words) with Porgy's loneliness theme.

Through such devices Gershwin conveys the message that the most effective way to overcome loneliness is to acknowledge it musically, then transform its character, also musically. Not only has Bess's love for Porgy at least momentarily conquered Porgy's loneliness, Catfish Row revels in this transformation. Ironically, at the end of this scene Bess does in fact leave Porgy, albeit at his urging, to join the community at their picnic, an act that sets up her eventual fall from grace. Nevertheless, the people of Catfish Row invite Bess to join them on Kittiwah Island, a strong sign of her successful integration into the community.

If Porgy's themes and their transformations in community songs serve to emphasize the unity between Porgy and Catfish Row, Sporting Life's central theme—both at his entrance in act II, scene 1, and in the main melody of "It Ain't Necessarily So" in act II, scene 2—demonstrates his separation and estrangement from this same community (Example 4.2). Just as Cap'n Andy's shrewish wife Parthy possesses a melody that cannot live in harmony with the other themes that dwell within the secure perfect fourths of the Mississippi River (Example 2.3, p. 31), Sporting Life's attempt to be a part of Catfish Row is demonstrably false, musically as well as dramatically.

Example 4.2. Sporting Life's themes
  (a) Sporting Life
  (b) Jewish prayer ("Boruch attah adonoi")
  (c) Happy Dust theme

Like Porgy's theme, the melody that Gershwin assigned to Sporting Life is encompassed within a perfect fifth and concludes with a prominent minor (or blue) third. What betrays Sporting Life as an unwelcome outsider, however, is the prominence of the diminished fifth (the same sound as Parthy's dissonant augmented fourth, or tritone), an interval that has been associated with the devil since the Middle Ages when it was known as the *diabolus in musica*. The chromatic machinations of Sporting Life's theme appropriately enough suggest the movements of a snake-in-the-grass, analogous to the serpent who manages to tempt Eve out of the Garden of Eden. The agent of Sporting Life's evil, his "happy dust" (cocaine), receives a suitably chromatic, serpentine theme (Example 4.2c).[80] Even if one takes the optimistic view that Porgy will eventually find Bess after the final curtain, it must be acknowledged that both Bess and Porgy have been forced to leave Eden and search elsewhere for the Promised Land.

The third principal male character, Crown, exhibits a highly charged orchestral theme that contrasts markedly with Porgy's theme (Example 4.3).

Example 4.3. Crown's theme

Crown's strength and restless vitality, like those of a caged animal, are evident in the relentless syncopation of his theme. Musically, Crown's theme is also confined, within the narrow limits of a minor third. Further, in keeping with his dominating presence, whenever Crown appears all other themes are subordinate. His music even dominates the final struggle with Porgy in act III, scene 1, before Porgy states his musical supremacy and manages to overcome and kill his nemesis. In act II, scene 1, however, Crown, who has been absent a month from Catfish Row, does not exert any dramatic influence on the actions or thoughts of Porgy and Bess, and his musical theme is appropriately absent from this peaceful scene.

What about Bess? Does she not merit a theme of her own? Commentators on the opera have without exception neglected to assign her one.[81] Crown's music dominates his fight to the death with Porgy, but Bess's musical identity is less assertive and strongly influenced by the man she is with at the time (Porgy, Crown, or Sporting Life). Although Bess certainly holds her own musically, the two songs that she sings to her men, "What You Want

Wid Bess?" (to Crown) and "I Loves You Porgy" (to Porgy) (Example 4.4), bear striking melodic or rhythmic resemblances to Porgy's themes, the former a paraphrase of Porgy's central theme (Example 4.1a) and the latter a new melody that uses the rhythms of "They pass by singin'" (Example 4.1b). When she sings "Summertime" to Clara's orphaned baby in act III, scene 1, Bess demonstrates her hard-won acceptance into the Catfish Row community by singing one of their songs.

Example 4.4. "I Loves You Porgy"

It is not surprising, then, that Bess's weaknesses and chameleon-like nature as a character have caused writers to overlook (with good reason) that Gershwin did in fact associate a specific theme with his heroine, albeit privately and ultimately unrecognizably. We know this only from Heyward's original libretto typescript, which he sent to Gershwin, where on page 2–17 Gershwin indicated in a handwritten notation that a "Bess theme" should accompany the words sung by Bess, "Porgy, I hates to go an' leave you all alone."[82] At this point in the genesis of the work the idea of a love duet between the principals, the future "Bess, You Is My Woman Now"—which does not have a counterpart in the play *Porgy*—may have been an embryo in Gershwin's mind but it had not yet been hatched.

Earlier it was noted that the eventual insertion of "Bess, You Is My Woman Now" was the most substantial alteration to Heyward's typescript for this scene. Perhaps it is possible to conjecture, after all, even without the benefit of Gershwin's handwritten notes, that the principal tune of this famous duet (even if Porgy sings it) might belong to Bess (Example 4.5).[83] And of course it is reasonable (and egalitarian) that Bess, who is capable at this point in the drama of dispelling Porgy's loneliness, deserves her own theme, especially since she is deprived of a solo aria in act III, scene 3. Surely it is significant that her opening intervals consists mainly of consonant major thirds and

sixths and that her principal minor third is gently completed by an intervening step, just as Bess fills in the gap of Porgy's lonely existence. Interestingly,
Bess's theme also figures prominently in the orchestra in the opera's final
scene, act III, scene 3, when Porgy inquires for Bess upon his return from
jail and she is not there to sing her theme. In the last moments of the opera
Bess's theme—again presented in the orchestra in her absence—connects
with Porgy's own central theme for the first time to seal their fate.[84]

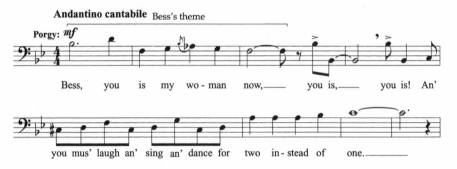

Example 4.5. Bess's theme ("Bess, You Is My Woman Now")

Act II, scene 1, provides abundant evidence of Gershwin's skill in making dramatic connections and distinctions through his use of musical signa-
tures or leitmotivs. Once he has shown, for example, that Bess's theme and
the Catfish Row songs can at least temporarily transform Porgy's loneliness
into hope, Gershwin's motivic transformations reveal a great deal about the
meaning and significance of future dramatic events. One such scene, act II,
scene 3, which takes place one week after Bess left Porgy to join the Catfish
Row picnic on Kittiwah Island, offers a particularly vivid demonstration of
Gershwin's ability to establish dramatic meaning through motivic transformation and paraphrase.

For the week that followed Bess's meeting with Crown on the island in
the previous scene (act II, scene 2), Bess was "out of her head" back in Catfish
Row. She remains in precarious condition at the opening of scene 3. Before
we see Bess, however, we hear Jake's melody and a reprise of "It Take a Long
Pull to Get There." In a passage cut from the New York production Bess
sings "Eighteen mile to Kittiwah, eighteen mile to trabble," a musical line
that might be interpreted as another of the many transformations of Porgy's
central theme. Like Porgy's theme (Example 4.1a), it is encompassed within
a perfect fifth and contains a prominent descending minor third (at the end
of its second measure). It also reuses the syncopated rhythm of Porgy's

loneliness (on "trabble") and combines this rhythm with the half-step interval that dominated the "Buzzard Song" (Examples 4.1c and 4.1d).

Bess's recitative also shows the influence of Sporting Life with its glaring and ominous augmented fourth (A-D♯) (the same sound as the diminished fifth (G-D♭) in Example 4.2). When she returns to this phrase moments later with the words, "Oh, there's a rattle snake in dem bushes," one can imagine the devilish and serpentine Sporting Life lurking in the bushes as well. After Bess sings this brief passage she collapses and Porgy sings his first words of the scene, "I think dat may-be she goin' to sleep now," an easily perceptible transformation of his central theme untarnished by any intrusion of Sporting Life. The devil is taking a nap and Bess will recover.

Serena prays on Bess's behalf and in answer to these prayers Catfish Row comes back to life with Jake's theme and the music of street vendors hawking their wares.[85] We know that Bess has recovered when we hear the orchestra play the opening of her theme (unsupported by harmony), and her conversation with Porgy is underscored by the continuation of "Bess, You Is My Woman Now." In their conversation Porgy tells Bess that he knows she has "been with Crown" on Kittiwah Island, because "Gawd give cripple to understan' many thing he ain' give strong men." Bess, too, understands many things about herself, including the fact that when Crown comes for her, she will be incapable of resisting him. When, near the end of "I Loves You Porgy," she sings, "If you kin keep me I wants to stay here wid you forever.—/ I got my man" (Example 4.4), she uses the rhythm of "They pass by singin'" (Example 4.1b) to plead with Porgy to keep her safe from a man who possesses a harmful power over her.

Although Bess survives her illness and is able to express her love for Porgy once again, the moment of hope that concluded "Bess, You Is My Woman Now" has vanished forever (along with the key of F♯ major reserved for their brief moment of bliss). With her realization that the irresistible Crown, who was conspicuously absent in the earlier scene, now represents a menace to her future happiness with Porgy and that she is now unworthy of the man she loves, Bess has been rendered incapable of defusing Porgy's loneliness. Gershwin conveys this dramatic point simply and effectively when he gives Bess a new melody that is rhythmically identical to Porgy's loneliness theme. Bess has now become so overwhelmed by Porgy's loneliness that its rhythm has become a consuming obsession for her as well. She cannot sing anything else, despite Porgy's assurances of a better life and a sturdy statement of Porgy's central theme to conclude their duet.[86]

Later, in act III, scene 2, Sporting Life mocks the hero (who is about to lose the love of his life) by singing the short-long rhythm of Porgy's loneliness themes (Examples 4.1b and c) no less than four times in the first six measures of his "There's a Boat Dat's Leavin' Soon for New York." But it is Bess's fatalistic sense of defeat in act II, scene 3, rather than Sporting Life's powers of mockery and seduction that enables us to understand why she is so easily persuaded she belongs in New York rather than in Catfish Row.

We will meet Ira Gershwin again five years after *Porgy and Bess* as Kurt Weill's lyricist for *Lady in the Dark* (see chapter 7). For the first two of these years, George was only able to compose a pair of film scores, *Shall We Dance* (1936) and *A Damsel in Distress* (1937), and start a third, *The Goldwyn Follies*, which was completed by Vernon Duke after Gershwin's sudden death of a brain tumor in July 1937.

Assessments on the relative merits of Gershwin's twenty musicals and one opera continue to vary, even among music historians. For example, while H. Wiley Hitchcock concludes that *Porgy and Bess* was "a more pretentious but hardly more artistically successful contribution" than Gershwin's musical comedies and political satires, Hamm writes unreservedly that Gershwin's opera "is the greatest nationalistic opera of the century, not only of America but of the world."[87] Unfortunately, from Gershwin's time to ours, the comedies and satires have seldom been revived in anything approaching their original state, even though nearly all contain one or more songs of lasting popularity and extraordinary musical, lyrical, and dramatic merit. In contrast, Gershwin's sole surviving opera, a work that began its career on Broadway, has, despite its pretensions and attendant artistic and political controversies, long since demonstrated a stage worthiness matched only by the memorability of its tunes.

CHAPTER FIVE

ON YOUR TOES AND PAL JOEY

Dance Gets into the Act and "Sweet Water from a Foul Well"

The historic collaboration of Richard Rodgers (1902–1979) and Lorenz Hart (1895–1943) began inauspiciously, shortly after their first meeting in 1919, when one of their first songs, "Any Old Place with You," was interpolated into a Broadway show. Hart was twenty-four and Rodgers only seventeen. The next year the new partners produced the first of three varsity shows at Columbia University and placed seven interpolated songs in a modestly successful Sigmund Romberg musical, *The Poor Little Ritz Girl*. After five years of failures and frustrations (Rodgers was on the verge of quitting show business to become a babies'underwear wholesaler), the duo enjoyed two big hits in 1925, *The Garrick Gaieties*, a revue that included among its seven Rodgers and Hart songs the still-popular "Manhattan," and *Dearest Enemy*, a romantic musical set during the Revolutionary War.

These two shows launched a succession of popularly received musicals, each containing at least one future perennial song favorite: *Peggy-Ann* in 1926 ("Where's That Rainbow?"), *A Connecticut Yankee* in 1927 ("My Heart Stood Still" and "Thou Swell"), *Present Arms* in 1928 ("You Took Advantage of Me"), and *Evergreen* in 1930 ("Dancing on the Ceiling"). In 1930 the pair began a five-year sojourn in Hollywood where they produced the much discussed but still relatively unknown *Love Me Tonight* (1932), directed by Rouben Mamoulian, the future stage director of *Porgy and Bess*, *Oklahoma!*, and *Carousel*. A circus musical spectacular, *Jumbo*, marked their return to Broadway in 1935 and the beginning of their greatest successes: *On Your Toes*

(1936), *I'd Rather Be Right* and *Babes in Arms* (1937), *I Married an Angel* and *The Boys from Syracuse* (1938), *Pal Joey* (1940), *By Jupiter* (1942), and a revised *A Connecticut Yankee* (1943).

Before the belated triumphs of 1925, Rodgers, who like Hart had dropped out of Columbia University without earning a degree, decided at the age of twenty that he needed to acquire a more rigorous musical education. As an adolescent Rodgers had received informal instruction both from his mother, an amateur pianist, and from his father, an enthusiastic amateur singer. Over three academic years, 1920–21, 1921–22, and 1923–24, he studied piano, theory, and ear training, including a special harmony class limited to five students with the noted theorist and author Percy Goetschius his final year at the Institute of Musical Art (which became the Juilliard School of Music in 1926).

Complementing this musical training was a legendary facility in the creation of melody. Rodgers's early biographer David Ewen reports that after Hammerstein had labored many hours and sometimes weeks, Rodgers needed only about twenty minutes to compose "June Is Bustin' Out All Over" and another twenty minutes for "Happy Talk"; the complex "Soliloquy" from *Carousel* allegedly occupied "about three hours."[1] Although in his autobiography, *Musical Stages*, Rodgers emphasizes the months of precompositional discussions with Hammerstein rather than his own speed, he corroborates the story that "Bali Ha'i" "couldn't have taken more than five minutes."[2] It therefore comes as something of a shock, and perhaps a relief, that the opening of the chorus to "I Could Write a Book" in *Pal Joey* took Rodgers the three tries illustrated in Example 5.1 before he found a version that satisfied him.

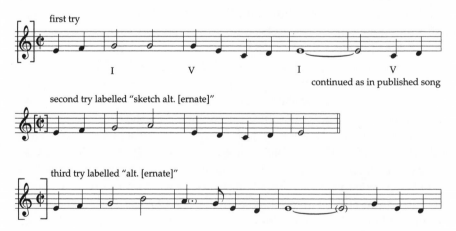

Example 5.1. "I Could Write a Book," three sketches for the opening four measures

Throughout his long career Rodgers placed innovation and integration among his loftiest goals for a musical. In *Musical Stages* he writes with pride that *Dearest Enemy* (1925), his first book musical with Hart, gave his team the welcome "chance to demonstrate what we could do with a score that had at least some relevance to the mood, characters and situations found in a story."[3] Rodgers took similar pride the following year in *Peggy-Ann*'s distinction as the first musical comedy to express Freud's theories on the stage "by dealing with subconscious fears and fantasies."[4]

Rodgers prefaces his remarks concerning the ill-fated musical about castration, *Chee-Chee*, a musical that received an all-time Rodgers and Hart low of thirty-one performances in 1928, with the suggestion that long before *Pal Joey* (1940) and *Oklahoma!* (1943), Rodgers with Hart "had long been firm believers in the close unity of song and story."[5] *Chee-Chee* provided their first opportunity "to put our theories into practice," as Rodgers explains:

> To avoid the eternal problem of the story coming to a halt as the songs take over, we decided to use a number of short pieces of from four to sixteen bars each, with no more than six songs of traditional form and length in the entire scene. In this way the music would be an essential part of the structure of the story rather than an appendage to the action. The concept was so unusual, in fact, that we even called attention to it with the following notice in the program: NOTE: The musical numbers, some of them very short, are so interwoven with the story that it would be confusing for the audience to peruse a complete list.[6]

On Your Toes

By the time Rodgers and Hart returned from Hollywood in 1935, their desire to create innovative musicals reached a new level. One year later they wrote *On Your Toes*. The genesis of the show can be traced to the Hollywood years, however, when Rodgers and Hart conceived the idea of a movie musical about a vaudeville hoofer (to be played by Fred Astaire) who becomes involved with a Russian ballet company.[7] Astaire, then busy with his series of films with Ginger Rogers, declined the role and Hollywood rejected their scenario. Soon, however, Broadway bought the idea as a vehicle for a new dancing sensation, Ray Bolger, the scarecrow in Hollywood's *The Wizard of Oz* in 1939, and the star of Rodgers and Hart's final Broadway show, *By Jupiter*, in 1942 and Frank Loesser's first Broadway triumph, *Where's Charley?* in 1948. Boston tryouts took place between March 21 and April 8, 1936, and

On Your Toes. Ray Bolger and Tamara Geva (1936). Photograph: White
Studio. Museum of the City of New York. Theater Collection.

On Your Toes opened at the Imperial Theatre three days later. When it concluded its run at the Majestic Theatre the following January 23, the hit show
had been performed 315 times.

The history of *On Your Toes* after its initial critically and popularly acclaimed
run differs markedly from the history of its more popular predecessor, Porter's
Anything Goes (discussed in chapter 3). The first major revival of *Anything Goes*
in 1962 offered a new book and many interpolated songs, and made a respectable Off-Broadway run of 239 performances; the first revival of *On Your Toes*
in 1954, with one interpolation and several other modest alterations, folded
after only sixty-four showings. More incriminatingly, the work itself, not the
production, was considered the principal reason for its failure.

In 1936 Brooks Atkinson had written that "if the word 'sophisticated' is not
too unpalatable, let it serve as a description of the mocking book which Richard Rodgers, Lorenz Hart and George Abbott have scribbled."[8] By 1954, the

integrated musicals of Rodgers and Hammerstein and even Rodgers and Hart's recently revived *Pal Joey*—which Atkinson had reviewed disparagingly in 1940 before extolling its virtues in 1952—had created new criteria that musicals such as *On Your Toes* did not match. Thus eighteen years after his initially positive assessment Atkinson attacked as "labored, mechanical and verbose" the book he formerly had deemed sophisticated. For Atkinson and his public "the mood of the day," which had recently caught up to *Pal Joey*, had "passed beyond" *On Your Toes*. The "long and enervating" road to the still-worthy "Slaughter on Tenth Avenue" ballet at the end of the second act simply was not worth the wait.[9]

In the 1936 *On Your Toes* Rodgers and Hart attempted an integration of music and drama that went beyond their successful innovations in *Peggy-Ann* and their unsuccessful ones in *Chee-Chee*. In *Musical Stages* Rodgers discusses his ambitious new artistic intentions:

> One of the great innovations of *On Your Toes*, the angle that had initially made us think of it as a vehicle for Fred Astaire, was that for the first time ballet was being incorporated into a musical-comedy book. To be sure, Albertina Rasch had made a specialty of creating Broadway ballets [for example, *The Band Wagon* of 1931], but these were usually in revues and were not part of a story line. We made our main ballet ["Slaughter on Tenth Avenue"] an integral part of the action; without it, there was no conclusion to our story.[10]

Despite such claims, the degree to which co-authors Rodgers and Hart and Abbott succeeded in their attempt to integrate dance, especially "Slaughter on Tenth Avenue," has been questioned by Ethan Mordden:

> Much has been made of "Slaughter on Tenth Avenue"'s importance as a book-integrated ballet, but it was, in fact, a ballet-within-a-play...*not* a part of the story told in choreographic terms. Only towards the ballet's end did plot collide with set piece when the hoofer learned that two gangsters were planning to gun him down from a box in the theatre at the end of the number. Exhausted, terrified, he must keep dancing to save his life until help comes, and thus a ballet sequence in *On Your Toes* turned into the *On Your Toes* plot.[11]

Mordden's challenge does not obscure the fact that *On Your Toes* treats a vexing artistic issue: the conflict and reconciliation between classical and popular art. Much of the plot and the comedy in *On Your Toes* evolves from the tensions between the cultivated and the vernacular, between highbrow and lowbrow art. Even the barest outlines of the scenario reveal this.

When in act I, scene 3, we meet Phil Dolan III ("Junior") as an adult, he is employed as a music professor at a W.P.A. [Work Projects Administration] Extension University, having renounced his career as a famous vaudeville hoofer sixteen years earlier at the insistence of his parents (scenes 1 and 2). His student and eventual romantic partner, Frankie Frayne, writes "cheap" (1936) or "derivative" (1983) popular songs, including "It's Got to Be Love," "On Your Toes," and "Glad to Be Unhappy"; another student, Sidney Cohn, who supposedly possesses greater talent (to match his pretensions and ambition), has composed "Slaughter on Tenth Avenue," which will be performed by the Russian Ballet in act II.

The Cat and the Fiddle, a 1931 hit with lyrics by Otto Harbach and music by Kern, had explored the tensions and eventual accommodation of classical and popular music in a European setting in which a "serious" Romanian male composer and a jazzy American female composer—at the beginning of the show she is already well known as the composer of "She Didn't Say Yes"—eventually produce a harmonious hybrid. *On Your Toes* contrasted the cultivated and vernacular traditions through dance, two full-length ballets, both choreographed by the revered George Balanchine (1904–1983), who in the previous decade starred in Diaghilev's ballet company: a classical ballet to conclude act I ("La Princesse Zenobia") and a jazz ballet ("Slaughter on Tenth Avenue") as a climax for act II. In the title song, tap dancing and classical ballet alternate and compete for audience approbation in the same number. Further, the Russian prima ballerina (Vera Baranova) and her partner (Konstantine Morrosine) have important dramatic (albeit non-singing) parts as well as their star dance turns. By contrast, in the dream ballet that concludes act I of *Oklahoma!*—the musical which almost invariably receives the credit for integrating dance into the book—the dancing roles of Laurey and Curley are played by separate and mute dancers.

That *On Your Toes* is a musical about Art is frequently evident in the dialogue, especially its original 1936 manifestation. For example, in her efforts to convince the Russian ballet director, Sergei Alexandrovitch, that Sidney Cohn's ballet is worthy of his company, manager and principal benefactress Peggy Porterfield explains the case for branching out: "Your public is tired of *Schéhérazade, La Spectre de la Rose*—they've seen all those Russian turkeys at the Capital for 40 cents—this is something different—it's a jazz ballet—they can't understand the music without the story and nobody can understand the story—they'll say it's art."[12] Vera considers herself "a great artist" because she has convinced Junior that her "dancing [has] a virginal charm."[13] And when Morrosine tells a gangster that he "must wait till he [Junior] stops dancing" before shooting him, Art takes precedence over jealousy and revenge.[14]

The libretto also explores conflicting attitudes on the relative merits of classical and jazz dance. Frankie questions Junior's priorities in giving up his potential as "a headliner in vaudeville" to be a supernumerary in the Russian ballet.[15] In the 1936 libretto Morrosine's infidelities and obnoxious behavior toward his partner and paramour Vera are acceptable, but he is denied the lead role in the jazz ballet for artistic reasons: "he does not understand American Jazz Rhythm" and "does not know how to dance on the off beat."[16]

On Your Toes *in 1936 and 1983*

In 1983, nearly thirty years after it had previously stumbled in its first Broadway revival, *On Your Toes* was again revived, this time with a new book from nonagenarian Abbott, the principal contributor to the original book. Echoing Atkinson's condemnation of the earlier production, Frank Rich of the *New York Times* wrote that the 1954 failure "was no fluke" and that "its few assets as entertainment are scattered like sweet and frail rose petals on a stagnant pond."[17] With the exception of Rich, the new production received mostly favorable reviews and ran 505 performances, after the 1952 revival of *Pal Joey* (542 performances) the second longest running Rodgers and Hart production and, like *Porgy and Bess, Pal Joey, Candide,* and in the 1990s, *Guys and Dolls, Cabaret,* and the still-running *Chicago,* one of the relatively few musical revivals to surpass its initial run.

What made the 1983 *On Your Toes* revival especially newsworthy was the approach of the revivalists. In contrast to the drastic book revisions and interpolated songs of the 1962 and 1987 revivals of *Anything Goes,* the 1983 *On Your Toes* in most respects closely followed its 1936 model. And unlike the 1954 revival, which had contained the interpolated "You Took Advantage of Me" (originally heard in *Present Arms* of 1928) in act II, scene 3, and dropped the first number, "Two a Day for Keith," soon after opening night, no interpolations or deletions in 1983 disturbed the "authenticity" of the original. That the 1983 production attempted to offer a faithful reenactment of the 1936 show is evident also in the reinstatement of the original dance and vocal arrangements, for the most part uncut and unedited, and the resuscitation of Hans Spialek's 1936 orchestrations. Although some of the original choreography was lost, "Donald Saddler, who restaged the non-ballet numbers, took care to use only movements that belong to the dance of the time."[18]

The considerable success of the 1983 revival prompted the publication of the first complete vocal score two years later with the following introductory remarks from Theodore S. Chapin, President of the Rodgers & Hammerstein Organization:

This score corresponds to the 1983 production of ON YOUR TOES which used the orchestrations and arrangements created for the original production in 1936. A few slight changes were necessary and were made by Hans Spialek, the man who orchestrated the show forty-seven years earlier. Therefore, what you have in your hands is a record of a 1936 Rodgers and Hart score as it sounded when first presented to the public, as well as a documentation of a successful revival. That a score of this nature could be presented as its creators intended, and that those intentions could seem as vital today as they were in 1936, is a testament not only to the timelessness of Rodgers and Hart, but to the dedication and affection lavished on the 1983 production.[19]

Chapin neglects to mention that the vocal score issued in 1985 by Chappell does not entirely preserve the original order of these authentic 1936 orchestrations and arrangements. The brackets and other emendations in the lists of scenes and songs from the 1936 Broadway production and 1983 revival in the online website reveal, for example, that "The Heart Is Quicker Than the Eye" (sung in 1936 by Peggy and Junior in act I, scene 6) has been transferred to the first scene of the second act to replace "Quiet Night" so that Ms. Porterfield would have something to sing in both acts. "Quiet Night" in 1936 opens act II, sung by a character identified only as Crooner; in 1983 "Quiet Night" is sung one scene later by a named nonentity (Hank J. Smith) and a female trio and reprised in scene 4 by the Russian ballet impresario Sergei Alexandrovitch and an offstage chorus.

Gone also is the act II reprise by Sergei and Peggy of Junior's and Frankie's "There's a Small Hotel." Even if one refrained from asking how Sergei and Peggy came to know this song, its second act appearance in 1936 seemed somewhat gratuitous. In 1983 Sergei and Peggy sing a reprise of "Quiet Night" instead. Both productions allow everyone to learn "There's a Small Hotel" well enough to sing it at the end of the show.

The 1983 version also changed the locale of a few scenes. For example, the schoolroom scene in act I, scene 5, originally took place in Central Park at night, a setting for "There's a Small Hotel" that even the staunchest advocates of authenticity might consider laughable in 1983. But these changes do not contradict Chapin's assertion that for the most part Abbott & Co. as well as Chappell & Co. remained faithful to their musical source to a degree that was remarkable for a 1980s revival of a 1930s musical.

Thirty years earlier, as a result of his dissatisfaction with director Dwight Wiman, Abbott left for Palm Beach before rehearsals had begun in February, returning after Rodgers reminded him that as co-(de facto principal) author Abbott had an "obligation to come and protect it."[20] In his autobiography Abbott explains his reaction and solution:

Arriving in Boston, where *On Your Toes* was playing its final week, I found things in better shape than I had expected. Ray Bolger was sensational in the lead, and "Slaughter on Tenth Avenue" remains in my memory as one of the best numbers I've ever seen in the theatre, both musically and choreographically. The book, however, was a mess; the story line had been destroyed by experimenting, and the actors were out of hand. I behaved ruthlessly to the cast to force them to play parts instead of fighting for material, and I straightened the book out by the simple device of putting it back the way I had written it in the first place.[21]

When he returned to the script in 1983, Abbott (now ninety-five) had had time to rethink and reinterpret his responses and actions of 1936. He now recalled the situation somewhat differently than in both his and Rodgers's published autobiographies: "I respected Rodgers and Hart so much in that field...I didn't do as much as I should have done....I threw out three sets....In the old days, if they wanted to sing a song, they set it in Central park or the Palladium. What for? To sing a song like 'Quiet Night'? I made 'Quiet Night' part of the plot."[22]

In order to further integrate plot and music as well as to establish greater credibility (and, of course, accessibility) for a 1980s audience, Abbott altered his original libretto. In 1936 Sergei and Vera had been several times married; in 1983 Sergei is given some romantic potential with Peggy (as revealed in their reprise of "Quiet Night," now "part of the plot") and Vera and Konstantine are lovers both on and off the stage. Also in 1983 the original meeting between Junior and Peggy is made more understandable; Frankie now knows a friend of Peggy's uncle who can introduce them.

The main changes between the 1936 and 1983 books, however, deal less with plot than with language. The earlier version is more sexually suggestive and, still more surprisingly, perhaps even funnier. Here, for example, is what 1936 audiences heard in the dialogue that precedes Vera's meeting with Junior in act I, scene 4:

PEGGY: You're to be a strip tease girl in a burlesque show.
VERA: Well, if he's got ideas like that, why should I bother to dress?
PEGGY: Darling, he thinks you are an actress. He doesn't know we are casting to type.

In 1983 Vera is cast as a primmer prima ballerina who has the *potential* to play a striptease character when given time to consider such an outrageous thought. Abbott is clearly no longer casting to type:

PEGGY: You're going to love the part—it's a striptease girl in a burlesque show. It will shock the dance world. It will show us as the
progressive ballet company I want us to be.

VERA: What about Sergei Alexandrovitch? He will say no.

PEGGY: First you have to like it. This young man who is coming will
play the music and tell you all about it.

VERA (*Begins to play the part*): Sure, a striptease girl—why not?

As a sexually liberated goddess of the ballet world, the original Vera is
allowed to conclude the scene in her apartment with a risqué punch line that
indicates her desire to see more of Junior. After the foreplay of dancing to the
"Zenobia" ballet with Junior, they climb on her bed and she takes his glasses
off. When Junior tells Vera his real name and his nickname, Vera replies with
a line that could have been stolen from a Mae West film: "But I'll call you
Phillip. I can't call you Junior. For very soon you will be a great big boy."[23]

The original book of *On Your Toes* had fewer Groucho Marx–Margaret
Dumont–type exchanges than the 1934 *Anything Goes*, but those that
remained were carefully expurgated. Thus in Abbott's 1983 revised book
(act 1, scene 6) Sergei learns of the glitch that will pave the way for Junior to
escape from his role as a supernumerary to become a star of the "Zenobia"
ballet: the dancer Leftsky has been detained in jail. This change obscures the
politically topical nature of the 1936 version which finds Lefsky (less obviously named than his 1983 counterpart) in a hospital.

SERGEI: He got in fight with union delegates—All afternoon we are
waiting and waiting for him—

PEGGY: Waiting for Lefsky![24]

Theater audiences in 1936 would not have had any trouble relating this reference to Clifford Odets's then widely known union play produced the previous year, *Waiting for Lefty*, in which members of a taxi drivers' union are
waiting in vain for their leader, who has been killed.

The Classroom Scene

A comparison between the 1936 and 1983 versions of the first classroom
scene, act I, scene 3, further demonstrates evolving social attitudes. In 1936
Junior not only derogates as "cheap" the musical ditty Frankie has composed, but he also displays a favoritism toward his "serious" jazz (and, not
incidentally, male) student composer Sidney Cohn. In fact, he is so engrossed
in his protégé that he is oblivious to Frankie's feelings. Although Frankie is

still the one who will return to apologize for leaving so abruptly, by 1983 Junior has learned something from the feminist movement of the intervening years. At least he realizes that he has hurt her feelings.

Gone from both the lyrics and the vocal score of "The Three B's" in 1983 are Hart's virtuosic and delectably absurd rhymes in 1936 that called attention to their brilliance: "Who are the three 'B's' of music? / Name the holy trinity / Whose true divinity / Goes stretching to infinity / No asininity / In this vicinity / Who are the three "B's" of music?"[25]

In 1983 Junior offers the following interpretation of romantic lieder: "And thus we note the painless transition into the next phase. The early 19th century brought forth a renaissance of what we could term singing composers. The great music of that period was idealized folk song. Chopin, Schumann, Mendelssohn, and, last but not least, Franz Schubert."[26]

The following dialogue from 1936 (abandoned in 1983) introduces "The Three B's" from quite a different perspective:

> JUNIOR: You will notice I am careful of the pronunciation, Schu-*bert*, not Shubert [a reference to the organization which, then as now, owned a considerable number of Broadway theaters]. (*Walks to piano*) Let us take this lovely melody. (*He plays the* Ständchen *and sings*) "Dein ist mein Herz" which means "Yours is my heart." We are all familiar with that melody but I wonder is there anyone who can tell me what life force may have inspired Franz Schubert? (*Hands are raised by some of the class*) Yes, Miss Wasservogel?
>
> MISS WASSERVOGEL: A beautiful girl.
>
> JUNIOR: Miss Frayne?
>
> FRANKIE: A handsome young man.
>
> SEVERAL STUDENTS: A girl—a girl.
>
> OTHERS: A boy.
>
> JUNIOR: No—a pork chop, a glass of beer and liverwurst; Schubert should be very close to our hearts here for he was born poor with no W.P.A.[27]

Abbott's 1936 dialogue lets audiences know unequivocally that Frankie—a contemporary Schubert—is the one inspired by "a handsome young man."[28] Also in 1936, with a remark that would mean more to Depression audiences, Junior disregards love as a motive and attributes Schubert's inspiration to a good meal. "The Three B's" in the 1936 version (renamed "Questions and Answers" in 1983) also demonstrates the essence of the conflict between classical music and jazz so central to *On Your Toes*. Classical music, with its "charms of Orpheus," throws lovers of popular music "right into the arms of Morpheus." Although the scholarly establishment would not lower itself in 1936 (or even a 1983 version of 1936) to explain the artistic merits of jazz in a university classroom, classical music is characterized as boring for all its artistic pretensions while jazz, a "cheap" (or "derivative") pseudo-art, provides much greater entertainment.

Throughout "The Three B's" the jazz-loving W.P.A. Extension University class unabashedly reveals its ignorance of and derision for art music. To the strains of the Symphony in D Minor and *Les Préludes* they mispronounce César Franck's name as Seezer Frank and convert Liszt's popular classic into a drinking song (Example 5.2).[29] Next they add ignorance to sacrilege when they confuse Shostakovich's recently banned opera, *Lady Macbeth of Mtsensk*, with celebrity stripper Gypsy Rose Lee's burlesque house Minskys, and reach a "new low" (to rhyme with "Von Bülow") when they assert that Puccini wrote the popular song classic "Poor Butterfly" instead of *Madame Butterfly*. In exclaiming in the chorus of "Bach, Beethoven, and Brahms" that "two of them wrote symphonies and one wrote psalms," they add the sin of a weak rhyme "Brahms/psalms" to a tenuous historical claim (Bach wrote chorales, after all, not psalms). But the students show that they are not complete dunces when they place "the man who wrote *Sari*"—the now-obscure Emmerich Kálmán (1882–1953)—on a par with Bernardino Molinari (1880–1952).[30] To paraphrase a line from *Pal Joey's* "Zip," "Who the hell is Molinari?"

Example 5.2. "Questions and Answers (The Three B's)"
(a) with Franck's Symphony in D Minor and Liszt's *Les Préludes* borrowings
(b) Liszt's *Les Préludes*

Example 5.2. Continued

The dramatic context of the song "It's Got to Be Love" in act I, scene 3, is a pretext for Frankie to sing the song she wrote (with Junior in mind). Here is the exchange that leads to it in 1936:

> JUNIOR: Well, I seem to remember that primarily you wanted to talk about the song of yours.
>
> FRANKIE (*cross to desk*): Oh, no, not really. It's so unimportant. Just look at the title, "It's Got to Be Love"—that's unimportant to start with, isn't it?
>
> JUNIOR: I wish I knew.

FRANKIE: What?

JUNIOR: I mean, well, perhaps if you play it for me a few times, I'll change my mind.[31]

Following a five-measure introduction and a tuneful verse of twenty-three measures, which provides a smooth musical transition between spoken dialogue and a song hit—Frankie has indeed composed a hit worthy of Rodgers—Frankie and Junior sing two thirty-two-bar choruses. The melody of the first chorus (the first A of an A-A form) is shown in Example 5.3.

Example 5.3. "It's Got to Be Love" (chorus, mm. 1-18)

A	a	[It's] got to be love! [upbeats in brackets]
		It couldn't be tonsillitis;
		It feels like neuritis,
		But nevertheless it's love.
		(8 measures, mm. 1–8)
	b	[Don't] tell me the pickles and pie à la mode
		(2 measures, mm. 9–10)
	á	[They] served me
		Unnerved me,
		And made my heart a broken down pump!
		(6 measures, mm. 11–16)

The first eight measures start off conventionally enough and present what anyone familiar with the standard popular song form would inter-pret as the beginning of an A section. Instead of the more conventional repeat of A, however, the words that continue the song, "Don't tell me the pickles and pie à la mode" during the next two measures, inaugurate something new, which in retrospect we can call *b'* (we can call the first part of A, "*a*"). More surprisingly, two measures later, beginning with "served me," Rodgers interrupts b' and returns to a new version of *a* (more accu-rately *a'*), a version much transformed through condensation. Probably relatively few listeners would recognize that *a'* (mm. 11–16) is fundamen-tally the same as *a* (mm. 1–8), albeit stripped of all but the bare essential notes of the earlier phrase. Together *a*, *b*, and *a'* make up the sixteen mea-sures of the first A.

After the first eight measures of the second A (*a*), Rodgers offers another surprise when he returns to *b*, 'but doubles its length from two measures to four (mm. 25–28, not shown). The added measures (mm. 27–28), for which Hart wrote the words "sinking feeling," stand out from the rest of the song as the only occasion (other than the ends of phrases) where a note is held longer than a single beat. Hart understood that the descending melodic line of these measures, D-C♯-B-B♭, aptly fits the sentiment of the lyric here, just as in the previous line he set the melody that turns around the note E to capture the feeling of "spinning around above" (m. 23). When he arrives at the phrase that inspired Hart's "sinking feeling," Rodgers also presents a harmonic rhythm dramatically altered from everything that came before in the song. Instead of allowing several melody notes for each chord, he now allots one note per chord.[32] The final *a"* (mm. 29–32) starts off like *a* before returning to the opening lyrical idea and a new concluding musical phrase, "But nevertheless it's only love!," to conclude the song.

"It's Got to Be Love" contains a characteristic Hartian sentiment about love as an unwelcome malady and its negative effect on the body and spirit. Two years later in *The Boys from Syracuse*, Rodgers and Hart composed a sequel, "This Can't Be Love." Why not? Because Luciana and Antipholus of Syracuse "feel so well—no sobs, no sorrows, no sighs...no dizzy spell." In the earlier lament from *On Your Toes* Rodgers and Hart present a love song composed by a woman so smitten that her lover's hair, even if it "couldn't possibly be duller," would be perceived as pure gold. Since at this stage in the show Frankie cannot admit that Junior is the reason her heart has become "a broken down pump," the jazzy tune, like the lyrics (with the exception of "that sinking feeling"), creates a surface lightness that masks the underlying truth: Frankie is literally as well as figuratively lovesick. Perhaps even more ingeniously than in Vera Simpson's open admission of her obsession with

Joey in "Bewitched," discussed later in this chapter (Example 5.6), "It's Got to Be Love" displays a descending two-note figure in alternate measures (for example, m. 1, A-B; m. 3, G-A; m. 5, F♯-G; m. 7, E-F♯) that subtly but surely betrays Frankie's obsession with her teacher Junior.

Organicism in On Your Toes

In his notes to the 1983 revival, recording conductor John Mauceri writes tantalizingly of musical organicism in *On Your Toes*: "The score is full of musical 'cross-references'" like the theme of the pas de deux in 'Princesse Zenobia' having the same rhythmic structure as 'There's a Small Hotel' [Example 5.4]. The great composers of the American musical theater were not merely tunesmiths but composers of songs, ensembles and occasionally

Example 5.4. "There's a Small Hotel" and "La Princesse Zenobia" Ballet
  (a) "There's a Small Hotel," original song
  (b) transformation in "La Princesse Zenobia" ballet

larger structures, like Schumann, Mendelssohn and Schubert a century before them."[33]

Mauceri's message is that great works of theatrical art such as *On Your Toes* possess unity and structural integrity not usually associated with musical comedy—and, by implication, that large works are more worthy of praise than "mere" tunes. And certainly "There's a Small Hotel" and "Princesse Zenobia" have much in common melodically as well as rhythmically. Since this song has previously served as the love duet between Junior and Frankie, it is dramatically convincing when Rodgers uses a transformed version of this song for a *pas de deux* (the balletic equivalent of a love song) that depicts the love between the Beggar (Morrosine) and the Princesse (Vera).

Additional examples of organicism include the rhythmic and sometimes melodic connections between the release or B section of "There's a Small Hotel" (which, unlike "It's Got to Be Love," displays the more usual A-A-B-A thirty-two-bar form with each letter representing eight measures) and the first phrase of "The Heart Is Quicker Than the Eye" (also A-A-B-A) shown in Example 5.5. Mauceri might have noted that Rodgers reuses the dotted rhythmic accompaniment of "Small Hotel" to accompany the main theme of "Slaughter" for the jazzy duet between Junior (who knows the tune pretty well by now) and the stripper Vera. He might also have mentioned that the accompaniment of the second half of the verse, beginning with the words "see...looks gold to me" of "It's Got to Be Love" also anticipates the rhythmic accompaniment throughout "There's a Small Hotel" and the *pas de deux* between Junior and Vera in "Slaughter." Nevertheless, in contrast to the vast network of connections previously observed in *Show Boat* and *Porgy and Bess*, examples of organicism in *On Your Toes* are comparatively rare. More

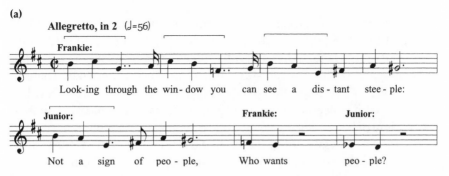

(a)

Example 5.5. "There's a Small Hotel" and "The Heart Is Quicker Than the Eye"
(a) "There's a Small Hotel" (B section, or release)
(b) "The Heart is Quicker Than the Eye" (opening of chorus)

(b)

Example 5.5. Continued

important, Rodgers, although he does employ the musical device of fore-shadowing for dramatic purposes, especially of his second ballet, "Slaughter on Tenth Avenue," for the most part does not exploit the dramatic potential of his musical connections as he would later with Hammerstein.[34]

Musical comedies before *Oklahoma!* and *Carousel* are almost invariably criticized for their awkward transitions from dialogue into music. The segue into "There's a Small Hotel" (act I, scene 6), a big hit song in the original production, provides a representative example by its absence of any references in the dialogue that lead plausibly, much less naturally or inevitably, to the song. In his 1983 revision Abbott tries to remedy this:

> FRANKIE: Oh, Junior, I wish we were far away from all this.
> JUNIOR: Yes, so do I. With no complications in our lives.
> FRANKIE: Yes.
> JUNIOR (*Goes to her*): Oh yes...very far away...Paris maybe.[35]

If the revised dialogue constitutes an improvement over the Central Park setting of the 1936 original, where "There's a Small Hotel" almost literally comes out of nowhere, it does not fully solve the problem of how a librettist or an imaginative director can successfully introduce a song like "There's a Small Hotel." "It's Got to Be Love" may subtly reflect Frankie's disguised obsession with veiled descending melodic sequences, but not even with all the wisdom of his advancing years could a genius such as Abbott make these songs grow seamlessly out of the dramatic action. But perhaps the point is that if we think of the song and its performance *as the show* rather than an interruption that "stops" the show, so-called integrated dramatic solutions are less necessary?

Pal Joey

Several days before *Pal Joey*'s 1952 revival, Rodgers wrote in the *New York Times* that "Nobody like Joey had ever been on the musical comedy stage before."[36] In his autobiography Rodgers concluded that of the twenty-five musicals he wrote with Hart, *Pal Joey* remained his favorite, an opinion also shared by his lyricist.[37] Porter's *Anything Goes* may be more frequently revived. Several Rodgers and Hart shows, including *A Connecticut Yankee* (1927) in its revised 1943 version, *Babes in Arms* (1937), and *The Boys from Syracuse* (1938) can boast as many or even more hits. The scintillating *On Your Toes* can claim two full-length ballets and an organic unity unusual in musical comedies. Despite all this, only *Pal Joey* has proven that it can be successfully revived without substantial changes in its book or reordering of its songs.

The genesis of the musical *Pal Joey*, based on John O'Hara's collection of stories in epistolary form, can be traced to 1938 when a single O'Hara short story, "Pal Joey," was published in the *New Yorker*. By early 1940, shortly after Rodgers had received O'Hara's letter suggesting a collaboration on a musical based on his collection, an additional eleven Joey stories (out of a total of thirteen) had appeared.[38] A normal five-week rehearsal schedule began on November 11 and tryouts took place in Philadelphia between December 16 and 22. Directed by Abbott and starring Gene Kelly as Joey and Vivienne Segal as Vera Simpson, the musical made its Broadway premiere at the Ethel Barrymore Theatre on Christmas Day and closed 374 performances later at the St. James Theatre on November 29, 1941.[39]

In his now-infamous review *New York Times* theater critic Brooks Atkinson found *Pal Joey* "entertaining" but "odious." Referring to the disturbing subject matter, including adultery, sexual exploitation, blackmail, the somewhat unwholesome moral character of the principals, and a realistic and unflattering depiction of the seamy side of Chicago night life, Atkinson concluded his review with the question, "Although it is expertly done, can you draw sweet water from a foul well?"[40] Other critics greeted *Pal Joey* as a major "advance" in the form. Burns Mantle, for example, compared it favorably with the legitimate plays of the season and expressed his delight "that there are signs of new life in the musicals."[41] And in *Musical Stages* Rodgers proudly quotes Wolcott Gibbs's *New Yorker* review as an antidote to Atkinson: "I am not optimistic by nature but it seems to me just possible that the idea of equipping a song-and-dance production with a few living, three-dimensional figures, talking and behaving like human beings, may no longer strike the boys in the business as merely fantastic."[42] Some reviewers noted weaknesses in the second act, but most praised O'Hara for producing a fine book. John Mason Brown described the work as "novel and imaginative."[43] Sidney B. Whipple lauded the "rich characterizations" and concluded that it was "the first musical comedy book in a long time that has been worth the bother."[44]

Pal Joey appeared several years before the era of cast recordings, but in September 1950, ten years after its Broadway stage debut, a successful recording was issued with Vivienne Segal, the original Vera Simpson, and with Harold Lang as a new Joey. The recording generated considerable interest in the work and soon led to a revival on January 3, 1952, a sequence of events that foreshadowed the trajectories of several Andrew Lloyd Webber musicals of the 1970s and 1980s that were introduced as record albums and later evolved into stage productions. The 1952 *Pal Joey* became the second major revival (after Cheryl Crawford's 1942 revival of *Porgy and Bess*) to surpass its original run, and at 542 performances remains the longest running production of any Rodgers and Hart musical, original or revival. Even Atkinson, while not exactly admitting that he had erred in his 1940 assessment, lavishly praised the work as well as the production in 1952, including "the terseness of the writing, the liveliness and versatility of the score, and the easy perfection of the lyrics."[45]

Pal Joey. Gene Kelly in right foreground (1940). Photograph: Vandamm Studio. Museum of the City of New York. Theater Collection.

After two successful revivals at the New York City Center in 1961 and 1963 (both with Bob Fosse in the title role), the artistic and commercial failure of a 1976 revival at New York City's Circle in the Square—abandoned by New York City Ballet star Edward Villella shortly before opening night—would not cause *Pal Joey* to lose its place as a classic American musical, a place firmly established by the 1952 revival. As another sign of its artistic stature *Pal Joey* became the earliest musical to gain admittance in Lehman Engel's select list of fifteen canonic musicals.[46] For Engel, *Pal Joey* inaugurated a Golden Age of the American musical.[47]

Pal Joey *in 1940 and 1952*

Compared to the liberties taken with the 1962 *Anything Goes* and the 1954 *On Your Toes*, the 1952 *Pal Joey* revival followed its original book and song content and order tenaciously. Nevertheless, some of what audiences heard and saw in 1952 departs from the original Broadway production. For example, in the 1952 revival, "Do It the Hard Way" is placed outside of its original dramatic context (act II, scene 4), when it is sung by Joey to Vera in their apartment; in 1940 this song is presented as a duet between Gladys and Ludlow Lowell in Chez Joey one scene earlier.[48]

The 1952 lyrics also depart in several notable ways from O'Hara's 1940 typescript.[49] In 1940 Hart concluded the chorus of "That Terrific Rainbow" (act I, scene 3) with the following quatrain: "Though we're in those GRAY clouds / Some day you'll see / That terrific RAINBOW / Over you and me" (preserved on the pre-revival recording); for the 1952 revival someone (presumably not Hart) replaced two lines of this lyric with one that is grammatically incorrect, perhaps to emphasize the amateurish nature of the song. Thus "Some day you'll spy" now rhymes with "Over you and I" (Hart rhymed "someday you'll see" with "over you and me"). This alteration was adopted in the 1962 vocal score published by Chappell & Co.

The topical "Zip"—a song in which newspaper reporter Melba Snyder (played in the revival by Elaine Stritch) acts out her interview with Gypsy Rose Lee, "the star who worked for Minsky"—also underwent several lyrical changes in 1952. In the revival Melba opened the song with Hart's earlier version of the first lines when she recalls her interviews with "Pablo Picasso and a countess named di Frasso." It is possible that Picasso and di Frasso were more recognizable to an early 1950s audience than the revised 1940 lyric that paired Leslie Howard and Noël Coward. In the final chorus the then-better-known Arturo Toscanini replaced Leopold Stokowski as the leader of the "the greatest of bands," and one stripper (Lili St. Cyr) replaced another (Rosita Royce). Even present-day trivia buffs could not be expected to know who either stripper is (although it might be said that Lili St. Cyr has achieved immortality by being mentioned in "Zip"). The 1952 version of "Den of Iniquity" (act II, scene 2) replaced Tchaikovsky's *1812 Overture* with Ravel's *Boléro* and added a final lyrical exchange between Joey and Vera after their dance.[50]

In his autobiography Abbott somewhat exaggeratingly refers to a preliminary script by librettist O'Hara as "a disorganized set of scenes without a good story line [that] required work before we would be ready for rehearsal."[51] In fact, although it contains no lyrics among its indications for songs and displays several notable deletions and departures from his Broadway typescript in 1940 (including an ending in which Linda and Joey are reconciled), in most respects O'Hara's preliminary typescript follows the story line of the 1940 version closely.[52]

Some songs that became part of the Broadway draft, "That Terrific Rainbow," "Happy Hunting Horn," and even "Bewitched," were not given any space at all in O'Hara's preliminary script. Further, the early typescript offers no indication for a ballet, an idea that Abbott credits scene and lighting designer Jo Mielziner for suggesting during rehearsals.[53] The dialogue that precedes "The Flower Garden of My Heart" in the published libretto is also missing from the earlier draft, but in this case O'Hara's description of this production number (original draft, beginning of act II) leaves no room for doubt that he was responsible for the idea of the ballet:

> The song is Richman corn [Harry Richman, who introduced Irving Berlin's song "Puttin' on the Ritz" in the 1930 film also called *Puttin on the Ritz*], the flower number kind of thing—every girl reminds me of a flower; here is a hydrangea, here is a crocus, etc. a YOUNG MAN stays in the spotlight, holding out a hand for Hydrangea, who is in silly nudish costume. He never quite lets her get all the way in the light, but hands her away with one hand as he reaches for Crocus with the other. He looks at the fannies etc. in a way to make them ridiculous, and is mugging terribly, even in rehearsal.

Song and Story

O'Hara's typescript of the 1940 Broadway libretto (I-6–36) contains handwritten changes for "Bewitched," the biggest song hit from *Pal Joey*. Here are the typed lyrics as they once appeared in the B and final A sections of the third A-A-B-A chorus.

B   We can fight—we start *shrieking*
      Always end in a *row*,
      Horizontally *speaking* is not the whole thing *now*,
A   I'm *dumb* again
      And *numb* again
      Like Fanny Brice singing "Mon *Homme*" again.
      Bewitched, bothered and bewildered am I.

The draft poses a cultural literacy problem for those who might not know, even in 1940, that Fanny Brice sang "My Man" in *Ziegfeld 9 O'Clock Frolic* (1920) and *Ziegfeld Follies* (1921), or that this song was originally the French song "Mon Homme" by Maurice Yvain and Channing Pollock.[54]

Fortunately this lyric was abandoned. The first three lines were crossed out and replaced with the following handwritten script for the B section with the forced rhyme **pal** / verti-**cal**:

When your dream boat is *leaking*
And your pal ain't your **pal**
Geometrically *speaking* just keep it verti**cal**

The final version published in 1940 with its paired rhymes in B, is not indicated in the O'Hara typescript:

B   Though at first we said, *"No sir,"*
      Now we're two little **dears**.
      You might say we are closer
      Than Roebuck is to **Sears**.
A   I'm *dumb* again
      And *numb* again,
      A rich, ready, ripe little *plum* again—
      Bewitched, bothered and bewildered am I.

All of these versions are variations on a theme that Hart explored in numerous songs, including "It's Got to Be Love" discussed earlier: love as a sickness. Vera, the restless wife of the wealthy Prentiss Simpson, is generally in control of her emotions and entertains no delusions about the cause of her sleepless nights. In the verse that precedes the chorus she even refers to Joey as a "fool" and a "half-pint imitation," but even this realization does not prevent her from catching the dreaded disease.

In his autobiography Rodgers recalls what he learned from his training in Goetschius's class of five students: "Whenever Goetschius talked about ending a phrase with a straight-out tonic chord (the first, third and fifth step of any scale), he would call it a 'pig,' his term for anything that was too easy or obvious. Once I heard the scorn in Goetschius' voice I knew that I'd avoid that 'pig' as if my life depended on it."[55] In "Bewitched" (Example 5.6) Rodgers avoids the infelicitously named "pig" at the end of the second eight-measure A section. He does this by moving to an A in measures 15 and 16 on the word "I" rather than the expected first note of the scale, F (also on the word "I"), that he set up at the end of the first A section in measures 7 and 8. The harmony, however, add interest as well as richness but not following the expectations of the melody. When the melody resolves to F (mm. 7–8), Rodgers harmonizes this note, not with F but with D minor (D-F-A, with F as

Example 5.6. "Bewitched" (chorus)
  (a) Chorus, mm. 1-16.
  (b) B section, or release, mm. 17-20

the third rather than an F major triad, F-A-C, with F as the root); when the melody closes on A at the end of the second A section (mm. 15–16), the note that avoided the "pig," Rodgers offers the F harmony expected eight measures earlier (but now a surprise), with A as the third. Only at the conclusion of the final A section (mm. 31–32) does Rodgers join melody and harmony (the note C in the melody matches the C major chord in the harmony) to conclude the song with a satisfying close.

Rodgers also finds an effective musical means to capture Hart's virtuosic depiction of Vera's obsession. Hart conveys the society matron's idée fixe by giving her thrice-repeated lyrics to conclude the first three lines of each A section, as in "I'm wild *again!* / Beguiled *again!* / A whimpering, simpering child *again*" (with the internal rhymes *wild, beguiled,* and *child*) before delivering the "hook" of the song's title, "bewitched, bothered and bewildered" (always unrhymed) to conclude each A section. It is tempting to conclude that Rodgers's musical characterization of Vera's emotional state corresponds with uncanny accuracy to the lyrics. But since the lyrics apparently followed the music—in contrast to Rodgers's subsequent modus operandi with Hammerstein—it is more accurate to admire Hart's special sensitivity to Rodger's music, which presents an equally repetitive musical line, the note B ascending up a half-step to C. By inverting the musical line (turning it upside down) in the B section (mm. 17–24), Rodgers manages to maintain Vera's obsession while providing welcome musical contrast to the repetitive A sections.

Vera's ability to rhyme internally also reflects her complexity and sophistication—or, as Sondheim would say, her education.[56] In other songs Hart's lyrics convey literal lyrical parallels to Rodgers's music. Examples of textual realism include Joey's monotonous recitation of the alphabet and numbers to match the repeated notes in the verse of "I Could Write a Book," the word "blue" in the phrase "but I'm blue for you" to match Rodgers's "blue note" (a blue seventh) in the first period of "That Terrific Rainbow," and the hunting imagery that corresponds to the horn-like fifths in "Happy Hunting Horn." Other pictorial examples include the gunshot at the end of this last song to suggest fallen prey, the graphic chord each time Melba Snyder sings the word "Zip!," and the dissonant chord cluster after she mentions "the great Stravinsky."

Perhaps in an effort to musically integrate his *Pal Joey* songs, Rodgers maintains his obsession with the prominent half-steps that characterized "Bewitched." No less than three other songs in *Pal Joey* prominently employ various melodic permutations of the half-step interval. Can we attribute any dramatic meaning to this? By emphasizing this interval in both of Vera's solo songs, "Bewitched" and "What Is a Man?" (Examples 5.6 and 5.7), Rodgers

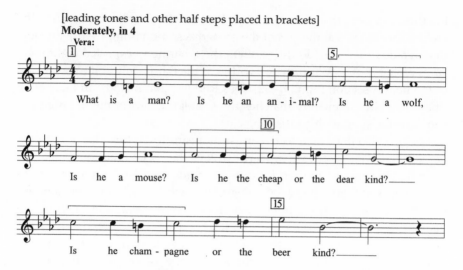

[leading tones and other half steps placed in brackets]

Moderately, in 4

Vera:

Example 5.7. "What Is a Man?" (chorus, mm. 1-16)

helps establish the musical identity of a woman who has allowed herself the luxury of an obsession. When Vera is with her paramour and sings with him, she has no need to obsess about him. Consequently, the half-step is absent in her duet with Joey, "Den of Iniquity." Why Joey should sing half-steps so often in "Plant You Now, Dig You Later" is less explicable.[57] What remains consistent is that the songs prominently displaying the half-step are the "offstage" songs, not the songs sung in rehearsal or as part of the entertainment in Mike Spears's nightclub or Chez Joey.

The seemingly irresistible musical and psychological pull that characterizes the move from the seventh degree of a major scale (aptly labeled the leading tone) to the tonic, one half-step higher (e.g., B-C in the key of C), was also used to produce meaningful dramatic effects in other shows. In *South Pacific* (1949) Rodgers (with Hammerstein) greases rather than avoids the "pig" (an F) for the sake of verisimilitude in "I'm Gonna Wash That Man Right Outa My Hair." In this well-known song Rodgers conveys Nellie Forbush's delusion by introducing the oft-repeated title line with an equally repetitive ascending scalar phrase (C-D-E-F) that relentlessly and obsessively returns to the central key and thereby exposes her failure to accomplish her task. Later in the show when she admits to herself and her fellow nurses that she is, in fact, "in love with a wonderful guy," Nellie sings an exaggerated eighteen repetitions of the half-step interval (again from the leading tone up to the tonic) on the repeated words "love, I'm in" (B-C-C, B-C-C, etc.). In "Bali Ha'i," also from *South Pacific*, Rodgers convincingly conveys the mysterious quality and seductive call of the exotic island by its emphasis on repeated half-steps (e.g., "Ha'i may call you" becomes F♯-F♯-F♯-G).

Not to be overlooked is Rodgers and Hart's ability in *Pal Joey* to write first-rate songs appropriate for their second-rate surroundings, a delicate balancing act that will also be used by Frank Loesser in the Hot Box numbers of *Guys and Dolls*. In "That Terrific Rainbow," for example, Hart presents a wide array of trite and clichéd images to create his rainbow.

> I'm a RED-hot mama,
> But I'm BLUE for you.
> I get PURPLE with anger
> At the things you do.
> And I'm GREEN with envy

After moving from red, blue, purple, and green, the object of the lyric's affection burns the protagonist's heart with an ORANGE flame. Before the end of the next stanza, the RED-hot mama with a heart of GOLD accuses her love object of being WHITE with cold, an unfortunate situation which creates GRAY clouds that, hopefully, will eventually make way for "That Terrific Rainbow."

When Mike Spears's club is converted to Chez Joey in act II, the lyrics of the more elaborate and pretentious new opening production number, "The Flower Garden of My Heart," read like a parody of the hackneyed and formulaic Mother Goose rhyme "Roses Are Red": "In the flower garden of my heart / I've got violets blue as your *eyes*. / I've got dainty *narcissus* / As sweet as my *missus* / And lilies as pure as the *skies*." In the same chorus Hart gives Gladys the couplets, "Just to keep our love *holy* / I've got *gladioli*," and in ensuing choruses "Oh, the west wind will *whisk us* / The scent of *hibiscus*," and "You will look like sweet *william* / And smell like *a trillium*." Was Rodgers perhaps too successful in achieving conventionality and mediocrity in this song? Perhaps. In any event, it was one of only two numbers—the other is "A Great Big Town"—excluded from the pre-revival cast album?

Pal Joey's successful original run was surpassed by Rodgers and Hart in their final collaboration, the now largely forgotten *By Jupiter* (1942), which received 427 performances. After that, Hart possessed neither the interest nor the will to tackle a setting of Lynn Riggs's play, *Green Grow the Lilacs* (1931). Rodgers therefore left his "partner, a best friend, and a source of permanent irritation," and turned to Hammerstein to create *Oklahoma!* in 1942 and early 1943. In the increasingly small intervals between drinking binges Hart managed to create a few new songs for the successful 1943 revival of the 1927 hit *A Connecticut Yankee* (including the bitingly funny "To Keep My Love Alive"), but within a few months of *Oklahoma!*'s historic debut he was dead.

The new team of Rodgers and Hammerstein and the integrated ideal would dominate the American musical until Hammerstein's death in 1960. But something irreplaceable was also lost when the Rodgers and Hammerstein era replaced Rodgers and Hart. The new partners would continue to compose excellent songs that, although integrated, can be sung successfully outside of their carefully considered contexts. Only rarely, however, would Rodgers recreate the rhythmic energy and jazzy melodic vernacular that distinguished so many of his songs with Hart, songs such as "You Mustn't Kick It Around," "Happy Hunting Horn," "Plant You Now, Dig You Later," and "Do It the Hard Way" in *Pal Joey* and "It's Got to Be Love" "Slaughter on 10th Avenue," and the title song in *On Your Toes*.

Alec Wilder addresses this point in *American Popular Song: The Great Innovators 1900–1950*, an idiosyncratic survey that for years was the only book seriously to discuss the musical qualities of popular songs.[58] Although Wilder treats the songs show-by-show, he scrupulously avoids discussing their dramatic context or even their texts and consequently evaluates them solely on their autonomous musical merits. For this reason he remains impervious to the psychological insights in "Bewitched" and instead berates Rodgers's repetitive "device" that was "brought to a sort of negative fruition in that it finally obtrudes as a contrivance."[59] Nevertheless, Wilder devoted fifty-three pages to Rodgers and Hart and only six to Rodgers and Hammerstein, and he tells us why:

> Though he wrote great songs with Oscar Hammerstein II, it is my belief that his greatest melodic invention and pellucid freshness occurred during his years of collaboration with Lorenz Hart. The inventiveness has never ceased. Yet something bordering on musical complacency evidenced itself in his later career. I have always felt that there was an almost feverish demand in Hart's writing which reflected itself in Rodger's melodies as opposed to the almost too comfortable armchair philosophy in Hammerstein's lyrics.[60]

Musical comedies in general, like their nonmusical stage counterparts, stand unfairly as poor relations to tragedies—musicals that aspire to nineteenth-century tragic operas filled with thematic transformations and conspicuous organicism. *Pal Joey* is a brilliant musical comedy that has not lost its relevance or its punch since its arrival in 1940. Despite its many virtues, however, this first musical in "long pants," as Rodgers described it in 1952, and the first major musical to feature an anti-hero, lacks the great themes of *Show Boat* and *Porgy and Bess* and their correspondingly ambitious and complex dramatic transformations of musical motives. The transformation of "Bewitched" in Joey's ballet from a ballad in duple meter to a fast waltz in triple meter—an idea that likely originated with the dance arranger rather than Rodgers—for example, does not convey the dramatic meaning inherent in Kern's transformations of Magnolia's piano theme, nor does it come close to attaining Gershwin's dramatic application of his melodic and rhythmic transformations and paraphrases.

In contrast to Porter's *Anything Goes* and Rodgers and Hart's *On Your Toes*, however, *Pal Joey* possesses a book that could be revived in nearly its original state (even though some modern productions, including its 2008 Broadway revival, tend to treat the work as though it were *Anything Goes*). Its songs, nearly all gems, grow naturally from the dramatic action and tell us something important about the characters who sing them. For some, including Lehman Engel, if by no means most discerning critics, the bewitching *Pal Joey* deserves a chance to survive on its own terms as an enduring Broadway classic of its genre and of its time.

CHAPTER SIX

THE CRADLE WILL ROCK

A Labor Musical for Art's Sake

arc Blitzstein (1905–1964) remains an obscure figure. With few exceptions his music either was never published or is only gradually coming into print. As late as the early 1980s, one decade before her company, under new leadership, revived the work, Beverly Sills of the New York City Opera was rejecting *Regina*, Blitzstein's 1949 adaptation of Lillian Hellman's *Little Foxes*, as "too old-fashioned" for present-day tastes.[1] Bertolt Brecht scholar Martin Esslin had already dismissed Blitzstein's "sugar-coated" English translation of Brecht and Weill's *The Threepenny Opera*—the version that during the years 1954–1960 became the longest Off-Broadway musical of its era and Blitzstein's best-known achievement—as unworthy of Brecht's vision.[2]

Although he is seldom treated as a major figure, the authors of most comprehensive histories of American music, as well as more idiosyncratic surveys, offer Blitzstein some space and a generally good press.[3] Aaron Copland gives Blitzstein equal billing with Virgil Thomson in a chapter in *Our New Music*.[4] Wilfrid Mellers presents Blitzstein along with Ives and Copland as one of three distinguished and representative American composers in *Music and Society* (1950).[5] In *Music in a New Found Land*, published the year of Blitzstein's death and dedicated to his memory, Mellers focuses on *Regina* in a laudatory chapter which pairs it with Bernstein's *West Side Story*.[6] Blitzstein's Broadway opera *Regina* (1949), successfully revived and recorded in 1992 by the New York City Opera, was poised for the possibility of future enshrinement.

Marc Blitzstein. © AL HIRSCHFELD. Reproduced by arrangement with Hirschfeld's exclusive representative, the MARGO FEIDEN GALLERIES LTD., NEW YORK. WWW. ALHIRSCHFELD.COM

Several years earlier the composer of *The Cradle Will Rock* was the subject of the longest biography up until that time of an American composer.[7]

Historians and Broadway enthusiasts relatively unfamiliar with either Blitzstein or *The Cradle Will Rock* may nevertheless know something of the circumstances behind this work's extraordinary premiere on June 16, 1937 (directed by Orson Welles). As reported on the front page of the *New York Times* the next day—and almost invariably whenever the work is mentioned for the next seventy years—the show, banned from a padlocked Maxine Elliot theater, its government sponsorship revoked, moved its forces and its assembled audience twenty blocks uptown to the Venice Theater. Once there, in conformance to the letter (if not the spirit) of the prohibitions placed upon its performance, cast members sang their parts from the audience while Blitzstein took the stage with his piano.[8]

After nineteen performances at the Venice, *Cradle* moved to the Mercury Theater for several months of Sunday evening performances. On January 3, 1938, the controversial show opened on Broadway at the Windsor for a short run of 108 performances (sixteen performances fewer than *Porgy and Bess* and in a smaller theater).[9] The play was published a few months later by Random House, and the following year *Cradle* was anthologized in a volume that included Clifford Odets's *Waiting for Lefty*, a play with which *Cradle* is frequently associated and compared.[10] A recording of the original production issued in 1938 became the first Broadway cast album, a historical distinction almost invariably and incorrectly attributed to *Oklahoma!*[11]

Reviews were generally positive. Although he wrote that the "weak ending" was "hokum" and a "fairy-tale," Thomson also concluded that after six months of the 1937 production "*The Cradle* was still a good show and its musical quality hasn't worn thin" and that the work was "the most appealing operatic socialism since *Louise*" [Gustave Charpentier's realistic opera that premiered in 1900].[12] Brooks Atkinson considered the musical "a stirring success" and "the most versatile artistic triumph of the politically insurgent theatre."[13] Edith J. R. Isaac wrote that the work "introduces a persuasive new theatre form."[14] Somewhat less sympathetically, the notorious George Jean Nathan concluded his acerbic review with the often-quoted barb that *Cradle* was "little more than the kind of thing Cole Porter might have written if, God forbid, he had gone to Columbia instead of Yale."[15]

In common with most of the musicals discussed in this survey *Cradle* has been revived with relative frequency, including a production in 1947 under the direction of Leonard Bernstein, who had presented the work at Harvard in 1939 while an undergraduate (playing the piano part from memory), a New York City Opera production in 1960 (the most successful work of their season), and an Off-Broadway production in 1964 that led to the first complete recorded performance of the work. In 1983, an Off-Broadway production and London run starring *Evita* superstar Patti Lupone (doubling as Moll and Sister Mister) and directed by John Houseman, who produced the premiere, generated a second complete recording and a television broadcast.[16] Of all these performances, only the 1960 production resuscitated the orchestral score that Blitzstein had completed in May 1937 and Lehman Engel conducted at the dress rehearsal before the eventful opening night. The performances with Blitzstein alone on his piano launched a tradition that has long since become entrenched and seemingly irrevocable.[17]

Singing a Song of Social Significance

Authentic avant-garde works achieve their status in part by their continued ability to shock audiences out of their complacency and to bite the hand that feeds. For this reason, the purposeful retraction of government funding when the political wind began to blow in a different direction in 1937—even if the government was not initially targeting *Cradle*—arguably gives *Cradle* more credibility than those works that were ideologically safe, including Blitzstein's earlier modernistic works. *Cradle* also joins other works of the 1930s, most notably the Gershwins' *Of Thee I Sing* (1931) and *Let 'Em Eat Cake* (1933) and composer-lyricist Harold Rome's *Pins and Needles* (1937), in its representation of politically satirical or antiestablishment themes.

Contributing to the continued problematic taxonomic status of *The Cradle Will Rock* is its musical incongruity with both the avant-garde and the conventional popular theater of the 1930s. Particularly jarring is *Cradle*'s conflicting allegiances to vernacular song forms and styles and modernistic characteristics and emblems, the latter including harsh dissonances and chords that thwart expectations. How many musicals would encourage the musically shrill hysteria of Mrs. Mister in the Mission Scene (scene 3) when she asks Reverend Salvation in 1917 to pray for war in order to support her husband's military machine? What other musicals would permit the dissonance of the recurring gavel music that proclaims order in the Night Court before a new flashback? On the other hand, although the work is for the most part through-sung and contains proportionally far less talk than most *Singspiels*, including Mozart's *The Magic Flute, Cradle*'s treatment of popular vernacular and its non-reliance on opera singers contributes further to the difficulty of placing the work with one genre or another.

In contrast to Gershwin, who began as a popular songwriter before transforming his popular music into art music, Blitzstein, like Copland and Weill, began his musical career as a modernist who then converted to populism. As a student of both Stravinsky-advocate Nadia Boulanger in Paris and Schoen-berg in Berlin, Blitzstein became intimately acquainted early in his career with the two primary tributaries to the modernist mainstream and reflected their values in early works such as his Piano Sonata (1927) and Piano Con-certo (1931). Blitzstein's modernist phase prior to 1933 also embraces the "art for art's sake" ideology that he would soon come to loathe and indict in his first major populist work, *The Cradle Will Rock*.

One month after he had completed *Cradle*, Blitzstein, a prolific essayist, published an article in the left-wing magazine *New Masses* on July 14 (Bastille Day) in 1936 in which he viewed modernism as an inevitable reaction against the excesses required of "a capitalist society turning imperialist."[18] Although Blitzstein thought that Schoenberg and Stravinsky wrote "the truth about the dreams of humanity in a world of war and violence," he concluded this essay by asserting that these premier modernists were limited by their inability to confront the social issues of their time: "It is too much to say that the new men sought deliberately and fundamentally to battle the whole conception. They were still the 'art-for-art's-sake' boys, they didn't see much beyond their artistic vision."[19]

One week later, in *New Masses*, Blitzstein praised the *Gebrauchsmusik* movement (variously translated as "utility music" or "music for use") for its sense of direction and its topicality. At the same time, he faulted it because its exponents—principally Paul Hindemith, who at that time was only slightly less highly regarded than Schoenberg and Stravinsky—"had little politi-cal or social education."[20] The value of *Gebrauchsmusik* for Blitzstein was its spawning of men such as Brecht who possessed the necessary education and who "saw the need for education through poetry, through music."[21]

Earlier in 1936, in an article published in *Modern Music*, Blitzstein concluded that Hanns Eisler and Weill, two of Brecht's musical collaborators, "write the same kind of music, although their purposes are completely at variance.... Weill is flaccid (he wants to 'entertain'); Eisler has spine and nerves (he wants to 'educate')."[22] By the time he composed *Cradle*, Blitzstein revealed in print that he shared Eisler's ideology and had become a card-carrying member of the musical-theater proletariat led by Brecht. He ends his *New Masses* mani-festo with a call to political action. Blitzstein himself had taken such action the previous month when he had completed his *Cradle* after five weeks of composing at "white heat." "The composer is now willing, eager, to trade in his sanctified post as Vestal Virgin before the altar of Immutable and Undefil-able Art, for the post of an honest workman among workmen, who has a job to do, a job which wonderfully gives other people joy. His music is aimed at the masses; he knows what he wants to say to them."[23]

Contributing to the changes in Blitzstein's thinking was his meeting several months earlier (probably in December 1935) with Brecht, at which the playwright and poet shared his response to Blitzstein's song "Nickel under the Foot." The scene was reported by Minna Lederman, the editor of *Modern Music*: "Marc said to Brecht, 'I want you to hear something I've written,' and, sitting at his piano, played and sang 'The Nickel under the Foot.' This immediately excited Brecht. He rose, and I can still hear his high, shrill voice, almost a falsetto, exclaiming, 'Why don't you write a piece about all kinds of prostitution—the press, the church, the courts, the arts, the whole system?' "[24] *Cradle's* dramatic structure follows Brecht's suggestion to the letter, and most of the work's ten scenes in "Steeltown, U.S.A. on the night of a union drive" focus on the metaphoric prostitution of various prototypes.[25] The only incorruptible figures are Moll, who literally prostitutes herself but does not metaphorically sell out to Mr. Mister and at least has something genuine to sell, and Larry Foreman, who refuses to be corrupted by Mr. Mister and eventually leads the unions to thwart the union buster's corrupt use of power.

Undoubtedly, the ideological nature of *The Cradle Will Rock* has obscured its artistic significance. That the work deserves its frequently designated status as an agit-prop musical is evident by the degree to which it was imitated by life. Only a few months after its opening, America seemed to heed its call to action with the formation of a strong national steel union, Little Steel. If *Cradle's* pro-unionist and anti-capitalist stance now seems dated, its central Brechtian theme, the indictment of a passive middle class that sells out to the highest bidder, continues to haunt and disturb. As Blitzstein wrote: " 'The Cradle Will Rock' is about unions but only incidentally about unions. What I really wanted to talk about was the middleclass. Unions, unionism as a subject, are used as a symbol of something in the way of a solution for the plight of that middleclass."[26]

With the exception of "Nickel under the Foot," which observes Brecht's call for an epic theater and "the strict separation of the music from all the other elements of entertainment offered," Blitzstein, in contrast to Brecht and Weill, created a work in which music and words were inseparable from the axis of the work.[27] Despite this aesthetic discrepancy, the integrated songs of *The Cradle Will Rock* remain faithful to Brecht's larger social artistic vision. Consequently, the *Cradle* songs, like those of Brecht and Weill, both embrace the didactic element espoused by Brecht's epic theater and reject the "hedonistic approach" and "senselessness" common to operas (and of course musicals as well) before *The Rise and Fall of the City of Mahagonny* of 1930.[28]

Two Scenes: Lawn of Mr. Mister and Hotel Lobby

Lawn of Mr. Mister: "Croon-Spoon"

Scene Four, which contains four songs ("Croon-Spoon," "The Freedom of the Press," "Let's Do Something," and "Honolulu") opens on the lawn of Mr. Mister's home, where his children, Junior and Sister Mister, are lounging on hammocks.[29] The stage directions describe Junior as "sluggish, collegiate and vacant; Sister is smartly gotten up and peevish." Unlike most of the characters in Blitzstein's morality tale, Junior and Sister Mister have nothing to sell and therefore cannot be indicted for selling out. But they do possess vacuous middle-class values that Blitzstein targets for ridicule in their duet that opens the scene, "Croon–Spoon" (Examples 6.1 and 6.2), a spoof of the type of trivial and ephemeral popular song on recordings, dance halls, and non-didactic Broadway shows.

Blitzstein's opinion of the idle rich, who spend their time singing songs that do not convey a message of social significance, is apparent from the opening lyrics to "Croon–Spoon" when Junior sings, "Croon, Croon till it *hurts*, baby, / Croon, My heart *asserts*, baby, / Croonin' in *spurts*, baby, / Is just the *nerts* for a tune!"[30] True, Blitzstein permits Junior to begin on a note that belongs to a chord in the key of the song, an F♯ (the third of the tonic D major triad). But this F♯ is the last note in a tonic chord that Junior manages to assert in his opening seven-measure phrase (one measure less than the nearly ubiquitous eight of Tin Pan Alley and Broadway songs). The "conventional" theater song (e.g., "Anything Goes") would present four eight-measure phrases to create an A-A-B-A or thirty-two-bar song form. Blitzstein's altered phrase lengths (A[7]-A[7]-B[6+6+2]-A[7+4] measures) within the A-A-B-A structure manage to acknowledge convention at the same time he defies and ridicules it.

In contrast to Junior Mister, who concludes his first A section a half-step too low for the accompanying harmony (E♯ against a D-major chord), Sister Mister, in her complementary seven-measure phrase (the second A of the askew A-A-B-A), manages to conclude correctly on a tonic D in the melody. Blitzstein, however, subverts the harmonic implication of Sister's more self-assured D (again on the word "spoon") with harmony that will rapidly depart from the home tonic. The B section, which begins in F♯ minor (Example 6.2) and consists of two nearly melodically identical six-bar phrases followed by Sister Mister's two-bar patter that leads back to the final A section, is remarkable for the C♮ in measure 17 (on "-la-" of "pop-u-la-tion") and measure 23 (on "nev-" of "nev-er"), a lowered or blue fifth that is relatively rare in Broadway songs (and even somewhat unusual in jazz before the 1940s).

Example 6.1. "Croon-Spoon" (beginning)

The punch line of the final A derives from the inability of either Junior or Sister Mister to successfully resolve the harmony. After six measures, Junior should be ready to conclude the song one measure later to preserve the odd but symmetrical seven-bar units of the first two A sections. Instead, Sister Mister, after a fermata (a hold of indefinite length), repeats her brother's last three measures and Junior, after another fermata, repeats the third measure one more time before the siblings screech out the original tonic to conclude the thirty-nine-measure tune.

Following Brecht and his own evolution as a reformed modernist with a social agenda, Blitzstein is of course telling us to avoid singing what he considers to be vapid songs about croon, spoon, and June, even as Junior tells us in the bridge of this song that "Oh, the crooner's life is a blessed one, / He makes the population happy." Junior concludes his song with his own didactic message directed toward the poor who are "not immune" to the wonders of croon spoon. "If they're [the poor] without a *suit*, / They shouldn't give a *hoot*, / When they can *substitute*—CROON!" In *Pins and Needles*, the inspired and phenomenally popular revue presented by the International Garment Workers Union the same year as *Cradle*, Rome asks

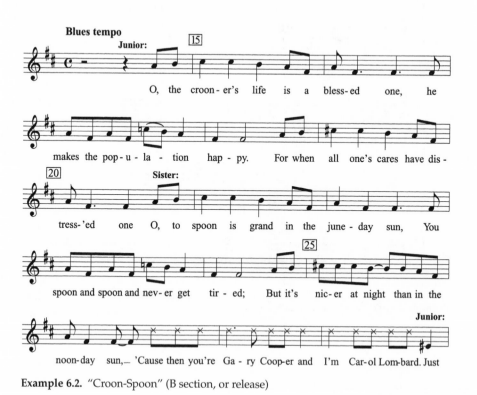

Example 6.2. "Croon-Spoon" (B section, or release)

his audience to "Sing a Song of Social Significance." "Croon–Spoon," a song far removed from social significance, serves as a forum in which Blitzstein can lambaste songs that do not respond to his call for social action and provides the composer-lyricist with an irresistible opportunity to ridicule performers who sing socially useless songs.[31]

Lawn of Mr. Mister: "The Freedom of the Press" and "Honolulu"
During the Windsor run of *Cradle*, Blitzstein concluded an article, "On Writing for the Theatre," with some remarks on the relationship between theory and practice in this work.

> When I started to write the *Cradle* I had a whole and beautiful theory lined up about it. Music was to be used for those sections which were predominantly lyric, satirical, and dramatic. My theories got kicked headlong as soon as I started to write; it became clear to me that the theatre is so elusive an animal that each situation demands its own solution, and so, in a particularly dramatic spot, I found the music simply had to stop. I also found that certain pieces of ordinary plot-exposition could be handled very well by music (*The Freedom of the Press* is a plot-song).

"The Freedom of the Press" begins immediately (*attacca subito*) after Mr. Mister excuses Junior and Sister Mister, an exit underscored by the vamp that began "Croon-Spoon." Blitzstein called this duet between Mr. Mister and Editor Daily a plot-song because the song narrates (or plots) the entire process by which Daily reinterprets the meaning behind its title: the freedom of the press can be a freedom to distort as well as to impart the truth. The plot is as follows: Daily reveals that he is willing to sell out to the highest bidder (first stanza, A); Daily expresses his willingness to change a story, that is, "if something's wrong with it [the story] why then we'll print to fit" (second stanza, B); and Daily learns that Mr. Mister had purchased the paper that morning (third stanza, Mr. Mister's final A).

Following a vigorous six-measure introduction, the form of the song is strophic in three identical musical stanzas. Blitzstein subdivides each stanza into an *a-b-a-b-c-d* form, in which the melody of the rapid ($\quarternote$=160) *a* sections (eight measures each) sung by Mr. Mister are tonally centered in F (concluding in C minor) and the equally fast *b* sections (also eight measures) are answered by Editor Daily in a passage that begins abruptly one step higher in D major ("All my gift...") and modulates to A major (on "very kind") before Mr. Mister returns to the *a* section and a D-minor seventh with equal abruptness (Example 6.3 on next page).[32]

When Editor Daily returns to his *b* section ("Just you call..."), Blitzstein has him sing a whole step higher than his original D major (in E major) for greater intensity. In the brief *c* section Mr. Mister departs from the relentlessness and speed of his (and Editor Daily's) earlier material and for four measures sings, *"lento e dolce"* (slow and sweetly), the menacing words "Yes, but some news can be made to order" to match the menacing underlying harmony. In the *d* section (twenty measures) the music resumes the original tempo, starting with E major (followed by shifts to C♯ major, G♯ major, among other less clearly defined harmonies), and Mr. Mister and Editor Daily sing the main refrain. "O, the press, the press, the freedom of the press... for whichever side will pay the best!"[33]

After "The Freedom of the Press," the music stops for the first time in the scene, and in spoken dialogue Editor Daily quickly agrees with his new boss that Junior "doesn't go so well with union trouble" and would be a good candidate for a correspondent's job "out of town, say on the paper." Junior and Sister enter to a brief and frenetic dance and jazzy tune, "Let's Do Something." Editor Daily, now firmly ensconced as a stooge of his new

(a)

Example 6.3. "The Freedom of the Press"
  (a) *a* section
  (b) *b* section

Example 6.3. Continued

boss, proposes the "something" that might satisfy Mr. Mister and appear palatable to Junior: "Have you thought of Honolulu?"

In his survey of American music, H. Wiley Hitchcock writes that the first twelve measures of "Honolulu" illustrate "Blitzstein's subtle transformation of popular song style," in which "the clichés of the vocal line are cancelled out by the freshness of the accompaniment."[34] Hitchcock singles out the "irregular texture underlying" the "hint of Hawaiian guitars" in the first eight measures (a four-measure phrase and its literal repetition), the "off-beat accentuation of the bass under the raucous refrain," which produces a phrase structure of 3+4+1+3+4+1, and an "acrid" harmony (in technical terms, an inverted dominant ninth) on the word "isle." If the first four measures are labeled A and measures 9–12 B (Example 6.4) the overall form of the song looks like this:

A A B A'   A' A' A B   A A A' A'   B A' A' A'   A' B A A'
4 4 4 4   4 4 2 4   4 4 6 4   4 4 4 4   6 4 6 3

The irregularity of the form and the unpredictability of the less frequent B entrances go a long way to save "Honololu" from the banality it is trying to satirize, just as the unconventional phrase lengths and unorthodox relationship between melody and harmony earlier spared "Croon-Spoon" from a similar fate.

Hotel Lobby: "The Rich" and "Art for Art's Sake"

If "Croon–Spoon" and "Honolulu" ridicule the vapidity of ephemeral popular music and some of the people who sing these tunes, the songs in the Hotel Lobby Scene (scene 6) convey a more direct didactic social message about the role of artists and their appropriate artistic purposes. Blitzstein saves his sharpest rebuke for the artists themselves, the painter Dauber and the violinist Yasha who meet by accident in a hotel lobby in scene 6.[35] Like the other members of Mr. Mister's anti-union Liberty Committee, Dauber and Yasha have sold themselves to the highest bidder, in this case to the wealthy Mrs. Mister. The painter and the musician, like the poet Rupert Scansion to follow, have come to the hotel to curry favor with their patroness in exchange for a free meal and perhaps a temporary roof over their heads.

Blitzstein presents Dauber and Yasha as caricatures of artists who, in their espousal of art-for-art's-sake, have rejected nobler socially conscious artistic visions. The audience learns immediately that they are second-rate artists who fail whenever they are forced to rely on their talent alone. Then, in the course of their initial exchange (a combination of song and underscored dialogue), Dauber and Yasha learn that both of them have appointments with Mrs. Mister. In the ensuing tango (shades of Brecht and Weill),

Example 6.4. "Honolulu"
 (a) A phrase
 (b) B phrase

appropriately named "The Rich," they expose the foibles and inadequacies of the "moneyed people" in such lines as "There's something so damned low about the *rich*!" and "They've no impulse, no fine feeling, no great *itch*!" The answer to the question "What have they got?" is money; the answer to the question "What can they do?" is support you. Clearly Dauber and Yasha hate the rich as much as Blitzstein does.

At this point, the object of their scorn, Mrs. Mister, enters to the accompaniment of the horn motive from Beethoven's *Egmont* Overture based on Goethe's play of the same name: "you know: ta, ta, ta-ta-ta, ta-ta-ta, yoo hoo!" (Example 6.5). In Blitzstein's satire of *Gebrauchsmusik*, Goethe's tale of a great man who loses his life in his efforts to overcome the tyrannical bonds of political oppression is demeaned: Beethoven's heroic horn call now serves as the horn call on Mrs. Mister's Pierce Arrow automobile. This horn also includes the violin answer that was interpreted by nineteenth-century Beethoven biographer Alexander Wheelock Thayer as depicting the moment when Egmont was beheaded.[36] Clearly, the Pierce Arrow usurpation of Beethoven's horn motif constitutes a sacrilegious use of an art object.

That Mrs. Mister expects Dauber and Yasha to pay a price and kiss the hand that feeds these untalented artists becomes clear near the end of the scene, when she asks them to join her husband's Liberty Committee, formed to break the unions led by Larry Foreman, a heroic figure analogous to Egmont. This is the same committee of middle-class prostitutes of various professions who were mistakenly rounded up in scene 1 and taken to night court in scene 2 before the flashbacks began in scene 3. Dauber and Yasha are only too eager to oblige, and when Mrs. Mister asks them, "But don't you want to know what it's all about?" they reply that they are *artists* who "love art for art's sake."

Example 6.5. Scene Six, Hotel Lobby
Entrance of Mrs. Mister and Beethoven's *Egmont* Overture

It's *smart*, for Art's sake,
To *part*, for Art's sake,
With your *heart*, for Art's sake,
And your *mind*, for Art's sake—
Be *blind*, for Art's sake,
And deaf, for Art's sake,
And dumb, for Art's sake,
Until, for Art's sake,
They *kill*, for Art's sake
All the Art for Art's sake![37]

As shown in Example 6.6a, Blitzstein's choice to state each of these lines with a nearly monotonal melody reinforces the pervasiveness of Dauber's and Yasha's political vacuity. The fact that Blitzstein reharmonizes the B on the downbeat of each measure with increasingly dissonant chords bears some similarity to the notorious nineteenth-century "Art" song by Peter Cornelius, "Ein Ton," in which a single pitch is harmonized to an almost absurd degree by evolving chromaticism. Through his relentless dissonant harmonization of the Johnny-one-notes, Blitzstein creates a musical equivalent to support his single-mindedly vitriolic text.

Because Blitzstein himself is a genuine artist, in contrast to Dauber and Yasha, he cannot resist using Beethoven for his own artistic purposes as well. He does this by making two simple rhythmic alterations that effectively disguise the *Egmont* horn motive. The first allusion to *Egmont* occurs in the second chorus of their initial vaudeville routine when Dauber sings "Your lady friend does resemble a lot / Some one, and that's very queer." By adding

Example 6.6. Scene Six, Hotel Lobby
(a) "Art for Art's Sake"
(b) "The Rich"

(b)

Example 6.6. Continued

one beat to the first note of the horn motive Blitzstein accommodates the difference between the triple meter of Beethoven's original motive and the duple meter of the vaudeville routine, a subtle but recognizable rhythmic transformation (Example 6.6b). In the second allusion, the art-for-art's-sake passage previously discussed in Example 6.6a, Blitzstein keeps the rhythmic integrity of Beethoven's motive but distorts it almost (but not entirely) beyond recognition in a duple context with contrary accentual patterns.

It is possible, albeit unlikely, that Blitzstein's rhythmic distortions, which parallel his bizarre atonal harmonizations of the B♮ ("*Art* for Art's sake," "*smart* for Art's sake," etc.) can be interpreted as a critique of Beethoven's noble purposes in *Egmont* as well as an indictment of Yasha and Dauber's art. In any event, Blitzstein's incorporation of Beethoven into his Hotel Lobby Scene goes beyond the conventions and expectations of a musical. It also shows that a revered European master can serve Blitzstein's artistic as well as satiric purposes.

In contrast to *Show Boat* and *Porgy and Bess*, Blitzstein's *Cradle* does not offer a grand scheme of musical symbols and musical transformations that reflect large-scale dramatic vision and character development. Unlike their counterparts in the other musicals discussed in this survey, the characters in *Cradle* for the most part sing their songs and then either assume a secondary role, merge into a crowd, or vanish entirely from the stage. The work is episodic within a structured frame; the characters, vividly outlined, are not filled in.[38]

It is significant that Moll, the pure prostitute, and Larry Foreman, who represents the juggernaut of the oppressed, are the only characters permitted to recycle musical material. In fact, both of the Moll's songs are reprised.

The melody of "I'm Checkin' Home Now," the first music heard in the show, returns as underscoring for Moll's spoken introduction to her song "Nickel under the Foot" in scene 7.[39] Before her big scene Moll had sung most of "Nickel" (using other words) in her conversation with Harry Druggist in scene 2. "Nickel" returns a last time in scene 10 against a din of conversation before Larry Foreman and the chorus of union workers concludes the work with a reprise of the title song.

Although *Cradle* has been called "the most enduring social-political piece of the period" and has generally received high marks as the musical equivalent of *Waiting for Lefty*, its didacticism has unfortunately overwhelmed its rich intrinsic musical and dramatic qualities.[40] If other musicals of the time rival *The Cradle Will Rock* as a work of social satire, few musicals of its time (for example, those by Brecht and Weill the previous decade or E. Y. Harburg and Harold Arlen in the next) and few works since combine Blitzstein's call for social action with a vernacular of such musical sophistication and, yes, artistry.[41] In contrast to many avant-garde works eventually absorbed into the mainstream, *The Cradle Will Rock*, despite its intent to reach a wider public, has managed to sustain its anomalistic status remarkably well. After more than seventy years it continues to resist artistic classification within a genre. It also continues to offend its intended audience of middle-class capitalists through its messages, its devastating caricatures of clergy, doctors, and even university professors, and its occasionally difficult and unconventional score. With due respect to Blitzstein's sincere didacticism, Blitzstein's *Cradle*—cult musical, historical footnote, and agent of social change—might, even as it agitates and propagandizes, someday achieve the recognition it deserves as a work of musical theater art (for art's sake).[42]

CHAPTER SEVEN

LADY IN THE DARK AND ONE TOUCH OF VENUS

The Broadway Stranger and His American Dreams

Within a year after Kurt Weill (1900–1950) emigrated to America his *Johnny Johnson* (1936) had appeared on Broadway. By the time he ended his brief but productive American career with *Lost in the Stars* (1949), the German refugee had managed to produce no less than eight shows in his adopted homeland, including two certifiable hits, *Lady in the Dark* (467 performances) and *One Touch of Venus* (567 performances). At the risk of minimizing such a notable achievement, it must be said that Weill's hits did not run significantly longer than the disappointing 315 performances suffered by Rodgers and Hammerstein's *Allegro* (1947), which closed only a few months after *Oklahoma!*'s five-year run.

Furthermore, while all three of Rodgers and Hammerstein's 1940s hits, *Oklahoma!*, *Carousel*, and *South Pacific*, have gone on to form part of the nucleus of the Broadway repertory, Weill's two contemporaneous hits have nearly vanished. With the escalating success of *Street Scene* (1947) and *Lost in the Stars* and the championing of his previously neglected European music from both sides of the Atlantic, however, Weill's critical and popular star continues to rise. At the same time, with the notable exception of the perennially popular *Threepenny Opera* (Off-Broadway 1954–1960), the once-popular Broadway Weill remains largely overlooked in the Broadway survey literature as well as in Broadway revivals.[1]

Weill, like Bernstein to follow, entered the world of Broadway after rigorous classical training. In contrast to Bernstein, Weill made his mark as an avant-garde composer *before* succumbing to the siren song of a more popular musical theater. The trajectory of Gershwin's career perhaps better exemplifies the more usual evolutionary pattern of the Tin Pan Alley composer who harbored more lofty theatrical ambitions. Unlike most of his Broadway colleagues (including Gershwin), Weill, years before his arrival in America, had established himself as a reputable classical composer from Germany in what Stravinsky called the "main stem" of the classical tradition. At fifteen he began studying theory and composition as well as piano, at sixteen he was creating "serious" compositions, and by seventeen he was acquiring skills in instrumentation, orchestration—unlike most Broadway composers Weill would score his own shows—and score-reading. In 1918 he enrolled at Berlin's Hochschule für Musik to study composition with Engelbert Humperdinck, the composer of *Hänsel und Gretel*. Conducting and counterpoint studies with equally distinguished teachers would continue.

At twenty, Weill was accepted as one of Ferruccio Busoni's six composition students at the Prussian Academy of Arts in Berlin. After composing an impressive series of instrumental as well as stage works, Weill made his pivotal decision to devote his career to the latter in 1926. The next year he began his most famous collaboration with Bertolt Brecht, a collaboration that over the next six years yielded the works by which Weill remains best remembered and most appreciated, at least in classical circles: *Die Dreigroschenoper* (*The Threepenny Opera*) (1928), *Happy End* (1929), and *Aufstieg und Fall der Stadt Mahagonny* (*The Rise and Fall of the City of Mahagonny*) (1930).

Those who saw the collaborations with Brecht as the summit of Weill's creative life concluded that when Weill immigrated to America after a two-year Parisian interregnum, he traded in his artistic soul for fourteen years of hits—and still more misses—in the cultural wasteland of Broadway. Even writers sympathetic to his American musicals recounted the compromises that Weill was forced to make to reach the lowest common Broadway denominators.[2] Just as politicians frequently do not survive a change of party allegiance or a conspicuous change of mind on a sensitive issue, composers who abandon the trappings of "high culture" for the commercial marketplace can be expected to pay a price for their pact with Mammon. Schoenberg's idea that great works are inherently inaccessible to general audiences and that audiences who like great works cannot possibly understand them, died a slow and lingering death.

In a reflective entry in *The New Grove Dictionary of Music and Musicians* Weill authority David Drew helped to place the transplanted German's "divided" career in perspective when he pointed out that even with his sharper-edged collaborations with Brecht, Weill had also aimed to please a particular audience in a particular time and place.[3] According to Drew, Weill discovered with

Die Dreigroschenoper "that a 'serious' modern composer could still reach the broad masses without sacrifice of originality or contemporaneity." Similarly, when discussing the Broadway works, Drew helped to clarify the altered aesthetic transformation between the "cultural implications" of a work like *Mahagonny* and the Broadway period: "The creation of 'works of art' was not Weill's primary concern.... Weill now attempted to subordinate all aesthetic criteria to purely pragmatic and populist ones. Musical ideas, and dramatic ones too, were not to be judged in terms of originality or intrinsic interest...but in terms of their power to evoke, immediately and unambiguously, the required emotional response from a given audience."

Drew went on to remark that Weill continued to take risks on Broadway in dramatic form or subject matter. Even in the conventional *One Touch of Venus* Weill took a risk by allowing dance to tell a story and by teaming up with Broadway newcomers, librettist S. J. Perelman (1904–1979) and lyricist Ogden Nash (1902–1971). But Drew seemed to share the view held by even those sympathetic to Weill's American adventure when he wrote that Broadway "exacted from him a degree of self-sacrifice greater than any that would have been demanded by a totalitarian ministry of culture." In Europe, Weill was a leading modernist and a composer "accustomed to measure his talents and achievements against those of the most eminent of his German contemporaries, Paul Hindemith." In America, "the composer whom he now saw as his chief rival was Richard Rodgers." Nevertheless, Weill's "aural imagination" and "highly cultivated sense of musical character and theatrical form" enabled him to secure "a special place in the history of American popular music."

Drew and other Weill biographers assumed that Weill sacrificed his potential for growth and artistic achievement (albeit willingly) in order to serve "a larger interest than his own, namely that of the American musical theatre." In any event, the absence of subsidized American theater and the scarce opportunities for new works to be performed in what he viewed as artistically stagnant American operatic institutions allowed Weill no place to turn but to the somewhat restricted world of Broadway.

In its English translation by Blitzstein, *Die Dreigroschenoper* has demonstrated its durability in the American musical theater repertory as *The Three-penny Opera*. Of the works originally composed for American audiences perhaps only *Street Scene* (1947), a modest success in its own time with 148 performances, and the comparably successful *Knickerbocker Holiday* (1938) and *Lost in the Stars* (1949) (168 and 273 performances, respectively) have gained increasing popular and critical acclaim (in the years since the first edition of *Enchanted Evenings*, Weill performances have become increasingly common). In fact, *Street Scene* has achieved a reasonably secure place in the operatic repertory. Meanwhile, despite an increasing number of performances on American and European stages, neither of Weill's wartime hits, *Lady in the Dark* and *One Touch of Venus*, has returned for a full-scale staged Broadway production. It is indeed a peculiar legacy that Weill's popularly designed American works remain unrevived, if not revivable.[4]

Despite its long neglect, *Lady in the Dark* can be found in nearly every list of notable musicals. While it failed to make Lehman Engel's short list, this pioneering critic confidently predicted that it "will come back again and again."[5] *One Touch of Venus* was greeted as "an unhackneyed and imaginative musical that spurns the easy formulas of Broadway" and "the best score by Mr. Weill that we recall."[6] Even Weill, in a letter to Ira Gershwin, expressed the opinion that he had for the most part succeeded in producing an audience-worthy show: "I was rather pleased to find, looking at it cold-bloodedly, that inspite [*sic*] of all the faults and mistakes it is a very good and interesting show and that it holds the audience all through once they sit through the first 15 minutes which are pretty awful."[7] Despite such public and private endorsements, *Venus*, like its wartime predecessor, has so far failed to establish itself in the Broadway repertory. The issues raised by *Venus*'s demise deserve more attention than they have so far received.

In his final years Weill himself seemed to repudiate his Broadway hits when he interpreted his creative evolution in America to show its culmination in *Street Scene*. In his notes to its recording the composer confesses that he "learned a great deal about Broadway and its audience" as a result of his first effort, *Johnny Johnson*, "a continuation of the [European] formula."[8] According to Weill's revisionism, *Lady in the Dark* and *One Touch of Venus*, the former especially "with its three little one-act operas," were merely way stations on the road to the development of "something like an American opera."[9] Just as Gershwin opted for a Broadway home for *Porgy and Bess* and Rodgers was content to present his brand of opera (*Carousel*) on the Great White Way, Weill concluded that his Broadway operas "could only take place on Broadway, because Broadway represents the living theatre in this country."[10] Weill continues: "[It] should, like the products of other opera-civilizations, appeal to large parts of the audience. It should have all the necessary ingredients of a 'good show.' "[11]

Additional evidence that Weill appreciated, or at least understood, audience-pleasing shows can be found in his remarks to Ira Gershwin regarding *Oklahoma!* Weill had seen the tryouts in New Haven and was surprised that "they still haven't got a second act" (although he quickly added that "they don't seem to need one").[12] After praising Rouben Mamoulian's work, the production as a whole, the direction and the songs ("just perfect for this kind of show"), and Hammerstein's singable lyrics, Weill made this final assessment: "On the whole, the show is definitely designed for a very low audience...and that, in my opinion explains the terrific success."[13]

Two Compromising Ladies

According to theater lore, Moss Hart (1904–1961) wrote *I Am Listening* when his psychiatrist advised him to cease his successful but inhibiting collaboration with George S. Kaufman and write a play of his own. As Hart tells it: "My psychoanalyst made me resolve that the next idea I had, whether it was good or lousy, I'd carry through."[14] In fact, three years before the creative crisis that led to *Lady in the Dark*, Kaufman and Hart had drafted the first act of a musical based on psychoanalysis starring Marlene Dietrich before settling on *I'd Rather Be Right* with Rodgers and Hart, and George M. Cohan as Franklin Roosevelt. *I Am Listening* also shares much in common with the Fred Astaire–Ginger Rogers film musical *Carefree* (1938), in which Rogers plays a woman similar to Liza Elliott who "can't make up her mind" about marriage, a problem solved in the film by psychiatrist Astaire when he falls in love with her.[15]

One Touch of Venus is based on Thomas Anstey Guthrie's novella *The Tinted Venus* (1885).[16] Sources disagree as to how Weill learned about this relatively obscure work of fiction by the man who published under the pseudonym F. Anstey, but most credit him as the person who persuaded Cheryl Crawford to produce the show.[17] Crawford then asked Sam and Bella Spewack, who had earlier worked on an abandoned Weill project, *The Opera from Mannheim* (1937), to write a libretto; light-verse poet Nash, a Broadway novice, would provide the lyrics. In August the Spewacks drafted the first act of *One Man's Venus*. After at least five lyrics and as many as eight songs, the Spewack libretto, now Bella's alone, was dismissed as beyond repair, and a new book was commissioned from Perelman, best known as the author of the Marx Brothers screenplays *Monkey Business* (1931) and *Horsefeathers* (1932), but untested in a book musical.[18]

Crawford articulates the causes for her dissatisfaction with Bella Spewack's libretto: "The idea that had enticed me was the irreconcilable differences between the world of mundane, conventional human beings and the free untrammeled world of the gods. But this theme had not been developed."[19] In Perelman's rewrite Anstey's Victorian England was transformed into contemporary Manhattan. Foremost among other significant alterations was the character of Venus herself, more threatening and forbidding than sensual in Anstey's novella, and a goddess who would return to her stone form for hours at a time. Rather than succumbing to her demands (as opposed to charms) the unfortunate barber (Leander Tweddle) remains steadfast in his love for his eventually understanding fiancée (Matilda

Moss Hart. © AL HIRSCHFELD. Reproduced by arrangement with
Hirschfeld's exclusive representative, the MARGO FEIDEN GALLERIES
LTD., NEW YORK. WWW. ALHIRSCHFELD.COM

Collum). By appealing to Venus's vanity, Leander in the end manages to
trick her into relinquishing the ring that gave her life.[20]

Throughout his career Weill rarely failed to surround himself with strong
artistic figures. In Germany he collaborated with Brecht and Georg Kaiser.
For the American musical stage he worked with a series of distinguished
partners as the following list attests: Paul Green (*Johnny Johnson*); Maxwell

Anderson (*Knickerbocker Holiday* and *Lost in the Stars*); Elmer Rice and Langston Hughes (*Street Scene*); and Alan Jay Lerner (*Love Life*). Similarly, the productions of *Lady in the Dark* and *One Touch of Venus* evolved under dynamic leadership, and his principal collaborators, Hart and Gershwin (*Lady*), Nash and Perelman (*Venus*), all possessed strong artistic personalities and identities. The *One Touch of Venus* team could boast an especially impressively deep talent roster. The previous year alone Crawford produced the immensely popular revival of *Porgy and Bess*, Elia Kazan directed his first memorable production, Thornton Wilder's *The Skin of Our Teeth*, and Agnes de Mille had choreographed Copland's ballet classic *Rodeo*. Only six months before *Venus* came to life in 1943 de Mille had gained enormous Broadway distinction as the choreographer of *Oklahoma!*[21]

Even in this venerable company the composer could still play a major role in the creative process of a musical, although he would not occupy the center stage enjoyed by Mozart and Da Ponte, Verdi and Boito, and Wagner. Theater critics appreciated the imagination of the *Lady in the Dark* and *One Touch of Venus* teams, but music critics who focused on Weill felt betrayed by his collaboration with the enemy, men and women of the theater who helped Weill to sell out. Critics Virgil Thomson and Samuel Barlow, respectively, accused Weill of banality and phoniness and wrote that the transplanted European had lost his sophistication and his satirical punch in his efforts to please the lower class inhabitants of Broadway.[22]

Considering the experience and prestige of his collaborators, especially Hart and Gershwin, it should come as no surprise that Weill would be asked to defer to the judgment of these collaborators during the writing of *Lady in the Dark*.[23] As a result, one complete dream in *Lady* (first described as the "Day Dream" and later as the "Hollywood Dream") was rejected before its completion, allegedly to help trim escalating costs. To add pizzazz (and perhaps to avoid racial stereotypes), the "Minstrel Dream" metamorphosed into the "Circus Dream." "The Saga of Jenny" was a response to Hart's and producer Sam H. Harris's assessment that Gertrude Lawrence's final number was not funny enough, and the patter number which preceded it, "Tschaikowsky," was added as a vehicle to feature the talented new star Danny Kaye.

Crawford credits de Mille with many of the small cuts in the *One Touch of Venus* ballets, summarizes the problem of the original ending, and explains how Weill's collaborators achieved a satisfactory solution:

> The bacchanal of the nymphs, satyrs, nyads and dryads who carry Venus off was very effective, but it left the audience hanging. It seemed very unsatisfactory for Venus to disappear into the clouds, leaving the poor barber all alone: the ending needed ooomph, something

upbeat. It was Agnes who thought of having Venus come back as an "ordinary" human girl, dressed in a cute little dress and hat—a sort of reincarnation.[24]

This new ending necessitated the shortening of Weill's Bacchanale ballet, which de Mille (as remembered by Crawford) considered "the best thing he'd done since *Threepenny Opera*" and Weill himself treasured as "the finest piece of orchestral music he had ever written."[25] But since Weill "wanted a success" and was "predominantly a theatre man," he acquiesced to de Mille's suggestion.

It is likely that the musical starting point for both *Lady* and *Venus* were songs that Weill had written for earlier contexts. Both of these songs, *Lady*'s "My Ship" and *Venus*'s "Westwind," would become pivotal to their respective musical stories. Since "My Ship" was originally the only song Hart had in mind when he drafted his play *I Am Listening*, it is not surprising that this was the first song Weill wrote for the show.[26]

In the midst of his sketches for *Lady*, including a draft for "My Ship," Weill sketched a tune that with some modifications would eventually become "Westwind" (Example 7.2a, p. 148). In the early stages Weill used its melody solely for the "Venus Entrance" music (and he would continue to label this tune as such throughout his orchestral score). Long after the entire show had taken shape, the music of the future "Westwind" was still reserved for Venus.[27] At a relatively late stage Weill decided to show Savory's total captivation with Venus musically by adopting her tune as his own. After their first meeting his identity is now fully submerged in the woman he idealizes.[28]

The extant manuscript sources and material of *Lady in the Dark* provide an unusually rich glimpse into the compositional process of a musical: Hart's complete original play *I Am Listening*, two revised scenes for this play, and two typescript outlines for two dreams not included in this play; Gershwin's lyrics drafts, including those for the discarded "Zodiac" song; and two hundred pages of Weill's sketches and drafts. Also extant are twenty letters between Weill and Gershwin exchanged between September 1940 and February 1944 ("with random annotations" by Gershwin in 1967) that occasionally reveal important information and attitudes about the compositional process.[29]

Gershwin had traveled from Los Angeles to New York in early May 1940 to work with Hart and Weill, and the letters from Weill began one or two weeks after Gershwin's return in August. The two Weill letters in September are especially valuable because they precede the opening night (the following January 23). On September 2 Weill sets the context for his following suggestions with a budget report: the show was $25,000 above its projected $100,000. Hart and

Hassard Short "read the play to the boys in the office," who were "crazy about the show" but thought "that the bar scene and the Hollywood dream had nothing to do with the play."[30] Hart asked Weill to cut the Hollywood Dream, and the composer agreed to do this if Hart agreed to delete the bar scene as well.

Did this compromise breach Weill's artistic sensibilities? Apparently Weill did not think so. He explains his positive reaction to the excision of the Hollywood Dream:

> I began to see certain advantages. It is obvious that this change would be very good for the play itself because it would mean that we go from the flashback scene directly into the last scene of the play. The decision which Liza makes in the last scene would be an immediate result of the successful analysis. The balance between music and book would be very good in the second act because we would make the flashback scene a completely musical scene.[31]

Although Weill regretted losing "an entire musical scene and some very good material," he saw artistic benefits as well as financial ones, and agreed to these changes.

After more discussion on the relationship between the Hollywood Dream and the Hollywood sequence, both eventually discarded, Weill turned to the "Circus Dream." Here Weill was less acquiescent to Short's suggestions. Although he understood that "Gertie" (Gertrude Lawrence) might remain dissatisfied until he provided "a really funny song" for her, Weill was not yet ready to abandon his "Zodiac" song and defended its place in the show to Gershwin. Although Weill acknowledged that the "Zodiac" song "is not the kind of broad entertainment which Hassard has in mind," he concluded that "it is a very original, high class song of the kind which you and I should have in a show and for which we will get a lot of credit." Because Weill also recognized "the necessity to give Gertie a good, solid, entertaining, humorous song in the Circus dream," he offered to make the "Zodiac" song "musically lighter, more on the line of a patter, and to think about another song for Gertie."

On September 14 Weill again commented on the evolving Circus Dream:

> So Moss and Hassard suggested that we give the Zodiak song back to Randy and I thought this might be good news for you because that's what we always wanted. Here is Moss's idea: the Zodiak song would become Randy's defense speech, just the way you had originally conceived it, but we should try to work Gertie into it.... When they have won over everybody to their cause, Liza should go into a triumphant song.... That would give Liza her show-stopping (??)

Lady in the Dark. "Circus Dream." Gertrude Lawrence sitting on the left, Danny
Kaye on the horse at right (1941). Photograph: Vandamm Studio. Museum of
the City of New York. Theater Collection. Gift of the Burns Mantle Estate.

song near the end of the dream and at a moment where she is triumphant and which allows her to be as gay or sarcastic as you want.[32]

From Ira Gershwin's 1967 annotations that accompany his manuscripts
as well his published comments in *Lyrics on Several Occasions*, we learn that
the "Circus Dream" was originally planned as a "Minstrel Dream" and "an
environment of burnt cork and sanded floor" was transformed "to putty
nose and tanbark."[33] Gershwin divides the "Zodiac" into two parts, "No
Matter under What Star You're Born" and "Song of the Zodiac," "both of
which were discarded to make way for "The Saga of Jenny."[34] He also notes
that he and Weill "hadn't as yet introduced 'Tschaikovsky.' "[35]

Weill's musical manuscripts add credence to the letters and Gershwin's
annotations and reveal that when most of the Circus Dream nearly reached its
final form, "The Saga of Jenny" was just taking shape. It is ironic that Gertrude
Lawrence's final number and Danny Kaye's patter show stopper that directly
preceded it were the only musical portions originally written for this dream. All
the other musical material—with the exception of some recitative—was borrowed from earlier shows. Even the lyrics to "Tschaikovsky" were borrowed

unchanged from a 1924 poem published in "the then pre-pictorial, humorous weekly *Life*" that Ira published under the pseudonym Arthur Francis.[36]

Weill's 1935 London box office debacle, *A Kingdom for a Cow*, served as an important musical link between the German Weill and the American Weill. In his *Handbook*, Drew lists thirteen major instances of Weill's recycling ideas from this most recent European venture into every American stage work from *Johnny Johnson* and *Knickerbocker Holiday* (two borrowings each) to *The Firebrand of Florence*.[37] The two *Kingdom for a Cow* borrowings in *Lady in the Dark* both occur in the Circus Dream: the opening circus march, "The Greatest Show on Earth," and "The Best Years of His Life." The single borrowing in *One Touch of Venus* occurs more obliquely in "Very, Very, Very."

Of the *Kingdom for a Cow* borrowings in *Lady* and *Venus* "The Best Years of His Life" comes closest to quotation. In fact, Kendall Nesbitt's melody in *Lady* is identical to the choral melody in the first act finale of *Kingdom*, and the rhythmic alterations are insubstantial. Weill takes significant transformational liberties, however, in adapting "Very, Very, Very" from *Kingdom* to *Venus* (where it is sung by Savory's assistant, Molly). On this occasion Weill uses two recognizable but highly disguised melodic fragments of "Madame Odette's Waltz" from the second act finale of *Kingdom*.

Weill's remaining borrowing falls between these extremes. "The Greatest Show on Earth," the rousing march that opens the Circus Dream, borrows significantly from the melody, rhythm, and dissonant harmonic underpinning of the refrain of *Kingdom*'s "Auftrittslied des General." When drafting his melody in its new context and new meter, Weill began by retaining the rhythmic *gestus* (to be discussed shortly) and symmetrical phrasing of its predecessor, altering only the pitch. By the time Weill completed his transformation, he had added a new syncopation at the ends of phrases and reinforced the sense of disarray by concluding his phrase one measure earlier than expected. In real (and especially military) life, marches contain symmetrical four-measure phrases; in Liza's confused dream message a seven-measure phrase makes more sense.

Partisans of Brecht may be disconcerted to hear the choral refrain "In der Jugend gold'nem Schimmer" from *Happy End* (1929) set to Nash's words in the opening verses of "The Trouble with Women." At the time Weill recast Brecht, he had abandoned the possibility of a staged revival of this show, although he had tried in 1932 to interest his publisher in "a kind of *Songspiel* with short spoken scenes."[38] Perhaps his sense that all was lost with *Happy End* prompted Weill to recycle no less than three numbers from this German show in his Parisian collaboration with Jacques Déval, *Marie Galante* (1934). One of these reincarnations is once again "In der Jugend gold'nem Schimmer," this time altered from triple to duple meter in the refrain of "Les filles de Bordeaux." Despite some modest melodic changes at the opening and closing and the metrical change from the German and American waltzes to the French fox trot, the two—or three—Weills are here much closer to one.[39]

The process by which *A Kingdom for a Cow, Happy End*, and *Marie Galante* would reemerge in *Lady in the Dark* and *One Touch of Venus* suggests a deeper than generally acknowledged connection between the aesthetic and working methods of the European and the American Weills. The connecting link is embodied in the concept of *gestus*, a term that eludes precise identification. According to Kim Kowalke, "the crucial aspect of *gestus* was the translation of dramatic emotion and individual characterization into a typical, reproducible physical realization."[40] In any event, the principle of a gestic music based on rhythm is demonstrable in the aesthetic framework and the compositional process of Weill's music in America as well as in Europe.

In his 1929 essay on this subject, "Concerning the Gestic Character of Music," Weill, after explaining that "the *gestus* is expressed in a rhythmic fixing of the text," makes a case for the primacy of rhythm.[41] Once a composer has located the "proper" *gestus*, "even the melody is stamped by the *gestus* of the action that is to be represented." Weill acknowledges the possibility of more than one rhythmic interpretation of a text (and, one might add, the possibility of more than one text for a given *gestus*). He also argues that "the rhythmic restriction imposed by the text is no more severe a fetter for the operatic composer than, for example, the formal schemes of the fugue, sonata, or rondo were for the classic master" and that "within the framework of such rhythmically predetermined music, all methods of melodic elaboration and of harmonic and rhythmic differentiation are possible, if only the musical spans of accent conform to the gestic proceeding."

Weill concludes his discussion of gestic music by citing an example from Brecht's version of the "Alabama-Song," in which "a basic *gestus* has been defined in the most primitive form."[42] While Brecht assigns pitches to his *gestus*—which may explain why he tried to assume the credit for composing Weill's music—Weill considers Brecht's attempt "nothing more than an inventory of the speech-rhythm and cannot be used as music."[43] Weill explains that he retains "the same basic *gestus*" but that he "composed" this *gestus* "with the much freer means of the musician." Weill's tune "extends much farther afield melodically, and even has a totally different rhythmic foundation as a result of the pattern of the accompaniment—but the gestic character has been preserved, although it occurs in a completely different outward form." Several compositional drafts and self-borrowings reveal that in America as well as in Germany, Weill, like Loesser to follow, continued to establish a rhythmic *gestus* before he worked out his songs melodically.

Kowalke suggests that eighteenth-century Baroque *opera seria* served as the aesthetic model for Brecht and Weill's music drama of alienation widely known as epic opera.[44] Kowalke goes on to describe more specific stylistic similarities, including the relationship between the Baroque doctrine of affections and Weill's interchangeable song types based on a related *gestus*.[45] An especially applicable example can be found in the genesis of "My Ship" from *Lady in the Dark*. Both the opening of the second sketch draft and the final version feature a rising diminished seventh, F♯-A-C-E♭ (a resemblance noted by bruce d. mcclung).[46] It is also clear that Weill had established a *gestus*, if not the melodic working out, by the time he drafted this second draft of five eventual versions.

Just as "Surabaya Johnny" (*Happy End*) constitutes a trope of the "Moritat" ("The Ballad of Mack the Knife") from *Die Dreigroschenoper*, the borrowed songs in *Lady* and *Venus* may be considered tropes from Weill's European output. Weill's practice of salvaging material from failed shows closely parallels the practice of other Broadway as well as European operatic composers as far back as Handel in the Baroque era.[47] What makes such salvaging possible for Weill is a shared *gestus* that might, like the Baroque affections, serve several dramatic situations with equal conviction. Weill would continue to develop this particular brand of transformation within his American works. *Lady* and *Venus* exhibit an especially notable example as shown in Example 7.1. Even the theater reviewer, Lewis Nichols, remarked after a single hearing in his opening night review of *Venus* that at the conclusion of act I, Savory "sings the sad story of 'Dr. Crippen' in a mood and a tune not unlike that of Mr. Weill's celebrated 'Saga of Jenny.' "[48]

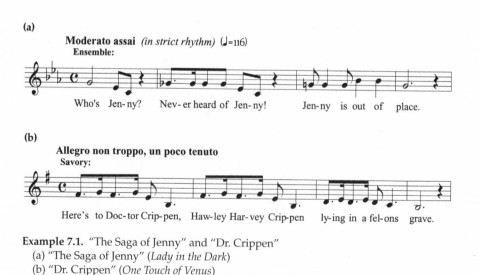

Example 7.1. "The Saga of Jenny" and "Dr. Crippen"
  (a) "The Saga of Jenny" (*Lady in the Dark*)
  (b) "Dr. Crippen" (*One Touch of Venus*)

Lady in the Dark *and* One Touch of Venus as *Integrated Musicals*

Despite his careful selection of librettists and lyricists and his devotion to theatrical integrity, Weill's Broadway offerings for the most part share the posthumous fate of such popular contemporaries as Kern, Porter, and Rodgers and Hart who are similarly remembered more for their hit songs in most of their shows.[49] Even in the case of *The Threepenny Opera*, an extraordinarily popular musical in its Off-Broadway reincarnation, "The Ballad of Mack the Knife," remains by far its most remembered feature.

It is additionally ironic that the ideal of Weill's most successful musical deliberately disregards the principle of the so-called integrated model popularized by Rodgers and Hammerstein, a principle that would hold center stage (with some exceptions) at least until the mid-1960s. In Europe, the apparent interchangeability of arias (providing the proper affects were preserved) in *opera seria* gave way to the increasingly integrated, albeit occasionally heterogeneous, operas of Mozart, Verdi, Wagner, Strauss, and Berg. Many Broadway shows before Rodgers and Hammerstein (and some thereafter), like their Baroque opera counterparts, emphasized great individual songs, stars, and stagecraft more than broader dramatic themes and treated their books and music as autonomous rather than integrated elements.

After *Oklahoma!* and *Carousel* the aesthetic goals of Broadway shifted. Two years after the disastrous *Firebrand of Florence* in 1945 (43 performances), Weill too composed an integrated dramatic work, *Street Scene* (148 performances), that would eventually achieve a commercial success roughly commensurate with its critical acclaim. The dream that Weill shared on his notes to the cast album of this Broadway opera, a "dream of a special brand of musical theatre which would completely integrate drama and music, spoken word, song and movement," was also the dream of his chief Broadway rival in the 1940s, Rodgers, who was composing *Oklahoma!, Carousel, Allegro,* and *South Pacific* during these years.[50]

In his notes to *Street Scene*, Weill acknowledges that he and his earlier collaborator Brecht "deliberately stopped the action during the songs which were written to illustrate the 'philosophy,' the inner meaning of the play."[51] It was not until *Street Scene*, however, that Weill achieved "a real blending of drama and music, in which the singing continues naturally where the speaking stops and the spoken word as well as the dramatic action are embedded in overall musical structure."[52] Three years before he completed his long and productive theater career, Weill appeared to repudiate the aesthetic he had worked out with Brecht and achieved his integrated American opera.

Thus Weill, by now a wayward branch from the German stem, did not begin his serious attempt to integrate drama and music until after he ceased collaborating with Brecht. On the other hand, Rodgers, in America, as early as Brecht and Weill's *Threepenny Opera*, was already somewhat paradoxically striving to compose integrated musicals in a marketplace somewhat indifferent to this aesthetic.[53] Weill's contemporary and posthumous success with *Threepenny Opera*, both its German production in the late 1920s and its Broadway adaptation by Blitzstein in the middle and late 1950s, rests in part in the alienation between and separation of music and story. Even those who remain impervious to the quality and charm of Weill's many other works acknowledge the artistic merits of *Threepenny Opera* and usually grant it masterpiece status.

Shortly before the debut of *Lady in the Dark* Weill informed William King in the *New York Sun* that in contrast to Schoenberg, who "has said he is writing for a time fifty years after his death," Weill wrote "for today" and did not "give a damn about writing for posterity."[54] Between the extremes of his two posthumous success stories, *Threepenny Opera* and, to a lesser degree, *Street Scene*, lie Weill's two greatest and—if posterity be damned—most meaningful hits. Both *Lady* and *Venus* exhibit integrative as well as non-integrative traits. On one level, *Lady in the Dark* might be considered the least integrated of any book show by any Broadway composer, since the play portions and the musical portions are unprecedentedly segregated. In this respect *Lady* shares much in common with film adaptations of musicals that remove the "nonrealistic" portions of their Broadway source.[55]

With the exception of "My Ship," virtually all the music of the show appears in three separate dream sequences that comprise half of the show— the Glamour Dream and the Wedding Dream in act I and the Circus Dream in act II—and nowhere else. In each of these dreams virtually everything is sung or underscored by continuous music, while the other half is composed entirely of spoken dialogue. Hart's original intent, evident in his draft of the play *I Am Listening*, was to have a play with a small amount of musical interjections rather than "three little one-act operas."

Once Hart had decided to create a play that could accommodate Weill's music, he fully embraced the integrated ideal (for the dreams) that within a few years would dominate Broadway. In his prefatory remarks to the published vocal score, Hart expressed the desire for himself and his collaborators not only to avoid "the tight little formula of the musical comedy stage" but to create a show "in which the music carried forward the essential story." "For the first time...the music and lyrics of a musical 'show' are part and parcel of the basic structure of the play."[56]

With due respect to Hart, the music in *Lady in the Dark* might more accurately be described as a conscious interruption of a play. But since an important component of the story is the disparity between Liza Elliott's drab quotidian existence and the colorful pizzazz of her dream world, it makes sense for her to speak only in her waking life and reserve music for her dreams. The dream pretext also allows Weill to present the interruptions within the discontinuity of a dream, since, after all, audiences should not expect dreams to be totally logical. Dreams, as Weill wrote in his thoughts on dreams that he typed out in preparation for *Lady in the Dark*, "are, at the moment of the dreaming, very realistic and don't have at all the mysterious, shadowy quality of the usual dream sequences in plays or novels."

Liza's dreams differ no more from her daily life than escapist musicals of the late 1930s differed from the daily lives of their audiences.[57] The musical and dramatic non sequitur that launches "Tschaikowsky" may be equally abrupt as the opening gambits in 1930s musical comedies, for example, "There's a Small Hotel" in *On Your Toes*. After Liza, accompanied by a chorus, concludes her musical defense—"Tra-la—I never gave my word"—in the breach of promise suit for failing to marry Nesbitt (clearly reminiscent of Gilbert and Sullivan's *Trial by Jury*), the music comes to a halt with a soft cymbal. The Ringmaster (*Allure* photographer Randy Paxton in real life) then breaks the silence with "Charming, charming, who wrote that music?"; the Jury answers, "Tschaikowsky!," and the Ringmaster says, "Tschaikowsky? I love Russian composers!" Part of the joke, of course, is that Tchaikovsky did not compose "The Best Years of His Life" (Weill himself had composed this song several years earlier in *Kingdom for a Cow*). Moreover, in the slightly askew chronology of dreamland, the exchange between the Ringmaster and the Jury actually anticipates a real, albeit small, dose of Tchaikovsky's "Pathétique" Symphony (third movement).

While a major theme of *Lady in the Dark* is the disparity between Liza Elliott's real and dream worlds (although she retains her name in her dreams), her co-workers often appear in her dreams as metaphors for their roles in Liza's waking life. The metaphors also become increasingly obvious as Liza comes to understand the meaning of her dreams. Of the four men in her life, the "mildly effeminate" Paxton (Danny Kaye) plays a neutral role in Liza's romantic life and serves the dreaming Liza with equal neutrality (a chauffeur in the Glamour Dream and the ringmaster in the Circus Dream). Nesbitt (Bert Lytell), who "waits" for Liza in real life, plays the role of a head waiter in a night club in the Glamour Dream and the real-life role of Liza's expectant groom in the Wedding Dream before appearing as the first witness for the prosecution in the Circus Dream. The glamorous movie star Randy Curtis (Victor Mature), who appreciates and defends

Liza's lack of glamour, naturally appears as Liza's defense attorney in the Circus Dream.

Similarly, Hart captures the complexity of Liza's relationship with her obnoxious advertising manager, Charley Johnson (MacDonald Carey). In the Glamour Dream Johnson plays the marine who paints Liza's portrait for the two-cent stamp, not as Liza sees herself in the dream but as others see her in real life. Already in the first dream he has established himself as firmly grounded in reality and the person who truly sees Liza for what she is (significantly, Johnson's realism is bound to speech and he never sings in the dreams, although he will eventually sing "My Ship" for Liza). In the Wedding Dream Johnson appears twice, first as the salesman who offers a dagger instead of a ring and then as the minister who, merely by asking the standard question, "If there be any who know why these two [Liza and Nesbitt] should not be joined in holy wedlock let him speak now or forever hold his peace," prompts a truthful response from his congregation that exposes the wedding as a sham: "This woman knows she does not love this man."

In the Circus Dream, Johnson acts as the prosecuting attorney and as a surrogate for Dr. Brooks when he repeats the psychiatrist's diagnosis nearly word for word, adding a new accusatory tone at the end of the dream: "You're afraid. You're hiding something. You're afraid of that music aren't you? Just as you're afraid to compete as a woman—afraid to marry Kendall Nesbitt—afraid to be the woman you want to be—afraid—afraid—afraid!" "That music" is of course the song "My Ship," or rather the opening portion of this song that either leads to dreams (Glamour and Wedding Dreams) or makes a dream come to a stop (the Circus Dream).

In her final session with Dr. Brooks, Liza manages to recall the entire song as she formerly sang it to a boy named Ben. Ben, the Handsomest Boy at Mapleton High, many years earlier had abandoned the teenage Liza, the Most Popular Girl, to return to the Most Beautiful Girl. While she waits for Ben to return, another boy asks to take Liza to dinner (Liza prefers to wait). The boy's name is Charles, yet another clue that someday a prince named Charley will come. In the final scene, Charley Johnson offers more substantive evidence that he is indeed Mr. Right for Liza Elliott: he knows "My Ship" and will sing it with her as their ship sails off into the golden sunset.

The central unifying musical element of *Lady in the Dark* is certainly "My Ship," the opening portion of which appears in various harmonizations in each dream before Liza manages to sing it completely in the otherwise musically silent Childhood Dream.[58] The musical material of the three main dreams is internally "unified" around a characteristic rhythm (a rumba for the Glamour Dream, a bolero for the Wedding Dream, and a march for the Circus Dream). The Glamour dream contains the greatest use of internal thematic transformation. Beyond the reuse and development of "My Ship," however, organic unity is not especially prominent from one dream to the next.

In *One Touch of Venus* the use of song to musically interrupt rather than continue the action may be a characteristic shared with the non-integrated musicals of Porter before *Kiss Me, Kate*. It also suggests a return structurally, if not ideologically, to Weill's epic creations with Brecht (*Threepenny Opera, Happy End*, and *Mahagonny*). Venus's final song, "That's Him," is representative of Weill's earlier ideal by distancing the singer from the object and providing a commentary on love rather than an experience of it. Venus even speaks of her love object in the third person.

Dramatic unity in *One Touch of Venus*, outwardly more conventional than the intricate continuous dream scenes in *Lady in the Dark*, nevertheless corresponds closely to the contemporary *Oklahoma!* model based on such devices as thematic transformation in narrative ballets and the use of strong rhythmic profiles to reflect character.[59] These two techniques converge in Weill's recasting of Venus's (Mary Martin's) jazzy and uninhibited opening song, "I'm a Stranger Here Myself" moments later in the ballet "Forty Minutes for Lunch," described in the libretto as "a series of formalized dance patterns parodying the tension of metropolitan life."[60]

Like the composers of *Anything Goes, Carousel, Guys and Dolls*, and *West Side Story*, Weill uses quarter-note triplets when he wants to show his characters moving emotionally beyond their metrical boundaries.[61] Weill uses the quarter-note triplet most prominently in Whitelaw Savory's love song "Westwind" (Example 7.2a), previously noted as based, appropriately enough as it turns out, on Venus's Entrance Music. Even Rodney Hatch, when serenading his fiancée Gloria Kramer in his characteristically rhythmically square fashion, manages a few quarter-note triplets in the release of his "How Much I Love You" when he sings "I love you" and "I yearn for you." But by the time he sings of his "Wooden Wedding" near the end of the show, quarter-note triplets have vanished, and Venus will soon follow.

Venus herself, who tells Savory at their first meeting that "love isn't the dying moan of a distant violin—it's the triumphant twang of a bedspring," generally prefers swing rhythms, but quarter-note triplets remain a prominent part of her musical character (as well as of the Venus Theme).[62] She sings them prominently in the swinging and highly syncopated "I'm a Stranger Here Myself" and even opens the verse of the waltz "Foolish Heart" with a quarter-note triplet group. By the time Venus sings "Speak Low" with Rodney, every phrase of both the main portion and the release

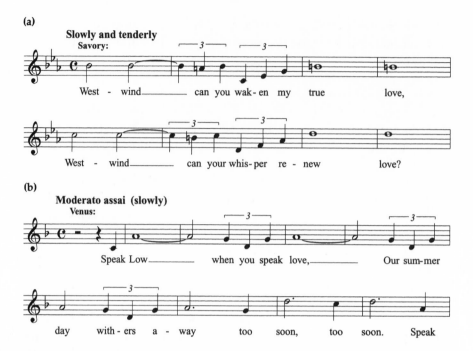

Example 7.2. Quarter-note triplets in *One Touch of Venus*
  (a) "Westwind"
  (b) "Speak Low"

includes quarter-note triplets (Example 7.2b), and her characteristic swinging rhythms are submerged in the accompaniment.

In the spoken dialogue that prepares for her final song Venus confesses that while the ring brought the statue to life, it was not responsible for making her love him. Nevertheless, Venus wastes no time in asking Rodney to part his hair on the other side. The song itself, "That's Him," lyrically and musically captures Venus's ambiguity toward Rodney. On one hand, Venus literally compares her potential mate to Gershwin's *Rhapsody in Blue*, she could "pick him out" from the millions of men in the world, and she concludes her A sections by singing "wonderful world, wonderful you." On the other hand, despite his endearing qualitites, Rodney remains an unlikely romantic partner, especially for a Venus. He is "simple," "not arty," "satisfactory," and appreciated primarily for his functionality, "like a plumber when you need a plumber" and "comforting as woolens in the winter."

In order to musically express less exalted feelings for her conventional barber, Venus must be deprived of the musical identity she has established for herself in her other songs. Weill conveys this underlying conflict when he does not allow the accompaniment, significantly filled with Venus's characteristic swinging rhythms, to share the implied harmony of Venus's melody. Additionally, although Venus's melodic line contains several telling vocal leaps, it mainly consists of stepwise motion, again in contrast to her previously established melodically disjunct character portrayed in "I'm a Stranger Here Myself" and "Speak Low." Only at the end of the A' sections—the song forms an unusual arch, A-A'-B-A-A' rather than A-A-B-A—do melody and harmony resolve to the C major that Weill has Venus avoid so assiduously for thirty-three measures. Although throughout this B section Venus returns to her jazzy swing rhythms, she will abandon her unrealistic dream of an unambiguous C major existence with Rodney after three measures. Venus may be in love with a wonderful guy, but a marriage with Rodney would be like Pegasus pulling a milk truck.[63]

At the end of the song, the delusion can no longer be sustained. When Rodney finishes singing his description of their "Wooden Wedding" with its "trip to Gimbel's basement, / Or a double feature [pronounced fee'-tcha]

One Touch of Venus, act I, scene 4. Mary Martin in the center behind the dressing screen (1943). Photograph: Vandamm Studio. Museum of the City of New York. Theater Collection.

149

with Don Ameche," Venus must say, "Rodney, I hope I'll be the right kind of wife for you."[64] Venus's nightmarish vision of herself as a conventional "housewife" in the concluding ballet, "Venus in Ozone Heights," finally convinces her to rejoin the gods.

The Possibility of Revival

We have previously noted that in contrast to the other musicals discussed in this survey, *Lady in the Dark* and *One Touch of Venus* have yet to receive fully staged Broadway revivals. Although both musicals have enjoyed a number of regional performances in America and in Great Britain, they remain shortchanged and underappreciated. Do they need revised books or more Weill hit songs to succeed like Porter and Rodgers and Hart revivals? The final section of this chapter will address the problems and possibilities of revival.

The first of several alleged problems with *Lady in the Dark* is its dependence on a star. After exhibiting indecisiveness equal to Liza Elliott, the versatile Gertrude Lawrence consulted with her friend and oracle Noël Coward as well as her astrological charts and accepted the demanding title role. When Lawrence left for the summer the show closed, and, unlike most shows, including Mary Martin's *Venus*, Lawrence's *Lady* never went on the road. A second problem is expense. Three revolving sets and the attendant costs of the three dream ballets do not travel cheaply.

But certainly these red herrings mask deeper problems. When Hart wrote the libretto to *Lady*, for example, psychiatry was still a relatively novel subject for a musical, and the endless series of obligatory dream ballets in musicals were mostly in the future. Nevertheless, even by the standards of the early 1940s, Hart's treatment of psychiatry is simplistic and predictable.

More problematic than the dated treatment of psychiatry are the increasingly volatile subjects of sexism and sexual harassment. To be sure, the sexism in *Lady in the Dark* is rather unpalatable, especially as displayed in the character of Liza's eventual Mr. Right, the fanny-pinching, male-chauvinist Charley Johnson, who tries to give Maggie "a wet kiss" against her will. When Johnson accuses Liza of having "magazines instead of babies and a father instead of a husband," he may be telling it like it was (or how he saw things), but his remarks were not destined to please modern Broadway audiences.[65] Instead of getting the girl, Johnson today might be obtaining the services of an attorney who specializes in sexual harassment suits; he certainly does not deserve a woman like Liza. The non-singing Kendall Nesbitt hardly seems a better alternative: "Somehow—I don't know why—it's different for a man, but a woman can have no sense of fulfillment—no real peace and serenity as a woman, living out her life this way."[66] In a later era, the story of a bright, successful, and powerful woman whose achievement comes at the expense of her feminine identity does not bode well for a box office bonanza, even with Madonna in the title role.

Sexual stereotyping is not reserved for the heterosexual members of the *Lady in the Dark* cast. Russell Paxton, the "mildly-effeminate-in-a-rather-charming-fashion" photographer for Liza's fashion magazine, *Allure*, is introduced as "hysterical, as usual." He also freely acknowledges his physical admiration for male beauty when he describes Randy Curtis: "He's got a face that would melt in your mouth....He's heaven."[67] Although some mystery will remain as to which of Liza's suitors (Curtis, Nesbitt, or Johnson) will eventually win out, Paxton is removed at the outset as a romantic contender.[68]

The reasons for the demise of *One Touch of Venus* are less explicable. The premise of a cultural alien examining America from another perspective has proven remarkably durable in numerous films over the past two decades and includes aliens from another country (*Moscow on the Hudson*) and extraterrestrial aliens (*E.T.*) in its wide orbit. A genuine and liberated sex goddess adrift amid overly romantic types like Whitelaw Savory and prosaic practical types like Rodney Hatch provide for a potentially engaging story, a story wittily realized by Perelman, Nash, and Weill.

While Weill is criticized for abandoning his social conscience in his Broadway musicals, *Venus* manages to effectively satirize a host of American values. We know from the first song that Savory is more than a little eccentric because, in contrast with nearly anyone who loves popular musicals, he firmly believes that (with the notable exception of the classical Anatolian Venus) "New Art Is True Art": "*Old* art is *cold* art, / The new art is *bold* art; / The best of ancient *Greece*, / It was centuries behind *Matisse*, / Who has carried us beyond Re*noir*, / Till our bosoms are tri-an-gu-*lar*."

The largest target of the Perelman-Nash satire is the contrasting moral values of the very, very rich and the common folk. The loose morals of the wealthy are comically portrayed in the song "Very, Very, Very," when Molly explains that "It's a minor pecca*dillo* / To patronize the wrong *pillow*, / When you're very, very, very rich." It was previously noted that Venus dismisses Savory's idealistic and bourgeois love by favoring the twang of a bedspring over the moan of a violin. In contrast, Venus's earthbound inamorata, Hatch, expresses his love for his fiancée Gloria through a series of negative prosaic images, for example, "I love you more than a wasp can sting, / And more than a hangnail hurts." Although Venus helps Hatch to rid himself of his shrewish intended—"*sic transit* Gloria Kramer"—the simple barber retains his desire to live in Ozone Heights, where "every bungalow's just the same" and each has "a radio that looks like a fireplace—and a fireplace that looks like a radio."[69]

If *Street Scene* is the American Weill stage work that posterity has voted retrospectively most likely to succeed, *One Touch of Venus*, the most Broadway-like of any Weill show, may turn out to be the most revivable—the sleeper musical of the 1940s. In short, *Venus* is a first-rate traditional Broadway show, packed with an unprecedented number of song hits and other fine songs by Weill, lyrics that reveal the idiosyncratic Nash at his cleverest, and engaging dialogue by Perelman.

After *Venus*, Nash would abandon Broadway and go back to the more intimate world of comic verse. Perelman's next (and last) musical, three years after *Venus*, closed out of town; he would take time off from his prolific output of comic literary fiction on one more occasion to write the script for Porter's last effort, the television musical *Aladdin* (1958). Hart ended his distinguished Broadway career with a successful play, *Light Up the Sky* (1948), and as the director of *My Fair Lady* and *Camelot*. Between *Light Up the Sky* and *My Fair Lady* he also wrote distinguished musical screenplays for *Hans Christian Andersen* (lyrics and music by Loesser) and *A Star Is Born* (lyrics by Ira Gershwin and music by Harold Arlen). One year after his failed collaboration with Weill, *The Firebrand of Florence*, Gershwin completed his Broadway career with the poorly received *Park Avenue* (music by Arthur Schwartz). He concluded his career by writing lyrics to several successful films, most notably *A Star Is Born*, then spent three decades in creative retirement as the guardian of his famous brother's legacy. After *Venus* and *Florence*, Weill would compose the music to *Street Scene*, *Love Life*, and *Lost in the Stars*, dying before he could realize his next American dream with Maxwell Anderson (his lyricist-librettist on *Knickerbocker Holiday* and *Lost in the Stars*), a musical based on Mark Twain's *Huckleberry Finn*.

CHAPTER EIGHT

STAGE VERSUS SCREEN (1)

Before Rodgers and Hammerstein

Adapting to Hollywood

Show Boat marks one possible starting point for a study of the modern Broadway musical. Fortuitously, its arrival in December 1927 closely followed the opening of a landmark in the history of one of the quintessential modern media of the twentieth century, *The Jazz Singer*, the first American feature film with sound. Although most of this historic film was still "silent"—accompanied by a live pit band—Al Jolson's songs were reproduced via a recorded soundtrack, tube amplifiers, and loudspeakers placed behind the movie screen at selected theaters. Seemingly traveling at the speed of sound, if not light, talking and singing film adaptations of popular Broadway stage works soon became rapidly, abundantly, and relatively cheaply available to national then worldwide audiences. Masses of movie enthusiasts could view film adaptations of major and minor works that until the end of the 1920s were accessible only on Broadway stages and in touring productions. Audiences could also view a large body of original film musicals not based on a stage work.

During the early decades of sound film, musical film adaptations were usually remote from their stage sources, and it would often be a challenge to discern the difference between an adaptation and an original musical film without prior knowledge. Before the Rodgers and Hammerstein era, film adaptations tended to be footloose and fancy free and at times unrecognizable vis-à-vis their stage counterparts. The musical films high-lighted in later chapters of this study tend to be relatively faithful, perhaps too respectful, of their Broadway origins.

In any event, the two film "Stage versus Screen" chapters at the end of acts I and II in this Broadway survey work from the premise that it is intrin-sically unfair to value a film adaptation in direct or indirect proportion to its fidelity to what audiences saw and heard onstage—the musical theater scholar's own version of the early and traditional music "authenticity" and "historically informed performance" debates. An Alfred Hitchcock sus-pense thriller roughly based on a novel or short story might be considered an improvement over its source or at least an excellent film in its own right. At the same time, readers of a survey on the Broadway musical deserve to know the connection between what they see on the silver screen and what they are likely to see on a stage. Film adaptations such as *The Gay Divorcée, On the Town*, and *Funny Face* may be worthy exponents of the film genre, but students of musical theater should know that these films only imperfectly approximate their stage counterparts.

One of the central purposes of the two "Stage versus Screen" chapters will be to inform fans of Broadway shows what they are getting into when they rent or purchase a film adaptation of a show they have seen on a stage or heard on a cast album. Just as quoting obscenity is not the same thing as being obscene, those who study musical film adaptations, and even those who occasionally shout *vive la différence* should not be accused of wantonly sleeping with the enemy or other acts of traitorous activity. While some, erroneously, treat stage and screen versions of Broadway shows as inter-changeable, other musical theater advocates regard even the act of adap-tation with suspicion, if not disdain. One articulate adversary of the film musical adaptation, Kim Kowalke, encapsulated this position: "The generic deformation inherent in adapting stage musicals as movies left few intact and most virtually unrecognizable, except for title, some songs, and perhaps a few actors in common."[1] Even if Kowalke's blanket indictment is read as hyperbolic, the term "generic deformation" unfortunately more than occa-sionally applies.

There are many subtle cultural dimensions to the transition from live to recorded performance with which any musician familiar with a real-life per-forming tradition will be familiar. Creeping in on little cat feet, media craft workers and modern-minded audiences have revolutionized performances and their reception. The result, as Kowalke implies, is a change in the *genre*, or *kind* of a musical theater work—or, to use his carefully chosen term, a deformed *genre*. To return to the more straightforward structural dimensions of book and score, film adaptations of musicals from *Show Boat* to *Oklahoma!*

generally, but by no means invariably, do retain recognizable story lines and more than just "some songs."

On the other hand, with distressing frequency, departures and alterations from Broadway story lines result in the elimination of half or more than half of the songs people heard when they saw the show on the stage. To cite one extreme but not unique example, the musical film of George and Ira Gershwin's *Strike Up the Band* managed to salvage only the title tune from this wonderful score. In another frequent practice that we will witness shortly in the 1936 film adaptation of *Show Boat*, the original composer and lyricist will add one or more songs expressly for the show's new incarnation. Perhaps because only new songs are eligible for Best Song Academy Awards, this practice has continued until the present day, even if the new song is not heard until the final credits, as happens in the case of *The Phantom of the Opera* in the 2004 film version. Another common scenario is the practice of interpolating songs into a show from *different* shows by the original composer-lyricists, a practice that parallels the distortions we have come to expect in *stage* revivals (for example, in the revivals of *Anything Goes* on Broadway in 1962 and 1987). The 1957 film of *Pal Joey* exemplifies this widespread approach.

Before the Rodgers and Hammerstein era it was also a common practice to bring in new composers and lyricists who were under contract with the studio producing the film as collaborators after the fact. The 1936 film adaptation of *Anything Goes* provides a good example of this scenario. Another adaptation type is the 1937 film version of the show *Rosalie*, which has an entirely new score. The original double story (the Lindbergh flight and a visit from the Queen of Romania) was preserved, but the double compositional duties between George Gershwin and Sigmund Romberg were instead relegated solely to Cole Porter, a composer who was not even remotely involved in the Broadway version of 1928. Not until the 1950s did Broadway composers and lyricists begin to exert the kind of creative control over films they had begun to show decades earlier on Broadway. Since then, composers and lyricists have usually exerted the right to share their opinion about which songs to cut—although they can be overridden as we will see in producer Samuel Goldwyn's version of Frank Loesser's *Guys and Dolls*. Songwriters also gained the frequent privilege of contributing their own new songs.

A large percentage of Broadway shows were adapted into films. Among the highlights of the adaptation subgenre are Ernst Lubitsch's *The Merry Widow* (MGM 1934), the series of eight freely adapted operettas (and the occasional musical comedy) with Jeanette MacDonald and Nelson Eddy from 1935 to 1942, and *On the Town* (produced by Arthur Freed for MGM in 1949), not all of which are cherished for their fidelity to their stage sources.

The most consistently memorable musical films to appear in the era between *Show Boat* and *Oklahoma!*, however, were original film musicals. A short list in this latter category would be remiss if it did not include the following: *The Love Parade* (1929); *Love Me Tonight* (1932); *42nd Street*, *Gold Diggers of 1933*, and *Footlight Parade* (1933); *The Great Ziegfeld* and *Born to Dance* (1936); *Snow White and the Seven Dwarfs* (1937); *Alexander's Ragtime Band* (1938); *The Wizard of Oz* (1939); *Pinocchio, Broadway Melody of 1940*, and *Fantasia* (1940); *Yankee Doodle Dandy* and *Holiday Inn* (1942); and *Cabin in the Sky, Stormy Weather*, and *This Is the Army* (1943).

Of the eight classic films that paired Fred Astaire and Ginger Rogers between 1933 and 1938, only three were based even in part on Broadway shows. *The Gay Divorcée*, which was based, but not quite nominally, on *Gay Divorce*, starring Astaire, retained but one Porter tune, "Night and Day." This movie, which has genuine merit on its own terms, gave film audiences an opportunity to see comics Erik Rhodes and Eric Blore, as well as Astaire, replay their stage roles and offered the attractive new face of Betty Grable. It also concludes with perhaps the most elaborate and certainly the longest of the dance duets in the Fred and Ginger series, "The Continental" (more than 16 minutes). With its relatively lengthy medium shot, this dance (and future Fred and Ginger dances) also showcased the dancers from head to toe, with only an occasional close-up, a directorial concession Astaire routinely demanded (and got).[2] Despite these genuine merits, the film version of *Gay Divorce* is as different from its source as, well, night and day. The plot of *Follow the Fleet* (1936), like that of *The Gay Divorcée*, is also loosely derived from a Broadway show, *Hit the Deck!* from 1927, with music by Vincent Youmans (also the principal composer of the first of the Fred and Ginger films, *Flying Down to Rio*). With *The Gay Divorcée*, at least one song was composed by its original composer. *Follow the Fleet*, however, met *Rosalie*'s fate. Youmans's entire score was thrown overboard, and Irving Berlin, who composed the music and lyrics to *Top Hat* and would soon do the same for *Carefree* (both films also in the first eight Fred and Ginger films), was brought in to write the complete score.[3]

James Whale's 1936 *Show Boat* remains arguably the most successful relatively faithful transfer of operetta-leaning genre (with significant touches of musical comedy) from stage to screen in the 1930s. Kern's *Roberta*, with lyrics by Otto Harbach, and yet another from the first Fred and Ginger eight, also deserves consideration as one of the finest contemporary film adaptations of a staged musical comedy (with significant touches of operetta). It also demonstrates how it is possible to retain a story line and much of a score while at the same time transforming leading acting roles into dancing stars. Onstage, the non-dancing role of Huck Haines, played by then-newcomer comedian Bob Hope, was now played by Astaire, while Rogers replaced the non-dancing Lyda Roberti (who as Countess Tanka Schwarenka was not even attracted to Haines in the stage version). The playful roles of Haines and the Countess were expanded both dramatically and musically and offered a sharp comic contrast to the ingénue elegance of Russian Princess Stephanie, played by romantic lead Irene Dunne, who now got to sing both big ballads, "Smoke Gets in Your Eyes" and "Yesterdays" (the latter originally sung onstage by her Aunt Minnie, Fay Templeton). Other songs retained from the original score included the lively and jazzy "Let's Begin" and "I'll Be Hard to Handle."

The film dropped "Something Had to Happen" and used "The Touch of Your Hand" and "You're Devastating" as orchestral underscoring for the fashion-show sequence. As part of the musical enhancement for Huck and the Countess (Fred and Ginger), the film added two new swing dance numbers for this pair: "I Won't Dance," a reworking of a song by Dorothy Fields and Jimmy McHugh from Kern's recent London flop with Hammerstein, *Three Sisters*, and a song composed expressly for the film, "Lovely to Look At."[4] The winning combination of romantic elegance (operetta) and catchy popular vernacular (musical comedy) and their signature songs (Dunne) and dances (Astaire and Rogers) captured the best of both worlds. Despite the outrageous notion of an exiled Russian princess living in Paris in 1935, the screen form of *Roberta*, with its great new roles for dancers, might even make a good candidate for a stage revival.

Given the 80–120 minute fixed time frame, a technical requirement for early films, reasonably faithful and complete adaptations would not be possible until the film adaptations of classic shows in the mid-1950s. If one expects fidelity of dialogue and score, all the film adaptations made before the 1950s are destined to disappoint. Looking at four of the shows treated in act I of *Enchanted Evenings*, we find a range of possible connections to the original stage versions:

- The 1936 film version of *Show Boat* featured several cast members who had appeared either in the original 1927 stage version or subsequent productions over the next nine years; a screenplay by the original librettist, Oscar Hammerstein; songs exclusively written for *Show Boat* by Hammerstein and Jerome Kern (but not all the songs heard onstage); and three new songs written expressly for the film.[5] In a practice that would become increasingly common after *Oklahoma!*, two of these new songs, "Ah Still Suits Me" and "I Have the Room above Her" would reappear in future Broadway productions.[6]

- The 1936 Paramount *Anything Goes* retains much of the original plot, a surprising amount of dialogue from the 1934 libretto, the original star Ethel Merman, a small sampling of the songs Porter wrote for the stage version, and more than an equal number of new songs by other composers and lyricists.

- The 1959 *Porgy and Bess* presents a condensed "Broadway" version that replaced most of the recitative with spoken dialogue and like most musical comedies of the era also reduced the role of the chorus. Nevertheless, while heavily reduced, few songs were cut entirely, and no new songs by the Gershwins or others were added. It was not until 1993 that one could view a *Porgy and Bess* that, with two omissions, presented a filmed adaptation of a production (based on Glyndebourne in 1986) that offered what audiences heard during the Boston tryouts in the weeks before its 1935 Broadway debut, that is, a virtually uncut *Porgy and Bess*.

- The 1957 film version of *Pal Joey*, like the 1962 and 1987 stage versions of *Anything Goes*, presented, in addition to a few songs from the 1940 stage production, other songs created only by the original composer-lyricists Rodgers and Hart. Unlike the film *Anything Goes*, however, the *Pal Joey* film takes extensive liberties with the stage plot and script and features no actors or actresses from the original Broadway production.

Unfortunately, the *Show Boat* and *Anything Goes* 1930s adaptations discussed here are often harder to find than their 1950s remakes, probably because they are shot (albeit gorgeously) on black and white film.[7] The readily attainable 1951 Technicolor *Show Boat* followed the basic plot outline, at least for the portion that corresponds to act I, and most of the major songs from the original stage version. On the other hand, it removes most of Hammerstein's dialogue and eliminates or greatly reduces the African-American themes and characters that gave the stage and first film so much meaning. Gone entirely is the black chorus, gone after ten minutes is Queenie, Julie no longer has a revealing kinship with "Can't Help Lovin' Dat Man," and the exchange of blood between Julie and Steve is so underplayed that it would go unnoticed unless one were expressly on the lookout for this potentially powerful moment. Even "Ol' Man River" is heard only twice, which is perhaps a dozen fewer times than patrons of the Harold Prince 1994 revival would experience. Howard Keel (a baritone) as Ravenal, Joe E. Brown as Cap'n Andy Hawks, and William Warfield as Joe are excellent in their roles, but not enough to compensate for the film's infelicities. Although the film has its entertaining moments, in the end it does disservice to the stage version we examined in chapter 2 and does not begin to measure up to the 1936 film directed by Whale, the version of *Show Boat* that will be discussed in this chapter.

Similarly, given a choice between using the 1956 remake of *Anything Goes* and nothing at all (assuming that the 1936 version cannot be located), the suggestion offered here is to try to wait until one of the various stage revivals arrives at a theater near you, which should happen soon. Aside from taking place on a boat, nearly all vestiges of the plot have vanished in this version. Although in vastly altered contexts, the 1956 version delivers a little more of Porter's score than the 1936 original, including "All through the Night" and "Blow, Gabriel, Blow," excised in the earlier film; the complete title song, "I Get a Kick Out of You"; "You're the Top"; and a new Porter song, "It's De-Lovely" six years before it would reappear in the 1962 Off-Broadway revival. It also offers Bing Crosby reprising his earlier film role under the assumed name of Bill Benson, joining co-star Donald O'Connor in two new songs by Jimmy Van Heusen and Sammy Cahn in addition to those by Porter. But the excessive liberties with plot disqualify the film from being a fair representation of any of the many possible stage versions.

Show Boat *(1936)*

The difficult-to-obtain Universal 1936 *Show Boat*, directed by the critically acclaimed James Whale, is almost without exception regarded as far superior to the 1929 sound-silent hybrid *Show Boat* of 1929 or the 1951 version. Stephen Banfield goes as far as to praise the 1936 film as the best of all possible *Show Boats*: "Shortened to less than two hours, the score, including three new songs (plus two more that were cut and are lost), and the new, tighter, closer-to-the novel screenplay provided by Hammerstein together offer the most satisfying, balanced, and compelling version of *Show Boat* as drama achieved up to the present day. In almost every way it is superior to the stage version and its variants." For Banfield, the stage *Show Boat* of 1927 constitutes a rough draft and the 1936 film a finished and culminating destination.

Although the film added three new songs ("I Have the Room above Her," "Gallivantin' Aroun,'" and "Ah Still Suits Me"), time constraints required deletions or condensations of other songs and dialogue. Gone entirely are Ellie's stage number "Life on the Wicked Stage" and Ellie's duet with Frank, "I Might Fall Back on You"; Queenie's ballyhoos in each act, "C'mon Folks"

Show Boat, 1936 film. The marriage of Magnolia (Irene Dunne) and Ravenal (Allan Jones) (left) with Cap'n Andy (Charles Winninger) and Parthy (Helen Westley). For a stage photo of this scene see p. 25.

and "Hey Feller"; Ravenal's "Till Good Luck Comes My Way" in act I; and three songs from the Chicago Fair scene that opens act II, "At the Fair," "Why Do I Love You?," and "In Dahomey." Although this is a lot of songs at the expense of Queenie and Frank and Ellie, the latter relegated to singing non-Kern duets at the Trocadero, the new songs add considerable substance and nuance to the romantic principals and to Joe, now played by the iconic Paul Robeson, the 1928 London and 1932 New York Joe.

Even the canonic and complex opening scene, which introduced no less than five couples, was subjected to considerable pruning in the film. In the 1988 McGlinn recording, which includes both dialogue and music for the entire scene, it runs twenty-nine minutes; in the film, this scene runs a little over eighteen minutes. We will look at these eighteen minutes in greater detail, starting with the opening of "Cotton Blossom," which offers new words to the verse, B section, and the inversion of "Ol' Man River," all appearing over the credits.[8]

While the film charmingly (and cinematically) shows the universal effect on humans and animals generated by the arrival of the show boat, it leaves out some of the meaningful underscoring that characterized the stage version. Also missing from the stage are the choruses of town beaux and belles and their counterpoint with the black chorus. During the opening conversation between Magnolia and Ravenal, for example, stage audiences heard the orchestra interrupt with Parthy's theme (which had already clearly been associated with Parthy, Cap'n Andy Hawk's grumpy spouse). We can presume that Magnolia heard her mother's theme calling—that is what prompts her to say she has to leave. The absence of Parthy's theme in the film at this same point in the conversation makes Magnolia's sudden desire to interrupt the conversation inexplicable.

An even more dramatically significant effect of an underscoring omission occurs during the short scene in which Pete confronts Queenie about where she got her brooch (which we soon learn was a gift from Julie who rejected Pete's gift). The conversation appears in both the stage and film versions. In the stage version the underscoring of "Can't Help Lovin' Dat Man" connects this song with Queenie and sets up its use in the next scene, where we learn that Julie somehow picked up a song closely associated with black culture. In the film, Pete's confrontation with Queenie is accompanied, not by "Can't Help Lovin,'" but by Magnolia's piano theme. This important theme will not be associated with Magnolia until Ravenal asks her if she is a player.[9] Although the 1936 *Show Boat* certainly exhibits expert plotting and dramatic consolidation, it discards some of the dramatic connections that the music of the 1927 stage original provided.

The opening number contains substantial cuts, and much of "Cap'n Andy's Bally-hoo" is either deleted or spoken. The next two songs in the scene contain significant omissions as well. Among the most drastic and dramatically significant reductions are those in Ravenal's entrance and first song, "Where's the Mate for Me?" Those familiar with the stage version here (discussed in chapter 2) may recall that Ravenal sings a melody in AABA form in which the B section, "Magnolia's Piano Theme," forms the inspiration of Ravenal's B section. Ravenal asks where his mate might be. He hears Magnolia, her theme enters his consciousness and his music, and when he repeats the question, Magnolia herself appears to answer the question before Ravenal is able to finish it in song. After Ravenal almost finishes the second of the first two A sections in the film version he is interrupted as well, but not by Magnolia's piano theme. The interruption is in the form of a short film cutting to a conversation in which Frank contradicts Ellie's assumption that Ravenal must be an aristocrat by pointing out the cracks in his shoes (after which Ravenal, now discredited, proceeds to complete the song with the final phrase). Together, the song and the dialogue interjection occupy a not-so-grand total of thirty seconds.

Although it no longer begins as the interruption of a song, the ensuing dialogue between Magnolia and Ravenal follows the stage version closely (with

Parthy's interrupting theme now absent). In the 1936 film, "Make Believe" is also deprived of its second section.[10] With the time saved by the reductions of "Cotton Blossom," "Where's the Mate?," and "Make Believe," "Ol' Man River," sung by Paul Robeson accompanied by an inventive filmic montage of stevedores toting barges, lifting bales, Joe getting drunk and landing in jail, rolls along uninterrupted for more than four minutes to create a powerful conclusion to a magnificent if somewhat shorter scene. This change in emphasis surely reflects both Robeson's star quality and the fact that since 1927, "Ol' Man River" had become the signature song of the show and a deeply resonant reflection on American history. Indeed, in the MTV era, this filmic version of an iconic song can come across like a marvelous music video.

The 1936 film introduces to us a practice that becomes extremely common if not ubiquitous in films that discard significant amounts of musical material from the stage version. This is the practice of using fragments of abandoned songs as underscoring. Some examples include the appearance of the second section of "Make Believe" to underscore Julie's departure, the use of "Till Good Luck Comes My Way" when Ravenal is seen gambling, and "Life on the Wicked Stage" when Frank and Ellie are seen together. "Why Do I Love You?" is also reduced to an orchestral fragment. Only if one knew the song would someone realize the significance of the words "Because I love you," a lyric from this song and a line that appears in Ravenal's farewell letter which Ellie reads out loud (or that the musical line that accompanies this lyric and the line in the letter are synchronized).

Since nearly every *Show Boat* ends differently, it should come as no surprise that major changes have transpired between the 1927 stage and 1936 screen versions. Due largely to the show's excessive length, the role of Magnolia's daughter Kim, a successful young singing and dancing star on the stage in the tradition of her mother, was removed during the tryouts along with her song, "It's Getting Hotter in the North," in which Magnolia's piano theme is transformed into a jazzy '20s tune in the general style of Gershwin's *Rhapsody in Blue*. Although the growing length of the film forced a curtailment of Kim's transformation of her mother's "Gallivantin' Aroun'" (sung earlier in the film in blackface), film viewers see a lot of Kim in 1936 from birth to young adulthood. Audiences witness her birth in a scene taken from the novel, we meet Kim again when Ravenal sings "Make Believe" to her at her convent school before his disappearance, and the adult Kim appears in several later scenes, including the happy reunion of her parents after twenty years who conclude the film with a reprise of their duet, "You Are Love." The film also fleshed out the role of Joe, not only by giving him the rare full version of a song, "Ol' Man River" and a new song later in film, but in some new dialogue with Queenie. Audiences also gain a richer sense of

Joe's character, when, in a demonstration of courage and resolve that belies Queenie's accusations of laziness, Joe takes it upon himself to find a doctor in a hazardous storm so that Magnolia will give birth to Kim safely.

Even if one does not find the 1936 filmed *Show Boat* a dramatic improvement on the 1927 stage original (or other versions), the opportunity to see so many actors associated with this musical in one film will help give a new generation of film viewers a renewed appreciation of this show. The characters understand and believe in their material. Charles Winninger's enactment of *The Parson's Bride*, assuming all the roles when his cast was scared off the stage by a backwoodsman who thought the villain was real, may be reason enough to seek out this film, one of the great film adaptations of a stage classic.

Anything Goes *(1936)*

Those who come to expect earlier musical film adaptations to abandon the original stage book and most of the songs will only be half mistaken when it comes to the first movie version of the 1930s hit show *Anything Goes*. For

Anything Goes, 1936 film. Billy Crocker (Bing Crosby, left), Reno Sweeney (Ethel Merman, upside down center), and Rev. Dr. Moon (Charles Ruggles, right).

163

starters, viewers of the 1936 Paramount film will only hear about twenty seconds of the title song at the film's beginning, albeit sung by Merman, followed by instrumental fragments of "All through the Night" and "Blow, Gabriel, Blow." After that tantalizing morsel, the only Porter tunes from *Anything Goes,* or from any other Porter show for that matter in the film will be "I Get a Kick Out of You" sung by Merman, "There'll Always Be a Lady Fair" sung by the Avalon Boys quartet, and "You're the Top," a duet for Merman and rising film star Bing Crosby. Due to the controversial nature of some of Porter's lyrics, "sniffing cocaine" was not an option as a "kick" in "I Get a Kick Out of You," replaced by "that perfume from Spain." The new lyrics for "You're the Top" were assigned to Ted Fetter. Joseph Breen, the new enforcer of the Hollywood Production Code, objected to suggestive lyrics such as "you and your love give me ecstasy," which resulted in the total removal of the show's central love ballad, "All through the Night." The rousing "Blow, Gabriel, Blow," which might be interpreted as a slur on religion (and knowing Porter, perhaps also intended as a sexual double entendre), also bit the dust. If it was once shocking to catch a glimpse of a stocking (as the verse of "Anything Goes" went), when adapting a 1934 stage hit into a Hays Code–era Hollywood film in 1936, the phrase "anything goes" did not necessarily apply.

The Paramount film does offer a lot to be thankful for. Although she's confined in a slow-moving swing in a nightclub, it's a treat to see and hear a young Merman convey the words and the rhythms of "I Get a Kick Out of You," including the tricky half-note triplets that pervade the opening of each A section over a rumba beat.[11] Even with the altered lyrics it's also a delight to see and hear Merman and Crosby share "You're the Top." Crosby—replacing the original Billy Crocker, William Gaxton, who never enjoyed much of either a recording or film career, and displacing Merman as the star of the show—was a marvelous singer, a natural actor, and well suited for the part. The comic role of Public Enemy No. 13, originated onstage by the bumbling Victor Moore, was played in the film by comedian Charles Ruggles in the non-singing role of Reverend Dr. Moon (Moore got to "Sing like the Bluebird").[12] The Avalon Boys' rendition of "There'll Always Be a Lady Fair," joined by Crosby in a reprise, is another highlight; performed at about half the speed of the John McGlinn reconstructed recording, the film rendition of this song belies the myth that 1930s tempos are always faster than modern ones, a valuable lesson in historical performance practice.

Since Crosby, not Merman, was the big screen star, he needed more material—new songs. Merman's songs, "Anything Goes" and "Blow, Gabriel, Blow," were textually out of bounds as was Billy's "All through the Night," while "Gypsy in Me," sung in the Broadway show by his inamorata Hope Harcourt, was not the right song for Crosby. Lewis Milestone, who had previously directed the Academy Award–winning *All Quiet on the Western Front* (1930) but no musicals, brought in three interpolated songs expressly written for Crosby to sing in the film: "Sailor Beware" (Richard Whiting and Leo Robin), "My Heart and I" (Frederick Hollander and Robin), and "Moonburn" (Edward Heyman and Hoagy Carmichael). They may not have possessed the lyrical wit of "You're the Top"—neither did the new and rewritten lyrics of this song in the film—but all three are top-tier songs, engagingly crooned by Crosby.

The 1936 Paramount *Anything Goes* may have less of Merman and significantly less of Porter than the stage original, but it does offer a book that, aside from a few twists here and there, is remarkably similar to the stage plot from two years earlier. Even more remarkably, despite a number of plot deviations that will go unmentioned here, the film retains a considerable portion of the original dialogue, including many of the corny jokes. That they go over as well as they do—even the silly misunderstanding of "in door" China for Indo-China—is due to Ruggles's impeccable delivery. The "putting on the dog" joke is retained in the film script. So is the scene that leads to "calling all pants" that director Jerry Zaks found incomprehensible but kept in the 1987 Vivian Beaumont version because people still laughed. The 1936 film clears this matter up once and for all. During the strip poker game with the surprisingly adept Chinese missionaries, Billy bets his coat and Wang bets his pants. When Moon asks Billy if he calls pants, Billy calls pants, the missionaries call pants, and Moon calls pants. This exchange fully explains why Moon concludes the scene by shouting, "CALLING ALL PANTS." Even though only the relatively ancient viewers of the film (or trivia buffs) would make the connection between calling all pants and *Calling All Cars*, a popular crime and police radio drama that ran from 1933 to 1939, it's still a funny scene. Another surprise. The exchange between Moon and Mrs. Wentworth, the kind of stream-of-consciousness banter that Groucho and "straight man" Margaret Dumont excelled in (excerpted in chapter 3), can be found in the film between Ruggles as Groucho and the redoubtable Margaret Dumont as herself. By the way, Billy really does put on the dog, Mrs. Wentworth's newly shaved Pomeranian. PETA watchdogs should take note.

Although much of the dialogue was retained in the scenes that remained, some of the subtext regrettably did not manage to escape the cutting floor. For example, in the 1934 libretto, when Reno arrives unannounced in Evelyn Oakleigh's stateroom in order to frame him for a phony seduction, Evelyn, expecting the steward and without turning around, asks the visitor to "just put it down on the bed," expresses his hope that "it's good and hot," and states his desire that whatever the visitor has to offer he wants to receive before he is dressed. In response to this proposition, Reno asks whether she is early or late. In the screenplay, the tea is replaced by a dozen martini cocktails, presumably not hot, and when Reno arrives unseen Evelyn simply asks his visitor to leave the drinks there to which Reno simply responds, "I beg your pardon." The somewhat suggestive "not a grope" becomes "not a try" when Reno complains to Billy that he shouldn't have led her on by *not* getting her drunk, *not* asking her to his apartment to see his etchings, and *not* making a move on her in a taxi. "Hell" and other fiendish words, including "hot pants," may be banished, but Reno's basic complaint to Billy onstage, "You never even laid a hand on me, and I'm not used to men treating me like that!," was repeatable in the film. Similarly, although the details remain unspecified, Reno is allowed to confirm that Evelyn does "things" to her. One line that has, if anything, increased its topicality and resonance in the early twenty-first century is Moon's claim that he left the con artist game when the mortgage companies arrived.[13]

Although it often offers tangential connections with the 1934 stage version of *Anything Goes*, this film should be put back in circulation without delay where it can be criticized and enjoyed on its own terms.

Porgy and Bess

Samuel Goldwyn, 1959

As we have seen (see chapter 4), Rouben Mamoulian, with Gershwin's acquiescence, if not approval, managed to cut about forty minutes before *Porgy and Bess* launched its career on Broadway in 1935. Despite the cuts, what audiences heard at its Broadway debut was a full-scale opera, with sparse amounts of spoken dialogue reserved mainly for white characters. A few years later, the Cheryl Crawford Broadway revival of 1942 turned the opera into a more conventional musical with many cuts and spoken dialogue replacing much of Gershwin's recitative. Ten years after that, the Blevins Davis and Robert Breen production starring Leontyne Price as Bess, William Warfield as Porgy, and Cab Calloway as Sporting Life brought the opera closer to its operatic roots, style, and length. The historic Houston Grand Opera production of 1976 completed this process. In fact, Houston returned the work to what it looked like during the tryouts prior to its Broadway

Porgy and Bess, 1959 film. Porgy (Sidney Poitier) and Bess (Dorothy Dandridge) inside Porgy's room.

Porgy and Bess, 1959 film. Porgy (Poitier) and Bess (Dandridge) outside Porgy's door, with goat.

opening, that is, an uncut *Porgy and Bess* that included the forty soon-to-be-discarded minutes.

Between the Davis-Breen and the Houston production lies the shadow of the first film version of *Porgy and Bess*, produced by Samuel Goldwyn (his eightieth and final picture), and after its first director Mamoulian was fired, directed by Otto Preminger. Playing but not singing the part of Porgy was Sidney Poitier, at the time still in the early stages of his career as America's leading black actor and box office draw. Dorothy Dandridge, a rising star who had played the title role in Preminger's *Carmen Jones* a few years earlier, was cast as Bess. The film marked a return to the type of presentation not seen since Crawford's production, a shorter version in which the dialogue is mostly spoken rather than sung and with less activity from the chorus. Some critics lauded the film, including Bosley Crowther of the *New York Times*. Others were highly critical, especially of the sets, which seemed too theatrical and unrealistic. In "Why Negroes Don't Like 'Porgy and Bess,'" Era Bell Thompson, writing for the African-American magazine *Ebony* faulted the film for its anachronistic continuities with the opera.[14] Both works, this reviewer felt, reinforced stereotypes. For Bell, the Goldwyn-Preminger extravaganza was merely "the same old catfish." This is a topic to which we must return.

The film was a triumph of love over money. Goldwyn had seen the opera in 1935 and wanted to bring it to the screen practically ever since, and he spared no effort to attract the finest African-American stars of the day. When the warehouse containing the sets was destroyed on the eve of production, he built new sets from scratch. In the end the film lost half of its $7 million investment and received only one of the three Academy Awards for which it was nominated, a Best Scoring award shared between André Previn and Ken Darby. When it was first released, Ira Gershwin was quoted as saying, "It is everything we hoped for."[15] Other early supporters of the film included Dorothy Heyward, who exclaimed that "the film exceeds our highest expectations."[16] George Gershwin's great friend Kay Swift was enthusiastic about the film and agreed to give lectures and interviews on its behalf in twelve cities over a period of fifteen weeks.[17] The film was broadcast on national television in 1967 and then withdrawn, along with the soundtrack, at the insistence of the Gershwin estate owners Ira and Leonore Gershwin in 1974, two years before the work returned to its operatic roots with the Houston Opera production. Sometime between 1959 and 1974, Ira and Leonore, or at least Ira, experienced a change of heart about the work.

Since neither Poitier nor Dandridge was a singer, their songs were dubbed. Goldwyn attempted to complement their speaking voices musically and to use African-American opera singers whenever possible for all the major roles.

The voice of Porgy was Robert McFerrin. Although today less well known than his son Bobby McFerrin, in his own time the senior McFerrin had an impressive and distinguished career. Among other achievements, he became the first black male to sing at the Metropolitan Opera—in January 1955, the same month that the first African-American female to perform there, Marian Anderson, made her debut. The following year McFerrin sang the title role, in Verdi's *Rigoletto*, at the Met. The voice of Bess was Adele Addison, a versatile singer of opera and concert literature, perhaps best known today for her recordings of Baroque literature. Leontyne Price, the much-acclaimed Bess of the Breen-Davis stage Bess, was invited but declined to dub the role for Dandridge. In any event, Addison, whose operatic roles included Gilda and Micaela (Price was noted for her Aïda onstage and Carmen on recordings), possessed a lighter lyric soprano sound than Price and thus matched Dandridge's speaking voice more closely.

Sammy Davis Jr., Sporting Life, widely praised for his "new sinister spin to the character (thus establishing a precedent for later interpretations)," did his own singing for the film.[18] Since contractual agreements precluded the use of his voice on Columbia records, however, Cab Calloway, the Breen-Davis Sporting Life, is the voice heard on the album soundtrack. Brock Peters (Crown), who played the falsely accused rapist in the film adaptation of *To Kill a Mockingbird* (1962) and sang the lead role in the Broadway revival and the screen version of *Lost in the Stars* in the 1970s, sang for himself in the *Porgy and Bess* film. The Maria was Pearl Bailey, the role created both in the 1927 play and the opera by the non-singing precocious rapper Georgette Harvey. Unlike Harvey, Bailey, a leading popular singer and one of the stars of *St. Louis Woman* on Broadway in the 1940s, was featured as a soloist to augment what was a choral number onstage, "I Can't Sit Down." One year earlier, in the film adaptation of *South Pacific*, Juanita Hall, acclaimed on Broadway for her creation of Bloody Mary, had suffered the indignity of being replaced on the soundtrack. Diahann Carroll as Clara, the mother who sings "Summertime," did not sing Clara onstage, but she was nonetheless an able singer who before long would record an album of *Porgy and Bess* songs and even starred in a Tony Award–winning performance of Richard Rodgers's *No Strings*; even so, she was similarly replaced on the *Porgy* soundtrack. Peters, Bailey, and Carroll, along with Dandridge were all alumni of Otto Preminger's 1954 film *Carmen Jones*, the film adaptation of Hammerstein's 1940s Broadway hit reinterpretation of Bizet's opera *Carmen*.

Sammy Davis Jr. eagerly campaigned for the role of Sporting Life but others, most prominently Harry Belafonte, who had played Joe (Don José) in Preminger's *Carmen Jones*, turned down offers to appear in Goldwyn's *Porgy and Bess*. Whether as a result of manipulation by his agent or Goldwyn, threats to his career, or a combination of these, the initially reluctant

Poitier eventually capitulated. This is what he said at a news conference held on December 10, 1957, six months before shooting was scheduled to begin:

> I have never, to my conscious knowledge, done anything that I thought would be injurious to anyone—particularly to my own people. Now this is a personal choice. I do not pretend to be the conscience of all Negroes....I was convinced irrevocably that it will be a great motion picture and tremendous entertainment and that it will be enjoyed by everyone—little and big—people of all races and creeds.[19]

Poitier even went as far as asserting that Goldwyn and Mamoulian were "almost as sensitive" as he was to the dangers of portraying racial stereotypes in popular culture.

The film inevitably shared some of the stereotypes that characterize the opera. The characters are uneducated; Sporting Life is a pimp, drug dealer, and an atheist; and Bess is a former prostitute and drug addict, but nonetheless a relatively sedate progenitor of Mimi in Jonathan Larson's *Rent*.[20] Crown is a murderer. Sporting Life's evil qualities may have been magnified in the film, but Dandridge's Bess was accused of being too elegant and gentle. In response to the Production Code, if not the demands of the story, Porgy seems to be sleeping on the floor and not directly adjacent to his own bed, which is occupied by Bess. Missing from the film are not only the "Buzzard Song" but other remnants of Porgy's superstitions. Serena refuses Bess's money for the burial of her husband Robbins, who was murdered in a drunken rage by Bess's Crown; she later accuses Bess of being unfit to mother Clara's baby. The film introduces a genuine Christian preacher on Kittiwah Island as a foil for Sporting Life's blasphemous "It Ain't Necessarily So" (followed by an exuberant, almost orgiastic dance that was not in the opera, in a jazz arrangement more 1950s than 1930s in style). These added touches clarify that Christian values are preferred to those of Sporting Life and his followers. The crooked lawyer Frazier is entirely absent, as is Archdale, the benevolent white man whose parents were slave owners who once owned the parents of Peter, the Honey Man. The film also greatly reduced the amount of dialect heard in both the spoken dialogue and the songs themselves. In short, *Porgy and Bess* may be rightly interpreted as full of arguably demeaning stereotypes, but the film version was demonstrably far less so. Nevertheless, after its initial release and nationally televised broadcast in 1967, the Gershwin estate chose to suppress this historic cinematic version of Gershwin's masterpiece.

Ostensibly, the film was not withdrawn for its controversial depictions of African Americans but for artistic reasons. It was withdrawn, they said in effect, because the surviving Gershwins did not want a Broadway version of *Porgy and Bess* to represent George and Ira's opera in a film. Michael Strunsky, the nephew of Ira and his wife Leonore and their executor after the latter's death in 1991, summarized Leonore's strong position on the subject: "My aunt didn't want it distributed. She and my uncle felt it was a Hollywoodization of the piece. We now acquire any prints we find and destroy them."[21] It is also clear that Ira's wife Leonore, who lived to see *Porgy and Bess* produced on the prestigious stages of the Metropolitan and Glyndebourne, did not want a filmed stage version to represent the work and for this reason did not even approve a filmed operatic *Porgy and Bess* until nearly a decade after Ira's death in 1983. This was the television studio production directed by Trevor Nunn (not a videotaped live performance in front of an audience) that eventually appeared in 1993 and will be discussed shortly, nearly sixty years after the opera's Broadway debut.

Certainly, the Goldwyn-Preminger film poorly represents the work when compared with the operatic form intended by Gershwin. This may be reason alone for lovers of the opera to avoid the film. But the change of approach from an operatic to a more conventional Broadway musical conception of the work does not result in a film that is disrespectful of the work or a failure on its own Broadway-Hollywood terms. Much of the recitative and large stretches of the choral numbers have vanished, and Robbins and Crown fight in silence. But nearly all of the many songs are present and often complete. If one can believe the timings offered by A. Scott Berg or Howard Pollack, the film actually runs *longer* than the version Broadway audiences saw in 1935 (after the 40 minutes of cuts).[22] It might be constructive to compare the Preminger *Porgy and Bess* with the Franco Zeffirelli *Otello* (1986), which reduced Verdi's opera to 123 minutes (including long stretches of elaborate montages with neither music nor dialogue). Marcia Citron offers a list of what is absent from this adaptation, including the seemingly indispensable "Willow Song."[23] Compared to Zeffirelli, Preminger is a purist.

Preminger's accomplishment was to reveal the opera's vital Broadway roots, and to reveal them in an idiomatic cinematic form. One fascinating by-product of the non-operatic approach becomes evident in the decisions of what besides the songs needed to be sung. Although Gershwin offers many degrees and varieties of nuance in his recitatives, Preminger's decision to replace most of the recitatives with spoken dialogues allows the ones that remain to become increasingly meaningful, especially since most of these are given to central characters at strategic moments in the work. One telling example is the expressive passage that begins with "They pass by singin,'" in which Porgy incorporates his own signature theme as well as his loneliness to explain why he is resigned to life without a woman. Another occurs a little later in the opening scene during Porgy's musical foreshadowing of "I Got Plenty o' Nuttin' " as he rolls the dice. Still another place where impassioned recitative takes over speech occurs during Bess's confrontation with Crown on Kittiwah Island in act II, scene 2 ("It's like dis, Crown"). As the film progresses, the use of recitative at other lyrical musical moments when dialogue can no longer suffice creates an aura around these moments that is less evident when *everything* is sung. One might miss the addition of Serena and Maria that converts Porgy's great third act aria, "Oh, Bess, Oh Where's My Bess," into a magnificent operatic trio in the stage version, but the direct, uncluttered, and obsessive quality of his solo plea in the film has an effect that is admittedly slightly reduced in an ensemble.

The filming was interrupted by a devastating fire that destroyed two million dollars worth of sets and costumes and nearly brought production to a permanent halt. One of the casualties of the fire was Mamoulian as director, who was fired after he continued to insist on using actual settings in Charleston, South Carolina, and expressed other ideas that were at odds with Goldwyn's vision of the film. In the end, only the Kittiwah scene was filmed on location. His employment terminated, Mamoulian was nonetheless paid in full for his work, which did stop him from taking legal action. Mamoulian's firing marked the end of a brilliant career that included his direction of *Love Me Tonight, Golden Boy, Oklahoma!*, and *Carousel* as well as both the play and opera based on the story of Porgy and Bess.

Although allegedly none of the surviving footage was shot by Mamoulian, one fascinating likely remnant occurs in the part of the film that corresponds to the final scene of the opera (the part of the scene that occurs prior to Porgy's return from prison where he was jailed for a week because of his refusal to look directly at Crown's dead body). The published vocal score contains most of the material that was cut during the tryouts, an unusual situation that has greatly contributed to the resistance by music directors to cuts in the opera. One part missing from this score, a rhythmic sequence added by Mamoulian, opened the final scene onstage in 1935. A description of the sequence appears in a production script now housed in the New York Public Library. The concert performance under conductor John Mauceri that was performed by the Nashville Symphony Orchestra in 2006 not only followed Gershwin's cuts but restored this sequence. The 1959 film offers something similar at the beginning of the scene before the chorus enters with "How are you dis mornin' "?[24]

The film, long unavailable in theaters or on video, made a rare guest appearance in 1998, on the occasion of a Gershwin Centennial Festival sponsored by the Institute of Studies in American Music in Gershwin's beloved New York City. At this screening, Foster Hirsch, a professor of film studies at Brooklyn College, where the film was shown, offered appreciative reflections on the film. His thoughtful appraisal implicitly contradicts the attitudes of Leonore Gershwin that continue to be enforced by the Gershwin estate:

> Preminger's direction is intensely cinematic, his approach far more sophisticated than that of a filmed play. Replacing passages of recitative with dialogue, he has made no attempt to present the material as an opera.... With his august presence and speaking voice, Poitier is a remote, dignified Porgy, a survivor. In effective contrast, Dandridge is an anguished Bess victimized by her beauty as well as her race and gender. Quite contrary to its tarnished reputation, Preminger's film is a magisterial pageant, a ceremonial work deeply respectful both to the intentions of Gershwin and his collaborators and to its black subjects.... This "forbidden" text demands to be shown exactly as it is here, on a large screen and with a sound system that can do justice to what may well be the most glorious theatrical work by an American composer.[25]

The overview in this chapter seconds Hirsch's opinion. Despite its flaws, Goldwyn's *Porgy and Bess* should not be sequestered in the Library of Congress. It deserves to be seen and heard.

EMI Classics, 1993

The first version of *Porgy and Bess* (1959) marked a return to the approach popularized in the Crawford revival in the early 1940s. The 1970s introduced the first recorded uncut *Porgy and Bess*, and the 1980s brought the uncut opera to the stages of the Metropolitan and Glyndebourne. But it was not until 1993 that this increasingly preferred version of the work reached the screen. This film, videotaped in a television studio, was based on the 1986 Glyndebourne production staged by Trevor Nunn, known to the world of Broadway through his direction of *Cats* and most recently *Sunset Boulevard*.

By filming in a studio, Nunn was able to visually expand the world of Catfish Row, especially by taking advantage of a television studio's ability to depict realistic waterways and other humanly constructed natural surroundings. In an unusual move, the cast—with few exceptions the same as that of the 1986 stage production—lip-synched to their own voices in the acclaimed 1989 London Philharmonic recording conducted by Simon Rattle.

Porgy and Bess, 1993 film. Porgy (Willard White) casting away his crutches.

Porgy and Bess, 1993 film. Porgy (White) begins his long journey to New York City.

Four singers, most importantly Bruce Hubbard (Jake) who had died, were replaced by new actors.

For the most part, the television film, unlike its 1959 predecessor readily available on DVD, for the first time offered the complete opera as seen and heard onstage a few years earlier. All that is missing is the "Buzzard Song" in act II, scene 1, one of the cuts made shortly before the Broadway debut, and the opening of the final scene, act III, scene 3, which shows the citizens of Catfish Row waking up just prior to Porgy's return from his week in jail for refusing to look at Crown's dead body (ironically a scene partly visible in the otherwise heavily cut version of this scene in the Preminger film).[26] It is not clear whether the stage version also cut these opening moments of act III, scene 3, but the 1989 recording and probably the Glyndebourne staging did contain the "Buzzard Song." Surely its deletion cannot be attributed to its length or the possible strains it might place on a dubbed singing voice. The absence of the "Buzzard Song" and perhaps the opening of the final scene explains why the 1993 DVD clocks in at five minutes less than the 189 minutes of the 1989 recording, which provided the soundtrack for both.

In addition to the film's nearly complete performance state, some of its length can be attributed to tempos slower than those of recordings made between 1935 and 1942. The faster tempos of these older recordings hold to the historical performance movement truism that older is faster, a belief that is belied by the Avalon quartet's leisurely film rendition of Porter's "There'll Always Be a Lady Fair" (see the discussion of the 1936 film *Anything Goes*). At the outset of the opera, Harolyn Blackwell's performance of "Summertime" runs two minutes and forty seconds; this is nearly a minute longer than it took the original Clara, Abbie Mitchell, to sing the song at a rehearsal performance recorded on July 19, 1935. The first commercially recorded Clara, Helen Jepson, one year later clocked in at six seconds slower than Mitchell, and when the first Bess, Anne Brown, recorded the song in 1942, her time was ten seconds longer than Mitchell.[27] Like "Ol' Man River" before it, this particular song had by then become the signature moment of the entire work, and slowing it down gives it more dramatic weight, if not always more interest.

A central decision in Nunn's stage and film versions was to raise Porgy off his knees and take away his goat and his goat cart. Although Nunn's Porgy is deformed and limps around on crutches, his standing posture presents a new view of the character, symbolically and literally raising his stature. At the end of the opera Porgy even throws down the crutches as he begins his slow and painful journey (on foot rather than by goat cart) to retrieve Bess in New York City. The removal of the goat necessitated a few line changes (e.g., in the final scene the coroner refers to Porgy as the beggar man instead of the goat man), but the effect is largely a visual and psychological one. Other dramatically significant visual revisions include Bess's unmistakable flirtation with Robbins, which provides a motivation for Crown to murder him in the first scene that goes beyond a simple argument over a crap shoot as well as the decision to show Crown hobbling on to Kittiwah Island at the end of the first act, two scenes before he prohibits Bess from leaving the island to return to her Porgy. At the end of act II, scene 2, Nunn shows Jake's boat leaving to meet its fate in the storm and a close-up of Maria's anguished face. In act II, scene 4, he illustrates Crown's attempted rescue and Clara's death, neither of which are seen when the opera is staged. Finally, before we hear the music of act III, scene 1, we see Sporting Life lurking around, and later in the scene Nunn makes it clear that Sporting Life is complicit in Crown's murder, a brutal murder by strangling that Sporting Life observes and tacitly encourages. In the 1935 stage directions, Porgy uses a knife (there are also no witnesses). In the 1959 film version, both methods of murder are combined.

For those unable to see the opera *Porgy and Bess* in their neighborhood, the Nunn film provides an innovatively filmed and well-sung opportunity to see and hear what the work has become to most audiences and recording aficionados since the late 1970s. It is a most welcome addition to the short list of filmed adaptations of Broadway classics before *Oklahoma!*

Pal Joey *(1957)*

By the time a Hollywood studio got around to making a film version of *Pal Joey* in 1957, the show had completed both its first run, begun in 1940, and its 1952 Broadway revival. The Rodgers and Hart era was long past, and the Rodgers and Hammerstein era was nearing its own finale with *Flower Drum Song* and *The Sound of Music*. However, film versions of *Oklahoma!*, *Carousel*, and *The King and I* had appeared within the past two years, the film version of *South Pacific* was only one year away, and it must have looked like a good time to mine the riches of Rodgers's past achievements with his first lyricist.

The film adaptation of *Pal Joey* provided vivid proof that the makers of Broadway musicals could do more, show more, and say more onstage in the early 1940s than it was possible to do, show, and say on film in the late 1950s. Portraying behavior such as adultery was possible, but the Hollywood Production Code, which had expurgated Porter's lyrics two decades earlier, had by now determined that a character engaging in such objectionable behavior would have to pay a clear price for such conduct. A musical

Pal Joey, 1957 film. Joey Evans (Frank Sinatra) and Vera Simpson (Rita Hayworth) take the gloves off.

based on two sleazy characters, Joey Evans and Vera Simpson, who use one another for sexual and financial gain, would not be permitted in a major motion picture in the United States for yet another decade—until the Code was finally cast off in the turbulent 1960s. It is also possible that the censorship was seconded by the projected onscreen Joey, Frank Sinatra, who may have recoiled from playing such a fundamentally foul character for fear of tarnishing his maturing public image, which was of concern to the broader Italian-American ethnic community as well. In the current era of media multiple choice, it may be hard to fathom the contradictory strictures in a social world with only one source of prestigious public audiovisual entertainment (Hollywood), and only three fledgling television networks still broadcasting only in black and white (CBS, NBC, and the upstart ABC).

In any event, Vera, the flagrant adulteress in the stage version, is now a rich widower, and Joey, the heartless philanderer, at the end of the film marries the innocent Linda English instead of walking offstage to catch a fresh "mouse." Linda, now a show girl infatuated with Joey instead of a stenographer he happens to meet in front of a pet shop, agrees to do a strip number, but in the end the uncharacteristically gallant Joey does not let her go through with it and does not take advantage of her sexually off-camera. Making Vera a *former* stripper sets up an opportunity to have her sing "Zip" to raise money for a charity. Onstage the song was delivered by the newspaper reporter Melba, who uses the song to describe her interview with the famous Gypsy Rose Lee, in which the surprisingly intellectual stripper shared her musings (including her considered opinion that the philosopher Schopenhauer was right) while zipping off her clothes. The seedy world of blackmailers, strippers, and other low-life characters is now replaced by likable show people and a likable ex-stripper socialite.

Placing Frank Sinatra in the title role removed the dancing component associated with the role first played by Gene Kelly and in the revival by Harold Lang. The non-singing and for the most part non-dancing Kim Novak played Linda English. Novak, then at the peak of her popularity—one year before she starred in Alfred Hitchcock's *Vertigo*—and a major money earner for Columbia pictures, gained additional national exposure when she appeared on the July 29 cover of *Time* magazine shortly before the release of *Pal Joey* in September. Perhaps due to the star power of Sinatra and Novak, the film earned nearly five million dollars, one of the ten highest grossing films of the year.

Appealing to a slightly older film audience, the role of Vera Simpson was played by one of the most popular World War II pinups and the major Columbia pictures star of the 1940s, Rita Hayworth. Hayworth herself had been featured on both *Time* and *Life* covers in 1941, the latter in one of the most famous photographs of the era (her image even appeared on an atomic nuclear bomb dropped on Bikini Atoll shortly after World War II). In 1957, she was a mature but still beautiful woman at thirty-nine and appropriate in her new role as the older woman. "Zip" gave Hayworth the opportunity to sing a suggestive but refined strip number without taking off more than her gloves. Its referential gesture to her similar glove-strip in *Gilda* would be familiar to anyone who had seen both films.[28] Unfortunately, Hayworth, the first of an exclusive group to have partnered with both Fred Astaire and Gene Kelly, only dances a little with Sinatra here.

Not only is the Columbia 1957 *Pal Joey* bowdlerized, with little remaining from Frank O'Hara's lively dialogue. It also plays havoc with the score. Nearly every song is either missing, buried in underscoring, or placed in a new and misleading context. Songs retained include the following:

- "That Terrific Rainbow," originally sung by the main showgirl Gladys and now with Novak as Linda dubbed by Trudi Erwin (about 5 minutes into the film).

- "A Great Big Town" (or "Chicago") for the showgirls, but only lasting a few seconds (about 9 minutes into the film). On Broadway, Joey sang this song as an audition number to open the show and the girls reprised the song at the opening of the actual nightclub act, which featured "That Terrific Rainbow." Since the milieu was changed to San Francisco, the few preserved lyrics did not reveal the earlier town's identity.

- "Zip" for Vera (Hayworth) once known as "Vanessa the undressa" (dubbed by Jo Ann Greer about 15 minutes into the film). As noted earlier, in the stage version the song is delivered by newspaper reporter Melba Snyder in act II.

- "I Could Write a Book" (about 25 minutes into the film). In the stage version, this was the song Joey sang to Linda English after spinning his yarn about the dog that was killed when Joey was young. Onstage, the fictitious childhood dog was named Skippy; in the film, the dog's name is Snuffy and their stories are similar. Onstage, Skippy stays in the pet store, but in the film Snuffy remains a continuous presence. Much later, about seventy minutes into the film, the song returns as a waltz which sets up Linda's striptease (stopped by Joey before it gets out of hand long before Linda runs out of clothes to discard).[29]

- "Bewitched" (about 48 minutes into the film). The staged context is changed in the film from a tailor shop where Vera is outfitting Joey in style to Vera's boudoir. This occurs not long, we infer, after Vera and Joey have finished the early rounds of their non-adulterous and monogamous love making. As a way to stem the shock of moving from speech to song, Vera speaks rather than sings the lyrics of the opening verse before, again dubbed by Erwin, she sings the next part of the verse and the chorus (she also spoke the verse of "Zip"). Some of the less provocative lyrics she sings are not by Hart.

- "Pal Joey" ("What Do I Care for a Dame?"). Onstage Joey dreams of his new club at the end of act I; in the film the dream sequence, which will soon depict Vera and Linda along with the music of "Bewitched," occurs in the last four minutes of the film (at about 83 minutes).[30]

Of these five songs and one fragment, which occasionally recur as underscoring, only one song is delivered by its rightful character ("Pal Joey") and only one song ("That Terrific Rainbow") shares a context familiar from the stage version. Other fragments of other songs from the great original *Pal Joey* score appear as fragments, ironically as if to remind those who know the score well of what they are missing. These include "Do It the Hard Way" at the beginning of the film, a brief orchestral statement of "Happy Hunting Horn" (about 27 minutes and again 54 minutes into the film), orchestral underscoring of "Plant You Now, Dig You Later" (at about 31 minutes), and "You Mustn't Kick It Around" for the orchestra (at 60 minutes). Spaced out during the film to round out the decimated score are a small collection of hit Rodgers and Hart songs, one from *One Your Toes* and two from *Babes in Arms*.

- "There's a Small Hotel," Joey (Sinatra) (*On Your Toes*, 1936) (11 minutes into the film)

- "The Lady Is a Tramp," Joey, dancing with Vera (Hayworth) (*Babes in Arms*, 1937) (41 minutes); a brief reprise returns late in the film (73 minutes)

- "My Funny Valentine," Linda's strip number (Novak) (*Babes in Arms*) (56 minutes into the film); a shorter version is reprised by Joey on a sofa a few minutes later (61 minutes)

With the addition of "The Lady Is a Tramp" and "My Funny Valentine" in their new homes, the least that can be said of *Pal Joey* as a film adaptation is that it included one more song from *Babes in Arms* than the 1939 film adaptation of this earlier, equally song-studded and richly crafted Broadway 1937 score. It's a sad commentary on the gulf between the creative worlds of Broadway and Hollywood in the 1950s that such a potentially golden era of film musicals is instead tombstoned with many might-have-beens. Happily, when the Golden Age of song was long past, in such television dramas and movies as Dennis Potter's *Pennies from Heaven* (BBC, 1978) and *The Singing Detective* (BBC, 1986), or Woody Allen's original film musical *Everyone Says I Love You* (Miramax, 1997)—and also prominently in most of Allen's richly musical comedy soundtracks from *Manhattan*'s Gershwin tribute to *Radio Days* and *Bullets over Broadway*—filmmakers returned to ancient Broadway melodies for inspiration and sometimes musically felicitous reinterpretation.

The Cradle Will Rock *(1999)*

The Cradle Will Rock (1937) inspired no Hollywood adaptations until in 1999 the left-leaning director and actor Tim Robbins gave the work considerable popular exposure in a film that used Marc Blitzstein's title and historic opening night as a plot fulcrum. Robbins's original script blends the making of

Cradle Will Rock, 1999 film. Marc Blitzstein (Hank Azaria at the piano)
is surprised to see Olive Stanton (Emily Watson) standing up from the
audience to sing the Moll's song on opening night.

Cradle Will Rock, 1999 film. A closer view of Olive Stanton (Watson) singing
the Moll's song from the audience on opening night.

Cradle Will Rock (without the *The*) with four other interweaving story lines. As the end credits roll we learn that the conversations at the Dies Committee Hearings in the film, which might appear to be fictional, especially the surrealistic debate about whether Christopher Marlowe was a communist, were in fact "taken directly from the Congressional Record." Throughout the film Zelig-like parabolic fictional characters interact with historical ones. For example, a major character in one of the subplots is the newly created Tommy Crickshaw (Bill Murray), a conservative vaudeville ventriloquist angry at the arty and (to him) shockingly socialistic Federal Theatre. The character he teams up with to fight the communists, Hazel Huffman (played by Joan Cusack), was based on an actual historical figure, an anti-communist clerk employed by the WPA who testified against the Theatre for three days. Hallie Flanagan, the real-life head of the Federal Theatre played by Cherry Jones, was granted only six hours to reply to Huffman's marathon of testimony. The film points out this imbalance. Another invented character was Aldo Silvano (John Turturro), an Italian American who opposed Mussolini's fascist regime and is consequently kicked out of his parents' apartment where he is living with his wife and family. Casting Silvano as the principled Larry Foreman thus made an effective connection between life and art within the complex plot world of the film.[31]

In addition to inventing or reinterpreting characters and situations, the film takes the artistic liberty of compressing and conflating historical events from the six years between 1932 and 1938 into the months between the time Blitzstein was finishing his *Cradle* (fall 1936) and the evening of its historic and dramatic premiere on June 16, 1937 (described simply as "Summer 1937" in the script). The commission (by Nelson Rockefeller) and destruction of a politically incendiary mural by Mexican artist Diego Rivera (played in the film by the brilliant Panamanian Harvard-educated attorney/actor/singer/songwriter Rubén Blades) in the new Rockefeller Center actually happened, but in 1932–33. Since the Dies Hearings took place in 1938, Huffman's testimony did not actually play a role in the termination of federal funds and the closing of the *Cradle*'s scheduled theater. In Robbins's film, Flanagan's abbreviated hearing, the obliteration of Rivera's mural commissioned and destroyed by Rockefeller (John Cusack), and the opening night drama of *Cradle* all take place on the same fateful summer day.

Robbins's *Cradle Will Rock* does not attempt to present a performance of Blitzstein's musical. Nevertheless, viewers hear more music from this show over the course of the film's 134 minutes than in several of the putative adaptations previously discussed in this chapter. Early in the film we see Blitzstein (Hank Azaria) hard at work composing the opening, sung by Olive Stanton, about whom little is known, as the Moll (Emily Watson). Olive is also the first person we see in the film. In an effective but by necessity speculative demonstration of life imitating art, the film begins as she wakes up in a theater, an unemployed homeless street person who goes up to strange men offering to sing a song for a nickel (early in the film viewers also see and hear the character Blitzstein trying out the song based on this idea, "Nickel under Your Foot"). The idea and the music come full circle when, during the performance that concludes the film, Moll (played by Olive), finally sings this plaintive melody. A sympathetic Huffman helps Olive find a job as a stagehand for Project 891, now about to embark on the production of *Cradle*. Although ineligible to act in the work, she is helped by John Adair (Jamey Sheridan). Later, Adair plays the Gent, the man the Moll solicits in the musical and Olive beds in the film. Olive's first song, the "Moll's Song" which opens with the words "I'm Checkin' Home Now," is heard again when she auditions and continues seamlessly in the film as the time shifts to five months later (where she sings the same song without improvement). Reinforcing Moll's importance in the musical as well as dramatic components of the film, both of her songs will return in the filmed version of the opening night performance.

Before we arrive at this culminating moment, we also see and then hear Blitzstein in Union Square conceiving yet another song, "Joe Worker." In a moment of magical realism, the song is overheard by the spirit of Bertolt Brecht, who had inspired Blitzstein when he played "Nickel" for Brecht in 1935, along with the ghost of Blitzstein's wife and Brecht translator Eva Goldbeck, who died of anorexia earlier in the year. As he allegedly did in real life in 1935, Brecht in the film inspires Blitzstein to make his musical address the reality that none of us, artists included, are immune to at least metaphorical prostitution via moral dilemmas around money and patronage, encapsulated in the biblical adage, "the love of money is the root of all evil."

During its last portion the film focuses mainly on the *Cradle* performance, albeit with occasional and brief cuts away to subplots. The film is faithful to the spirit and many of the details of what happened that night, including the banning of the performance onstage, and the twenty-block-long (one mile) march uptown to the Venice Theater. In addition to most of the Moll's opening tune and her "Nickel under the Foot," we hear announcements of sample scenes, portions of dialogue, fragments of solo songs, and a harmonious sextet belting out the phrase "We don't want a union in Steeltown." The performance concludes with Larry Foreman's powerful refusal to be co-opted, or metaphorically prostituted, by Mr. Mister and the stirring title song that concludes the show.

Despite its historical and artistic veracities, those who were present do not completely concur with Robbins about what actually happened on the historic opening night. The actual proceedings began with some conciliatory remarks by Houseman, who wanted to make it clear that the production "was a gesture of artistic, not political, defiance."[32] Orson Welles then spoke about his admiration for Blitzstein's musical, informed those present about what they would have seen if the scheduled theater "had not been taken over by the Cossacks of the WPA," and introduced the scene and the characters.[33] In the film, Houseman (Cary Elwes) does not appear here and the two introductions are reduced to a few sentences by the character playing Welles (Angus Macfadyen), who acknowledges the unusual circumstances of the performance, refers to the "sinister force at work" in the play that "frightens people in Washington," and then ironically introduces "the monster behind *The Cradle Will Rock*: Mr. Marc Blitzstein."[34]

Perhaps because what happened next was as dramatic as any fictional portrayal could be, the next part of the film follows life quite closely. This is how Houseman described these moments in his memoir, *Run-Through*:

> *The Cradle Will Rock* started cold, without an overture. A short vamp that sounded harsh and tinny on Jean Rosenthal's rented, untuned upright, and Marc's voice, clipped, precise and high-pitched: "A Street corner—Steeltown, U.S.A." Then, the Moll's opening lyrics: [first three lines]. It was a few seconds before we realized that to Marc's strained tenor another voice—a faint, wavering soprano— had been added. It was not clear at first where it came from, as the two voices continued together for a few lines—[next three lines of lyrics]. Then, hearing the words taken out of his mouth, Marc paused, and at that moment the spotlight moved off the stage, past the proscenium arch into the house, and came to rest on the lower left box where a thin girl in a green dress with dyed red hair was standing, glassy-eyed, stiff with fear, only half audible at first in the huge theatre but gathering strength with every note.[35]

Houseman continues, relating that at the conclusion of the Moll's song and Blitzstein's introductory "Enter Gent," "a young man with a long nose rose from a seat somewhere in the front section of the orchestra and addressed the girl in green in the stage box."[36] The producer does not identify the man as John Adair. This may be because the man cast as the Gent was actually George Fairchild; Adair played the role of the Druggist, a character who does not appear in the film. In the film, Blitzstein introduces the Gent with the direction, "Enter a well-dressed gentleman," and after a shot of Adair *leaving* the theater, adds "on the make." When there is no response, he then interjects, "Enter me." Adair's film departure follows an invented but nonetheless heated disagreement between Olive and Adair over whether she should challenge the actors' union which, acting on federal instructions, forbade the actors to participate onstage in this production. When the Olive of the film sang her song, she was indeed once again on the street where we saw her in the opening scene, although now she is on the street in a performance as well as in real life. Adair's departure from the theater confirmed his threat that if she defied the union she would have to sleep somewhere else.

His dramatic exit stands as shorthand for what happened with the other characters that evening. According to Blitzstein biographer Eric A. Gordon, the real Adair, described by cast member Will Geer as a "rather reactionary young man," did not show up at all that night. Reverend Salvation, who was not, as in the film, played by the African-American actor Canada Lee, also did not sing.[37] Houseman recalled that "Blitzstein played half a dozen roles [Gordon says eight roles] that night, to cover for those who 'had not wished to take their lives, or rather, their living wage, into their hands.' Other replacements were made spontaneously, on the spot."[38]

The film treats a multitude of weighty political topics, including the conflict between unionism and management and communism and fascism. But the main issue is the complex relationships between art, artists, politics, and political theater. Although the political vantage point of the film leans leftward, it does make some effort to present other approaches to these issues. Just as *Cradle* continues to generate strong critical reactions pro and con, the film inspired a similarly wide span of responses ranging from positive reviews in the *New York Times, New Yorker*, and *National Review* to a spirited, unequivocally hostile attack by Terry Teachout in *Commentary*, a periodical with strong anti-communist roots.[39] At the conclusion of his indictment of Robbins and Blitzstein, Teachout goes as far as to forge a link between this pair of creators and the evils of Stalinism:

> Evidently, in Robbins's moral calculus, prostituting one's art in the name of the foremost mass murderer of modern times does not in the least derogate from one's idealism and courage, any more than utter ignorance of the crosscurrents of cultural politics in the 30's disqualifies one from making a relentlessly preachy movie about that decade's complex history.[40]

Although the music of *Cradle* serves as a backdrop rather than the main event, surprisingly few songs from the musical go entirely unheard in Robbins's film. And during the long credits, the soundtrack returns once again to "Nickel under the Foot," sung by Polly Jean Harvey and Bob Ellis, followed by a charming rendition of "Croon-Spoon," unheard in the film, sung by Eddie Vedder (the lead singer of the Pacific Northwest band Pearl Jam) and Susan Sarandon (who in the film played Mussolini's former mistress Margherita Sarfatti). At the end of the credits the last sound we hear is the bitter refrain of "Art for Art's Sake." It is not necessary to agree with Blitzstein or Robbins to be fascinated by their portrayals of an American world roiled by the economic and political crises of the 1930s, so similar in some ways to our own time.

Lady in the Dark *and* One Touch of Venus

Lady in the Dark *(1944)*

Unfortunately, neither the film version of *Lady in the Dark* (Paramount 1944) nor that of *One Touch of Venus* (Universal 1948) did much to maintain the short-lived legacy of these two major contemporary Broadway successes. While both films preserved the basic plot structure, the scores in each case were severely truncated.

To compensate for time lost in largely preserving the play component in the film adaptation of *Lady in the Dark*, a film lasting only 100 minutes, the three dream sequences, half of the music of the stage show, were drastically cut. Only fractions of the Glamour Dream and Wedding Dream were retained. The latter dream also offers a new song interpolation not by Weill, "Suddenly It's Spring" by Johnny Burke and Jimmy Van Heusen, as a replacement for "This Is New," the dramatic center of the original stage dream. The Circus Dream was shorn of both Danny Kaye and "Tschaikowsky."

Most egregious is the elimination of "My Ship." Since its completion is necessary to resolve Liza Elliott's dramatic conflicts, its fragmentary instrumental-only and hummed presentation throughout the film is never resolved nor explained. According to bruce d. mcclung, who offers the most substantial historical and critical overview of the film, the executive producer, B. G. (Buddy) DeSylva, who earlier co-wrote the lyrics for the hit show of the 1920s, *Good News!* as part of the team of DeSylva, Brown, and Henderson, did not like the song (or much of the score, for that matter) and overruled director Mitchell Leisen's wishes.[41] Despite its flaws, the film succeeded at the box office where "it racked up $4.3 million, making it the fourth-largest grossing film of 1944."[42] After that, its fate rivaled that of its stage successor by retreating even more deeply into darkness and near oblivion.

One Touch of Venus *(1948)*

The initial idea was a film musical starring the original Venus, Mary Martin, and featuring the original dances of Agnes de Mille. Mary Pickford, a leading actress from the silent era and early talkies and a co-founder of United Artists in 1919, had purchased the screen rights while the hit show was still running in 1943. After a series of delays, the rights were sold to Universal in 1947 and the revamped film, directed by William A. Seiter and produced by Seiter and Lester Cowan, was released in 1948 without the services of either Martin or de Mille, or even much of Weill and Nash, a torso of the show's full form as seen on the Broadway stage.[43] Perhaps the greatest disappointment is that viewers of this adaptation hear only three songs from the tuneful score, "Speak Low," "That's Him," and "Foolish Heart," none of which are placed in their stage contexts and are only partially sung by their rightful owners. To add injury to insult, in the song last named, the words of Ogden Nash are replaced by those of Ann Ronell, including a new title ("Don't Look Now but My Heart Is Showing"). Even though the total film length adds up to only eighty-two minutes, one will have to wait thirty-three minutes before hearing the first of these songs, "Speak Low." "That's Him" appears about forty-four minutes into the film, "Foolish Heart" ("Don't Look Now") about sixteen minutes later, and a reprise of "Speak Low" appears five minutes before the end.

Although the story is roughly equivalent to the stage version, several of the plot machinations are quite different. Rodney (renamed Eddie) Hatch has been given a new male friend Joe Grant, played by one of the two actors whose actual voices are heard on the soundtrack, Dick Haymes, a popular singer of the day who played a major character in Rodgers and Hammerstein's *State Fair* three years earlier.[44] Considering how little they sing together, Rodney spends a considerable amount of time onscreen with Venus (Ava Gardner). Onstage, Gloria (Olga San Juan, the other singer in the film) disappears for long stretches; now she shares music of the film with Joe, and, not surprisingly, they gradually fall in love. As in the stage version, Rodney will end up with a Venus look-alike, this one by the name of Venus Jones (also played by Gardner just as Mary Martin played Venus and her earthling surrogate onstage) after the real Venus has returned to the land of the Gods and her earthly remains have become re-solidified as a statue. The popular Haymes naturally sings in two of the three songs, the second of which, formerly a solo for Venus (Martin), is now a double duet in two juxtaposed scenes, one between Eddie and Venus, the other between Joe and Gloria, an interesting cinematic flourish. The other major new plot wrinkle revolves around Whitfield (onstage Whitelaw) Savory's gradual awareness that the love of his life is not Venus but his assistant Molly, played with characteristic acerbic wit by Eve Arden.

The role of Hatch was assigned to the non-singing Robert Walker. In recent years Walker had acted the role of two great songwriters, Jerome Kern in *Till the Clouds Roll By* (1946) and Johannes Brahms in *Song of Love* (1947) and was convincing as the milquetoast window dresser who brings the statue of Venus to life with an impulsive kiss. Gardner's voice was dubbed by Eileen Wilson; three years later in the 1951 remake of *Show Boat*, Gardner's Julie LaVerne would be dubbed by Annette Warren on screen (although strangely Gardner's own voice is heard on the *Show Boat* soundtrack album). Not long after making her first major film impression playing opposite Burt Lancaster in *The Killers* (1946), based on a Hemingway story, Gardner was invariably assigned to roles where physical beauty was a major prerequisite. Ephraim Katz in *The Film Encyclopedia* offers the following description that might help explain why Gardner was chosen to play Venus: "A sensuous, sloe-eyed beauty, with a magnetic, tigresslike quality of sexuality, she replaced Rita Hayworth in the late 40s as Hollywood's *love goddess* [italics mine] and occupied that position until the ascent of Marilyn Monroe in the mid-50s."[45]

Although it remains not only a poor replica of the *Venus* book, lyrics, and score seen and heard onstage four years earlier, the musical film *Venus* is not without its charms as a story. Walker, Arden, and Tim Conway as Whitfield carry off their respective characters with aplomb, Haymes sings his two songs mellifluously, and the visual fluctuations between Venus/Eddie and Gloria/Joe in "Foolish Heart" are welcome. The film also contains some chase scenes that recall the early Keystone Cops routines, which may be attributed to the fact that the film's director William Seiter was himself once a Keystone Cop.

After experiencing the indignity of having songs deleted and, even worse, replaced, in *Lady in the Dark*, composer Kurt Weill insisted on a contract for *One Touch of Venus* that would include a "non-interpolation clause," in which no music by other composers could be inserted. As he explained in a letter to his agent, Leah Salisbury, "All the songs in the picture have to be taken from the score, and the underscoring has to be based on themes from the original score."[46] The studio honored these conditions to the letter; the end result was a film adaptation that contained only the shell of the original score (and no new songs by others to fill in) and a few Weill songs inserted here and there between long stretches of dialogue.

This survey of film adaptations from *Show Boat* to *One Touch of Venus* reveals much about Hollywood's response to their Broadway sources. The goal during these years was to entertain and engage a film audience, not to offer a replica of a sacrosanct stage artifact. Only the Nunn version of *Porgy and Bess*, which appeared nearly sixty years later, comes close to depicting a Broadway stage version, but even here the very completeness of the film, ironically, belies its "authenticity" (a problematic term) since in 1935 attendees at the opera's first performances saw and heard a version of the work perhaps forty minutes shorter. Most of the films discussed in this chapter present heavily revised books and brutally abbreviated scores, sometimes with additional music by the original or newly contracted composers, and sometimes with recycled music from the original songwriter's trunk placed in new contexts. It is probably not an exaggeration to assert that with the exception of *Show Boat*, these adaptations fall short of the best original films that use the music of the composers and lyricists featured in act I of *Enchanted Evenings*. We will conclude this chapter with a summary of other adaptations in relation to the original musicals with scores by Kern, Porter, the Gershwins, and Rodgers and Hart.[47]

• KERN
Of this quartet, Kern was probably the most frequently adapted with reasonable success. In fact, a number of films retained a significant amount of his music, including *The Cat and the Fiddle* and *Music in the Air* in 1934 and *Sweet Adeline* and *Roberta* in 1935.

• PORTER
We have already noted that the adaptation of *Gay Divorce* (renamed *The Gay Divorcée*) salvaged only one song, "Night and Day." Film adaptations of *Something for the Boys* and *Mexican Hayride* contained no songs by Porter; *Paris* and *Fifty Million Frenchmen* confined Porter's music to background noise; *Let's Face It* offered two songs; *Dubarry Was a Lady*, three; and *Panama Hattie*, four. For worthy films with Porter's music—prior to the 1953 adaptation of *Kiss Me, Kate* discussed in chapter 14—one would have to turn to the original film musicals *Born to Dance* (1936), *Rosalie* (1937), and *Broadway Melody of 1940*, and the modern-day biopic *De-Lovely* (2004), the latter chock full of stylistically updated Porter chestnuts starring Kevin Kline as the composer-lyricist.

• THE GERSHWINS
The films of George and Ira Gershwin were similarly disappointing as Broadway adaptations. *Strike Up the Band* offers only the title tune. At least the 1943 *Girl Crazy*, also starring Judy Garland and Mickey Rooney, had the sense to retain six of the 1930 original's fourteen songs, plus the Gershwin hit originally composed in 1924 for Fred Astaire in *Lady, Be Good!*, "Fascinating Rhythm." *Funny Face* (1957), with Astaire reprising his original stage role thirty years later, satisfies as a film musical, but with only five songs

from the original, "Clap Yo' Hands" from another show, three interpolated song numbers by Roger Edens and Leonard Gershe, and a new scenario and script, it falls far short as a reliable adaptation of the Gershwin musical as it appeared onstage. Fortunately, George lived long enough to complete outstanding film scores the year he died (1937) for *Shall We Dance* with Astaire and Rogers and *Damsel in Distress* with Astaire, George Burns and Gracie Allen, and the non-dancing Joan Fontaine. Long after George's death his music and Ira's lyrics served as the centerpiece for another fine original musical, *An American in Paris* (1951), produced by Arthur Freed, directed by Vincente Minnelli, to an award-winning screenplay by Alan Jay Lerner, and starring its choreographer Gene Kelly.

• RODGERS AND HART

Of the many films adapted from the stage musicals of Rodgers and Hart, none rivaled the increasingly recognized classic original film *Love Me Tonight* (1932), produced and directed by Rouben Mamoulian and starring Maurice Chevalier, Jeanette MacDonald, and Charles Ruggles. Of the rest, *Too Many Girls*, directed by its Broadway director George Abbott and starring four members of the original stage cast, managed to salvage half of the score, seven songs—if you have been counting, this is close to a record for film adaptations. *Girls* also added a new instant classic by Rodgers and Hart, "You're Nearer," and even kept much of the original libretto intact. Five of the six songs from Rodgers and Hart's *Jumbo* can be heard in the 1962 film, which retains the basic plot and, twenty-seven years after its Broadway debut, its original star, Jimmy Durante.

In the film adaptation of *On Your Toes* (Warner Bros. 1938) none of the songs are sung, and only four tunes are heard in unobtrusive underscoring ("There's a Small Hotel," "Quiet Night," and "On Your Toes"). On the other hand, *Toes* does contain the "Princesse Zenobia" and "Slaughter on Tenth Avenue" ballets with the original choreography by George Balanchine and featuring Vera Zorina. About thirty seconds of the latter can be seen in the documentary *Richard Rodgers: The Sweetest Sounds*, but the film itself was never released on either VHS or DVD.[48] The best place to find "Slaughter" on film is the athletic duet between Rodgers and Hart stage alums Gene Kelly (the original Pal Joey) and Vera Ellen (Mistress Evelyn in the 1943 revival of *Connecticut Yankee*) on the easily obtainable Rodgers and Hart biopic *Words and Music* (1948).[49]

Although three of the films discussed in this chapter are difficult to locate and all offer distortions of one kind or another, these film adaptations offer their share of compensations. In particular, *Show Boat* and *Anything Goes* let us see some of the original stars or other actors and actresses associated with early productions. Seeing and hearing Charles Winninger, the original Broadway Cap'n Andy, Paul Robeson, the original London Joe, or Ethel Merman, the original Reno Sweeney sing their songs in a film that is roughly contemporaneous to their theatrical performances is worth the time it takes to find these films. Some of the shows have even retained a surprising amount of original dialogue, even when the plots are greatly altered. Although they are destined to disappoint musically they are worth getting to know, as long as you know what you're missing.

· Act II ·

The Broadway Musical After *Oklahoma!*

CHAPTER NINE

CAROUSEL

The Invasion of the Integrated Musical

Working under the premise that success begets success, Rodgers and Hammerstein followed the phenomenal triumph of *Oklahoma!* (1943) by assembling much of the same production team for their second hit, *Carousel* (1945). Like their historic opening salvo, *Carousel* was produced by the Theatre Guild and supervised by Theresa Helburn and Lawrence Langner, the pair who had given Rodgers and Hart their big break in 1925, *The Garrick Gaieties*. For their director the Theatre Guild selected Rouben Mamoulian, who had directed *Oklahoma!* as well as Rodgers and Hart's classic film *Love Me Tonight* in 1932, the play *Porgy* in 1927, and the opera *Porgy and Bess* in 1935 (both of the latter were also Theatre Guild productions). Agnes de Mille was again asked to choreograph, and Miles White designed the costumes.

Ferenc Molnár's play *Liliom*, which premiered in Hungary in 1909, had been successfully presented by the Guild in 1921 with the legendary Eva Le Gallienne and Joseph Schildkraut, and more recently in 1940 in a production that starred Ingrid Bergman and Burgess Meredith. After some initial resistance, Molnár, who had allegedly turned down an offer by Puccini (and Weill and perhaps Gershwin as well) to make an opera out of his play, reportedly agreed in 1944 to allow the Theatre Guild to adapt his play: "After fifteen months, all the legal technicalities involved in the production of the musical version of *Liliom* were settled last week."[1] The *New York Post* went on to say that "the smallest percentage, eight tenths of one percent, go to Ferenc Molnár, who merely wrote the play."

Rodgers and Hammerstein. © AL HIRSCHFELD. Reproduced by
arrangement with Hirschfeld's exclusive representative, the MARGO
FEIDEN GALLERIES LTD., NEW YORK. WWW. ALHIRSCHFELD.COM

The idea for setting Molnár's play came from the Theatre Guild, who
naturally wanted to reproduce a second *Oklahoma!* Writing in the *New York
Times* four days before the birth of the new sibling, Hammerstein recalled
Helburn and Langner propositioning the creators of their previous blockbuster in Sardi's "toward the end of January, 1944." The main obstacle for
Hammerstein was the Hungarian setting. When, the following week, the persistent Helburn offered a more promising alternative locale in Louisiana, the
required dialect also proved to be "a disconcerting difficulty" for the librettist. Sources agree that the workable idea to "transplant the play to the New
England coast" came from Rodgers and that the starting point for the show
was Billy Bigelow's "Soliloquy." In *Musical Stages* Rodgers wrote that once the
team had conceived "the notion for a soliloquy in which, at the end of the first

act, the leading character would reveal his varied emotions about impending fatherhood," the central problem of how to sing *Liliom* was resolved.[2]

Although their contract allowed Rodgers and Hammerstein considerable latitude in their adaptation, they were nonetheless relieved to learn during an early rehearsal run-through that the playwright had given his blessing to their changes, including a greatly altered ending.[3] In the play, a defiant Liliom does not regret his actions and is doomed to purgatory for fifteen years. He is then required to return to earth for a day to atone for his sins. While on earth, disguised as a beggar, Liliom slaps his daughter when she refuses the star he stole from heaven; she sends him away, and the play ends on this pessimistic note. In the musical a much more sympathetic Liliom, renamed Billy Bigelow, comes to earth by choice, appears as himself, and can choose either to be seen or to remain invisible. As in the play he has stolen a star and slaps his daughter Louise, but now the slap feels like a kiss (in the play it felt like a caress). In stark contrast to the play, the musical's final scene shows Billy, in his remaining moments on earth, helping his "little girl" at her graduation to overcome her loneliness and misery. To the inspirational strains of "You'll Never Walk Alone," with its somewhat dubious advice if taken literally ("when you walk through a storm keep your chin up high"), Louise finds the courage to live, Julie realizes that her marriage—in Molnár's less family-oriented play she remained Billy's mistress—was worth the pain. Billy redeems his soul, and even the most jaded of contemporary audiences find themselves shedding real tears.

Auditions began in February 1945 and tryouts took place the following months in New Haven (March 22–25) and Boston (March 27–April 15). Elliot Norton describes the principal dramatic alteration made during the Boston tryouts:

> The original heaven of *Carousel* was a New England parlor, bare and plain. In it sat a stern Yankee, listed on the program as He. At a harmonium, playing softly, sat his quiet consort, identified as She. Later some observers [including Rodgers] referred to this celestial couple as Mr. and Mrs. God....
>
> Richard Rodgers, walking back to the hotel with his collaborator afterwards, put it to Oscar Hammerstein bluntly:
>
> "We've got to get God out of that parlor!"
>
> Mild Oscar Hammerstein agreed.
>
> "I know you're right," he said. "But where shall I put Him?"
>
> "I don't care where you put Him," said Richard Rodgers. "Put Him up on a ladder, for all I care, only get Him out of that parlor!"
>
> So Oscar Hammerstein put Him up on a ladder. He discarded the sitting room too, and put his deity into a brand new sequence.

On a ladder in the backyard of heaven, He became the Star-Keeper, polishing stars which hung on lines strung across the floor of infinity, while a sullen Billy Bigelow looked and listened to his quiet admonitions.[4]

Carousel's premiere took place at the Majestic Theatre on April 19, and the show closed a little more than two years later on May 24, 1947, after a run of 890 performances. Following a successful national tour, *Carousel* began another impressive run of 566 performances at London's Drury Lane on June 7, 1950 (closing on October 13, 1951). Major New York revivals took place at the New York City Center Light Opera in 1954, 1957, and 1967; at the Music Theater of Lincoln Center in 1965; and in 1994 with an acclaimed New York staging based on the Royal National Theater of Great Britain production.

Almost without exception *Carousel* opened to rave reviews. Nevertheless, most critics could not resist the temptation to compare the new work to *Oklahoma!*, then beginning its third year on Broadway. Although an anonymous reviewer in the *New York World-Telegram* found "the distinct flavor of 'Oklahoma!'" in "A Real Nice Clambake," persistent rumors that the latter song once belonged to the former and titled "A Real Nice Hayride," are unsubstantiated.[5] Ward Morehouse's review in the *New York Sun* is representative in its conclusion that the laudatory *Carousel* could not quite match the earlier masterpiece: "'Carousel,' a touching and affecting musical play, is something rare in the theater. It's a hit, and of that there can be no doubt. If it is not the musical piece to challenge 'Oklahoma' for all-time honors it is certainly one that deserves its place in the 44th Street block. The team of Rodgers and Hammerstein will go on forever."[6]

A handful of reviewers regarded the new musical more favorably than its predecessor. According to John Chapman, "'Carousel' is one of the finest musical plays I have seen and I shall remember it always. It has everything the professional theatre can give it—and something besides: heart, integrity, an inner glow."[7] Although reviewers then and now found the second-act ballet too long, Robert Garland wrote that "when somebody writes a better musical play than 'Carousel,' written by Richard Rodgers and Oscar Hammerstein, Richard Rodgers and Oscar Hammerstein will have to write it."[8]

By the time it returned to New York in 1954 the climate of critical opinion had shifted further, and Brooks Atkinson could now write that *Carousel* "is the most glorious of the Rodgers and Hammerstein works." Atkinson continued: "Three of the Rodgers and Hammerstein shows have had longer runs than 'Carousel.' It is the stepchild among 'Oklahoma!' 'South Pacific,' and 'The King and I.' But when the highest judge of all hands down the ultimate verdict, it is this column's opinion that 'Carousel' will turn out to be the finest of their creations. If it were not so enjoyable, it would probably turn out to be opera."[9]

Carousel would also remain the pride and joy of its creators. For Rodgers, especially, the second musical with Hammerstein stood as his personal favorite among all his forty musicals. Without any false sense of modesty he conveyed his reasons: "Oscar never wrote more meaningful or more moving lyrics, and to me, my score is more satisfying than any I've ever written. But it's not just the songs; it's the whole play. Beautifully written, tender without being mawkish, it affects me deeply every time I see it performed."[10]

The above critical reception and the judgment of its authors partially explains why *Carousel* and not *Oklahoma!* was selected for examination in the present survey. But given the importance attributed to *Oklahoma!* as the "Eroica" Symphony of the American musical, the question "Why not *Oklahoma!*?" nevertheless lingers and needs to be addressed. The simple answer is that *Oklahoma!*'s incalculable historical importance as the musical that changed all musicals is equaled and arguably surpassed dramatically and musically by *Carousel*. Not content to merely duplicate their earlier success, Rodgers and Hammerstein in their second musical attempted to convey a still richer dramatic situation with characters who were perhaps more complexly realized, through music, than the inhabitants of the Oklahoma Territory.

Further, the artistic ambitions in *Carousel* are matched by a deeper relationship between music and drama. The integrated songs in *Oklahoma!* grow naturally from the action and reflect each character's idiosyncratic nature. But, like *Show Boat* and *Porgy and Bess* before it and *West Side Story* after, the music of *Carousel* develops action and explores nuances of characterization that frequently transcend what the characters themselves understand.[11] The analysis that follows will suggest how Rodgers and Hammerstein's imitation may have surpassed (artistically if not in popularity) not only its model but many other musicals that have had their two or more hours' traffic on the Broadway stage.

The "Bench Scene"

In several respects Julie Jordan, who moves us by her ability to see the good qualities in her abusive husband, Billy Bigelow, and by her uncompromising loyalty to his memory, bears a stronger kinship to Hammerstein's *Show Boat* heroine Magnolia Ravenal than to *Oklahoma!*'s Laurey. Even the message of its central song, "What's the Use of Wondrin,'" like that of *Carousel* as a whole, echoes Hammerstein's theme in *Show Boat* as embodied in the song "Can't Help Lovin' Dat Man": once fate brings two lovers together "all the rest is talk." Julie shares with Magnolia rather than her Oklahoma cousin a common destiny—to love a man who will eventually generate much unhappiness. Like Magnolia, Julie will also meet the man she will love early in her show.[12]

Also like Magnolia and Ravenal, Julie and Billy—as well as Laurey and Curley in the analogous "People Will Say We're in Love"—describe a hypothetical rather than an acknowledged love, at least at the outset of their duets. The romantic leads in *Show Boat*, however, declare their love in the waltz "You Are Love" at the emotional climax of act I and offer additional explanations for their feelings early in act II when they sing "Why Do I Love You?" (at least before Hal Prince gave this song to Parthy in the 1994 Broadway revival). In contrast, Julie and Billy, more tragically, are unable to express their love directly, not only in their first duet, "If I Loved You," but at any point in the drama, at least while Billy is alive.

In an extremely poignant moment that immediately follows Billy's suicide in act II, scene 2, Julie finally manages to share her feelings with her deceased husband: "One thing I never told you—skeered you'd laugh at me. I'll tell you now—(*Even now she has to make an effort to overcome her shyness in saying it*) I love you. I love you. (*In a whisper*) I love—you. (*Smiles*) I was always ashamed to say it out loud. But now I said it. Didn't I?"[13]

Outside Julie's cottage three scenes later, Billy, whose presence is felt rather than seen or heard, finally sings his love in the following reprise (release and final A section) of "If I Loved You." According to Rodgers, this inspired new idea was, after the removal of Mr. and Mrs. God, the only other major change made during the tryouts. "Longing to tell you, / But afraid and *shy*, / I let my golden chances pass me *by*. / Now I've lost you; / Soon I will go in the mist of day, / And you never will know / How I loved you. / How I loved you."[14]

Just as Kern conveys Magnolia's penetration into Ravenal's being by merging her music with his, Rodgers finds subtle musical ways to let audiences know that Julie's love for Billy is similarly more than hypothetical. During the opening exchange between Carrie and Julie, for example, Julie's friend makes it clear that she knows why Julie is behaving so "queerly." First, Carrie describes Julie's recent habit of rising early and sitting silently by the window. Julie lamely denies this circumstantial evidence of love sickness ("I like to watch the river meet the sea"), but Carrie's next and more telling observation of Julie's behavior on the job, the "Mill Theme" (Example 9.1) is incontrovertible: "When we work in the mill, weavin' at the loom, / Y' gaze absent-minded at the *roof*, / And half the time yer shuttle gets twisted in the threads / Till y'can't tell the warp from the *woof*!"[15]

Although Julie denies even this evidence with a "'Tain't so!," her strangeness, even more than Frankie's in *On Your Toes*, cannot be attributed to

Example 9.1. The "Mill Theme"

tonsillitis or to the combination of pickles and pie à la mode: it's got to be love. The sensitive Carrie, now that Julie has a "feller," can inform Julie of her own romantic good fortune in being courted by the young entrepreneur Enoch Snow. This time Julie does not attempt to deny Carrie's presumption. When Julie explains to Billy minutes later how she would behave, hypothetically, "if she loved him," Rodgers and Hammerstein have her describe, again to the "Mill Theme," the behavior that Carrie has in fact already observed. Julie's denial of love may satisfy Billy, but it fails to convince either Carrie or a knowing audience who has more than sufficient textual and musical evidence to catch Julie in her self-deception.

The spark that will eventually set fire to Julie and Billy has already been lit in the pantomimed prelude to act I.[16] During this prelude we see that Billy "takes his mind off his work" when he watches Julie and that she gains his attention in part by being the only person who does not "sway unconsciously with the rhythm of his words." The description of the prelude's action points out (parenthetically) that "Billy's attitude to Julie throughout this scene is one of only casual and laconic interest." Although he makes a point of finding the last place on the carousel for Julie, he then "dismisses her from his mind." When he later waves "patronizingly," the omniscient description notes that "it means nothing to him," but that "it means so much to her that she nearly falls!"[17]

"If I Loved You," the climactic moment in the following Bench Scene (act I, scene 1), reinforces these discrepancies in emotional intensity and awareness between the principals. Julie sings as a young woman already in love; Billy, although he admits to having noticed Julie at the carousel "three times before today" (she has actually been there far more often) sings, if not about a hypothetical love, about a love that he does not yet comprehend. Thus Billy can truthfully assert that if he loved Julie he would be "scrawny and pale," and "lovesick like any other guy." So far none of these symptoms has appeared. In fact, Billy does not realize until act II, scene 5, what Mrs. Mullin, the jealous, older, and less desirable carousel proprietress, has understood only too well as early as the prelude. Already in the pantomimed introduction Mrs. Mullin has demonstrated that, like Julie, she is enamored of Billy. Also in the prelude Mrs. Mullin has observed his unique attraction to Julie. We learn later that Mrs. Mullin correctly perceived that this peculiar young woman posed a serious threat both to her business—the other young women would

Carousel, prelude to act I. Jan Clayton and John Raitt on the carousel (1945). Museum of the City of New York. Theater Collection.

patronize the carousel less ardently if Billy were romantically attached—and to any more personal relationship she might enjoy with her favorite barker.

Although Rodgers and Hammerstein have the two love-struck mill workers, Carrie and Julie, sing the same tune, "You're a Queer One, Julie Jordan," Rodgers musically differentiates the sharp character distinctions drawn by Hammerstein. He does this by contrasting Carrie's even eighth-note rhythms ("You are quieter and deeper than a well") with Julie's dotted eighths and sixteenths ("There nothin' that I keer t'choose t' tell") (Example 9.2a); revealingly, Billy will whistle Julie's dotted rhythms rather than Carrie's even ones (Example 9.2b). A clue to Rodgers's intention might be found in his autobiography, *Musical Stages*, where he discusses how "It Might as Well Be Spring," from the Rodgers and Hammerstein film musical *State Fair* (Example 9.2c), serves as "a good example of the way a tune can amplify the meaning of its lyric."[18] Rodgers continues: "The first lines are: 'I'm as restless as a willow in a wind storm, / I'm as jumpy as a puppet on a string.' Taking its cue directly from these words, the music itself is appropriately restless and jumpy."[19]

Example 9.2. "Jumpy" rhythms in *Carousel* and *State Fair*
    (a) Julie and Carrie Sequence (*Carousel*)
    (b) Scene Billy and Julie (*Carousel*)
    (c) "It Might As Well Be Spring" (*State Fair*)
    (d) Julie and Carrie Sequence (*Carousel*)

(c)

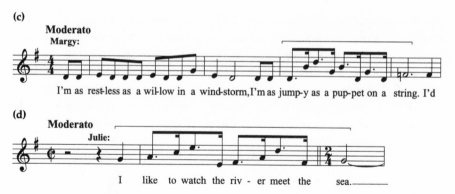

(d)

Example 9.2. Continued

Clearly, Julie's dotted rhythms when she sings "There's nothin' that I keer t' choose t' *tell*," almost identical in pitch to Carrie's "You are quieter and deeper than a *well*," successfully contrasts Julie's restlessness with Carrie's stability. When Julie tells Carrie that she likes "to watch the river meet the sea" (Example 9.2d), Rodgers presents a dotted melodic line filled with wide leaps that are unmistakably "jumpy as a puppet on a string." Once Rodgers has established Julie's sharp rhythmic profile in her opening exchange with Carrie, he shows Julie's influence over her friend when Carrie adopts dotted rhythms to conclude their sung exchange ("And as silent as an old Sahaira Spink!"). More significantly, Julie's dotted rhythms return when Billy reprises "You're a queer one" after Carrie's "Mister Snow" and Julie repeats her dotted jumpy melodic line to the words "I reckon that I keer t' choose t' stay."

In the closing moments of the first act, Billy's imaginary daughter, appropriately enough, will share Julie's restlessness and her dotted rhythms. By the time Billy sings the "My little girl" portion of his "Soliloquy," dotted rhythms have acquired a strong association with Julie, and by extension her as-yet-unborn daughter, Louise. Thus when Billy imagines his daughter as "half again as bright" and a girl who "gets hungry every night," Rodgers has the future father sing Julie's dotted rhythms. True to her character, in the second act Julie's "What's the Use of Wondrin'" also makes persistent use of dotted rhythms. On this occasion, however, Rodgers captures Julie's newly acquired inner peace when he replaces with more sedate scales the jumpy melodic leaps that characterized her conversations with Carrie and Billy in act I, scene 1.

Rodgers also gives dramatic meaning to another distinctive rhythm in *Carousel*: the triplet. The main association between triplets and the principal lovers occurs when each attempts to answer what would happen if they loved the other in the song "If I loved you." The "hidden" triplets in their response to this subjunctive (Example 9.3a) reinforce the unreality and hesitation that matches the lines "Time and again I would try to say" and "words wouldn't come in an easy way." Not only do these words appear on the weak beats (second and fourth) of their measures–in marked contrast to the triplets in "Many a New Day" from *Oklahoma!* (Example 3.1b)—they are invariably tied to the stronger beats (first and third).

Of course, the imagined musical responses of Julie and Billy nevertheless reveal the truth that Julie is hiding from Billy and Billy from himself: the two misfits in fact are already in love. Although their desire for verbal communication is great ("Time and again I would try to say all I'd want you to know" or "Longing to tell you, but afraid and shy"), the pair must rely on music to express their deepest feelings. Words do not "come in an easy way." Most poignantly, as if to reflect the painful truth of the few words they do sing, within a few months Billy indeed will be leaving Julie "in the mist of day."

Just as Billy adopts Julie's dotted rhythms in his "Soliloquy," he will adopt in this central (and earliest-composed song) the triplets that he shared with Julie in "If I Loved You." In contrast to the hesitant tied triplets of his duet with Julie, however, Billy in his private "Soliloquy" sings "Many a New Day"-type triplets that stand alone when he envisions having a daughter (compare Example 9.3b with Example 3.1b).[20] After Billy's death, triplets also

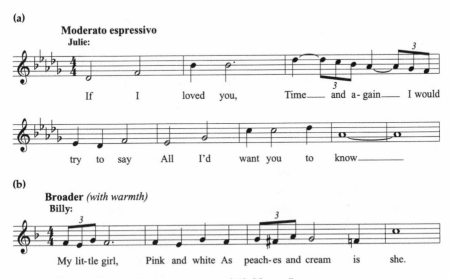

Example 9.3. Triplets in "If I Loved You" and "Soliloquy"
(a) "If I Loved You"
(b) "Soliloquy"

provide a brief but distinctive contrast in the release of Julie's "What's the Use of Wondrin'" to the ubiquitous dotted rhythms of the main melody.

It makes musical sense, of course, for Rodgers to fill his prelude with waltzes to accompany the swirling of the carousel. But marches and polkas would be equally suitable. Rodgers knew, however, that waltzes, although capable of expressing a variety of meanings and emotions, had been associated with love ever since Viennese imports had dominated Broadway in the decade before World War I.[21] The most familiar waltz musical then and now was and is Lehár's *The Merry Widow*, the work that launched an operetta invasion on Broadway in 1907. But waltzes had also figured prominently in 1920s operetta. Several of these featured lyrics by Hammerstein himself, including "You Are Love" in *Show Boat*. Later, in *The King and I*'s "Hello, Young Lovers" and *South Pacific*'s "A Wonderful Guy" Rodgers gives Anna Leonowens and Nellie Forbush waltzes when they sing of love, and Nellie's temporarily rejected suitor Emile De Becque sings a waltz lamenting a lost love in "This Nearly Was Mine."

In *Carousel* waltzes are associated either with the carousel itself, as in the procession of the several sharply defined waltzes that make up the panto-mimed prelude, or in the chorus of community solidarity that character-izes the main tune of "A Real Nice Clambake." Rodgers and Hammerstein therefore match the absence of directly expressed love between Billy and Julie by *not* allowing them to sing a waltz. Only when Billy sings his succes-sions of triplets in his "Soliloquy" does Rodgers suggest a waltz (Example 9.4a), a suggestion that is reinforced with a melodic fragment identical to the melody of the final carousel waltz (Example 9.4b). Characteristically, Billy must keep his waltzes, as well as his expression of love, to himself.

Rodgers and Hammerstein and the Integrated Musical

As early as the 1920s, Rodgers strove to create musicals in which songs were thoroughly integrated into a dramatic whole. In his finest efforts with Hart, including *On Your Toes* and *Pal Joey*, and in his first collaboration with Hammerstein, *Oklahoma!*, Rodgers often succeeded in making the songs flow naturally from the dialogue and express character. But it was not until *Carousel* that Rodgers created a thoroughly unified musical score which also achieved a truly convincing coordination (i.e., integration) between music and dramatic action. Earlier, in *On Your Toes, Pal Joey*, and *Oklahoma!* Rod-gers used the technique of thematic transformation for dramatic purposes, but the resulting musical unity did not always reinforce a drama generated by musical forces.

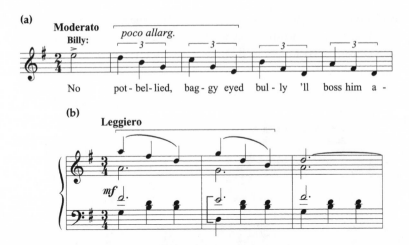

Example 9.4. "Soliloquy" and "The Carousel Waltz" (fifth waltz)
(a) "Soliloquy"
(b) "The Carousel Waltz" (fifth waltz)

In *Carousel*, many musical details, including the subtle reuse and transformation of rhythms that correspond to musical characters previously noted, frequently support dramatic details and generate dramatic themes. Some of these details serve more a musical than a dramatic purpose in their integration of disparate sections. For example, the parallelisms between the musical phrases that Carrie uses to describe Julie ("You are quieter and deeper than a well") and Mr. Snow ("He comes home ev'ry night in his round-bottomed boat") in the opening scene might be considered a musically meaningful but dramatically irrelevant unifying detail.

On the other hand, the primary accompaniment of "If I Loved You," in which three arpeggiated eighth notes follow an eighth rest, foreshadows the less breathless collection of four arpeggiated eighth notes that mark the first half of most measures of "Two Little People" (a melody which also not incidentally exhibits several prominent quarter-note triplets).[22] The musical link between the accompaniments of "If I Loved You" and "Two Little People" (Example 9.5a and b) shows up more clearly in the holograph manuscript on deposit at the Library of Congress, where the two songs share the key of C major.[23] Even those who refuse to see the accompaniment of "If I Loved You" as a foreshadowing of the accompaniment to "Two Little People" might acknowledge its connection with "You'll Never Walk Alone" (Example 9.5c). In this song the arpeggiated eighth-note figure is now continuous, not only for an entire measure but for nearly the entire song (Rodgers breaks the pattern in the final four measures). "If I Loved You" and

"Two Little People" demonstrate the unity between Billy and Julie; "You'll Never Walk Alone" signifies musically as well as dramatically that neither of these star-crossed lovers will walk alone as long as Julie carries Billy in her memory.[24]

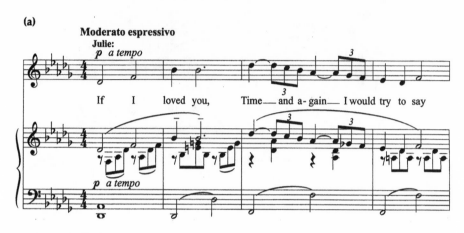

Example 9.5. Arpeggiated accompaniments
   (a) "If I Loved You"
   (b) "Two Little People"
   (c) "You'll Never Walk Alone"

(c)

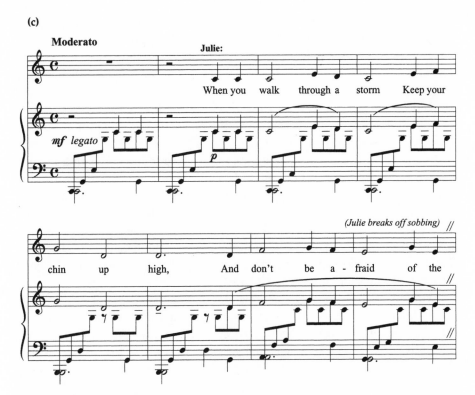

Example 9.5. Continued

Rodgers and Hammerstein also manage to convey a musical correspondence that matches the dramatic contrasts between two pairs of contrasting romantic leads (de rigueur in musicals for the next twenty years): Billy Bigelow and Julie Jordan on one end of the spectrum, Enoch Snow and Carrie Pipperidge on the other. In stark contrast to Billy (a baritone), Enoch (a tenor) is a man who plans ahead, whether he is building a fleet of herring boats or a fleet of children. With his irritating, self-satisfied laugh Enoch is reminiscent of Laurey's silly rival Gertie in *Oklahoma!* and embodies the negative as well as the positive consequences of conventionality and practicality.

When he gives Carrie flowers, Enoch, the builder and planner, gives her a package of geranium seeds to plant rather than the beautiful but ephemeral real thing. And when he tells Julie that he likes to "plant and take keer" of flowers, Julie replies that Billy "likes t' smell 'em," an impractical romantic trait that endeared the carousel barker to her in their first scene together. By the latter part of act II, Enoch has metamorphosed from an overbearing but essentially likable hard-working man with lofty plans for his sardine business and his family to an insufferable, condescending, and genuinely unsympathetic character. Unfortunately, his fleet of children are created in his image. Further, in opposition to Carrie's open appreciation for the less savory entertainments witnessed on their trip to New York, the pure-as-snow Enoch (the name is also uncomfortably close to eunuch) suggests that she discuss the Shakespeare play instead. Enoch's surreptitious visit to the burlesque house (where he runs into Carrie) adds hypocrisy to a growing list of negative characteristics, even if this action allows him a human vice that audiences might relate to.

In an age increasingly and justifiably less tolerant of wife-beating in any form and for any reason, Billy might be considered a much less wonderful guy than he was in 1945 (certainly than 1873), even if Rodgers and Hammerstein's Billy is less abrasive than Molnár's Liliom. Although his predilection for violence is indefensible—to satisfy his fragile ego he hits Julie because she is on the right side of their arguments—it is significant as part of the fantasy that his blows do not *hurt* either Julie or later Louise. In fact, when he slaps his daughter it feels like a kiss.

Without condoning Billy's actions Hammerstein seems to be telling us that other forms of abuse might take an even greater toll. By the end of act II, Mr. Snow's verbal abuse and condescension have at least partially stifled his formerly spunky bride, whereas Julie Bigelow never fears to stand up to her husband. When Mr. Snow and Carrie glorify their conventional and quotidian life in their duet, "When the Children Are Asleep," it is difficult not to notice that Enoch's love for Carrie is based on her maintaining a conventional image as the "little woman." Billy and Julie may each lose their jobs within minutes of their meeting, certainly a bad omen for their future stability, but their inarticulate and unexpressed love contains a richness lacking in the conventional courtship and marriage of Enoch and Carrie.

On the surface Enoch and Carrie conclude their act I duet "When the Children Are Asleep" in a close harmony that befits their harmonious image of marital bliss. Nevertheless, this happiness depends in large part on Carrie's willingness to overlook the fact that Mr. Snow makes all the plans for the two of them. Snow also adds musical injury to emotional insult by interrupting Carrie's turn at the chorus, ironically with the words "dreams that won't be interrupted." Billy may be a surly bully who occasionally strikes his wife offstage, but he never interrupts Julie when they sing. Unlike Snow, Billy allows his future bride to complete her song.[25] Perhaps more significantly, when he sings by himself, Billy allows Julie's character—musically depicted by dotted rhythms and triplets—to infiltrate his thoughts and become a part of him. The pretentiousness of Mr. Snow and his fleet of nine offspring may cause many in the audience to take pity on Carrie for having so many children, one more than she had agreed to when Snow presented his blueprint in the verse of "When the Children Are Asleep." Given the choice of negatives, it is certainly possible that one might prefer the fuller albeit deeply troubled lives of Billy, Julie, and, after Billy's death, their daughter Louise, to the deceptively happily-ever-after, rudely interrupted American dream of Mr. and Mrs. Snow and their brood.

Since revivals say as much about directors and their audiences as they do about the works being revived, it is not surprising that the *Carousel* of the 1990s emphasizes the show's "dark side," which was very dark indeed for the 1940s. It is also not surprising that the primary means to convey this dark side and thereby establish the work's modernity and contemporary relevance is through staging. In a bold rethinking of the work, director Nicholas Hytner took the liberty of opening his *Carousel* at the Vivian Beaumont Theater in Lincoln Center on March 24, 1994, not with the amusement park but at the Bascombe Cotton Mill. In this new setting (underscored musically by the "moderato" introduction to the sequence of fast waltzes) audiences could for the first time watch the young women mill workers "gaze absent-minded at the roof" and perhaps also at the large clock about to strike six o'clock. "As the waltz gains momentum," wrote Howard Kissel of the New York *Daily News*, "carousel horses begin circling the stage, the top of the carousel lowers into place, and the girls find release riding up and down under the admiring gaze of the handsome barker, Billy Bigelow. It takes your breath away."[26]

Reviewers were almost unanimous in praising "the most dazzling staging this musical is ever going to receive."[27] Two critics were even moved to repeat the old joke about leaving a show "humming the scenery." Others singled out the multiracial casting. Enoch and Carrie were a mixed-race couple in both the London and New York revivals; in a stylistic as well as a racial crossover, the role of Nettie was sung by the African American Shirley Verrett, a major opera star in the late 1960s and early 1970s.

Hytner's staging also intensified Billy's more sinister side. For example, no longer does Billy slap his daughter's hand when he returns to earth, he slaps her face. Thankfully, most critics, while rightly repulsed by a romanticized wife-beating hero who gains salvation (even though he does not get to sing his powerful musical plea, "The Highest Judge of All," in the second act), refused to confuse the message with the messenger. In the words of medieval scholar John Boswell, "To cite obscenity is not to be obscene."[28] In any event, Edwin Wilson concludes in the *Wall Street Journal* that "in the end, it is not Julie who can redeem Billy, but the musical alchemy of Richard Rodgers's score."[29]

In *Musical Stages* Rodgers speaks of a rhyming and rhythmic dialogue used in Mamoulian's films *Love Me Tonight* and *The Phantom President* in

1932 and the next year in *Hallelujah, I'm a Bum*. Rodgers, who preferred the term "musical dialogue" to describe the use of rhymed conversation with musical accompaniment, wrote that its purpose was "to affect a smoother transition to actual song" and to become "an authentic part of the action."[30] Twelve years later Rodgers transferred the device of "musical dialogue" to the stage to begin the Julie and Carrie sequence. In this new context the two friends begin each phrase with the rhythmic signature of Julie's name before it develops into a melodic theme, thus adding one additional layer to the dialogue-(spoken) verse-(musical speech) chorus (the main tune) progression from speech to song familiar from most theater songs of the 1920s and 1930s. By the time Billy arrives, her motive underscores their conversation before they even begin to sing. In the course of the scene the rhythm of Julie's name becomes the foundation for a series of questions (three or four syllables each) that Billy asks her about her love life: "Where'd you walk?," "In the woods?," "On the beach?," and "Did you love him?"

Also in his autobiography Rodgers reveals his sensitivity to potential word painting. In the discussion of "It Might as Well Be Spring" noted earlier and illustrated in Example 9.2c, Rodgers concludes that "since the song is sung by a young girl who can't quite understand why she feels the way she does, I deliberately ended the phrase ["I'm as jumpy as a puppet on a string"] on the uncertain sound of the F natural (on the word 'string') rather than on the more positive F sharp."[31]

Rodgers left it up to others to demonstrate how the musical details in *Carousel* support the lyrics and the libretto and create musical unity, and how such details create subtle correspondences between music, character, and drama. Nevertheless, his description of "musical dialogue" in *Love Me Tonight* and his analysis of his text-setting objectives in "It Might as Well Be Spring" reveal that Rodgers was fully conscious of how nuances can help a theater composer to achieve an artistic goal. In the light of his autobiography, a discussion of how dotted rhythms, triplets, and arpeggiated accompanimental figures reveal greater dramatic truths appears to be grounded in reality.[32] Rodgers is the first to admit that a number of his musicals created with Hart do not even aspire to, much less achieve, the goals he first enunciated in the late 1920s with *Dearest Enemy* and *Peggy-Ann*. His primary desire throughout his extraordinary career, however, was to create a musical theater in which the songs belong to their characters and determine their place within the dramatic action, and a musical theater in which dialogue, song, and dance are unified and integrated. These ideals did not suddenly appear with *Oklahoma!* and *Carousel*. After developing his vision and evolving technique as a dramatic composer with Hart, Rodgers found a collaborator who fully embraced the integrated ideal. Together, Rodgers and Hammerstein were a winning combination that forged a living and posthumous legacy of popular commercial works and a critical stature unmatched by any other body of work in the history of the American musical.

After the death of his second collaborator, Rodgers, who had by necessity ghost-written lyrics for Hart, decided to write his own lyrics for an entire show. The result, the biracial romance *No Strings* (1962) with Diahann Carroll and Richard Kiley in the principal roles, turned out to be Rodgers's final success (580 performances), albeit a modest one by the standards of *Oklahoma!, Carousel, South Pacific, The King and I,* and *The Sound of Music.* His next show, collaboration with Hammerstein's lyricist protégé Stephen Sondheim, produced the disappointing, if underrated, *Do I Hear a Waltz?* in 1965 (220 performances).

Rodgers remained active to the end. In the 1970s he managed to mount three final shows on Broadway: *Two by Two* (1970), with lyrics by Martin Charnin and starring Danny Kaye as Noah (343 performances); *Rex* (1976), with lyrics by Sheldon Harnick and starring Nicol Williamson as Henry VIII (49 performances); and *I Remember Mama* (1979), with lyrics by Charnin and Raymond Jessel and starring Liv Ullmann and George Hearn (108 performances).[33] Less than four months after his fortieth and final musical closed, Rodgers died on December 30, 1979.

Because they float at the center of the mainstream, the convention-shattering features of Rodgers and Hammerstein's adaptations of literary sources with their carefully constructed subplots (*Oklahoma!, Carousel, South Pacific,* and *The King and I*) seem less apparent than their more experimental and less successful works with original books. Among the latter are *Allegro* (1947), with its Greek chorus and abstract sets, and the back stager *Me and Juliet* (1953), in which audiences could see on- and offstage events simultaneously.[34] Just as it is often difficult for present-day listeners to appreciate the iconoclasm of the less noisy modernists (for example, the revolutionary Debussy), it requires a special effort in the post-Sondheim and Lloyd Webber era to understand just how unconventional and innovative Rodgers and Hammerstein musicals really were. Here is a glimpse of what was innovative (if not unprecedentedly new) in three of their shows, a body of work which helped to establish future conventions:

OKLAHOMA! (1943) eschews the usual opening chorus (or singer accompanied by an orchestra) and instead opens with a woman churning butter alone onstage and the hero singing "Oh, What a Beautiful Morning" (without even a piano to back him up) offstage. It also presents perhaps the first genuine, albeit pathetic, villain who dies in a struggle with a hero, and its full-length dream ballet moves several steps beyond *On Your Toes* in its integration of dance into the plot.

SOUTH PACIFIC (1949) offers the first major middle-aged romantic hero played by the first major defector from the Metropolitan Opera (Ezio Pinza). The younger romantic secondary male character dies, and the central romantic leads sing "Twin Soliloquies" to themselves "silently." The drama is conveyed through rapid and seamless scene shifts, and, most provocatively, the musical seriously explores the causes of racial prejudice in the song "Carefully Taught."

THE KING AND I (1951), based at least loosely on a true story and real people, is the first major musical in which the characters (if not the cast) are mostly Asian, a foreign language is conveyed by instruments rather than by speech, the principals never kiss and touch only once, when they are dancing, and the central male character dies at the end (and, unlike Billy Bigelow, stays dead).

Carousel (1945) was no less daring. It revolves around an unsympathetic character (when he is not singing) who hits his wife, sings a "Soliloquy" for nearly eight minutes before attempting a robbery, dies by suicide, and hits his daughter when he returns to earth (from purgatory) fifteen years later. Musicals of various types after *Oklahoma!* and *Carousel* would continue to be remembered by their songs, of course, but from now on their revivability would usually depend on integrated and more coherent books. Although by no means did they invent the so-called integrated Broadway musical (often referred to as the "sung play"), or even always adhere to the elusive integrated ideal, more than anyone else Rodgers and Hammerstein can be praised (or blamed) for demonstrating in their optimistic, homespun, and sentimental shows the commercial potential of the Rodgers and Hammerstein musical.

CHAPTER TEN

KISS ME, KATE
The Taming of Cole Porter

Two Tough Acts to Follow

Act I: Rodgers and Hammerstein

In the years following the success of *Anything Goes* in 1934 only Rodgers and Hart surpassed Porter in producing musical hits on Broadway. The Gershwins were unable to complete any more Broadway shows between *Porgy and Bess* in 1935 and George's death two years later, and Kern managed only one more new Broadway show, *Very Warm for May* (1939) in a final decade spent mainly in films. As Gershwin and Kern ebbed, Porter flowed for the remaining years of the 1930s with one successful (albeit now nearly forgotten) musical after another filled with unforgettable songs: "Begin the Beguine" and "Just One of Those Things" from *Jubilee* (1935); "It's De-Lovely" from *Red, Hot and Blue!* (1936); "Most Gentlemen Don't Like Love" and "My Heart Belongs to Daddy" from *Leave It to Me* (1938); "Well, Did You Evah!" and "Friendship" from *DuBarry Was a Lady* (1939).

In the mid-1940s, however, two successive failures, *Seven Lively Arts* (1944) and *Around the World in Eighty Days* (1946), prompted Porter and his backers to question the commercial vitality of the pre–Rodgers and Hammerstein–type musical. Earlier in 1944 Porter had produced his sixth successive old-fashioned Broadway hit, *Mexican Hayride*. But the tides had turned, and the examples of Rodgers and Hammerstein's second musical, *Carousel* (1945),

215

Irving Berlin's *Annie Get Your Gun* (1946), and Porter's own *Kiss Me, Kate* (1948) bear testimony to the power that *Oklahoma!* now exerted. Even these two old dog songwriters now felt the urgency of learning the new trick of writing integrated musicals.

Before the historic collaboration of Rodgers and Hammerstein was launched in 1943, both Berlin and Porter had achieved universal recognition as songwriters. Even today, as many of their shows drift into oblivion, these illustrious composer-lyricists unquestionably remain the most widely known and revered of their generation. After four decades of composing currently under-appreciated revues and musical comedies, Berlin was persuaded in 1945, after the sudden and unanticipated death of the intended composer Kern, to compose a full-fledged book show that to some extent paralleled the new objectives established in *Oklahoma!* and *Carousel*. Soon Porter attempted his first own "integrated" musical. The results, Berlin's *Annie Get Your Gun* (1946) and Porter's *Kiss Me, Kate* (1948) remain the only musicals by these great songwriters that occupy a firm position in the Broadway repertory (albeit with some book and song changes mainly in the case of *Annie*). Abandoned by his supporters and forced to sell his new work in degrading auditions, Porter celebrated his resurrection by creating one of the most highly regarded and popular musicals of all time.[1]

Shortly before his death in 1964 Porter publicly acknowledged the difficulty posed by the intimidating example of Rodgers and Hammerstein: "The librettos are much better, and the scores are much closer to the librettos than they used to be. Those two [Rodgers and Hammerstein] made it much harder for everybody else."[2] The specter of "those two" would haunt Porter for his remaining creative years. To add injury to insult they even managed to partially overshadow *Kiss Me, Kate* by depriving Porter of Mary Martin (the rising star of Porter's *Leave It to Me* ten years earlier and, more recently, the star of *One Touch of Venus*), who had auditioned for the lead but instead accepted the role of Nellie Forbush in *South Pacific*, which opened three months after Porter's classic.[3]

In a *New York Times* interview that he gave during the composition of *Can-Can* in 1953, Porter reveals that Rodgers and Hammerstein remained under his skin: "They [the songs] didn't come out of the book so much as now. Really, until Rodgers and Hammerstein, if you needed to change a scene, a girl could come out in front of the curtain and sing or dance or anything. But with *Can-Can*, I have worked since last June."[4]

Additional evidence that Porter suffered anxiety from the influence of *Oklahoma!* and *Carousel* appears amid the extensive unpublished manuscript material for *Kiss Me, Kate* housed in the Music Division of the Library of Congress in a packet labeled "Unfinished Lyrics."[5] Although some of these lyrics are in fact unfinished and others only barely begun, including one tantalizing title, "To Be or Not to Be," most lyrics in this packet are alternate versions of known *Kiss Me, Kate* songs. One such draft belongs with the song "Bianca," a late addition to the show. In the staged (and published) verse of this song Bill Calhoun the Baltimorean and, as Lucentio, the Shakespearean suitor of Lois Lane/Bianca, sings the following lyric: "While rehearsing with Bianca, / (She's the darling I *adore*), / Offstage I *found* / She's been a*round* / But I love her *more* and *more*; / So I've written her a love song / Though I'm just an ama*teur*. / I'll sing it *through* / For all of *you* / To see if it's worthy of *her*. / Are yuh list'nin'?"

In the "Unfinished Lyrics" the private Porter can be observed working with an alternate idea: Bill Calhoun himself as an aspiring Broadway lyricist. Porter's surrogate lyricist, however, is not merely a suitor for the fair Lois/Bianca in this version. Porter has given his still-anonymous poet additional importance as "the dog who writes incog" for the great Berlin. In this alternative scenario, "Bianca" is one of the songs Bill has composed on behalf of Mr. Berlin.

Despite this subterfuge, Porter's draft labeled "Bianca 2nd Verse" on the second page arguably reveals more about Porter than it does about Bill Calhoun: "Ev'ry night I write for Irving [Berlin] / 'Til I nearly bust my *bean* / 'Cause Irving fears / Two rival peers / Known as Rodgers and Hammerstein. / I shall now repeat my ballad / Then I'll rush to Irving *quick* / And if he *thinks* / My ballad *stinks* / He'll sell it to Oscar [Hammerstein II] and *Dick* [Richard Rodgers] / Are you list'nin? (repeat refrain)."[6]

All available witnesses corroborate the story that it was not an easy task for Bella Spewack, herself only a recent convert to the somewhat heretical notion of setting Shakespeare's *Taming of the Shrew* musically, to convince her former collaborator on *Leave It to Me* that a Shakespeare musical would not be "too esoteric, too high-brow for the commercial stage."[7] In contrast to his modus operandi in *Anything Goes* and his other pre–Rodgers and Hammerstein musicals in which an often tenuous relationship existed between the songs and the librettos, the extant manuscript evidence reveals that from the time he began work on *Kiss Me, Kate* Porter was greatly concerned with creating a musical that integrated music with the book.

Also in contrast to *Anything Goes*, whose second act was barely a gleam in the eyes of Howard Lindsay and Russel Crouse at the time of their first rehearsal and with deletions and substitutions continuing into the Broadway run, *Kiss Me, Kate* could boast a completed book by the end of May 1948 before auditions would begin the following month.[8] Although much would be altered during auditions and rehearsals (between May and November), by the Philadelphia tryouts on December 2, *Kiss Me, Kate* as we know it today was nearly set. As Spewack reports:

I knew Cole had come through brilliantly. I knew what I had done and what Sam [co-librettist and spouse Samuel Spewack] had done was right. We had nothing to change. I knew it so I didn't have to be superstitious. In the history of American musicals this is the only one where they didn't have to touch a scene or a song. In rehearsals, changes were made. I wrote three versions, but I knew eventually we'd go back to the first one—and we did. There were disagreements over "Why Can't You Behave?" and over "Bianca," but the disagreements were all ironed out before we left town.[9]

After four weeks to "rehearse and rehearse," *Kiss Me, Kate* opened at the New Century Theatre on December 30, 1948, with nearly unequivocal endorsements from New York City reviewers.

When discussing the dramatic merits of *Anything Goes* (chapter 3) it was proposed that since Sir Evelyn Oakleigh does not sing, he does not deserve a woman like Reno Sweeney (Ethel Merman) who sings such hits as "I Get a Kick out of You," "You're the Top," "Anything Goes," and "Blow, Gabriel, Blow." At the very least, Sir Evelyn's non-singing status created a dramatic problem that future revivals tried to assuage. In *Kiss Me, Kate* the musically silent character does not get the girl. Fred Graham's rival, the powerful Washington diplomat Harrison Howell who, like Sir Evelyn, remains songless, gets caught napping and ends up barefoot on Fred's wedding day. Petruchio/Fred, who sings more songs than Kate/Lilli Vanessi, not only deserves to get a tamed Katherine at the end of the *Shrew* play, but he also gets a reformed spouse in real life.

It was also previously noted that Porter attempted to convey character musically in *Anything Goes*. Not only does Porter characterize his star Reno (Merman) with catchy syncopations and uncomplicated harmonies but he also conveys her spunky disregard for convention by having her sing triplets that clash with her duple meter, first and most consistently in "I Get a Kick Out of You" and later in "Blow, Gabriel, Blow." Once he makes this association, Porter then demonstrates how Hope Harcourt becomes more like the star when she adopts Reno's rhythmic signature in her own "Gypsy in Me."

Not surprisingly, in the wake of Rodgers and Hammerstein's *Oklahoma!* and *Carousel* Porter made a still greater effort in *Kiss Me, Kate* to channel music's power to establish character. He does this most noticeably by distinguishing the *Shrew* players from the Baltimore players. The former are given musical characteristics loosely associated with music of the Italian Renaissance. Bianca and her suitors are given an a cappella pseudo-madrigal in "Tom, Dick or Harry," the bluesy "Why Can't You Behave?" is transformed into a Renaissance dance (the pavane), and several of the *Shrew* songs display the long-short-short figure (♩♪♪) characteristic of the sixteenth-century Italian canzona.[10]

Example 10.1. "We Open in Venice" (closing orchestral tag) and "Miserere"
from Verdi's *Il Trovatore* (act 4)
(a) "We Open in Venice" (closing orchestral tag)
(b) "Miserere" from Verdi's *Il Trovatore* (act 4)

Porter's Italian evocations are not confined to the Renaissance. One
nineteenth-century appropriation occurs in the orchestral tag to "We Open
in Venice" (Example 10.1), where he quotes the opening of the "Miserere"
from Verdi's *Il Trovatore* (act 4). Perhaps Porter intended a musical pun
(the "misery" of an endless road tour and its associations with Verdi's
fourteenth-century Spanish troubadour, Manrico) or perhaps he simply
wanted to link a classic playwright with a classic Italian opera composer.[11]
Porter adopts a more contemporary Italian flavor in "I Sing of Love" and
"Where Is the Life That Late I Led?" and a more generalized Latin beguine
character in "Were Thine That Special Face," again to distinguish the *Shrew*
numbers from the more recognizably American Baltimore numbers. Representative American vernacular characteristics include the show biz and
jazzy quality of "Another Op'nin,' Another Show," the jazzy "Too Darn
Hot," the satire of Bowery waltzes in "Brush Up Your Shakespeare," and
the thirty-two-bar song form of a popularly styled ballad, "So in Love."

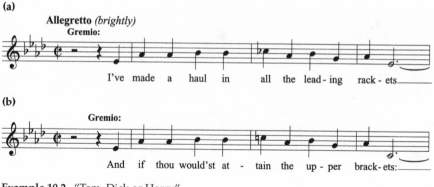

Example 10.2. "Tom, Dick or Harry"
(a) minor mode
(b) major mode

In his analysis of *Kiss Me, Kate,* Joseph P. Swain notes Porter's technique of moving from the major mode to the minor mode or vice versa to distinguish the Padua songs from their Baltimore counterparts.[12] Indeed, with one exception ("I'm Ashamed That Women Are So Simple") the texted songs sung in Padua juxtapose major and minor in dramatically purposeful ways. In "Tom, Dick or Harry" Porter distinguishes each suitor's past accomplishments from their rosy description of Bianca's future if she were to marry one of them by the simple juxtaposition of minor and major mode (Example 10.2). Similarly, Petruchio at the conclusion of "Were Thine That Special Face" moves from the minor to the major mode to capture the optimism of "then you'll be mine, all mine" that concludes the song. In Petruchio's "Where Is the Life That Late I Led?" Porter contrasts the life of the carefree bachelor in the main chorus

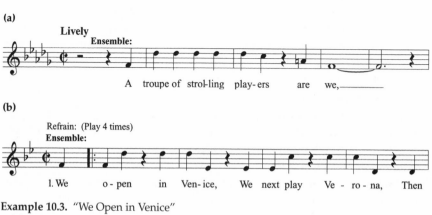

Example 10.3. "We Open in Venice"
(a) minor mode
(b) major mode

(major mode) with a mixture of minor and major modes that conveys his bittersweet nostalgia for the women he must now relinquish as a married man. Thus, in the slower second portion of the song Momo and Rebecca stir memories in the minor mode and Alice and Lucretia in the major, while memories of Carolina and Fedora contain elements of the two.

Porter lessens the dramatic contrast between Padua and Baltimore, however, when he contrasts major and minor modes in the latter songs as well. In fact, it might be said that this device—widely and effectively used by Schubert—not only serves as Porter's way of demonstrating parallels between the *Shrew* numbers and the Baltimore numbers. In the end, it functions primarily as a unifying musical device that shapes a musically integrated score. The Paduan "We Open in Venice," for example, was certainly intended to parallel "Another Op'nin,' Another Show" in Baltimore. In the Padua excerpts (Example 10.3) the players sing in the minor mode when describing themselves and in the major mode when they relate their circular itinerary. Conversely, "Another Op'nin'" opens in the major mode (E♭ major) and moves to G minor in the release (the B section) to convey the anxiety of the four weeks that lead to this opening ("Four weeks you *rehearse* and *rehearse* / Three weeks and it couldn't be *worse*"). Even a song as far removed from the drama as "Too Darn Hot" demonstrates a prominent move from minor (the "too darn hot" portion) to major (the "Kinsey report" portion).

Although the degree to which *Kiss Me, Kate* employs the major-minor juxtapositions is perhaps unprecedented in a Porter show, the roots of this idea can be found in Porter's pre–Rodgers and Hammerstein musical *Anything Goes* (and many other songs; see, for example its continuous presence in "Night and Day"). We have already observed that the verse of the title song in his earlier musical (Example 3.2, p. 56) clearly contrasts the past (minor mode) with the present (major mode). In another example, the sea chantey "There'll Always Be a Lady Fair" juxtaposes the modes to distinguish the hardships of a sailor's life in the verse (minor mode) from the fair ladies waiting on land (major mode). The intimidation by Rodgers and Hammerstein may have inspired Porter to explore additional and increasingly subtle ways to capture nuances in his characters and in their texts, but he did not suddenly discover textual realism or the dramatic potential of music after attending a production of *Oklahoma!*

Porter's efforts to demonstrate even more thematic unity for the purposes of dramatic credibility, however, do distinguish *Kiss Me, Kate* from his pre–Rodgers and Hammerstein shows, including *Anything Goes*. It also arguably surpasses *Oklahoma!*, if not *Carousel*, in this respect. Some musical material such as the reappearance of the repeated fourth that marks the opening of the

Example 10.4. "Why Can't You Behave?" transformed in the Pavane
(a) "Why Can't You Behave?"
(b) Pavane

main tune of "Another Op'nin'" as the vamp in the following "Why Can't You Behave?" (Example 10.4a, mm. 5–6), helps to create a smooth musical linkage between the first two numbers without conveying a comparable dramatic meaning.[13] But most connections do serve dramatic purposes. Bill and Lois, for example, share improper behavior. Bill is a shiftless yet likably dishonest gambler who signs an I.O.U. with Fred Graham's name; Lois is a shameless and fickle (and equally endearing) flirt who, in the role of Bianca, will mate with any Tom, Dick, or Harry and, as herself, date any man who asks her out for "something wet." It therefore makes sense that the verse of "Why Can't You Behave?" returns in "Always True To You in My Fashion." The transformation of "Why Can't You Behave?" (Example 10.4a) from the first act, when it is sung by Lois to Bill, into an orchestral pavane in act II (Example 10.4b) reinforces the commonality between Lois and Bill. At the same time it further identifies Lois and Bianca as the same character and clarifies the usurpation of the "Behave" theme in "Fashion."[14]

Another musical figure that links several songs first occurs in "I Sing of Love."[15] Not only does this song display a 6/8 meter that evokes popular Italian tarantellas such as "Funiculi, Funiculà," it also presents a melodic and harmonic shift from C major to F minor (on the words "We sing of [C major] love" [F minor]) that will resurface in two songs from act II (a progression

Kiss Me, Kate, act I, finale. Patricia Morison and Alfred Drake in the center (1948). Photograph: Eileen Darby. Museum of the City of New York. Theater Collection.

anticipated in "What Is This Thing Called Love?" from 1920). With only insignificant alterations this exotic, pseudo-Renaissance juxtaposition of major and minor harmonic shifts returns in the verse of "Where Is the Life That Late I Led?" (also in 6/8 meter). Here Petruchio describes the awakening of his desire and occasionally love for the opposite sex many years before ("Since I reached the charming age of [C major] puberty" [F minor]). In "Bianca" the progression appears in reverse, F minor to C major, when Bill as Poet expresses his love for Bianca in the verse of the song that bears her name ("While rehearsing with Bianca, / She's the darling I a- [F minor] dore" [C major]). In each case, love underlies the harmony and links the musical material.

Also dramatically motivated are the thematic recurrences between the finales of act I and act II. At the end of act I Petruchio, accompanied by "all singing principals (except Hattie) and chorus," serenades his shrewish new bride, who shrieks "No! Go! Nay! Away!" before breaking character and shouting "Fred!" The verbal battle between Kate/Lilli and Petruchio/ Fred that ensues is supported appropriately enough by a military march with dotted rhythms of a martial nature (Example 10.5a) before Kate sings a "quasi cadenza angrily" and the chorus concludes the act with a syncopated variant of "Another Op'nin.'"

Example 10.5. Transformation of act I finale into act II finale
(a) March
(b) Waltz

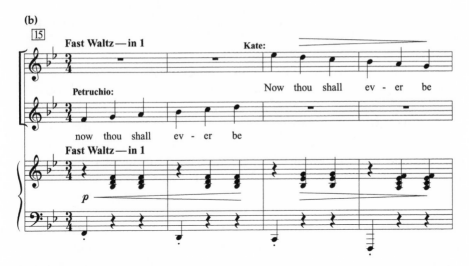

Example 10.5. Continued

Porter signifies his intent to parallel this ending when, at the outset of the second-act finale, he offers an unmistakable melodic transformation in triple meter of Petruchio's act I duple-metered serenade. Instead of insults, Kate/Lilli now interjects various terms of endearment in Italian. Petruchio's words, like Petruchio himself, remain unchanged from one act finale to the other, while Kate's dramatically contrasting response reinforces the significant change she had revealed moments before in her final song, "I Am Ashamed That Women Are So Simple."[16] Finally, the second melody of the act I finale (the march, Example 10.5a) returns transformed into a waltz, the dance of love (Example 10.5b). The transformation from a militaristic march to a romantic waltz succeeds simply but effectively in establishing musical equivalences for the dramatic changes that have taken place in the dynamics between Kate/Petruchio and Lilli/Fred.[17]

Act II: Shakespeare

After Rodgers and Hammerstein, the second tough act for Porter and his collaborators Bella and Sam Spewack to follow was "the bard of Stratford-on-Avon" himself, Shakespeare. As Bella Spewack writes in the introduction to the published libretto, "We hated to cut Shakespeare."[18] But when she received an unexpected and unwelcome new song from Porter, "Brush Up Your Shakespeare," both Spewacks acknowledged that they would have to adjust to the unpleasant idea that Shakespeare would be playing second fiddle to the demands of Broadway. Bella tells it this way in her introduction to the published libretto:

> We realized that according to the classic standards of Broadway it ["Brush Up"] was a "boff" number—a show-stopper, if you please. Perhaps not a New Art Form, but definitely a must for the male patron. So instead of any throat-cutting [Porter had written that "Belle will probably cut her throat when she gets this"], we dropped the final scene (all Shakespeare) and a beautiful dance for which the stairs had been built. We had exactly three minutes left in which to finish our show.[19]

According to Porter biographer George Eells, Porter's decision to add another song, "Bianca," for Harold Lang (Lucentio/Bill Calhoun) precipitated a strained correspondence between the Spewacks and the composer-lyricist.[20] Since Lang, then known primarily as a dancer, was not yet the star he would become four years later as the lead in Rodgers and Hart's *Pal Joey* revival, he was not given a solo when Porter and the Spewacks were planning their scenario. Patricia Morison, the original Kate/Lilli, recalls, however, that Lang "had it in his contract that he had to have a song in the second act" and "pulled a snit" until Porter decided "to write something that's going to be so bad they won't keep it in."[21] Silly and parodistic of the old Gillette razor jingle ("Look Sharp") as it is, "Bianca" added a great song and dance number for Lang and the show. Without "Bianca," Bill Calhoun would only sing "Gee, I need you kid" near the end of "Why Can't You Behave?" and a verse of "Tom, Dick or Harry," and would remain virtually indistinguishable in musical importance from Bianca's other suitors.[22]

Bella Spewack fought and won a battle with the producers to retain "Were Thine That Special Face" and persuaded Porter himself to leave "Tom, Dick or Harry" in the show. Nevertheless, the libretto that the Spewacks originally sent to Porter contained far more of Shakespeare's *The Taming of the Shrew* than audiences would eventually see in *Kiss Me, Kate*. Most notably, the May libretto included Shakespeare's lines in act IV, scene 5, when Kate capitulates to Petruchio and agrees that the sun is the moon or vice versa according to his whim, and Kate's complete final speech in act V, scene 2.[23] Porter would collaborate with the bard on an abbreviated version of this latter speech to produce "I Am Ashamed That Women Are So Simple." Gone entirely from the May libretto is the Induction (often cut from Shakespeare productions as well). Also removed from Shakespeare is the character of the Widow, the woman who eventually marries Bianca's suitor, Hortensio. The Widow's departure led to the demise of her counterpart in the Baltimore company as well, Angela Temple.[24]

The major dramatic departure from Shakespeare's play, however, occurred after the May libretto draft. In May, when Lilli learns from Fred that she is no longer under the custody of the two gunmen and therefore free to abandon the *Shrew* play, she informs her ex-husband (Fred), without hesitation, that she will *not* desert:

> FRED: Well, Miss Vanessi, you may leave now.
> LILLI: I am not leaving!
> FRED: Sleeping Beauty [Harrison] waits in your dressing room.
> LILLI: Let him NAP!
> FRED: Don't tell me the bloom is off (HE *sneezes*)—the rose?[25]

A few lines later Fred and Lilli reprise "We Shall Never Be Younger," a song that would soon be discarded. The two had sung a portion of this song together to conclude their duet in act I, scene 1, "It Was Great Fun the First Time," and Lilli sang the whole song alone in her dressing room two scenes later. Although the two stormy actors are not yet fully reconciled, an audience could reasonably infer from the reprise of their shared song that Fred and Lilli are on the verge of starting a happier third act together.

By December the Spewacks made a significant alteration in the dialogue to set up Fred's reprise of the newly added "So in Love" to replace "We Shall Never Be Younger" in act I:

> FRED: You're free to go. You don't have to finish the show....Aren't
>   you taking Sleeping Beauty with you?
> LILLI: Let him sleep.
> FRED: Don't tell me the bloom is off—the rose?...Lilli, you can't walk
>   out on me now.
> LILLI: You walked out on me once.
> FRED: But I came back.
> (LILLI *hesitates*)
> DOORMAN: (*From his cubbyhole*) Your cab's waiting, Miss Vanessi!
> (LILLI *leaves*.)

After Lilli has walked out on both Fred and her sleeping (and, more significantly, non-singing) fiancé, Harrison Howell, Fred, "alone, reprises 'So in Love.'" In the May libretto Lilli decides to stay in the show, the Spewacks were able to maintain their fidelity to Shakespeare, and Petruchio wins his wager in the last scene. In the revised libretto, however, Lilli leaves. What can Petruchio say if his offstage counterpart knows that he will lose the wager? Petruchio replies to Kate's father: "I know she will not come. / The fouler fortune mine and there an end." In contrast to both Shakespeare and the May libretto Lilli's reappearance in December as a tamed Kate who will follow Petruchio's bidding comes as much of a surprise to Petruchio as it does to the other *Shrew* players. To clarify the impact of her return, the stage directions tell us that Fred becomes "really moved, forgetting Shakespeare" and then utters a heartfelt "Darling" before returning to his Paduan character.

The circumstances that led to the addition of "So in Love" sometime between June and November remain a mystery. Neither Spewack nor any Porter biographer has anything definitive to say about its appearance during auditions, but Morison recalled in 1990 that " 'So in Love' was finished after I came into the show."[26] It is known, however, that "So in Love"—along with "Bianca" and "I Hate Men," the last songs to be added to the show—replaced "We Shall Never Be Younger," a song which all involved in the production agreed was a beautiful song but "too sad for a musical."[27] Like the song it superseded, the setting of "So in Love" is Lilli's dressing room in act I (after Fred's exit), and Lilli sings the song to herself unheard by her former husband. But the new song, unlike "We Shall Never Be Younger," is unknown to Fred as well as unheard. The once-married couple (the show opens on the first anniversary of their divorce) had sung a few lines of the sad earlier song as a mood-changing coda to their earlier duet, "It Was Great Fun" (also dropped after May). In the May libretto Fred does not hear Lilli sing her confession and remains oblivious of her hope that "my darling might even need me," but at least he knows the song that he has shared with his former romantic partner.[28]

In chapter 5 it was noted that in the original 1936 production of *On Your Toes*, Sergei Alexandrovitch and Peggy Porterfield sing the reprise of "There's a Small Hotel." Audiences were asked to accept a convention in which characters somehow know songs introduced privately by others, in this case Phil Dolan II and Frankie Frayne. In 1983 Sergei and Peggy sing a reprise of "Quiet Night" instead, a song that they have actually heard. Nevertheless, modern audiences still are expected to accept the idea that the entire cast can manage to learn "There's a Small Hotel" well enough to sing it the finale.

In *Kiss Me, Kate*, Porter continues the tradition of characters singing songs they're not really supposed to know. Certainly, the most significant example of this practice can be observed when Porter does not allow Lilli and Fred the opportunity to sing even a portion of "So in Love" together (as he did with the discarded "We Shall Never Be Younger"). Porter thus removes the means by which his characters can establish associations and connections with a song. When Fred reprises "So in Love" in act II, audiences might justifiably ask how he came to know it. Was he eavesdropping on Lilli when she sang it in act I?

In contrast to Rodgers and Hammerstein's powerful reuse of "If I Loved You" in *Carousel*, the reprise of "So in Love" puts the song above the drama, so that it becomes, as Joseph Kerman might say, a reprise "for the audience, not the play."[29] The dramatic impact of Billy Bigelow's reprise of "If I Loved You" in *Carousel* stems at least in part from the audience's memory of a shared interchange between Billy and Julie Jordan. The song belongs to them, they know it, and the audience knows that they know it. In this isolated but telling dramatic detail in *Kiss Me, Kate*, Porter returns to the era he himself had done so much to establish: once again a great song (and its reprise) takes precedence over the dramatic integrity of a book. Despite this criticism, it might also be said that Fred's reprise of "So in Love" demonstrates a credible bond and a communication with Lilli and serves a theatrical if not a literal truth.[30]

Kiss Me, Kate *and the Broadway Heroine*

In the revised ending Lilli (and, by extension, her *Shrew* counterpart, Katherine) willingly joins Fred and Petruchio in the final scene. She is free to leave both Fred (the frame of the musical) and his show (the musical within a musical). Although this ending took Porter and the Spewacks further away from their Shakespearean source, it also brought them perhaps a little closer to a modern view of the world. Lilli and Katherine return to their men as free agents, not as tamed falcons.

Nevertheless, Katherine's final Shakespearean speech, only "slightly altered by Cole Porter with apologies," creates a serious challenge to a feminist interpretation.[31] Katherine freely comes to Petruchio, but she then sings a speech almost invariably construed as degrading to women. Is *Kiss Me, Kate* therefore a sexist musical that should be banned, or at least restaged?

Long before feminism became part of the mainstream of intellectual thought and social action in the late 1960s and early 1970s, critics have been put off by Shakespeare's ending. For example, in 1897 George Bernard Shaw came to the following conclusion: "The last scene is altogether disgusting to modern sensibility. No man with any decency of feeling can sit it out in the company of woman without feeling extremely ashamed of the lord-of-creation moral implied in the wager and the speech put into the woman's own mouth. Therefore the play, though still worthy of a complete and efficient representation, would need, even at that, some apology."[32]

Nearly seventy years later Robert B. Heilman wrote that "the whole wager scene falls essentially within the realm of farce" and assumes that

Shakespeare accepted the idea that women are subservient to men even if modern theatergoers do not: "The easiest way to deal with it is to say that we no longer believe in it, just as we no longer believe in the divine right of kings that is an important dramatic element in many Shakespeare plays."[33] In the 1990s, David Thornburn, during a panel discussion on "The Remaking of the Canon," asked a conference speaker rhetorical questions that implicitly accused the Bard of harboring antediluvian views:

> Isn't it true that Shakespeare actually believes that women are subservient to men in *The Taming of The Shrew*? Now it is incumbent on people who offer the reified conception of the canon, as you, Professor [Gertrude] Himmelfarb, do, to explain how you can justify or defend texts whose obvious, explicit themes are so deeply offensive to what you as a thinker and as a moral person would regard as acceptable.[34]

Shakespeare has few modern defenders from the ranks of those who accept Katherine's speech at face value. But one unexpected apology might be noted—Germaine Greer's pioneering book on feminism, *The Female Eunuch*:

> The submission of a woman like Kate is genuine and exciting because she has something to lay down, her virgin pride and individuality: Bianca is the soul of duplicity, married without earnestness or good will. Kate's speech at the close of the play is the greatest defense of Christian monogamy ever written. It rests upon the role of a husband as protector and friend, and it is valid because Kate has a man who is capable of being both.[35]

Other critics offer interpretations that bring the apparently sexist playwright closer to modern feminism. As Martha Andresen-Thom writes: "Extraordinary individuals learn to play with wit and wisdom the roles of sex and class that at once bind them and bond them. Subordination of woman to man, in this view, is an opportunity for a brilliant and worthy woman to transform limitation into an incentive for play."[36] The "play" interpretation is supported in Shakespeare's text by the zeal with which Katherine takes the ball from Petruchio's court and pretends that Lucentio's elderly father Vincentio is a "young budding virgin, fair, and fresh, and sweet" (act IV, scene 5). At that moment Kate does not seem to be motivated by exhaustion and a realization that she cannot win, but by her newfound inspiration that play-acting can be fun rather than demeaning.[37]

Evolving sensitivities toward white and African-American racial relations have been explored briefly in the discussions of the history of *Show Boat* and *Porgy and Bess*. Two Rodgers and Hammerstein musicals introduced during the period of the present survey deal with relations between whites and Asians, *South Pacific* and *The King and I* (albeit on white terms), and the reworked books of *Anything Goes* revivals discussed in chapter 3 demonstrate a progressively less stereotypical approach toward Chinese Americans.

A discussion of sexism in *Kiss Me, Kate* opens the door to a broader discussion of how women featured in the present survey have fared. *Show Boat*'s Julie LaVerne and Magnolia Ravenal, *Carousel*'s Julie Jordan, and *West Side Story*'s Maria lose their men at some point in the musicals. *Porgy*'s Bess not only becomes a drug addict and a prostitute, she never gets to sing an aria by herself, even if she does have her own theme. The rich and powerful female executive in *Lady in the Dark*, Liza Elliott, must relinquish her post as head of a prestigious fashion magazine if she is to restore her lost glamour, femininity, and happiness, and complete her song, "My Ship." Liza Elliott has merely exchanged her unpleasant dreams for a living nightmare of submission to a sexist man, Charley Johnson, the advertising manager of Liza's magazine and her prosecuting attorney in the Circus Dream.

Compared to what happens to most nineteenth-century tragic European opera heroines, however, Broadway's women manage pretty well.[38] In contrast to her operatic sisters, none of these heroines dies, although Julie LaVerne is reduced to alcoholism and almost certainly a premature death (offstage) in response to the loss of her man. Before *Miss Saigon* in the 1990s many Cinderellas but no Madame Butterflys inhabited Broadway musicals. Even Maria in *West Side Story*, unlike her Shakespearean counterpart, survives and is thereby presumably able to effect societal changes that will lead to a less violent world. After losing her man, Magnolia gains fame as an actress, while Julie Jordan demonstrates enormous strength of character before and after Billy's death. Anna holds her own with the King of Siam and her actions lead to democratic reforms.

Among our musical heroines Adelaide (*Guys and Dolls*) and Eliza Doolittle (*My Fair Lady*) perhaps do the least to placate modern sentiments. Adelaide's saga of her fourteen-year engagement to Nathan Detroit ("Adelaide's Lament") and her advice to Sarah Brown to "marry the man today and change his ways tomorrow" might disappoint some. But audiences by and large have successfully distanced themselves from this cartoonish Runyonesque world and have been attending the Broadway and countless other revivals of this show in record numbers ever since. And although we shall see in chapter 12 that it is admittedly a tough call that Eliza should end up with (in the epilogue to Shaw's *Pygmalion* she marries Freddy), her decision to return to the barely repentant misogynist Higgins in *My Fair Lady* might cause many to cringe in their seats. Porter and Spewack's Katherine may, like Shakespeare, put her hand at Petruchio's feet, but at least she is not asked to fetch his slippers.

Porter never surpassed the brilliance or the popularity of *Kiss Me, Kate*. Two years later he completed *Out of This World*, a show that, before it was dropped during tryouts, included the now-perennial favorite "From This Moment On" (later interpolated by Ann Miller in the 1953 film version of *Kiss Me, Kate* discussed in chapter 14). After *Out of This World*, Porter created two successful Broadway shows, *Can-Can* (1953) and *Silk Stockings* (1955). He would complete his illustrious career with two film musicals, *High Society* in 1956 (which included "True Love," introduced by Bing Crosby and Grace Kelly in her final Hollywood role) and *Les Girls* in 1957. The next year, Porter's last eight songs appeared in the television production *Aladdin* (scripted by *One Touch of Venus* librettist S. J. Perelman). His creative spirit broken after the deaths of his mother and his wife and the amputation of a leg (he had already suffered more than thirty operations since 1937 when a horse he was riding crushed both his legs), Porter spent the remaining years before his own death in 1964 in self-imposed isolation.

CHAPTER ELEVEN

GUYS AND DOLLS AND THE MOST HAPPY FELLA

The Greater Loesser

For once nostalgia rings true. As Broadway and London revivals so frequently remind us, the 1950s were truly a glorious decade for the American musical. Following in their own luminous footsteps of the 1940s (*Oklahoma!*, *Carousel*, and *South Pacific*), Rodgers and Hammerstein continued to present their felicitous dramatic integrations of happy talk and happy tunes (and serious dramatic subjects) when they opened the new decade with their unprecedented fourth major hit musical, *The King and I* (1951), and closed it with a final hit collaboration, *The Sound of Music* (1959). In 1956, Lerner and Loewe presented *My Fair Lady*, a universally praised musical that eventually eclipsed *Oklahoma!* as the longest running Broadway musical. One year later the Laurents-Sondheim-Bernstein trilogy brought to Broadway *West Side Story*. The decade introduced many critical and popular successes, musicals like *Wonderful Town* (lyrics by Betty Comden and Adolph Green, music by Bernstein), *Kismet* (music and lyrics by Robert Wright and George Forrest with more than a little help from the nineteenth-century Russian composer Alexander Borodin), *Pajama Game* and *Damn Yankees* (music and lyrics by Richard Adler and Jerry Ross), *The Music Man* (music, lyrics, and book by Meredith Willson), *Fiorello!* (lyrics by Sheldon Harnick, music by Jerry Bock), and *Gypsy* (book by Laurents, lyrics by Sondheim, and music by Jule Styne); two of these by Frank Loesser, that have become classics—*Guys and Dolls* (1950) and *The Most Happy Fella* (1956)—were the toast of Broadway in the 1990s and *Guys and Dolls* returned yet again to Broadway in 2009.

Even those who love to hate Broadway musicals make an exception for *Guys and Dolls* and consider this show one of the most entertaining and perfect ever. Although Gershwin's *Porgy and Bess* and perhaps Bernstein's *Candide* would later overshadow Loesser's next show in popularity or critical approbation, *The Most Happy Fella* continues to boast the longest initial run, 678 performances, of any Broadway work prior to the 1980s that might claim an operatic rubric. As a tribute to its anticipated appeal as well as its abundance of music, its cast album was the first to be recorded in a nearly complete state, on three long-playing records.

In contrast to the instant and sustained appeal and unwavering stature of *Guys and Dolls*, however, the popularity and stature of *The Most Happy Fella* has evolved more slowly and less completely. In one prominent sign of its growing popularity and acclaim in the United States, the 1990–1991 Broadway season marked the appearance (with generally positive critical press) of two new productions, one with the New York City Opera and one on Broadway.[1] Despite lingering controversy regarding its ultimate worth, *The Most Happy Fella* is clearly gaining in both popular acclaim and critical stature and is even receiving some serious scholarly attention.[2]

Like fellow composer-lyricist Stephen Sondheim two decades later, Loesser (1910–1969) gained initial distinction as a lyricist.[3] Unlike Sondheim, who had been writing music to complement his lyrics since his teens, only after a decade of professional lyric-writing could Loesser be persuaded to compose his own music professionally. He scored a bull's eye on his very first try, "Praise the Lord and Pass the Ammunition" (1942), one of the most popular songs of World War II. Earlier he wrote his first published song lyrics, "In Love with the Memory of You" (1931), to music composed by William Schuman, the distinguished classical composer and future president of the Juilliard School and the Lincoln Center for the Performing Arts. In an unusual coincidence Loesser made his Broadway debut (as a lyricist) for the same ill-fated revue, *The Illustrator's Show* (1936), that marked the equally inauspicious Broadway debut of Frederick Loewe, twenty years before *My Fair Lady* and *The Most Happy Fella*.

Loesser began a decade of film work more successfully the next year with his song, "The Moon of Manakoora." Film collaborations with major Hollywood songwriters would soon produce lyrics to the Hoagy Carmichael chestnuts, "Heart and Soul" and "Two Sleepy People" (both in 1938), and song hits with Burton Lane and Jule Styne who, like Loesser, would soon be creating hit musicals on Broadway beginning in the late 1940s.[4] After "Praise the Lord," Loesser, a composer-lyricist in the tradition of Berlin and Porter, would go on to compose other World War II popular classics, including

Frank Loesser. © AL HIRSCHFELD. Reproduced by arrangement with Hirschfeld's exclusive representative, the MARGO FEIDEN GALLERIES LTD., NEW YORK. WWW.ALHIRSCHFELD.COM

"What Do You Do in the Infantry" (in "regulation Army tempo") and the poignant "Rodger Young," and later a string of successful film songs that culminated in the Academy Award–winning "Baby, It's Cold Outside," featured in *Neptune's Daughter* (1947).

Clearly, by the late 1940s Loesser was ready for Broadway. Drawing on the star status of Ray Bolger and the experience of George Abbott (the writer-director of Rodgers and Hart's *On Your Toes*, also starring Bolger, and the director of *Pal Joey*), fledgling producers Ernest Martin and Cy Feuer were prepared to take a calculated risk on Loesser's music and lyrics with Abbott's adaptation of Brandon Thomas's still-popular comedy, *Charley's Aunt* (1892). Unlike other musical settings of popular plays—including Loesser's *The Most Happy Fella*, adapted from Sidney Howard's Pulitzer Prize–winning but now mostly forgotten play, *They Knew What They Wanted* (1924)—*Where's Charley?* (1948) never managed to surpass its progenitor. Nevertheless, this extraordinary Broadway debut became the first of Loesser's four major hit musicals during a thirteen-year Broadway career (1948–1961). In the end, the composer-lyricist and one-time librettist would earn three New York Drama Critics Circle Awards (*Guys and Dolls, The Most Happy Fella,* and *How to Succeed in Business without Really Trying*), two Tony Awards (*Guys and Dolls* and *How to Succeed*), and one Pulitzer Prize for drama (*How to Succeed*).[5]

Where's Charley? was a well-crafted, old-fashioned Broadway show with sparkling Loesser lyrics and melodies. In order to show off a wider spectrum of Bolger's talents, the character of Lord Fancourt Babberley (who impersonated Charley's aunt in Thomas's play) was excised, and much of the comedy revolved around Charley's switching between two roles, Charley and his aunt, throughout the musical. Working against type, the opening duet, "Make a Miracle," between the central character, Charley Wykeham (Bolger), and Amy Spettigue was a comic number rather than a love song. More typically, Charley's formal expression of love, "Once in Love with Amy," was a show-stopper directed not to Amy but to the audience, which Bolger asked to participate in his public tribute.

One year before Rodgers and Hammerstein offered a serious subplot with Lt. Joseph Cable and Liat in *South Pacific*, the lyrical principals of *Where's Charley?* were the secondary characters, Jack Chesney and Kitty Verdun, who sing the show's central love song, "My Darling, My Darling." Despite this less conventional touch, at the end of the farce Charley (Bolger), without any dramatic justification other than his stature, was allowed to reprise and usurp his friend's "My Darling, My Darling." Such concessions were a small price to pay for a hit, even as late as 1948.

Guys and Dolls: *Life in Runyonland*

Although *Where's Charley?* was one of the most popular Broadway book musicals up to its time, the show hardly prepared critics and audiences for Loesser's next show two years later.[6] Reviewers from opening night to the present day have given *Guys and Dolls* pride of place among musical comedies. Following excerpts from nine raves, review collector Steven Suskin remarks that "*Guys and Dolls* received what might be the most unanimously ecstatic set of reviews in Broadway history."[7] In contrast to most musicals where some perceived flaw was manifest from the beginning (e.g., libretto weaknesses in *Show Boat*, the disconcerting recitative style in *Porgy and Bess*, the unpalatable main character in *Pal Joey*), *Guys and Dolls* was problem free. John McClain's epiphany in the *New York Journal-American* that this classic was "the best and most exciting thing of its kind since *Pal Joey*" is representative.[8] Indeed, after *Pal Joey* in 1940 Loesser's *Guys and Dolls* exactly ten years later is arguably the only musical comedy (as opposed to operetta) prior to the 1950s to achieve a sustained place in the Broadway repertory with its original book intact.

Although virtually no manuscript material is extant for *Guys and Dolls*, there is general agreement about the main outlines of its unusual genesis as told by its chief librettist Abe Burrows thirty years later.[9] After securing the rights to adapt Damon Runyon's short story "The Idyll of Miss Sarah Brown" (and portions and characters drawn from several others, especially "Pick the Winner"), *Where's Charley?* producers Feuer and Martin commissioned Hollywood scriptwriter Jo Swerling to write the book, and Loesser wrote as many as fourteen songs to match. Feuer and Martin then managed to persuade the legendary George S. Kaufman to direct. In a scenario reminiscent of *Anything Goes* and *One Touch of Venus*, where new librettists were brought in to rewrite a book, all of the above-mentioned *Guys and Dolls* collaborators concurred that Swerling's draft of the first act failed to match their vision of Runyonesque comedy. Burrows was then asked to come up with a new book to support Loesser's songs. As Burrows explains:

> Loesser's songs were the guideposts for the libretto. It's a rare show that is done this way, but all fourteen of Frank's songs were great, and the libretto had to be written so that the story would lead into each of them. Later on, the critics spoke of the show as "integrated." The word "integration" usually means that the composer has written songs that follow the story line gracefully. Well, we did it in reverse. Most of the scenes I wrote blended into songs that were already written.[10]

The legal aspects of Swerling's contractual obligations has generated some confusion regarding the authorship of *Guys and Dolls*. The hoopla generated by the Tony Award–winning 1992 Broadway revival of *Guys and Dolls* reopened this debate and other wounds.[11] When novelist William Kennedy credited Burrows as "the main writer" in a feature article in the *New York Times*, he inspired a sincere but unpersuasive letter from Swerling's son who tried to explain why the "myth" about Burrows's sole authorship "just ain't so."[12]

Although the full extent of Kaufman's contribution remains undocumented, his crucial role in shaping *Guys and Dolls* cannot be overlooked or underestimated. Just as his earlier partner in riotous comedy, Moss Hart, would work intensively with Lerner on the *My Fair Lady* libretto several years later and may be responsible for a considerable portion of the second act, the uncredited Kaufman had a major hand in the creation as well as the direction of the universally admired *Guys and Dolls* libretto. Even more than most comic writers, Kaufman was fanatically serious about the quality and quantity of his jokes, and under his guidance Burrows removed jokes that were either too easy or repeated. In addition, Burrows followed Kaufman's advice to take the necessary time to "take a deep breath and set up your story."[13] Burrows recalls that even six weeks after the show opened to unequivocally positive notices Kaufman "pointed out six spots in the show that weren't funny enough."[14]

In contrast to *Pal Joey*, with its prominent melodic use of a leading tone that obsessively ascends one step higher to the tonic (e.g., B to C in "Bewitched") as a unifying device, *Guys and Dolls* achieves its musical power and unity from the rhythms associated with specific characters. The "guys" and "dolls," even when singing their so-called fugues, display a conspicuous amount of syncopation and half-note and quarter-note triplet rhythms working against the metrical grain—illustrated also by Reno Sweeney in *Anything Goes* (Example 3.1, p. 56), Venus and Whitelaw Savory in *One Touch of Venus* (Example 7.2, p. 148), and Tony in *West Side Story* (on the words "I just met a girl named Maria" in Example 13.2b, p. 285).

The clearest and most consistently drawn rhythmic identity occurs in Adelaide's music. Even when "reading" her treatise on psychosomatic illness in "Adelaide's Lament," this convincing comic heroine adopts the quarter-note triplets at the end of the verses ("Affecting the upper respiratory tract" and "Involving the eye, the ear, and the nose, and throat"). By the time she translates the symptoms into her own words and her own song, the more common, rhythmically conventional eighth-note triplets are almost unceasing.[15]

In order for Loesser to convince audiences that Sarah Brown and Sky Masterson are a good match, he needed to make Sarah become more of a "doll" like Adelaide; conversely, he needed to portray Sky as more gentlemanly than his crapshooting colleagues. He accomplishes the first part of this task by transforming Sarah's rhythmic nature, giving the normally straitlaced and rhythmically even "mission doll" quarter-note triplets in "I'll Know" and syncopations in "If I Were a Bell."[16]

Sarah must also cast aside her biases against the petty vice of gambling and learn that a man does not have to be a "breakfast eating Brooks Brothers type" to be worthy of her love. In her first meeting with Sky, she discovers a person who surpasses her considerable knowledge of the Bible (Sky emphatically points out that the Salvation Army sign, "No peace unto the wicked" is incorrectly attributed to Proverbs [23:9] instead of to Isaiah [57:21]). Soon Sky will reveal himself to be morally sound, genuinely sensitive, and capable of practicing what the Bible preaches. Not only does he refuse to take advantage of her physically in act I, but he will even lie to protect her reputation in act II.

After audiences learn from his dialogue with Sarah that Sky's interest in and knowledge of the Bible sets him apart from the other "guys," his music tells us that he is capable of singing a different tune. His very first notes in "I'll Know" may depart from Sarah's lyricism, metrical regularity, and firm tonal harmonic underpinning, but after Sarah finishes her chorus, audiences will discover that Sky shares her chorus and verse as well as chapter and verse. Following Sarah's more "doll-like" acknowledgment of her changing feelings toward Sky in "If I Were a Bell," Sky is almost ready to initiate their second duet, "I've Never Been in Love Before." But first he needs to tell Sarah in "My Time of Day" (predawn) that she is the first person with whom he wants to share these private hours. The metrical irregularity, radical melodic shifts, and above all the harmonic ambiguity that mark his world before he met Sarah capture the essence of Sky's dramatic as well as musical personality.

The twenty measures of this private confession (the opening and closing measures are shown in Example 11.1) is stylistically far removed from any other music in *Guys and Dolls*. After the first chord sets up F major, Sky's restless nature will not allow him to find solace in a tonal center. By the end of his first phrase on the words "dark time," he is already singing a descending diminished fifth or tritone (D to A♭) which clashes with the dominant seventh harmony on C (C-E-G-B♭) that pulls to F major. Only when Sarah becomes the first person to learn Sky's real name, the biblical Obediah, will the orchestra—as the surrogate for Sky's feelings—return the music to F major. But now F is reinterpreted as a new dominant harmony instead of a tonic and serves to prepare a new tonal center, Bb major, and herald a new song, "I've Never Been in Love Before."

Even when Sky sings his own music rather than Sarah's, he shows his closeness to her by avoiding much of the metrical, melodic, and harmonic

Example 11.1. "My Time of Day"
(a) opening
(b) closing

Example 11.1. Continued

conventionality and syncopated fun of the other "guys." In his song for the souls of his gambling colleagues in act II, "Luck Be a Lady," syncopation is reserved for the ends of phrases, and his music, compared to the music of the tinhorns Rusty, Benny, and Nicely-Nicely, is contrastingly square. The marriage of Sarah and Sky at the end of the show is thus made possible (and believable) by the compromising evolution of their musical personalities. Just as Sarah becomes more like Sky and his world, Sky moves closer to Sarah's original musical identity.

Before their individuality is established Sky and Sarah are introduced more generically in their respective worlds in one of the most perfect and imaginative Broadway expositions, an opening scene that includes "Runyonland," "Fugue for Tinhorns," "Follow the Fold," and "The Oldest Established." The ancestor of "Runyonland" was Rodgers and Hammerstein's *Carousel*, which opened with an inspired pantomimed prologue—*Guys and Dolls* also includes an independent overture—that set up an ambiance and allowed audiences to place Julie Jordan's subsequent denial of her feelings in perspective. As we have seen in chapter 9, the *Carousel* pantomime focused on establishing the relationships between the central characters, Julie and Billy Bigelow, and the jealousy their romance will arouse in the carousel proprietress, Mrs. Mullin.

The musical component of the pantomimed "Runyonland" is a medley of the title song, "Luck Be a Lady," and "Fugue for Tinhorns" in various degrees of completeness and altered tempos. Inspired by Kaufman's admonition to "take a deep breath and set up your story," the opening devotes itself entirely through narrative ballet and mime to capturing the colorful world of Runyon's stories. The scene description in the libretto and the published vocal score details an intricate comic interaction of con artists, pickpockets, a man who pretends to be a blind merchant, naive tourists, bobby soxers, and a prizefighter who is inadvertently knocked down by the unimposing Benny Southstreet, the only named character to appear in this elaborate sequence. At the end of "Runyonland" we meet two other tinhorns, Rusty Charlie and Nicely-Nicely Johnson, the latter of whom will emerge, after Sky, as the leading male singer of the evening. In a transition that literally does not skip a beat, the trio introduce the first song of the show, "Fugue for Tinhorns."

Tinhorns are gamblers who pretend to be wealthier than they are. Burrows's and Loesser's tinhorns match this description with their pretense to a verbal and musical sophistication they do not possess. The verbal pretensions are evident throughout their dialogue, the musical ones are most clearly revealed in their opening song. Even the word "fugue" is pretentious, referring to a musical form associated with J. S. Bach in which similar melodic lines, introduced at the outset in staggered entrances of a principal melody (known as the fugue subject), are then heard simultaneously. True to type, what Rusty, Nicely-Nicely, and Benny sing is in fact not a fugue at all but a form that pretends to be a fugue, the lowlier round, known to all from "Three Blind Mice" and "Row, Row, Row Your Boat."

In the first of many departures from a fugue, the participants in a round begin by singing the identical (rather than a similar) musical line, albeit also

Guys and Dolls, Crap game in the sewer in act II. Robert Alda throwing the dice, Stubby Kaye kneeling to the left, Sam Levene to the right (1950). Museum of the City of New York. Theater Collection.

in staggered entrances. The whole tune of Loesser's "fugue" consists of twelve measures of melody, with the final eight measures containing additional repetition. Despite their relative simplicity, rounds are tricky to create, since they must be composed vertically (the harmonic dimension) as well as horizontally (the melodic dimension). In "Fugue for Tinhorns" Loesser therefore has constructed his twelve-bar tune so that it can be subdivided into three four-bar phrases (one complete phrase is shown in Example 11.2); each phrase is constructed so that it can be sung simultaneously with any of the others. In order to squeeze a horizontal twelve-bar melody comfortably into a vertical four-bar straitjacket, the harmony must not change. The entire musical content therefore consists of repetitions of harmonically identical four-bar phrases, alternated among the three participants, each of whom argues in favor of his chosen horse, Paul Revere, Valentine, and Epitaph.

Even though Loesser does not produce a real fugue, he does offer a degree of real counterpoint that is unusual in a Broadway musical, especially a musical comedy. In fact, the only substantial use of counterpoint among earlier musicals surveyed in this volume occurs, not surprisingly, in *Porgy and Bess* (a technique also demonstrated in earlier Gershwin shows not discussed here, perhaps most notably in "Mine" from *Let 'Em Eat Cake*). Prominent but relatively isolated additional examples can be found in Blitzstein's *The Cradle Will Rock* (scene 10) and Bernstein's *Candide* ("The Venice Gavotte") and *West Side Story* (the "Tonight" quintet). After 1970 this device would become more prominent in Sondheim (e.g., the combination of "Now," "Later," and "Soon" in *A Little Night Music*). Even straightforward harmonization between two principals is exceptional in the musicals of Kern, Rodgers, Porter, and Loewe. Interestingly, the only Broadway composer to rival Loesser at the counterpoint game was Berlin, another lyricist-composer with less formal musical training than the other composers discussed in the present survey, Loesser included. In songs that ranged throughout his career, most famously "Play a Simple Melody" from *Watch Your Step* (1914), "You're Just in Love" from *Call Me Madam* (1950), and his final hurrah as a composer, "An Old-Fashioned Wedding" from the 1966 revival of *Annie Get Your Gun*, Berlin created extraordinary pairs of melodies that could be sung simultaneously.

Example 11.2. "Fugue for Tinhorns" (one complete statement of three-part round)

Example 11.2. Continued

Loesser's predilection for counterpoint or overlapping musical lines can be observed as early as "Baby, It's Cold Outside." In *Where's Charley?* Loesser used counterpoint prominently in "Make a Miracle," and he would continue to present simultaneous melodies in ingenious new ways in more than a few songs in *Hans Christian Andersen, The Most Happy Fella,* and *How to Succeed.* Since it is usually hard to sing simultaneous melodic lines (or even harmony), actor-oriented musicals, especially those inhabiting musical comedy stages, use counterpoint relatively rarely, at least before Sondheim.

After the unison cadence that concludes "Fugue for Tinhorns," the orchestra is instructed to hold their final D♭ until the "Mission Band starts playing on Stage" one half-step lower on C major. In this next number, "Follow the Fold" (Example 11.3), the Save-a-Soul Mission Band and a quartet of missionaries led by Sarah provide a rhythmic and textural contrast to "Fugue for Tinhorns" that could hardly be more extreme. The tinhorns inhabit a world of syncopation, counterpoint, and lots of sharps and flats, while one jarring half-step lower the missionaries occupy a rhythmically unsyncopated, homophonic, C-majorish musical realm. The only conspicuous common denominator between these contrasting musical worlds is a shared underlying harmonic simplicity. In the fugue a measure of dominant harmony alternates with a measure of tonic harmony; the mission march also employs these two basic harmonies exclusively.[17] "Follow the Fold" also illustrates a rare "appropriate" use of a hymn-like style in Loesser's work. The concluding a cappella harmonies of the next song, "The Oldest Established," is far more typical of

Example 11.3. "Follow the Fold" (opening)

Loesser's predilection to translate the religious fervor of secular emotions with mock musical religiosity: gambling as a religious experience. In *Where's Charley?* Loesser had inserted a cadence (marked *"religioso"*) in several places to mark the miracle in "Make a Miracle." Later, in *How to Succeed*, J. Pierrepont Finch's faith in himself would inspire Loesser to musical religiosity and prayer at the punch line of "I Believe in You." The revival-tune quality of the concluding "Brotherhood of Man" in this show is designated "a la Holy Rollers." In all stages of his career Loesser would revisit the secular religiosity of his first hit, "Praise the Lord and Pass the Ammunition."

In addition to the touches inspired by Kaufman, the casting of the show also led to considerable changes of emphasis. This was not new. Earlier it was noted that the will of a star, Ethel Merman, led to the rejection of one song and a reprise of another in *Anything Goes*. Within the next five years, some of the songs of *My Fair Lady* would be composed *after* the non-singing Rex Harrison had been cast, and written accordingly. Strangely enough, with *Guys and Dolls* it was not discovered until casting Sam Levene as Nathan Detroit that the creative team had cast a star who would make Harrison sound like Ezio Pinza.[18]

Guys and Dolls follows the Rodgers and Hammerstein integrated model with the careful insertion of a comic subplot, in Loesser's show the fourteen-year engagement of Nathan and Adelaide and the debilitating psychosomatic symptoms brought about by this delay (described in "Adelaide's Lament"). Indeed, Nathan's role is truly a large one. Even much of "The Oldest Established [Permanent Floating Crap Game in New York]" is sung in his praises: "Why it's good old reliable Nathan, / Nathan, Nathan, Nathan Detroit.—/ If you're looking for action he'll furnish the *spot*.—/ Even when the heat is on it's never too *hot*, / Not for good old reliable Nathan."

But all that the musically unreliable Nathan is given to sing in act I is a speech-like chant in the verse to this song, rhythmically set almost exclusively to quarter-note triplets and virtually monotonal (all but three pitches are Cs): "And they've now got a lock on the *door*—/ Of the gym at Public School Eighty-*four*" and a couple of lines later, "And things being how they are, / The back of the Police Station is out." Later in act I, Levene as Nathan was not only deprived of leading the title song, but he was specifically instructed not to sing along.

In act II Nathan is finally—in number twenty-seven out of the thirty-two numbered selections in the vocal score—allowed to "sing" his waltz of love, "*Sue me, Sue me*, / What can you *do me*? / I love you." But before Kaufman & Co. discovered that Levene had meant what he said when he told them he could not sing, Nathan had also been designated to lead the song "Sit Down, You're Rockin' the Boat" at the prayer meeting.[19] Although this challenging song came to be indelibly associated with Stubby Kaye on stage and film in the expanded role of Nicely-Nicely Johnson, the reassignment of Nathan's music on the surface lessens his dramatic stature as well as his credibility as a romantic lead.

In any event, Nathan's romance with Adelaide certainly has a less comic side. How often must a major character undergo the indignity of a fourteen-year engagement (and fourteen years of a psychosomatic cold) and engage in a perpetual series of lies to her mother about her alleged husband's promotions and their inexorably growing family? To add insult to illness, on the one occasion she is aroused to anger, Adelaide remains the last to know that Nathan is for once telling the truth. Her fiancé is indeed on his way to attend a prayer meeting, Sky having successfully gambled to obtain his presence. After he reluctantly agrees to accept the inevitable deprivation of his freedom and mobility and marry Adelaide (now of course cured), Nathan expresses his feelings about this turn of events by appropriating his fiancée's former symptoms. Thus, after Adelaide describes the new Nathan "sitting there, beside me, every single night," he discharges an "enormous sneeze."

Adelaide and even Sarah are not above deceit and pretense. In the song that precedes Nathan's sneeze, "Marry the Man Today," the conniving pair reveal themselves as "dolls" who desire to change (in midstream) their chosen horses. A conspicuous and dramatically suitable resemblance to the pseudo-fugue tinhorn trio that opened the show is readily evident in the simple and static counterpoint of the following lines: "Marry the man today / Rather than sigh and *sorrow*, / Marry the man today / And change his ways *tomorrow*."

As we have observed, future book doctors of *Anything Goes* rightly questioned the 1934 premise in which a non-singing Sir Evelyn Oakleigh gets the girl. Their solution in the 1962 and 1987 revivals was to interpolate songs from other Porter shows. But Nathan's inability to sing as extensively as other secondary leads in other musicals (especially in the first act) should not be cause for alarm. Fortunately, by the end of the evening and faced with the imminent loss of Adelaide (no longer willing to be taken for granted), Nathan can and does finally demonstrate his love for his long-suffering fiancée when he breaks into song ("Sue Me"). In the Runyon story, "Pick the Winner," Cutie Singleton, a *nom de plume* for Adelaide, leaves Nathan for Professor Woodhead after a ten-year engagement and lives happily ever after with her new beau in their country house. By the simple but powerful act of singing, Nathan convinces us that Loesser's Adelaide need not have followed Cutie's example.

The Most Happy Fella: *"A Musical with a Lot of Music"*

During the long *Guys and Dolls* run, Samuel Goldwyn persuaded Loesser to compose the music for *Hans Christian Andersen* (1952), a Goldwyn-produced film starring Danny Kaye. In addition to its tuneful score, the movie is notable for its screenplay by Kaufman's former collaborator, Moss Hart. After his second consecutive Broadway success, Loesser was otherwise free to grow at his own pace and in his own way and to pursue his ambitious new Broadway show.

By the end of 1952 Loesser was simultaneously drafting sketches for his libretto, lyrics, and music in the first of sixteen sketchbooks of *The Most Happy Fella*. For more than the next three years he would work single-mindedly on his "musical with a lot of music" (calling it an opera would be the kiss of death).[20] His only other major creative project during these years was the composition of three new songs for the film version of *Guys and Dolls* (1955), also produced by Goldwyn (discussed in chapter 14).[21]

In contrast to the sparse documentary evidence for the compositional process of *Guys and Dolls*, *The Most Happy Fella* offers a cornucopia of dated and labeled material, all housed in the Music Division of the New York Public Library. These manuscripts shed some light on the embryonic mysteries and gestation of nearly every portion of the finished musical.[22] The sketchbooks tell us that Loesser had begun most of the major songs (i.e., the twenty-one musical numbers in the published vocal score and libretto (indicated by small capital letters in the online website) before September 1954. Most of these numbers would require additional work during the next fifteen months. In a striking demonstration of creative economy, Loesser managed to use nearly every scrap of sketchbook material—more than one hundred entries—usually in the final score, but at least in the longer version that opened in Boston.

From the sketchbooks we learn that Loesser's initial vision of the work allowed for even less spoken dialogue than the approximately fifteen minutes that would remain in the finished work. By far the most dramatically important material replaced by dialogue is the dramatic and climactic confrontation near the beginning of act III, when Rosabella tells Tony, the man she had come to love in act II, that she was willing to be seduced by his hired hand, Joe, at the end of act I. Relatively late in the compositional process (September and December 1955), in sketches marked "Angry Tony," Loesser revealed that the dialogue of this scene initially contained powerful and dissonant underscoring.[23]

The sketches also show that Loesser's titles for musical numbers, both large and small, were the generating force for the music to follow and that these titles generated rhythms (often indicated by X's) before the rhythms led to melodies. Those who admire Loesser's impeccable declamation of titles with strong profiles such as "The New Ashmolean Marching Society and Students' Conservatory Band" in *Where's Charley?* and "The Oldest Established" (the abbreviated title of "The Oldest Established Permanent Floating Crap Game in New York") in *Guys And Dolls* can observe firsthand how the melody of a song such as "Happy to Make Your Acquaintance" evolved from sketches that share the rhythmic rather than the melodic profiles of the finished product.

Without the sketchbooks, the process by which Loesser expanded arioso passages into full-scale arias would go undetected, nor would we understand how simple sequential musical patterns served Loesser as essential starting points of so many of the songs in this show. The sketchbooks reveal the creative effort that went into such nuances as the important elongated emphasis on the word "full" in Tony and Rosabella's big love duet, "My Heart Is So Full of You," after numerous compositional digressions over a ten-month period. The sketchbooks also help to identify one of the striking unifying musical features in *The Most Happy Fella*: Loesser's ubiquitous use of the melodic sequence, that is, short melodic phrases of symmetrical lengths repeated a step higher or lower. In *Guys and Dolls*, melodic sequences

The Most Happy Fella, act I, scene 2. Jo Sullivan and Robert Weede (1956).
Photograph: Vandamm Studio. Museum of the City of New York. Theater
Collection.

are noticeable in several songs, including the title song, "I'll Know," "I've
Never Been in Love Before," "Take Back Your Mink," and "Marry the Man
Today"; in *Fella*, sequences appear even more prominently and in nearly
every song. The first *three* phrases of "Happy to Make Your Acquaintance"
(Example 11.4), for example, open with Rosabella's thrice-ascending melodic
sequence.

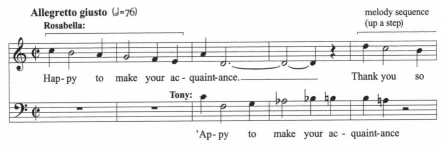

Example 11.4. Melodic sequence and counterpoint in "Happy to Make Your
Acquaintance"

Example 11.4. Continued

Not surprisingly, the sketchbooks reveal something about the process by which Loesser worked out ways to combine melodies. What is seemingly less explicable is that Loesser took the trouble early in his compositional work to notate the familiar English round, "Hey Ho, Nobody Home" on a sketch entry labeled "Lovers in the Lane" ("Hi-ho lovers in the lane" is how Loesser's text opens).[24] In the duet portions of "How Beautiful the Days," Tony and Rosabella alternate entrances of the same melody much as Charley and Amy shared their tune in "Make a Miracle" and the would-be lovers in "Baby, It's Cold Outside." When it came to "Abbondanza," the trio in which Tony's servants take stock of the wedding feast, Loesser could not decide whether he wanted exact melodic imitation in triple meter (3/4 time) or a freer melodic counterpoint in duple meter (2/4 time).[25] Eventually he opted for the freer counterpoint and triple meter found in the published vocal score.

Loesser also included several songs that featured two simultaneous statements of independent but equally important melodies à la Berlin (non-imitative counterpoint). As "I Like Ev'rybody" for Herman and Cleo attests, Loesser did not reserve such contrapuntal complexity for his central romantic characters. When the song is introduced in act II, scene 4, Cleo starts it off with her tune. Then Herman sings the "main" tune against Cleo's tune, now moved to the bass, where it was located in Loesser's sketchbook.[26] At the reprise of the song late in the show (act III, scene 1), the now-compatible Herman and Cleo simultaneously sing their compatible melodic lines (Example 11.5).

In a short essay printed in the Imperial Theatre playbill Loesser described his initial resistance to the idea of adapting Howard's play *They Knew What They Wanted*.[27] Before long, however, he realized that he could delete "the topical stuff about the labor situation in the 1920's, the discussion of religion, etc."[28] Loesser continues: "What was left seemed to me to be a very warm simple love story, happy ending and all, and dying to be sung and danced."[29]

Example 11.5. Two-part counterpoint in "I Like Ev'rybody"

Throughout his compositional work Loesser never lost sight of this central dramatic focus: the developing love and eventual fulfillment between the central protagonists, Tony and Rosabella.

In keeping with the generally warmer and fuzzier expectations of a Broadway musical, Loesser added Cleo, Rosabella's partner in waitressing drudgery in San Francisco, who receives a sitting job in Tony's Napa Valley to rest her tired waitressing feet. He also gives Cleo a partner not found in Howard's play, Herman, the likable hired hand who will win Cleo when he learns to make a fist. Cleo and Herman, like their obvious prototypes, Ado Annie and Will Parker in *Oklahoma!*, serve their function faithfully (in contrast to Adelaide and the relatively unsung Nathan in *Guys and Dolls*). They also make admirable comic lightweights (albeit with sophisticated counterpoint) to contrast with the romantic heavyweights, Tony and Rosabella.

Gone from the musical are not only the lengthy discussions about religion, but even the character of Father McGee, the loquacious priest who opposes the marriage between Tony and Amy (in the play Tony is in love with Amy rather than Rosabella). In Howard's play, Father McGee shows no apparent concern about their age differences, nor is he motivated by the jealousy that motivates his newly created counterpart in the musical, Marie, Tony's younger sister. Howard's Father McGee responds negatively to the marriage for religious reasons: Tony's mail-order bride is not a Catholic.

Other differences between the musical and the somewhat darker play might be briefly noted. Howard has Tony seek a mate outside his Napa

Valley Community because all the single women have slept with Joe, and he attributes Tony's accident to drunkenness rather than fear of rejection. In the play, but not the musical, we learn that Tony's fortune in the grape business stemmed from illegal earnings acquired during Prohibition. The play also contains a striking politically incorrect plot discrepancy. Only after the doctor tells Joe first that Amy (Rosabella) is pregnant does Joe tell Amy. In Howard's play Joe offers to marry Amy and take her out of the Napa Valley; in Loesser's adaptation Joe and Rosabella sing their private thoughts in the beginning of act II, but they never sing (or speak) directly after act I, and Joe leaves the community without knowing Rosabella's condition.

In his obituary for his friend and collaborator, Burrows recalled an exchange that took place after *The Most Happy Fella* premiere on May 3, 1956: "I came out of the theater in great excitement, dashed up to Frank and began chattering away about the marvelous, funny stuff. Songs like 'Standing on the Corner Watching All the Girls Go By.' 'Abbondanza,' 'Big D.' Suddenly he cut me off angrily. 'The hell with those! We know I can do that kind of stuff. Tell me where I made you cry.'"[30] Not content with the triumph of *Guys and Dolls*, Loesser wanted to do more in a musical than to entertain and write hit songs. He wanted to make audiences cry. And although the critical praise for Loesser's most ambitious show about the Napa wine grower and his mail-order bride was far more equivocal than that enjoyed by *Guys and Dolls*, the view espoused here is that the achievement of *The Most Happy Fella* is equally impressive and the work itself arguably even greater Loesser.[31]

Several New York tastemakers praised the show lavishly when it opened at the Imperial Theatre. Robert Coleman headed his review in the *Daily Mirror* with the judgment, "'Most Happy Fella' Is a Masterpiece" and subtitled this endorsement with "Loesser has performed a truly magnificent achievement with an aging play."[32] John McClain of the *New York Journal-American* encapsulated his reaction in his title, "This Musical Is Great," and underlying caption, "Loesser's Solo Effort Should Last as One of Decade's Biggest."[33]

In contrast to the unequivocal acclamation of *Guys and Dolls* and *My Fair Lady* (which opened less than two months before *Fella*), however, other New York critics then (and now) would respond negatively to the work's operatic nature, its surfeit of music, and especially its stylistic heterogeneity, much as they had two decades earlier with *Porgy and Bess*. Predictably, some New York theater critics wanted a musical to be a traditional musical comedy or a Rodgers and Hammerstein sung play—anything but an opera in Broadway garb.

For these critics, a Janus-faced musical was a sin in need of public censure. Walter Kerr's remarks in the *New York Herald Tribune* embody this distaste for works that combine traditional Broadway elements with features associated with European opera: "Still, there's a little something wrong with 'Most Happy Fella'—maybe more than a little. The evening at the Imperial is finally heavy with its own inventiveness, weighted down with the variety and fulsomeness of a genuinely creative appetite. It's as though Mr. Loesser had written two complete musicals—the operetta and the haymaker—on the same simple play and then crammed both into a single structure."[34]

Writing in the *New York Post*, Richard Watts Jr. notes the appropriateness of Loesser's decision that "most of the music ... suggests the more tuneful Italian operas."[35] Nevertheless, Watts is grateful that "the composer has wisely added numbers which, without losing the mood, belong to his characteristic musical comedy manner, and these struck me as the most engaging of the evening." By the end of his review Watts is urging Loesser to return to "his more successful American idiom." George Jean Nathan, another critic who regularly expressed disdain for operatic pretensions in a musical, wrote in the *New York Journal-American* that Loesser "is more at home on his popular musical playground and that the most acceptable portions of his show are those which are admittedly musical comedy."[36] Even *New York Times* theater critic Brooks Atkinson, who praised the "great dramatic stature" and "musical magnificence" of the show, voiced "a few reservations about the work as a whole" and concluded that the work "is best when it is simplest," namely, the songs that most clearly reveal Loesser's "connections with Broadway."[37]

Several weeks later the music critic Howard Taubman evaluated the work in the *New York Times*.[38] While he found much to praise in Loesser's score, including the operatic duet "Happy to Make Your Acquaintance" and the quartet "How Beautiful the Days," Taubman criticized in stronger terms than his theater colleague Loesser's failure "to catch hold of a lyrical expression that is consistent throughout." He also found fault with the composer-lyricist's capitulation "to the tyranny of show business" in such numbers as "Standing on the Corner" and "Big D." In the end Taubman defends his refusal to characterize *The Most Happy Fella* as an opera: "If it [music] is the principal agent of the drama, if the essential points and moods are made by music, then a piece, by a free-wheeling definition, may be called opera." Taubman writes that in a music column "it is not considered bad manners to discuss opera," but he agrees with Loesser's disclaimer. For Taubman, "*The Most Happy Fella* is not an opera."

Times have changed. Thirty-five years and one less-than-ecstatically received production (1979) later, Conrad Osborne, in an essay published several days before its 1991 New York City Opera debut, singled out *The Most Happy Fella* as one of three operatic musicals—the others were *Porgy and Bess* and *Street Scene*—that "have shown a particular durability of audience appeal and a growing (if sometimes grudging) critical reputation."[39] Like his predecessors in 1956 Osborne observed "a tension between 'serious' musicodramatic devices and others derived from musical comedy or even vaudeville," and noted perceptively that "this tension has been responsible for much equivocation about 'Fella.'"[40]

Rather than be disturbed by this clash between opera and Broadway, however, Osborne attributes "much of the fascination of the piece" to the same stylistic discrepancies that proved so disconcerting to Atkinson and Taubman.[41] Osborne also praises "Loesser's melodic genius," his "ability to send his characters' voices aloft in passionate, memorable song that will take hold of anyone," and contends that among musicals *The Most Happy Fella* ranks as "one of the few to which return visits bring new discoveries and richer appreciation."[42]

More frequently than not, heterogeneous twentieth-century classical music, especially American varieties, has been subjected to similar criticism. Music that combines extreme contrasts of classical and popular styles, of tonality and atonality, of consonance and dissonance, as found in Mahler, Berg, and Ives, often disturbs more than it pleases listeners who enjoy the more palatable stylistic heterogeneity of Mozart's *Magic Flute*. Before the 1970s most critics and audiences found *Porgy and Bess*, with its hybrid mix of popular hit songs and seemingly less-melodic recitative, at least partially unsettling. In the following chapter it will be suggested that even in *My Fair Lady* one song, the popular "On the Street Where You Live," whether or not it was inserted as a concession to popular tastes, clashes stylistically with the other songs in the show.

Similarly, the colliding styles of nineteenth-century Italian opera ("Happy to Make Your Acquaintance") and Broadway show tunes ("Big D") practically back-to-back in the same scene provoked strong negative reaction. What Loesser does in *The Most Happy Fella* is to use a popular Broadway style to contrast his Italian or Italian-inspired characters (and the operatic temperament of Tony's eventual match, Rosabella) with their comic counterparts and counterpoints, Rosabella's friend Cleo and her good-natured boyfriend Herman. Between the extremes of "How Beautiful the Days" and "Big D" lie songs like the title song and "Sposalizio," which are more reminiscent of Italian popular tarantellas such as "Funiculi, Funiculà" than of Verdian opera. Even those who condemn Loesser for selling out cannot fault him for composing songs that are stylistically inappropriate.

Nor will the accusation stick that Loesser undermined operatic integrity by inserting unused "trunk songs" from other contexts. The sixteen sketchbooks tell a different story. In fact, among all of the dozens of full-scale songs and ariosos, only one song, "Ooh! My Feet," can be traced to an earlier show.[43] The sketchbooks reveal that Loesser conceived and developed the more popularly flavored "Standing on the Corner" and "Big D" exclusively for his Broadway opera (what Loesser himself described as a "musical with a lot of music"). In the case of the latter, the solitary extant draft of "Big D" is a rudimentary one from March 1954 (two years before the Boston tryout) that displays most of the rhythm but virtually none of the eventual tune.[44] Early rudimentary sketches for "Standing on the Corner" appear in the first sketchbook (August 1953) and continue in several gradual stages (December 1953 and February, May, and June 1954) before Loesser found a verse and chorus that satisfied him.[45]

In "Some Loesser Thoughts," another playbill essay, the composer notes his "feeling for what some professionals call 'score integration,'" which for Loesser "means the moving of plot through the singing of lyrics."[46] Significantly, Loesser acknowledges that his comic songs do not accomplish this purpose when he writes in his next sentence that "in 'The Most Happy Fella' I found a rich playground in which to indulge both my 'integration' and my Tin Pan Alley leanings." His final remarks fan the fuel for those who would accuse Loesser of selling out by making "LOVE" the principal emphasis of his adaptation. For Loesser, not only is love "a most singable subject," it remains a subject "which no songwriter dares duck for very long if he wants to stay popular and solvent."

Loesser's judgment that the Tin Pan Alley songs do not contribute to the "moving of plot" shortchanges the integrative quality of songs such as Cleo's "Ooh! My Feet" and Herman's "Standing on the Corner," which tell us much about the characters who will eventually get together. Since one prefers to sit and the other to stand, even the concepts behind their songs reveal their complementariness. As a show-stopper in the literal sense, "Big D" ranks as perhaps the sole (and welcome) exception to the work's stature as an integrated musical.

The principal characteristics that unify *The Most Happy Fella* musically do not always serve dramatic ends. The first of Loesser's most frequent melodic ideas, the melodic sequence defined earlier (Example 11.4) provides musical unity without dramatic meaning.[47] With only a few small exceptions, however, Loesser consistently employs another melodic unifier. This second melodic idea serves as the basis of a melodic family of related motives, melodies in which a descending minor or major second (a half-step or a whole-step) is followed by a wider descending leap that makes forceful dramatic points. A small but representative sample of this ubiquitous melodic stamp is shown in Example 11.6. Loesser's keen dramatic instincts can be witnessed as the growing intensification of this large family of motives expands throughout the evening from "Benvenuta" (Example 11.6a) to "How Beautiful the Days" (Example 11.6b) and "Warm All Over" (Example 11.6c) to Rosabella's heartfelt arioso, "I Love Him," when a minuscule minor second twice erupts into a full and uninhibited octave (Example 11.6d).

Loesser introduces a less familial and more individually significant musical motive after Tony has asked Joe for his picture (see the "Tony" motive in Example 11.7a). Convinced by his sister Marie that he "ain't young no more," "ain't good lookin,'" and "ain't smart," the not-so-happy fella has the first of several chats with his deceased Mamma (act I, scene 2): "An' sometime soon I wanna send-a for Rosabella to come down here to Napa an' get marry. I gotta send-a Joe's pitch.'"[48] The music that underscores Tony's dialogue with his mother consists of a repeated "sighing" figure composed of descending seconds on strong beats (appoggiaturas), a familiar figure derived from eighteenth- and nineteenth-century operatic depictions of pain and loneliness, underneath a sustained string tremolo that contributes still further to the drama of the moment.[49]

(a)

(b)

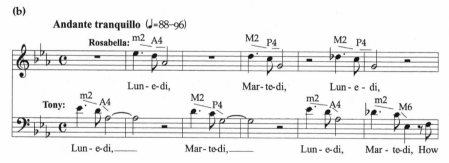

(c)

Example 11.6. The family of motives in *The Most Happy Fella* (M = major; m = minor; d = diminished; A = augmented; P = perfect)
(a) "Benvenuta"
(b) "How Beautiful the Days"
(c) "Warm All Over"
(d) "I Love Him"

(d)

Example 11.6. Continued

In act II, Marie again feeds her brother's low self-image despite Rosabella's assurance that Tony makes her feel "Warm All Over" (in contrast to the "Cold and Dead" response she felt after sleeping with Joe). Consequently, the still-unhappy central character "searches the sky for 'Mamma' and finds her up there," and the original form of his "sighing" returns to underscore a brief monologue. Tony then sings a sad reprise of his sister's didactic warning, "Young People," with still more self-flagellating lyrics: "Young people gotta dance, dance, dance, / Old people gotta sit dere an' watch, watch, watch. / Wit' da make believe smile in da eye. / Young people gotta live, live, live. / Old people gotta sit dere an' die."[50]

After the potent dramatic moment in the final scene of act II, Rosabella finally convinces Tony that she loves him, not out of pity for an aging invalid but "like a woman needs a man." To celebrate this long-awaited moment Tony and Rosabella sing their rapturous duet, "My Heart Is So Full of You." Tony announces that the delayed wedding party will take place that night, and everyone spontaneously dances a hoedown.

The newfound joy of this May-September mail-order romance is shortlived. Rosabella faints from the strain, discovers that she is pregnant with Joe's baby, and asks Cleo for advice. Tony, with a new self-confidence and

(a)

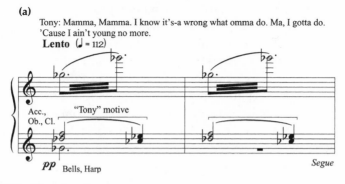

Example 11.7. "Tony" motive
(a) original
(b) transformed

(b)

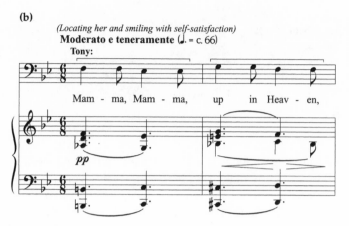

Example 11.7. Continued

overcome by love (he is also somewhat oblivious to Rosabella's internal anguish), again communicates with his mother over the returning string tremolo and the "sighing" "Tony" motive (Example 11.7a). This time, however, when Tony sings to his mother, Loesser ingeniously converts the "sighing" motive into a passionate arioso of hope and optimism, "Mamma, Mamma" (Example 11.7b). Tony's sighing motive will return briefly in the final scene of the show on the words "have da baby," as Tony, "reflecting sadly," decides to accept Rosabella's moment of infidelity as well as its consequences. And as he did in "Mamma, Mamma" at the end of act II, Tony successfully converts a motive that had previously reflected sadness, loneliness, and self-pity into positive emotions throughout the ten passionate measures of the abbreviated aria in act III, "She gonna come home wit' me."[51]

Just as Rosabella comes to express her growing love for Tony with ever-expanding intervals, Tony learns to channel the self-pity expressed in his sighing motive. By the end of the musical the "Tony" motive has been transformed into a love that allows him to put the well-being of another person ahead of himself and to understand how Rosabella's mistake with Joe was the consequence of Tony's own error when he sent Rosabella Joe's picture rather than his own. As part of this metamorphosis Tony finally stands up to his sister. When Marie once again points out his age, physical unattractiveness, and lack of intelligence, the formerly vulnerable Tony responds to the final insult in this litany in underscored speech: "No! In da head omma no smart, ma, in da heart, Marie. In da heart!"[52]

Loesser's *The Most Happy Fella*, smart in the head as well as in the heart, has managed to entertain and move audiences as much as nearly any musical that aspires to operatic realms (Loesser's denials notwithstanding).

Although it lacks the dazzling and witty dialogue, lyrics, and songs of its more popular—and stylistically more homogeneous—Broadway predecessor *Guys and Dolls*, Loesser's musical story of Tony and his Rosabella offers what Burrows described as "a gentle something that wanted to 'make them cry.'"[53] *The Most Happy Fella* makes us cry.

Four years later Loesser himself was crying over the failure (ninety-seven performances) of the bucolic *Greenwillow* (1960). The show contained an excellent score, the best efforts of Tony Perkins in the leading role, and a positive review by Brooks Atkinson in the *New York Times*. Despite all this, Donald Malcolm would ridicule the show's tone in the *New Yorker* when he wrote that the village of *Greenwillow* "makes Glocca Morra look like a teeming slum" and a village where "Brigadoon could be the Latin Quarter."[54]

The following year Loesser, again with *Guys and Dolls* librettist Burrows, succeeded in a more traditional urban musical comedy, *How to Succeed in Business without Really Trying* (1961). Unlike Tony in *The Most Happy Fella*, whose vulnerability and humanity, if not age, appearance, and intelligence, distinguishes him from other Broadway protagonists, the hero of Loesser's next (and last) Broadway hit, J. Pierrepont Finch, is a boyish and aggressively charming Machiavelli who sings the show's central love song to himself as he shaves before a mirror in the executive washroom ("I Believe in You").

As its well-received 1995 Broadway revival starring Matthew Broderick further demonstrated, *How to Succeed* deserves recognition as one of the truly great satirical shows. In how many musicals can we laugh so uproariously about nepotism, blackmail, false pretenses, selfishness, and the worship of money, among many other human foibles. One example of Loesser's comic originality and imagination in song is "Been a Long Day." In this number, which might be described as a trio for narrator and twin soliloquies, a budding elevator romance is described in blow-by-blow detail through a third party before the future lovebirds manage to express their privately sung thoughts directly.

For his remaining eight years Loesser was unable to bring a work to Broadway. *Pleasures and Palaces*, a show about Catherine the Great, closed out of town in 1965, and Loesser died before he could fully complete and begin to try out *Señor Discretion*. But Loesser's legacy remains large, and in his thirteen years on the Broadway stage he fared far better than Runyon's 6–5 odds against. As Loesser's revivals have shown, Broadway audiences, collapsing under the weight of musical spectacles, are reveling in the musicals of Loesser, the composer-lyricist who continues to give audiences and even musical and theater historians and critics so much to laugh (and cry) about and so little to sneeze at.

CHAPTER TWELVE

MY FAIR LADY

From Pygmalion *to* Cinderella

My *Fair Lady* was without doubt the most popularly successful musical of its era. Before the close of its spectacular run of 2,717 performances from 1956 to 1962 it had comfortably surpassed *Oklahoma!*'s previous record of 2,248.[1] And unlike the ephemeral success of the wartime Broadway heroines depicted in *Lady in the Dark* and *One Touch of Venus*, librettist-lyricist Alan Jay Lerner's and composer Frederick "Fritz" Loewe's fair lady went on to age phenomenally well. Most remarkably, over eighteen million cast albums were sold and profits from the staged performances, albums, and 1964 film came to the then-astronomical figure of $800 million. Critically successful revivals followed in 1975 and 1981, the latter with Rex Harrison (Henry Higgins) and Cathleen Nesbitt (Mrs. Higgins) reclaiming their original Broadway roles. In 1993 the work returned once again, this time with television miniseries superstar Richard Chamberlain as Higgins, newcomer Melissa Errico as Eliza, and Julian Holloway playing Alfred P. Doolittle, the role his father, Stanley, created on Broadway on March 15, 1956.

As with most of the musicals under scrutiny in the present survey, the popular and financial success of *My Fair Lady* was and continues to be matched by critical acclaim. Walter Kerr of the *Herald Tribune* told his readers: "Don't bother to finish reading this review now. You'd better sit down and send for those tickets to *My Fair Lady*."[2] William Hawkins of the *World-Telegram & Sun* wrote that the show "prances into that rare class of great musicals" and that "quite simply, it has everything," providing "a legendary evening" with songs that "are likely to be unforgettable."[3] In what may be the highest tribute paid to the show, Harrison reported that "Cole Porter reserved himself a seat once a week for the entire run."[4]

Opening night critics immediately recognized that *My Fair Lady* fully measured up to the Rodgers and Hammerstein model of an integrated musical. As Robert Coleman of the *Daily Mirror* wrote: "The Lerner-Loewe

My Fair Lady. George Bernard Shaw and his puppets, Rex Harrison and Julie Andrews (1956). © AL HIRSCHFELD. Reproduced by arrangement with Hirschfeld's exclusive representative, the MARGO FEIDEN GALLERIES LTD., NEW YORK. WWW. ALHIRSCHFELD.COM

songs are not only delightful, they advance the action as well. They are ever so much more than interpolations, or interruptions. They are a most important and integrated element in about as perfect an entertainment as the most fastidious playgoer could demand.... A new landmark in the genre fathered by Rodgers and Hammerstein. A terrific show!"[5]

Many early critics noted the skill and appropriateness of the adaptation from George Bernard Shaw's *Pygmalion* (1912). For *Daily News* reviewer John Chapman, Lerner and Loewe "have written much the way Shaw must have done had he been a musician instead of a music critic."[6] Hawkins wrote that "the famed *Pygmalion* has been used with such artfulness and taste, such vigorous reverence, that it springs freshly to life all over again."[7] And even though Brooks Atkinson of the *New York Times* added the somewhat condescending "basic observation" that "Shaw's crackling mind is still the genius of *My Fair Lady*," he concluded his rave of this "wonderful show" by endorsing the work on its own merits: "To Shaw's agile intelligence it adds the warmth, loveliness, and excitement of a memorable theatre frolic."[8]

Lerner (1918–1986) and Loewe (1901–1988) met fortuitously at New York's Lambs Club in 1942. Before he began to match wits with Loewe, Lerner's marginal writing experience had consisted of lyrics to two Hasty Pudding musicals at Harvard and a few radio scripts. Shortly after their meeting Loewe asked Lerner to help revise *Great Lady*, a musical that had previously met its rapid Broadway demise in 1938. The team inauspiciously inaugurated their Broadway collaboration with two now-forgotten flops, *What's Up?* (1943) and *The Day before Spring* (1945).

Documentation for the years before Loewe arrived in the United States in 1924 is sporadic and unreliable, and most of the frequently circulated "facts" about the European years—for example, that Loewe studied with Weill's teacher, Ferruccio Busoni—were circulated by Loewe himself and cannot be independently confirmed. Sources even disagree about the year and city of his birth, and the most reliable fact about his early years is that his father was the famous singer Edmund Loewe, who debuted as Prince Danilo in the Berlin production of Lehár's *The Merry Widow* and performed the lead in Oscar Straus's first and only Shaw adaptation, *The Chocolate Soldier*.[9]

As Loewe would have us believe, young Fritz was a child prodigy who began to compose at the age of seven and who at age thirteen became the youngest pianist to have appeared with the Berlin Philharmonic. None of this can be verified. Lerner and Loewe biographer Gene Lees also questions Loewe's frequently reported claim to have written a song, "Katrina," that managed to sell two million copies.[10] Loewe's early years in America remain similarly obscure. After a decade of often extremely odd jobs, including professional boxing, gold prospecting, delivering mail on horseback, and cow punching, Loewe broke into show business when one of his songs was interpolated in the nonmusical *Petticoat Fever* by operetta star Dennis King. Another Loewe song was interpolated in *The Illustrators Show* (1936).[11] The *Great Lady* fiasco (twenty performances) occurred two years later.

After their early Broadway failures, Lerner and Loewe produced their first successful Rodgers and Hammerstein–type musical on their third Broadway try, *Brigadoon* (1947), a romantic tale of a Scottish village that awakens from a deep sleep once every hundred years. By the end of the musical, the town offers a permanent home to a formerly jaded American who discovers the meaning of life and love (and some effective ersatz-Scottish music) within its timeless borders. The following year Lerner wrote the book and lyrics for the first of many musicals without Loewe, the modestly successful and rarely revived avant-garde "concept musical" *Love Life* (with music by Weill). Lerner and Loewe's next collaboration, the occasionally revived *Paint Your Wagon* (1951) was less than a hit on its first run. Also in 1951 Lerner without Loewe wrote the Academy Award–winning screenplay for *An American in Paris*, which featured the music and lyrics of George and Ira Gershwin. By 1952 Lerner, reunited with Loewe, was ready to tackle Shaw.

My Fair Lady *and* Pygmalion

The Genesis

It may seem inevitable that someone would have set *Pygmalion*, especially when considering the apparent ease with which Lerner and Loewe adapted Shaw's famous play for the musical stage. In fact, much conspired against any musical setting of a Shaw play for the last forty years of the transplanted Irishman's long and productive life. The main obstacle until Shaw's death in 1950 was the playwright himself, who, after enduring what he considered to be a travesty of *Arms and the Man* in Straus's *The Chocolate Soldier* (1910), wrote to Theatre Guild producer Theresa Helburn in 1939 that "nothing will ever induce me to allow any other play of mine to be degraded into an operetta or set to any music except its own."[12] As early as 1921, seven years after the English premiere of his play, Shaw aggressively thwarted an attempt by Lehár to secure the rights to *Pygmalion*: "a Pygmalion operetta is quite out of the question."[13] As late as 1948 Shaw was rejecting offers to musicalize *Pygmalion*, and in response to a request from Gertrude Lawrence (the original heroine of *Lady in the Dark*) he offered his last word on the subject: "My decision as to *Pygmalion* is final: let me hear no more about it. This is final."[14]

Much of our information on the genesis of *My Fair Lady* comes from Lerner's engagingly written autobiography, *The Street Where I Live* (1978), more than one hundred pages of which are devoted to the compositional genesis, casting, and production history of their Shaw adaptation.[15] Additionally, Loewe's holograph piano-vocal score manuscripts in the Music Division of the Library of Congress offer a fascinating glimpse into some later details of the compositional process of the songs.

From Lerner we learn that after two or three weeks of intensive discussion and planning in 1952 the team's first tussle with the musicalization of Shaw's play had produced only discouragement. Part of the problem was that the reverence Lerner and Loewe held for Shaw's play precluded a drastic overhaul. Equally problematic, their respect for the Rodgers and Hammerstein model initially prompted Lerner and Loewe to find an appropriate place for a choral ensemble as well as a secondary love story. While a chorus could be contrived with relative ease, it was more difficult to get around the second problem: Shaw's play "had one story and one story only," and the central plot of *Pygmalion*, "although Shaw called it a romance, is a non-love story."[16] In a chance meeting with Hammerstein, the great librettist-lyricist told Lerner, "It can't be done.... Dick [Rodgers] and I worked on it for over a year and gave it up."[17]

Lerner and Loewe returned to their adaptation of Shaw two years later optimistic that a Shavian musical would be possible. As Lerner explains:

> By 1954 it no longer seemed essential that a musical have a subplot, nor that there be an ever-present ensemble filling the air with high C's and flying limbs. In other words, some of the obstacles that had stood in the way of converting Pygmalion into a musical had simply been removed by a changing style....As Fritz and I talked and talked, we gradually began to realize that the way to convert *Pygmalion* to a musical did not require the addition of any new characters....We could do *Pygmalion* simply by doing *Pygmalion* following the screenplay [of the 1938 film as altered by director Gabriel Pascal] more than the [stage] play and adding the action that took place between the acts of the play.[18]

Instead of placing Higgins as a professor of phonetics in a university setting in order to generate the need for a chorus of students, Professor Higgins used his home as his laboratory and a chorus composed of his servants now sufficed. Since the move from a tea party at the home of Higgins's mother to the Ascot races provided the opportunity for a second chorus, it seemed unnecessary to insert a third chorus at the Embassy Ball. Although they did not invent any characters, Lerner and Loewe did provide a variation of a Rodgers and Hammerstein–type subplot by expanding the role of Alfred P. Doolittle, Eliza's father.[19] Despite these changes and other omissions and insertions that alter the tone and meaning of Shaw's play, Lerner's libretto follows much of the *Pygmalion* text with remarkable tenacity. In contrast to any of the adaptations considered here, Lerner and Loewe's libretto leaves long stretches of dialogue virtually unchanged.

By November 1954 Lerner and Loewe had completed five songs for their new musical. Two of these, "The Ascot Gavotte" and "Just You Wait," would eventually appear in the show. Another song intended for Eliza, "Say a Prayer for Me Tonight," would be partially salvaged in the Embassy Ball music and recycled in the film *Gigi* (1958).[20] Also completed by November 1954 were two songs intended for Higgins, "Please Don't Marry Me," the "first attempt to dramatize Higgins's misogyny," and "Lady Liza," the first of several attempts to find a song in which Higgins would encourage a demoralized Eliza to attend the Embassy Ball.[21] Rex Harrison, the Higgins of choice from the outset, vigorously rejected both of these songs, and they quickly vanished. The casting of Harrison, the actor most often credited with introducing a new kind of talk-sing, was of course a crucial decision that affected the musical characteristics of future Higgins songs.[22] A second try at "Please Don't Marry Me" followed in 1955 and resulted in the now familiar "I'm an Ordinary Man." "Come to the Ball" replaced "Lady Liza" and stayed in the show until opening night. Lerner summarizes the compositional progress of their developing show: "By mid-February [1955] we left London with the Shaw rights in one hand, commitments from Rex Harrison, Stanley Holloway, and Cecil Beaton [costumes] in the other, two less songs than we had arrived with ["Please Don't Marry Me" and "Lady Liza"] and a year's work ahead of us."[23]

Earlier Lerner reported that a winter's journey around the frigid Covent Garden had yielded the title and melody of "Wouldn't It Be Loverly." The genesis of Eliza's first song demonstrates the team's usual pattern: title, tune, and, after excruciating procrastination and writer's block, a lyric.[24] The lyricist details the agony of creation for "Wouldn't It Be Loverly," a process that took Loewe "one afternoon" and Lerner weeks of delay and psychological trauma before he could even produce a word. Six weeks "after a successful tour around the neighborhood with 'Wouldn't It Be Loverly?'" they completed Higgins's opening pair of songs, "Why Can't the English?" and "I'm an Ordinary Man."[25] These are the last songs that Lerner mentions before rehearsals began in January 1956.

Lerner's chronology accounts for all but four *My Fair Lady* songs: "With a Little Bit of Luck," "The Servants' Chorus," "Promenade," and "Without

You." All Lerner has to say about "With a Little Bit of Luck" is that it was written for Holloway sometime before rehearsals.[26] But although Lerner's autobiography provides no additional chronological information about the remaining three songs, we are not reduced to idle speculation concerning two of these. On musical evidence it is apparent that the "Introduction to Promenade" was adapted from "Say a Prayer for Me Tonight," one of the earliest songs drafted for the show.[27] It will also be observed shortly that the principal melody of "Without You" is partially derived from Higgins's "I'm an Ordinary Man," completed nearly a year before rehearsals.[28] Loewe's holograph piano-vocal score manuscripts of *My Fair Lady* songs verify Lerner's remark that this last-mentioned song underwent "one or two false starts."[29] Harrison described one of these as "inferior Noël Coward."[30] (In other differences with the published vocal score, the holograph of "You Did It" contains a shortened introduction and a considerable amount of additional but mostly repetitive material.)[31]

Of great importance for the peformance style of Higgins's role was the decision to allow the professor to talk his way into a song or a new phrase of a song. In "I'm an Ordinary Man," "A Hymn to Him," and "I've Grown Accustomed to Her Face," audiences have long been accustomed to hear Higgins speak lines that are underscored by orchestral melody; the pitches are usually indicated in the vocal part by X's, recalling the notation of Schoenberg's *Sprechstimme* in *Pierrot Lunaire*. The first of many examples of this occurs at the beginning of "I'm an Ordinary Man." This move from song to speech probably occurred during the course of rehearsals. In any event, the holograph scores almost invariably indicate that these passages were originally meant to be sung.[32]

A New Happy Ending

In their most significant departure from their source Lerner and Loewe altered Shaw's ending to allow a romantic resolution between Higgins and Eliza Doolittle. Shaw strenuously argued against this Cinderella interpretation, but he would live to regret that his original concluding lines in 1912 allow the *possibility* that Eliza, who has metamorphosed into "a tower of strength, a consort battleship," will return to live with Higgins and Pickering as an independent woman, one of "three old bachelors together instead of only two men and a silly girl."[33] While in his original text Shaw expresses Higgins's confidence that Eliza will return with the requested shopping list, for the next forty years the playwright would quixotically try to establish his unwavering intention that Higgins and Eliza would never marry.[34] Here are the final lines of Shaw's play:

MRS. HIGGINS: I'm afraid you've spoilt that girl, Henry. But never
    mind, dear: I'll buy you the tie and glove.
HIGGINS: (*sunnily*) Oh, don't bother. She'll buy 'em all right enough.
    Goodbye.
(*They kiss.* MRS. HIGGINS *runs out.* HIGGINS, *left alone, rattles his cash in
his pocket; chuckles; and disports himself in a highly self-satisfied manner.*)

Despite Shaw's unequivocal interpretation—and long before Pascal's
Pygmalion film in 1938 or the *My Fair Lady* musical in 1956—the original
Higgins, Beerbohm Tree, had already taken liberties that would distort the
play beyond Shaw's tolerance. In reporting on the 1914 London premiere to
his wife Charlotte, Shaw wrote: "For the last two acts I writhed in hell. . . . The
last thing I saw as I left the house was Higgins shoving his mother rudely
out of his way and wooing Eliza with appeals to buy ham for his lonely
home like a bereaved Romeo."[35] Mrs. Patrick Campbell, for whom Shaw created the role of Eliza, urged the playwright to attend another performance
"soon—or you'll not recognize your play."[36]

When he summoned enough courage to attend the hundredth performance, Shaw was appalled to discover that "in the brief interval between
the end of the play and fall of the curtain, the amorous Higgins threw flowers at Eliza (and with them Shaw's instructions far out of sight)."[37] To make
explicit what he had perhaps naively assumed would be understood, Shaw
published a sequel to *Pygmalion* in 1916, in which he explained in detail
why Eliza and Higgins could not and should not be considered as potential
romantic partners.

Considering his strong ideas on the subject, it is surprising that Shaw
permitted Pascal to further alter the ending (and many other parts) of
Shaw's original screenplay for the 1938 *Pygmalion* film in order to create
the impression that Higgins and Eliza would in fact unite. Perhaps Shaw
was unaware that Pascal had actually filmed two other endings, including
Shaw's. In 1941, Penguin Books published a version of Shaw's screenplay,
which included reworked versions of five film scenes that were not part of
the original play:

1. Eliza getting in a taxi and returning to her lodgings at the end
   of act I;
2. Higgins's housekeeper, Mrs. Pearce, giving Eliza a bath in the
   middle of act II;
3. Eliza's lessons with Higgins at the end of act II;
4. The Embassy Ball at the end of act III (this scene is based on
   the Embassy Ball in the film—another Cinderella image—that

replaced the ambassador's garden party, dinner, and opera
that took place offstage in the play);
5. Eliza's meeting with Freddy when she leaves Higgins's
residence at the end of act IV.

In his book on Shaw's films, *The Serpent's Eye*, Donald P. Costello carefully
details and explains how the printed screenplay departs from the actual
film.[38] Perhaps not surprisingly, the most dramatic departure between what
was filmed and the published screenplay occurred at the work's conclusion.
This is what filmgoers saw and heard in the film:

> *Eliza's voice is heard coming out of the phonograph*:
> ELIZA'S VOICE: Ah-ah-ah-ah-ow-ow-oo-oo!! I ain't dirty: I washed my
> face and hands afore I come, I did.
> HIGGINS'S VOICE: I shall make a duchess of this draggletailed
> guttersnipe.
> ELIZA'S VOICE: Ah-ah-ah-ow-ow-oo!
> HIGGINS'S VOICE: In six months ... (*Higgins switches off the phonograph.*
> *Close-up of Higgins's sorrowful face.*) *Eliza enters the room, unseen by*
> *Higgins. He hears her voice, speaking with perfect lady-like diction, soft,*
> *gentle, lovingly.*
> ELIZA: I washed my face and hands before I came.
> *As Higgins turns to look at Eliza, the ballroom theme begins once*
> *more. Higgins looks at Eliza tenderly. Cut to a close-up of Eliza,*
> *looking back at him. Higgins just begins to smile; then he recol-*
> *lects himself, and says sternly, as the camera looks only at the back*
> *of his head*:
> HIGGINS: Where the devil are my slippers, Eliza?
> *As the ballroom theme swells into a crescendo, a fade-out from the*
> *back of Higgins's head. The lilting music of the ballroom waltz is*
> *heard as "The End" and the cast are flashed upon the screen.*[39]

Before the 1941 publication of the screenplay (as altered by Pascal), however, Shaw managed to have the last word. It appeared in a letter of correc-
tions from August 19, 1939:

> MRS. HIGGINS: I'm afraid you've spoilt that girl, Henry. I should be
> uneasy about you and her if she were less fond of Colonel Pickering.
> HIGGINS. PICKERING! NONSENSE: she's going to marry Freddy. Ha
> ha! Freddy! Freddy!! Ha ha ha ha ha!!!!! (*He roars with laughter as the*
> *play ends.*)

After submitting this final ending, Shaw parenthetically inserted the following remark: "I should like to have a dozen pulls of the corrected page to send to the acting companies."[40]

When asked in an interview why he acquiesced to a "happy" ending in Pascal's film, Shaw replied somewhat archly that he could not "conceive a less happy ending to the story of 'Pygmalion' than a love affair between the middle-aged, middle-class professor, a confirmed old bachelor with a mother-fixation, and a flower girl of 18."[41] According to Shaw, "nothing of the kind was emphasised in my scenario, where I emphasised the escape of Eliza from the tyranny of Higgins by a quite natural love affair with Freddy." Shaw even goes so far as to claim that Leslie Howard's "lovelorn complexion…is too inconclusive to be worth making a fuss about." Despite Shaw's desire to grasp at this perceived ambiguity and despite the fact that audiences of both film and musical do not actually see Eliza fetch Higgins's slippers, most members of these audiences will probably conclude that Freddy is not a romantic alternative.

Shaw's denial to the contrary, the romanticization of *Pygmalion* introduced by Beerbohm Tree during the initial 1914 London run of the play was complete in the 1938 film. As Costello writes: "What remains, after a great deal of omission, is the clear and simple situation of a Galatea finally being fully created by her Pygmalion, finally asserting her own individual soul, and, becoming independent, being free to choose. She chooses Higgins."[42]

The stage was now set for *My Fair Lady*, where the phonetics lesson introduced in the film would be developed still further, Alfred P. Doolittle would be observed on his own Tottenham Court Road turf (and given two songs to sing there, one in each act), and a new and more colorful setting at Ascot would replace Mrs. Higgins's home (act III of Shaw). Again following the film, *My Fair Lady* deleted many of Doolittle's lines, especially his philosophical musing on middle-class morality.[43]

If Lerner and Loewe did not invent a romantic pairing between Henry Higgins and Eliza Doolittle, they succeeded in contradicting Shaw still more completely (albeit more believably), a task made difficult by Higgins's extraordinary misogyny, rudeness, and insensitivity in Shaw's original play. Using the Pascal film as its guide, the Broadway *Pygmalion* therefore made Higgins less misogynist and generally more likable and Eliza less crude, more attractive, and more lovable than their counterparts in Shaw's play and screenplay and Pascal's film. Perhaps more significantly, Lerner and Loewe prepared the eventual match of Higgins and Eliza when they created two moments in song that depict their shared triumph, "The Rain in Spain" and Eliza's gloriously happy "I Could Have Danced All Night" that shortly follows.

Lerner and Loewe would also go beyond the film with several liberties of omission and commission to help musical audiences accept the unlikely but much-wished-for romantic liaison between the antagonistic protagonists. More important, not only did Lerner remove all references to Higgins's "mother fixation," but he gave Higgins compassion to match his brilliance. In order to achieve Higgins's metamorphosis from a frog to a prince, Lerner added a speech of encouragement—a song would be overkill—not found in either the film or published screenplay. Significantly, it is this newly created speech that leads directly to Eliza's mastery of the English language as she finally utters the magic words, "the rain in Spain stays mainly in the plain" with impeccable and lady-like diction.[44]

In this central speech, Higgins, in contrast to the play and screen versions, demonstrates an awareness of what his subject might be feeling and suffering: "Eliza, I know you're tired. I know your head aches. I know your nerves are as raw as meat in a butcher's window." After extolling the virtues of "the majesty and grandeur of the English language," Higgins for the first time offers encouragement to his human experiment: "That's what you've set yourself to conquer, Eliza. And conquer it you will....Now, try it again."[45]

A Cinderella Musical with an Extraordinary Woman

After conveying Higgins's humanity by the end of act I, Lerner and Loewe tried in their second act to make musically explicit what Shaw implies or omits in his drama. Not only does Eliza now possess the strength and independence of "a consort battleship" admired by Higgins in Shaw's play. After the Embassy Ball in *My Fair Lady* the heroine now in fact has the psychological upper hand as well. Clearly, Lerner and Loewe romanticized, and therefore falsified, Shaw's intentions. At the same time they managed to reveal Eliza's metamorphosis as Higgins's equal through lyrics and music more clearly than either Shaw's play or screenplay and Pascal's film. The playwright lets Higgins express his delight in Eliza's newfound independence, but he does not show how Eliza surpasses her creator (in this case Higgins) in psychological power other than by allowing Higgins to lose his composure (*"he lays hands on her"*). Lerner and Loewe accomplish this volte-face by taking advantage of music's power to reveal psychological change. Simply put, the Broadway team reverse the musical roles of their protagonists.

In act I of *My Fair Lady*, Eliza, in response to her initial humiliation prompted by her inability to negotiate the proper pronunciation of the letter "a" and to Higgins's heartless denial of food (recalling Petruchio's method

My Fair Lady, act I, scene 5. Julie Andrews and Rex Harrison ("In Hertford, Hereford, and Hampshire, hurricanes hardly ever happen.") (1956). Museum of the City of New York. Theater Collection. Gift of Harold Friedlander. For a film still of this scene see p. 321.

of "taming" Kate in *Kiss Me, Kate*), sputters her ineffectual dreams of vengeance in "Just You Wait" (Example 12.1a).[46] Eliza sings a brief reprise of this song in act II after Higgins and the uncharacteristically inconsiderate Pickering display a callous disregard for Eliza's part in her Embassy Ball triumph ("You Did It"). Eliza will also incorporate the tune at various moments in "Without You," for example, when she sings "And there still will be rain on that plain down in Spain" (Example 12.1b).

Just you wait, 'en - ry 'ig-gins, just you wait!_____ You'll be

Example 12.1. "Just You Wait" and selected transformations
  (a) "Just You Wait"
  (b) "Without You"
  (c) "I'm an Ordinary Man"
  (d) "I've Grown Accustomed to Her Face"

Example 12.1. Continued

The opening phrase of the chorus in "Without You," Eliza's ode to independence, consists of a transformation into the major mode of "Just You Wait." Its first four notes also inconspicuously recall Higgins's second song of act I, "I'm an Ordinary Man," when he first leaves speech for song on the words "who desires" (Example 12.1c). By this subtle transformation, audiences can subliminally hear as well as directly see that the tables have begun to turn as Eliza adopts Higgins's musical characteristics. At the same time Higgins transforms Eliza into a lady, by the end of the evening Eliza (and her music) will have successfully transformed Higgins into a gentleman.

To reinforce this dramatic reversal, Higgins himself recapitulates Eliza's "Just You Wait" material in both the minor and major modes of his final song, "I've Grown Accustomed to Her Face" (Example 12.1d). At this point in the song Higgins is envisaging the "infantile idea" of Eliza's marrying Freddy.[47] The verbal and dramatic parallels between Higgins's and Eliza's revenge on their respective tormentors again suggest the reversal of their roles through song.

Higgins's "I've Grown Accustomed to Her Face" in act II also offers a musical demonstration of a dramatic transformation needed to convince audiences that Eliza's return is as plausible as it is desirable. In the fast sections of "I'm an Ordinary Man" in act I, Higgins explains the discomforting effect of women on his orderly existence (Example 12.2a). Higgins's dramatic transformation in his final song is most clearly marked by tempo and dynamics, but the melodic change is equally significant if less immediately obvious.[48] As shown in Example 12.2b, no longer does Higgins move up an ascending scale to reach his destination like a "motor bus" (Eliza's description in Shaw's act V). For one thing, the destination of the opening line, "She almost makes the day begin," is the fourth degree of the scale (F in the key of C) on the final syllable rather than the first degree. For another, Higgins now precedes the resolution with the upper note G to soften the momentum of the ascending scale. Thus a lyrical Higgins, who sings more and talks less, conveys how he misses his Eliza. Eventually within the song this lyricism (to be sung *con tenerezza* or tenderly) will conquer the other side of his emotions, embodied in his dream of Eliza's humiliation.

The reuse of "Just You Wait" and the transformation of the "but let a woman in your life" portions of "I'm an Ordinary Man" into "I've Grown Accustomed to Her Face" provide the most telling musical examples of Higgins's dramatic transformation. The far less obvious transformation of "I'm an Ordinary Man" into "Without You" mentioned earlier (Example 12.1c) provides additional musical evidence of the power reversal between Higgins and Eliza in the second act of *My Fair Lady*.[49]

Example 12.2. "I'm an Ordinary Man" and "I've Grown Accustomed to Her Face"
(a) "I'm an Ordinary Man"
(b) "I've Grown Accustomed to Her Face"

Although they lack the immediate recognizability of these melodic examples, the most frequent musical unities are rhythmic ones, with or without attendant melodic profiles. The middle section of "Just You Wait," for example, anticipates the rhythm of "Get Me to the Church on Time" (Example 12.3). The eighteenth-century Alberti bass in the accompaniment of this section, which suggests the propriety of classical music, is also paralleled in the second act song of Eliza's father when he decides to marry and thereby gain conventional middle-class respectability.

It is possible that Lerner and Loewe intended to link the central characters rhythmically by giving them songs that begin with an upbeat. In act I, both parts of Higgins's "Ordinary Man," the main melody of Doolittle's "A Little Bit of Luck," and Eliza's "I Could Have Danced All Night" all begin with three-note upbeats. Eliza's "Just You Wait," Freddy's "On the Street Where You Live," and "Ascot Gavotte" each open with a two-note upbeat and "The Rain in Spain" employs a one-note upbeat.

Dramatic meaning for all these upbeats may be found by looking at the two songs in act I that begin squarely on the downbeat, "Why Can't the English?" and "Wouldn't It Be Loverly?" Significantly, these songs, the first two of the show, are rhetorical questions sung by Higgins and Eliza, respectively, before their relationship has begun. Clearly Higgins, in speaking about matters of language and impersonal intellectual matters, plants his feet firmly on solid ground. Similarly, the strong downbeats of Eliza's opening song demonstrate her earthiness and directness. Once Higgins has encountered Eliza in his study and sings "I'm an Ordinary Man," Lerner

(a)

Example 12.3. "Just You Wait" and "Get Me to the Church on Time"
(a) "Just You Wait" (middle section)
(b) "Get Me to the Church on Time" (opening)

(b)

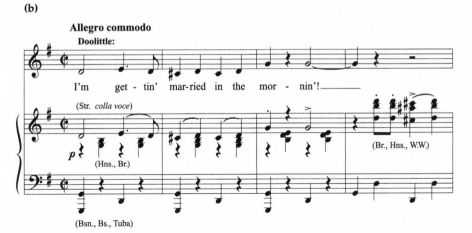

Example 12.3. Continued

and Loewe let us know that Higgins is on less firm territory and can no longer begin his songs on the downbeat. After Eliza begins her lessons with Higgins, she too becomes unable to begin a song directly on the downbeat. As Doolittle becomes conventional and respectable, he too will begin respectably on the downbeat in his second-act number, "Get Me to the Church On Time."[50]

Although Eliza transforms Higgins's "Ordinary Man" in "Without You," complete with upbeat, moments later she manages to demonstrate to Freddy that she can once again begin every phrase of a song on the downbeat, as she turns the Spanish tango of "The Rain in Spain Stays Mainly in the Plain" into the faster and angrier Latin rhythms of "Show Me." Tellingly, Higgins never regains his ability to begin a song on the downbeat. Especially revealing is his final song, "I've Grown Accustomed to Her Face," which retains the three-note upbeat of his own "Ordinary Man" ("but let a woman in your life") and Eliza's euphoric moment in act I, "I Could Have Danced All Night."

During the New Haven tryouts a few songs continued to present special problems. One of these songs, "Come to the Ball," Lerner and Loewe's second attempt to give Higgins a song of encouragement for Eliza prior to the Embassy Ball, was dropped after one performance.[51] Although Lerner never seemed to accept its removal, his more objective collaborators, Loewe and especially director Moss Hart, understood why the show works better for its absence: while it endorses Eliza's physical beauty, it simply does not offer her any other reason to attend the ball. Despite the current predilection of reinstating deleted numbers from Broadway classics, it seems unlikely that audiences will soon be hearing "Come to the Ball" in its original context.

The crucial role of Hart (the librettist of *Lady in the Dark*) in the development of Lerner's book should not go unnoticed. Even if the full extent of his contribution cannot be fully measured, Lerner readily acknowledged that the director went over every word with the official librettist over a four-day marathon weekend in late November 1955.[52] Several of Hart's major suggestions during the rehearsal and tryout process can be more accurately gauged. In addition to his requesting the deletion of "Come to the Ball," we know from Lerner's autobiography that Hart persuaded Lerner and Loewe to remove "a ballet that occurred between Ascot and the ball scene and 'Say a Prayer for Me Tonight.'"[53] To fill the resulting gap near the end of act I, Lerner "wrote a brief scene which skipped directly from Ascot to the night before the ball."[54]

The other major song marked for extinction after opening night in New Haven was "On the Street Where You Live." In both his autobiography and "An Evening with Alan Jay Lerner" presented at New York's 92nd Street Y in 1971, Lerner discussed the negative response to this song, his own desire to retain it, his failure to understand why it failed, and his solution to the problem several days later.[55] For Lerner, the "mute disinterest" that greeted this song was due to the fact that audiences were unable to distinguish Freddy Eynesford-Hill from the other gentlemen at Ascot.[56] Lerner's autobiography relates how he gave Freddy a new verse to help audiences remember him; in his "Evening" at the Y, Lerner explains a revision in which for the sake of clarity Freddy has the maid ask him to identify himself by name. In Lerner's view the positive response to this change was vindication enough. Certainly "On the Street Where You Live" remains the most frequently performed song outside the context of the show.

The rich afterlife of "On the Street Where You Live" as an independent song may provide a clue as to why everyone else concerned with the show (other than Lerner) was willing, even eager, to cut this future hit after it failed to register on its opening night audience. Lehman Engel, an astute and sensitive Broadway critic and a staunch proponent of the integrated musical, writes that when he sees a musical for the first time "the highest compliment anyone can pay is to not be conscious of the songs."[57] The absence of such awareness "indicates that all of the elements worked together so integrally that I was aware only of the total effect."

Engel's reaction to *My Fair Lady* expresses the problem clearly:

I had a similar response to *My Fair Lady* the first time [that like *Fiddler on the Roof*, the elements worked integrally], but I did hear "On the Street Where You Live" and I believe this happened for two reasons. In the first place, nothing else was going on when the song was sung; the singing character was simply (and intentionally) stupid—nothing complex about that.[58] But secondly I heard the song because I disliked it intensely. (I love everything else in the score. But this song, to me, did not fit.) It was the picture that shoved its way out of the frame with a bang. Suddenly there was a "pop" song that had strayed into a score otherwise brilliant, integrated, with a great sense of the play's own style and a faithful, uncompromising exposition of characters and situations.

Although much of *My Fair Lady* departs from Shaw's play, its Cinderella slant nevertheless constitutes an extraordinarily faithful adaptation to Pascal's filmed revision of Shaw's original screenplay. Moreover, the music of *My Fair Lady* for the most part accurately serves most of Shaw's textual ideas. Additionally, the songs themselves, which are carefully prepared and advance the action in the Rodgers and Hammerstein tradition, convey the dramatic meaning that underlies this action.

One critical quandary remains. Just as Higgins neglects to consider the question of what is to become of Eliza, Lerner and Loewe's popular adaptation of *My Fair Lady* poses the problem of what is to become of Shaw's *Pygmalion*, a play that noted literary critics, including Harold Bloom, consider to be the playwright's masterpiece.[59] The relative decline of Shaw's *Pygmalion* in the wake of *My Fair Lady* seems especially lamentable.[60]

But even measured by Shavian standards, Lerner and Loewe's classic musical is by no means overshadowed on artistic grounds. Readers of Shaw's play know, as Shaw knew, that Higgins would "never fall in love with anyone under forty-five."[61] Indeed, marrying Freddy might have its drawbacks, but marrying Higgins would be unthinkable. It is the ultimate achievement of Lerner and Loewe's *My Fair Lady* that the unthinkable has become the probable.

Two years after *My Fair Lady*, Lerner and Loewe completed *Gigi*, the Academy Award–winning film adaptation of a Colette novella. Not wishing to argue with success, *Gigi*, like *My Fair Lady*, tells the story of a young woman who ends up with an older man—Cinderella revisited. The final Broadway collaboration appeared two years later, *Camelot* (1960), a partially successful attempt to recycle a production team (director Hart and Julie Andrews as Guenevere, as well as a new, acclaimed, non-singing actor in the Harrison tradition, Richard Burton, as King Arthur). The box office magic of the *My Fair Lady* "team" and a long televised segment on the Ed Sullivan Show helped *Camelot*—the positive associations with President Kennedy came later—to survive its extraordinarily bad critical press, growing tensions between Lerner and Loewe, and Lerner's hospitalization for bleeding ulcers. Perhaps the most devastating blow of all was Hart's sudden heart attack and hospitalization, which forced the director to assume the unaccustomed role of patient rather than that of play doctor, a role he had performed so irreplaceably on *My Fair Lady*.

Even those who feel that Eliza should have gone off into the sunset (or the fog) with Freddy rather than the misogynist Higgins might have second thoughts about Guenevere's decision to abandon her likable and desirable husband Arthur for the younger but boorish and egotistical Lancelot. As Engel writes: "It is not lack of fidelity that makes for our dissatisfaction but an unmotivated, rather arbitrary choice that seemed to make no sense."[62]

After *Camelot*, Lerner and Loewe would adapt *Gigi* for Broadway in 1973 (it ran for only three months). One year later they would work together on new material for the last time in the film *The Little Prince*. With the exceptions of these brief returns, Loewe, who had collaborated exclusively with Lerner ever since *What's Up?* in 1943, retired on his laurels and died quietly in 1988. The more restless Lerner, who as early as the 1940s had teamed up with Weill on *Love Life* one year after *Brigadoon*, would collaborate with Burton Lane within five years after *Camelot* to create the modestly successful *On a Clear Day You Can See Forever*.

For his last twenty years, Lerner without Loewe—and, in some respects equally unfortunately, without Moss Hart, who died in 1961—would produce one failure after another. Not even the star quality of Katharine Hepburn in *Coco* (1970) could help this show with music by André Previn to run more than a year. A potentially promising collaboration with the brilliant Leonard Bernstein in *1600 Pennsylvania Avenue* (1976) closed within a week. Other short-lived post-*Camelot* musicals included *Lolita, My Love* (1972), *Carmelina* (1979), and *Dance a Little Closer* (1983) with music composed by John Barry, Lane, and Charles Strouse, respectively. At the time of his death in 1986, the indefatigable librettist-lyricist had drafted much of a libretto and several lyrics for yet another musical, this time based on the classic 1936 film comedy, *My Man Godfrey*.[63]

CHAPTER THIRTEEN

WEST SIDE STORY

The Very Model of a Major Musical

W*est Side Story*, a collaboration of four extraordinary individuals—Jerome Robbins (choreographer and director), Arthur Laurents (librettist), Leonard Bernstein (composer), and Stephen Sondheim (lyricist)—premiered on Broadway on September 26, 1957, and ran for 734 performances.[1] After a national tour that lasted a year, it returned to Broadway for an additional 249 performances. A bona fide hit but not a megahit like *Oklahoma!* or *My Fair Lady*, *West Side Story* eventually logged in as the twelfth longest running show of the 1950s (see "Long Runs: Decade by Decade 1920s–2000s" in the online website).[2]

In its initial run *West Side Story* received mostly favorable and respectful notices from our by-now familiar cast of critics. John McClain was the only critic who assessed the show as "the most exciting thing that has come to town since 'My Fair Lady.' "[3] Walter Kerr focused his attentions on the dancing, "the most savage, restless, electrifying dance patterns we've been exposed to in a dozen seasons," to the near exclusion of everything else, and concluded his review with a tribute to Robbins: "This is the show that could have danced all night, and nearly did. But the dancing is it. Don't look for laughter or—for that matter—tears."[4] Brooks Atkinson praised the blend and unity of the work and production and the authors for "pooling imagination and virtuosity" to create "a profoundly moving show that is as ugly as the city jungles and also pathetic, tender and forgiving."[5] Robert Coleman and John McClain predicted that the show would be a hit, and, in what was perhaps the most laudatory critical response, John Chapman opened his review in the *Daily News* by exclaiming that "the American theatre took a venturesome forward step" to present "a bold new kind of musical theatre."[6] Nevertheless, it was not until 1961, with the release of the Academy Award–winning film starring the glamorous box-office draw Natalie Wood (her singing dubbed by the ubiquitous Marni Nixon), that *West Side Story* finally became a certified blockbuster, with a soundtrack that Stephen Banfield reports "remains the longest ever number 1 on *Billboard*'s album charts."[7]

In the years since the film, *West Side Story* has appeared in revivals both at Lincoln Center's New York State Theater in 1968 (89 performances), on Broadway in 1980 (333 performances) and 2009, and in innumerable productions outside of New York. *West Side Story* has also acquired serious respect and attention from both theater and music historians and critics. While it shares with some of the other musicals in this survey a complex score rich in organicism and motivic and other musical techniques associated with the nineteenth-century European operatic ideal, as well as some songs that eventually became standards, it surpasses its European and Broadway predecessors in its reliance on dance and movement to depict dramatic action. The creators of *West Side Story* also managed to take a canonic and extremely well-loved Shakespeare play and adapt it for 1950s audiences while remaining faithful to the spirit of the original. Most significantly, the adaptation both provides dramatically credible and audible musical equivalents of Shakespeare's literary techniques and captures his central themes.

Musicals prior to *West Side Story* featured dance to advance the plot ("Slaughter on Tenth Avenue" in *On Your Toes*); to convey deeper psychological truths in dreams, in fantasies, or through mime (*Oklahoma!*, and *Carousel*); or to establish an ambiance at the beginning of the show (*Guys and Dolls*). Thanks to the choreographic vision of Jerome Robbins (1918–1998), the ability of Leonard Bernstein (1918–1990) to conceive extended dance music, and the willingness of Arthur Laurents (b. 1918) to let dance and music speak for a thousand words (his libretto is widely considered to be the shortest of any full-length Broadway show), *West Side Story* went beyond these early landmarks in expressing essential dramatic action through the medium of dance. At least four major moments in act I are told exclusively or nearly exclusively in dance (Prologue, The Dance at the Gym, the "Cool" Fugue, and The Rumble); act II features a dream ballet based on "Somewhere" and a violent Taunting ballet. Dances even figure prominently in most of the songs, especially "America."

West Side Story is also notable for increasing the tragic dimensions of a musical Jud Frye falls on his knife and dies in a fight with Curley in *Oklahoma!* Billy Bigelow takes his own life in act II in *Carousel*. Cable is killed on his military mission near the end of *South Pacific*, and the King dies at the end of *The King and I*. In *West Side Story* two principal characters, Riff and Bernardo, the respective leaders of the Jets and Sharks, are killed in a knife battle before the end of act I. Tony is shot and killed by Chino near the end of act II. In adapting what is arguably the most famous love story of all time, *Romeo and Juliet*, *West Side Story* presented a level of youthful violence, hatred, and death unprecedented in a Broadway musical.

The Making of a Masterpiece

Prior to its 1957 premiere, only Sondheim (b. 1930) among the principal creators of *West Side Story* had yet to distinguish himself on Broadway (Sondheim's career will be surveyed in chapter 15). More than a decade earlier librettist Laurents had written the critically lauded *Home of the Brave* (1945). Between Robbins's 1949 initial conception of a *Romeo and Juliet* musical with lots of dance and its working out, Laurents wrote his most successful play, *The Time of the Cuckoo* (1952).

In 1944 Robbins collaborated with Bernstein on both the ballet *Fancy Free* (as featured dancer and choreographer) and its inspired Broadway offspring later that same year, *On the Town*. Beginning with *High Button Shoes* in 1947 (lyrics by Sammy Cahn and music by Jule Styne), Robbins choreographed a quartet of musical comedies, mostly hits: Hugh Martin's *Look Ma, I'm Dancin'* (1948), Berlin's *Miss Liberty* (1949) and *Call Me Madam* (1950), and Rodgers and Hammerstein's *The King and I* (1951), with its innovative narrated ballet-pantomime "Small House of Uncle Thomas." As co-director with Abbott, Robbins helped to create Adler and Ross's *The Pajama Game* (1954); as director-choreographer he brought to life two shows with lyrics by Comden and Green and music by Styne, *Peter Pan* (1954) and *Bells Are Ringing* (1956), the latter one year before *West Side Story*.

Bernstein, like Gershwin, came to the piano at a relatively late age, in Bernstein's case, ten. He followed his undergraduate years as music major at Harvard (class of 1939) with studies in orchestration, piano, and conducting at the Curtis Institute in Philadelphia. In 1941 he began his private studies with Boston Symphony conductor Serge Koussevitzky. While an assistant to Artur Rodzinski (then conductor of the New York Philharmonic), Bernstein gained instant (and permanent) recognition when he filled in for ailing guest conductor Bruno Walter and conducted the orchestra on a national broadcast in November 1943.

Within the next three months Bernstein's first "serious" classical works were performed in New York: the song cycle *I Hate Music*, the "Jeremiah" Symphony, the ballet *Fancy Free*, and, by the end of 1944, when the composer was twenty-six, his first Broadway hit, *On the Town*. Between *On the Town* and *West Side Story* the phenomenally eclectic composer, conductor, pianist, and educator composed three major theater works of enduring interest: *Trouble in Tahiti* (1952; with his own libretto and lyrics), *Wonderful Town* (1953; book by Joseph Fields and Jerome Chodorov and lyrics by Comden and Green), and *Candide* (1956; book by Lillian Hellman, lyrics by Richard Wilbur, John Latouche, Dorothy Parker, Hellman, and Bernstein).

Several published personal remembrances help sort out the complicated genesis of *West Side Story*. The first recollection was recorded in 1949 in "Excerpts from a *West Side Story* Log," the year Robbins introduced his concept to two of his future collaborators, Laurents and Bernstein. Bernstein's log, which originally appeared in the *West Side Story Playbill*, identifies major events and ideological turning points between Robbins's initial idea and the opening night tryout in August 1957.[8] Nearly thirty years later the foursome (Robbins, Laurents, Bernstein, and Sondheim) met in 1985 as a panel to discuss their creation before an audience of the Dramatists Guild.[9] Valuable information on the genesis of *West Side Story* can also be found in excerpts from published interviews with those involved in the original production, a number of which appear in Craig Zadan's *Sondheim & Co.*[10] Other important sources on the compositional process are contained in Bernstein's letters to his wife, Felicia, who was visiting her family in Santiago, Chile, during the rehearsals and Washington tryouts; Sondheim's "Anecdote" published in the song book *Bernstein on Broadway*; and a Bernstein interview with theater critic Mel Gussow published shortly after the composer's death in 1990.[11]

Despite some minor discrepancies in their 1985 recollection of *West Side Story*'s genesis, the four collaborators shed a great deal of light on the evolution of their masterpiece.[12] Moreover, their memory of compositional changes is almost invariably vindicated by the eight libretto drafts and various lyric sheets housed among the Sondheim papers in the State Historical Society of Wisconsin. The first of the libretto drafts is dated January 1956, two months after Sondheim joined the entourage, and the last was completed on July 19, 1957, approximately midway through the unprecedentedly long eight-week rehearsal schedule (twice the usual length).[13] Earlier versions of Bernstein's holograph piano-vocal scores are also available both in Wisconsin and in the Music Division of the Library of Congress.

From Bernstein's log we learn that Robbins's original "noble idea" in January 1949 was "a modern version of *Romeo and Juliet* set in slums at the coincidence of Easter-Passover celebration."[14] Over the next four months Laurents drafted four scenes, and the original trio of collaborators discussed the direction of what was then known as *East Side Story*. Bernstein recorded that their goal was to write "a musical that tells a tragic story in musical-comedy terms...never falling into the 'operatic' trap," a show that would not "depend on stars" but must "live or die by the success of its collaborations."

The next log entries appear six years later when Robbins-Laurents-Bernstein returned to their dormant idea. On June 7, 1955, Bernstein reported that the group remained excited and hypothesized that "maybe I can plan to give this year to Romeo—if *Candide* gets in on time." By August 25 the trio had "abandoned the whole Jewish-Catholic premise as not very fresh," replacing Jews and Catholics with rival gangs, the newly arrived Puerto Ricans (the future Sharks) and the "self-styled 'Americans'" (the Jets). *East Side Story* had metamorphosed into *West Side Story*.

Since Robbins's balletic conception entailed an unusually extensive musical score, Bernstein, who until then thought he could handle the lyrics himself, decided that he needed a lyricist after all. On November 14 he wrote that they had found "a young lyricist named Stephen Sondheim," and described him as "ideal for this project."[15] In the 1985 symposium Sondheim added that when he was signed on as "co-lyricist" (in an unspecified month in 1955) Laurents "had a three-page outline."[16]

In the sole entry of 1956 (March 17) Bernstein announced that *Romeo* would be "postponed for a year" to make way for *Candide*.[17] Not unlike *Candide*'s Professor Pangloss, Bernstein tried to put the best possible face on this delay. He then described the "chief problem" of the new "problematical work": "To tread the fine line between opera and Broadway, between realism and poetry, ballet and 'just dancing,' abstract and representational," and to "avoid being 'messagy.'"[18]

On February 1, 1957, Bernstein noted briefly that with *Candide* "on and gone...nothing shall disturb the project." In the next entry (July 8), shortly after rehearsals had begun, Bernstein confirmed the wisdom of 1949 in not casting "'singers,'" since "anything that sounded more professional would inevitably sound more experienced, and then the 'kid' quality would be gone." On August 20, one day after the opening-night tryout in Washington, Bernstein made his final entry. With great enthusiasm and pride he assessed the successful artistic collaboration ("all writing the *same* show"). Together, the quartet had created a work that possessed a "theme as profound as love versus hate, with all the theatrical risks of death and racial issues and young performers and 'serious' music and complicated balletics."[19]

Shortly before his death Bernstein revealed that the melody of "America," portions of "Mambo" from "The Dance at the Gym" (both derived from a never-completed Cuban ballet called *Conch Town* begun in 1941), and the centrally important "Somewhere" and "Maria" were among the first musical ideas conceived.[20] Regarding the origins of "Somewhere" Bernstein explained: " 'Somewhere' was a tune I had around and had never finished. I loved it. I remember Marc Blitzstein loved it very much and wrote a lyric to it just for fun. It was called 'There Goes What's His Name.' "[21] Larry Kert (the original Tony) placed Bernstein's recollection about "Somewhere" more precisely when he remembered that "Somewhere" was "written about the time of *On the Town*" (1944), which would make this song the earliest musical antecedent of the future *West Side Story*.[22] Of equal importance is Bernstein's recollection that at the time the musical was still *East Side Story* he "had already jotted down a sketch for a song called 'Maria,' which was operable in Italian or Spanish."[23] Not only did Bernstein's sketch have a "dummy lyric," it "had those notes...the three notes of 'Maria' [that] pervade the whole piece—inverted, done backward."[24]

Stephen Sondheim (at piano) and Leonard Bernstein rehearsing *West Side Story* (1957). Museum of the City of New York. Theater Collection.

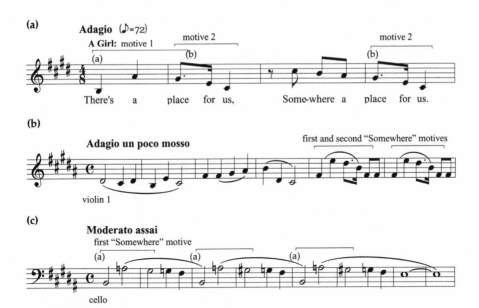

Example 13.1. "Somewhere" in Beethoven and Tchaikovsky
(a) "Somewhere"
(b) Beethoven: Piano Concerto No. 5, op. 73 ("Emperor")
(c) Tchaikovsky: *Romeo and Juliet*

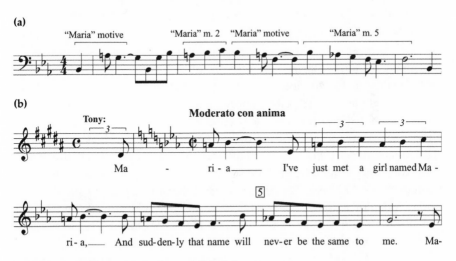

Example 13.2. Blitzstein's *Regina* and "Maria"
(a) Blitzstein's *Regina*, Introduction to act I
(b) "Maria"

In the light of their contribution to the organic unity of the work, the knowledge that "Somewhere" and "Maria" were the first two songs drafted provides invaluable historical confirmation of the analytical conclusions that follow. Also striking, even if perhaps coincidental, is the fact that both of these pivotal songs bear unmistakable resemblances to music of Bernstein's predecessors. The opening five pitches and rhythms of "Somewhere" (Example 13.1a) correspond closely to the fifth and six measures of the second movement of Beethoven's Eb major Piano Concerto, op. 73, known as the "Emperor" (Example 13.1b).[25] More significantly, the thrice-repeated three-note motive in the cello part at the conclusion of Tchaikovsky's *Romeo and Juliet* Overture (Example 13.1c) is identical to the first three notes of Bernstein's melody. Intended or not, "Somewhere" seems to begin where Tchaikovsky's overture leaves off. Unlike borrowed material in other shows, a number of Bernstein's central classical borrowings were apparently chosen for their programmatic and associative meaning.[26]

The main tune of "Maria" is more obviously indebted to an aria from the opera *Regina* (based on Hellman's *The Little Foxes*), composed by Bernstein's mentor and friend, Marc Blitzstein (Example 13.2).[27] Perhaps not coincidentally, *Regina* premiered in 1949, the year Robbins conceived his "noble idea." The exceedingly strong melodic, harmonic, and rhythmic similarities between "Maria" and the introductory music to act I of Blitzstein's lesser known opera should be readily evident, even to those previously unfamiliar with the model.

Before intensive collaborative work began in 1956, several months after the entrance of Sondheim, the tangible evidence of *West Side Story* included a draft of several scenes, an outline of the remaining scenes, and substantial compositional work on two dramatically and musically central songs, "Somewhere" and "Maria." The cross-fertilization between *West Side Story* and *Candide* of the previous year is also evident. In 1956 the comic duet now indelibly associated with Candide and Cunegonde, "Oh, Happy We," had been considered for the bridal shop scene in *West Side Story*, and the song that was eventually placed there, "One Hand, One Heart," was originally intended for *Candide*.[28] Until at least 1957, however, this future bridal shop song was located in the balcony scene, after which it was replaced by "Tonight" (see "Libretto Drafts 1 [January 1956] and 2 [Spring 1956]" in the online website). Another version of an unused *Candide* song, "Where Does It Get You in the End?," served as the basis for "Gee, Officer Krupke," a song that was not added until rehearsals in July.[29]

By the end of 1956 Laurents had completed his fourth libretto draft (out of eight), and much of the eventual version was fixed. The most significant changes in the months prior to and during the rehearsal schedule from mid-June to mid-August 1957 were the addition of two songs, "Something's

Coming" and "Gee, Officer Krupke," and considerable revamping of the opening Prologue. Also in 1957 more dance numbers would be added to the "Dance at the Gym" (only the "Mambo" was indicated for this section at the end of 1956); Tony's and Maria's "One Hand, One Heart" on the tenement balcony had still not been replaced by "Tonight."[30]

The Prologue and first scene, which had already undergone a number of changes in the first four librettos (all in 1956), required considerable revision before it achieved its revolutionary final version in the summer months of 1957. Although Bernstein exaggerates the ease with which he and his collaborators worked out the solution to the complex problems posed by this opening, the libretto and musical score drafts support his recollection in 1985 that the Prologue was originally intended to be sung: "It didn't take us long to find out that it wouldn't work. That was when Jerry [Robbins] took over and converted all that stuff into this remarkable thing now known as 'the prologue to *West Side Story*,' all dancing and movement."[31]

The three sung themes of "Up to the Moon" (Example 13.3) found their way into the instrumental Prologue and the instrumental portions of the "Jet Song" as we know it. A fourth theme (and much of the text) from "Up to the Moon" was salvaged in the eventual Broadway version of the "Jet Song," when the Jets sing "Oh, when the Jets fall in at the cornball dance, / We'll be the sweetest dressin' gang in pants!"[32] In Laurents's fourth libretto (Winter 1956) the opening scene had shifted from a clubhouse to an alleyway, but it is not until the similar fifth and sixth librettos (April 14 and May 1, 1957) that the first scene—none of the eight librettos indicate a Prologue distinct from a first scene—begins to resemble the final version shown in the online website.[33]

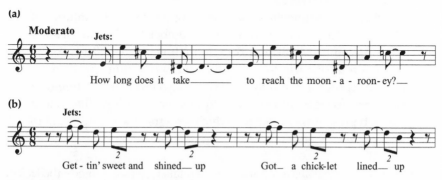

Example 13.3. Vocal passages from "Up to the Moon" reused in Prologue and "Jet Song"
(a) "How long does it take?"
(b) "Gettin' sweet and shined up"
(c) "Carazy, Daddy-O"

(c)

Example 13.3. Continued

Sondheim recalled in the 1985 Dramatists Guild symposium that *West Side Story* "certainly changed less from the first preview in Washington to the opening in New York than any other show I've ever done, with the exception of *Sweeney Todd*, which also had almost no changes."[34] In *Sondheim & Co.* he comments further on the extent of these alterations: "Our total changes out of town consisted of rewriting the release for the 'Jet Song,' adding a few notes to 'One Hand,' Jerry *potchkied* with the second-act ballet, and there were a few cuts in the book."[35]

Again, the evidence from the music manuscripts and libretto drafts substantiates Sondheim's recollection on all these points. Bernstein's early piano-vocal score reveals the rejected release for the "Jet Song" and two versions of "One," the original one-note-per-measure version and the familiar three-notes-per-measure version.[36] And in what is perhaps the most significant *potch* of the dream ballet sequence, "Somewhere" was originally intended to be danced rather than sung, at least until its conclusion when Tony and Maria reprise the final measures.

Sondheim also remembered Robbins's preoccupation during the tryouts with a number that would be eventually rejected:

> Jerry had a strong feeling that there was a sag in the middle of the first act [scene 6], so we wrote a number for the three young kids—Anybodys, Arab, and Baby John. It was called "Kids Ain't" and was a terrific trio that we all loved, but Arthur gave a most eloquent speech about how he loved it also but that we shouldn't use it, because it would be a crowd-pleaser and throw the weight over to typical musical comedy which we agreed we didn't want to do. So it never went in.[37]

During the July rehearsals Robbins & Co. had taken steps to remedy the lack of a comic musical number caused by the removal of "Kids Ain't." Although there had been a comic exchange between Officer Krupke and the Jets in act II, scene 2, in the four 1956 libretto drafts, no song had yet appeared in this space. Only in the final libretto draft did a recycled "Where Does It Get You in the End?" from

Jerome Robbins (second from left) rehearsing *West Side Story* (1957).
Museum of the City of New York. Theater Collection.

Candide materialize as "Gee, Officer Krupke." Sondheim recalled that Robbins staged this number "in three hours by the clock, three days before we went to Washington."[38] At the time, Sondheim thought that "Officer Krupke" would be better placed in act I, since its presence detracted from the serious developments in the drama. After viewing the 1961 film in which "Krupke" and "Cool" were reversed "and weren't nearly as effective," Sondheim came to accept Robbins's directorial decision and to acknowledge that "Krupke" "works wonderfully" in act II on the basis of its "theatrical truth" rather than its "literal truth."[39] Since its comic intent was meant to provide dramatic contrast and relief from the mostly tragic theme based on tritones and "Somewhere" motives (to be discussed), the absence of the latter and the softening of the former in "Krupke" is understandable and dramatically plausible and welcome.

After "Krupke," one final song, not indicated even as late as the final libretto draft of July 19, was added during rehearsals.[40] This song, newly composed to conclude act I, scene 2, after Tony promises Riff that he will attend the Settlement dance, is, of course, "Something's Coming." Bernstein describes the circumstances and motivation for this song:

"Something's Coming" was born right out of a big long speech that Arthur wrote for Tony. It said how every morning he would wake up and reach out for something, around the corner or down the beach. It was very late and we were in rehearsal when Steve and I realized that we needed a strong song for Tony earlier since he had none until "Maria," which was a love song. We had to have more delineation of him as a character. We were looking through this particular speech, and "Something's Coming" just seemed to leap off the page. In the course of the day we had written that song.[41]

At Robbins's suggestion, Laurents added the meeting between Tony and Riff in front of the drugstore, and in the course of the Washington tryouts the song "Something's Coming" replaced much of the dialogue.[42] Sondheim's recollection that the song ended with its eventual title is partially borne out by the Winter 1956 libretto, which concludes with the following exchange:

TONY: Now it's right outside that door, around the corner: maybe being stamped in a letter, maybe whistling down the river, maybe—
RIFF: What is?
TONY: (*Shrugs*). I don't know. But it's coming and it's the greatest.... Could be. Why not?[43]

In contrast to "Gee, Officer Krupke," the purpose of which was to provide a respite from the surrounding tragedy, the motive behind "Something's Coming" was to introduce a main character and to link this character to the ensuing drama.[44] This is accomplished musically by allowing Tony to resolve a dissonant and dramatically symbolic interval (the interval of hate, a tritone) at the beginning and conclusion of his song.

From Verona to the Upper West Side

In order to understand the Romantic qualities inherent in *West Side Story* it may be helpful to recall that the nineteenth century, an age obsessed by the theme of idealized youthful passionate love that realizes its apotheosis only with premature death, was irresistibly drawn to Shakespeare's *Romeo and Juliet*.[45] Not only did this play—in various degrees of fidelity to Shakespeare—occupy the European stage throughout most of the nineteenth century, numerous musical settings also made their debut. Just as revisions of Shakespeare's play from the late-seventeenth through the nineteenth centuries frequently included a happy ending, most of the musical adaptations strayed conspicuously from the original. Gounod's still-popular *Roméo et Juliette* (1867), for example, introduces a major female role (Stephano) that has no Shakespearean counterpart.[46]

Although these operatic, orchestral, and balletic versions, unlike *West Side Story*, retain the names of the major characters and basic plot machinations, they more often than not distort Shakespeare's tragic intention with the insertion of either a happy ending (like many play performances) or an ending that enables the principals to sing (or dance) an impassioned love duet before their demise. Consider Prokofiev's ballet (1935–36), one of the most popular of the twentieth century and most likely an inspiration for Robbins. After its premiere, Soviet Shakespearean scholars influenced censors to prohibit Prokofiev and his collaborators from allowing Romeo an extra minute in order to take advantage of his pyrrhic opportunity to witness Juliet alive. Prokofiev defended his original scenario: "The reasons that led us to such a barbarism were purely choreographic. Living people can dance, but the dead cannot dance lying down."[47]

Modern-day nonmusical versions of Shakespeare's play are similarly prone to alterations that can distort the meaning and tone of the Bard (or eliminate substantial portions of text), presumably for the sake of broader public palatability. The well-known 1968 film of *Romeo and Juliet* by director Franco Zeffirelli, probably the most popular film adaptation of Shakespeare ever made, serves as an instructive paradigm for the triumph of accessibility over authenticity introduced in chapter 1 (even though the eponymous principals die). One may acknowledge the need to make a Shakespeare movie cinematic and argue on behalf of the many artistic merits of Zeffirelli's considerable textual excisions, but the conclusion is nonetheless inescapable that Zeffirelli has succeeded more brilliantly in bringing himself rather than Shakespeare to a mass audience.[48]

Although it contains extensive transformational liberties, the tragic dramatic vision of *West Side Story* arguably corresponds more closely to Shakespeare than Zeffirelli's version or nineteenth-century musical adaptations that wear the garb of the Montagues and the Capulets. Robbins spoke of Laurents's achievement in following the "story as outlined in the Shakespeare play without the audience or critics realizing it," but most theatergoers familiar with the characters in Shakespeare's tale of "fair Verona" can easily recognize their West Side reincarnations.[49]

While preserving the central theme of youthful passionate love's Pyrrhic victory over passionate youthful hate and many of the central plot elements from the Shakespearean source, adapted to suit New York gang culture of the 1950s, the collaborators took four major transformational liberties:

1. Increased motivation for the conflict between the gangs
2. Decreased importance of adults
3. Substitution of free will for fate in the demise of Tony
4. Decision to keep Maria alive

Most obviously, the warring gangs, the Jets and Sharks, parallel the warring families, the Montagues and Capulets.[50] Like Romeo at the outset of Shakespeare's play, Tony, a Jet, has disassociated himself from the violent members of his clan. His friend, Riff, shares the fate and much of the mercurial character of Romeo's friend, Mercutio. Maria appears as an older and therefore more credible Juliet for modern audiences. Bernardo's death has a more direct emotional impact because he is Maria's brother rather than a literal counterpart to Juliet's cousin Tybalt. By 1957, New York City teenagers were less likely to share intimacies with an aging nurse. Consequently, Anita, a woman only a few years older than Maria, serves as a more credible counterpart to Shakespeare's elderly crone, a confidante to Maria, and of course an agile dancing partner for her lover, Bernardo. Chino, Maria's unexciting but eventually excitable fiancé and Bernardo's choice for his sister, corresponds closely to Juliet's parentally selected suitor, the County Paris.

All these changes reflect societal changes that transpired between the 1590s and the 1950s. For similar reasons, adult authority has been greatly reduced in the adaptation. Juliet's parents, who play a prominent role throughout the Shakespeare play (and in Laurents's early libretto drafts), are reduced to offstage voices in the musical; Tony's parents are represented metaphorically as dummies in the bridal shop where Tony and Maria marry themselves without benefit of clergy. Doc, a druggist who parallels the well-meaning but ineffectual Friar Laurence, serves far less as a catalyst for the plot than as an adult representative who can at least partially sympathize with troubled youth; Officer Krupke, although more abrasive than his counterpart, Prince Escalus, possesses less authority and earns even less respect.[51]

Other departures from Shakespeare's play were similarly motivated for the resulting accessibility. For example, in *Romeo and Juliet*, no Capulet or Montague can recall a specific cause for their senseless enmity.[52] *West Side Story* audiences learn that the Americans (the Jets) fear that the Puerto Ricans (the Sharks) are usurping jobs and territory. In contrast to the long-forgotten causes, the Jets and the Sharks know they are fighting for control over a few city blocks on the West side.

Perhaps the most dramatic departure from Shakespeare also developed because the collaborators of *West Side Story* realized they needed a "believable substitute for the philter." Laurents speaks of his imaginative solution to this problem with justifiable pride: "The thing I'm proudest of in telling the story is why she [Anita] can't get the message through: because of prejudice. I think it's better than the original story."[53]

Thus, whenever dramatically possible, the youthful characters in *West Side Story* make their own mistakes and generate their own fate. Tony's form of suicide, his vociferous public invitation for Chino to shoot him, contrasts with Romeo's quiet decision to take the poison he has purchased for this purpose. In Shakespeare, a tragic coincidence (an outbreak of plague) prevented the news of Juliet's magic sleep from reaching Romeo; the sleep itself was induced by Friar Laurence's herbal potions, a well-meaning, albeit imprudent, adult action. A much-provoked Anita sets the stage for Tony's death with her deliberate lie to the Jets that Maria is dead. By letting Maria live, the creators of *West Side Story* allow her to assume the authority previously delegated to the patriarchal figures of the Capulet and Montague families and to inspire reconciliation between the Sharks and Jets, who then carry Tony's body off the stage at the final curtain. Significantly, Maria leads the play's dramatic catharsis in front of adults as well as her peers.

Only the first two of Laurents's libretto drafts (January and Spring 1956) follow Shakespeare on this crucial dramaturgical point. Maria, thinking Tony dead, returns to the bridal shop and "sings passionately of her not wanting to live in a world without Tonio [at this point Tony was Italian-American], a world that has taken him from her." The scene description continues: "At the peak of this, she grabs up a pair of dressmaking shears and—with her back to us—plunges them into her stomach." Moments later Tony (Tonio) arrives and "cradling her in his arms, he starts to sing with her a reprise of their song from the marriage scene." The orchestra completes their song and after kissing her, Tony opens the door of the shop and cries out, "Come and take me! Come and take me too!"[54]

By the third draft (March 15, 1956), which also concludes at the bridal shop, Maria "tries to tear the wedding veil with her hands, cannot, picks up sewing shears and is about to cut the veil when a new thought [presumably suicide] enters her mind."[55] In this draft, as in the five others over the next sixteen months, a mortally wounded Tony finds Maria, and the lovers are able to share a few final moments together.

Robbins credits Rodgers for realizing how to "solve a problem like Maria" (two years before *The Sound of Music*'s Maria Von Trapp) and for keeping Maria alive: "I remember Richard Rodgers's contribution. We had a death scene for Maria—she was going to commit suicide or something, as in Shakespeare. He said, 'She's dead already, after this all happens to her.'"[56] All sources agree that Bernstein's collaborators wanted to convert Laurents's prose speech into music for Maria, just as Bernstein and Sondheim had raided the libretto for "Something's Coming" and "A Boy Like That." In the 1985 panel discussion Bernstein recalled that he discarded four or five attempts to create an aria for Maria from Laurents's dummy lyric that would become Maria's speech: "It's not that I didn't try." In an interview with Humphrey Burton, Bernstein offered a more detailed account:

> "It cries out for music," Bernstein said himself. "I tried to set it very bitterly, understated, swift. I tried giving all the material to the orchestra and having her sing an *obbligato* throughout. I tried a version that sounds just like a Puccini aria, which we really did not need. I never got past six bars with it. I never had an experience like that. Everything sounded wrong." So Maria's words, which Laurents had written merely as a guide to lyricist and composer, became the dramatic text. "I made," Bernstein confessed, "a difficult, painful but surgically clean decision not to set it at all."[57]

Despite these liberties, for the most part the collaborators of *West Side Story* preserve the spirit of the original as well as what is perhaps Shakespeare's central theme: the triumph of youthful passionate love over youthful passionate hate, even in death. They also incorporate Shakespeare's literary device of foreshadowing, for similar dramatic and musical purposes, to inform audiences of the inevitable, albeit mostly self-made, destiny facing the young lovers. Tony's somewhat more optimistic premonition in "Something's Coming" early in the musical can be seen, for example, as a parallel to Mercutio's famous Queen Mab speech: "My mind misgives / Some consequence, yet hanging in the stars, / Shall bitterly begin his fearful date / With this night's revels and expire the term / Of a despised life, closed in my breast, / By some vile forfeit of untimely death" (act 1, scene 4, lines 112–17).

Romeo's bittersweet, sorrowful premonitions in the first eleven lines of act V ("I dreamt my lady came and found me dead") clearly correspond to the Romantic message most clearly expressed in "Somewhere," introduced by an anonymous offstage "Girl" (opera stars Reri Grist on Broadway and Marilyn Horne on Bernstein's 1985 recording, handpicked by the composer) during the dream ballet sequence in act II.[58] By the end of Bernstein's musical counterpart to Shakespeare in the dream sequence, audiences know that the place and time for Tony and Maria will not be a flat on the Upper West Side. Rather, as in the tale of Tristan and Isolde, their passionate love will be fulfilled only after death. With great ingenuity Bernstein manages to discover a convincing musical equivalent to Shakespeare's foreshadowing of death, a musical transformation from youthful hate to youthful love.

A "Tragic Story in Musical-Comedy Terms"

As early as 1949, Bernstein, Laurents, and Robbins were consciously striving to write "a musical that tells a tragic story in musical-comedy terms" and to avoid "falling into the 'operatic trap.'" At the same time they—mainly Bernstein as the composer—borrowed freely from the European operatic and symphonic traditions.[59] The degree to which Broadway musicals could and should aspire to the condition of nineteenth-century tragic opera remains a controversial issue often vigorously and irreconcilably divided along party lines. Representing one side is Joseph P. Swain, who views Broadway generally as a series of "missed chances and unanswered challenges" that "made tragic drama in the American musical theater into an Olympus, beckoning beyond reach."[60] Not surprisingly for Swain, "Maria's last speech should indeed have her biggest aria."[61] Similarly, in the *West Side Story* entry in *The New Grove Dictionary of Opera* Jon Alan Conrad considers Bernstein's "failure to find music for Maria's final scene" one of the work's "weak points."[62] Those who interpret the dramaturgy of musicals as a workable alternative, perhaps even a corrective, to opera might conclude with Stephen Banfield that "whatever fears Laurents may have had that it would turn into a 'goddamned Bernstein opera,' one of *West Side Story*'s greatest strengths is that it did not."[63] Accordingly, "Maria's final speech works perfectly well as dialogue."[64]

The analytical remarks that follow will show that Bernstein borrowed from his European predecessors as well as from his American present. The varied score consists of three primary styles: a variant of cool jazz for the Jets; a cornucopia of Latin American dances associated with the Sharks, their girl friends, and Maria; and music that suggests European and American operatic traditions for much of the love music. The jazz can be heard most readily in the Prologue, "Jet Song," the Blues and Jump music in "The Dance at the Gym," "Cool," and The Rumble. Latin music is featured in the Promenade (paso doble), Mambo, and Cha-Cha dances in "The Dance at the Gym," the tango in "Maria," the seis and huapango in "America," and the cachucha in "I Feel Pretty." Of these song and dance prototypes only the seis can claim any authentic ties with Puerto Rico, which for some makes *West Side Story* about as Puerto Rican as Georges Bizet's *Carmen* is Spanish (or Cuban). Operatic dialects are most recognizable in "Tonight," "Somewhere," and the double duet "A Boy Like That / I Have a Love."

Combining techniques and ideologies of nineteenth-century opera and American and Latin vernacular styles, Bernstein forged his own dramatic musical hybrid. While the connections to Latin dance rhythms and cool jazz are immediately apparent and even labeled, the European technical procedures require more explanation. Although motivic melodic analysis no longer serves as the central analytical paradigm, the crucial role motivic development plays in some musicals, most notably *Show Boat*, *Porgy and Bess*, and *West Side Story*, is persuasive. More important, the principal motivic transformations are readily perceived (even to inexperienced listeners) and the more intricate melodic connections usually serve a demonstrable dramatic purpose.

Since the most famous exponent of nineteenth-century tragic drama was Wagner (his views were popular especially in the 1950s), it is not surprising that Bernstein, in setting the tragedy of Romeo and Juliet, borrowed melodic and harmonic elements most commonly associated with Wagner's operas (although certainly not limited to these works). The principal melodic technique is the pervasive use of leitmotivs (short themes that represent people, things, or abstract ideas) as source material for thematic transformation and organic unity.[65] Harmonically, Bernstein used the deceptive cadence, a sequence of chords in which a dominant fails to resolve to its tonic.[66] Also associated with Wagner and adopted by Bernstein is the technique of having the orchestra present an underlying dramatic commentary on the melodic line. Finally, the ensuing analytical discussion will suggest that Bernstein borrowed a central and specific leitmotiv from Wagner and used it for a related dramatic purpose.[67]

Bernstein's Wagnerian vision is most profoundly revealed in his use of the song "Somewhere," a song that, despite its early conception, did not achieve its vocal independence until a relatively late stage in the compositional process. As previously noted, until the production began its rehearsals in June, the piano-vocal score manuscript reveals that this song, eventually intoned by a woman offstage, was to be entirely danced. Only after the "Procession and Nightmare" did Tony and Maria return to sing the final eight measures of "Somewhere."[68]

Nearly all of the musical material in the thirty-seven-measure "Somewhere" is based on one of three brief motives: *(a)*, *(b)*, and three versions of *(c)*. See Example 13.4, which shows A and B of the overall form, A (8), A' (8), B (8), A" (8), and B" (5). Despite their brevity, each motive contains a distinctive rhythmic or melodic profile. More important, each motive will be purposefully foreshadowed. The first motive *(a)* which opens the song on "There's a place"—possibly derived from the second movement of Beethoven's "Emperor" Concerto or, more likely, from the final measures of Tchaikovsky's Fantasy-Overture on *Romeo and Juliet*—consists of three notes: a rising minor seventh (B up to A) followed by a descending half-step (A down to G♯). Bernstein uses this motive in the vocal part to mark the principal statements of the tune on the words "There's a place" (mm. 1—2 and A', mm. 25—26) and "There's a time" (A', mm. 9—10) that initiate each A section.

(a)

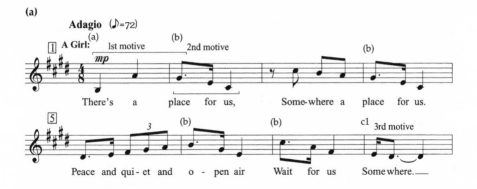

(b)

Example 13.4. "Somewhere" motives
(a) "There's a place for us" (motives *a* and *b*)
(b) "Some day! Somewhere" (motive *c*)

Bernstein elides the last note of this *a* motive with a second motive, *b*, on "place for us," composed of intervals that form a simple descending minor or, less frequently, major triad. This second motive with its idiosyncratic rhythmic signature is usually paired with its predecessor and occurs nine times in the first sixteen measures of the song and another four thereafter. The most frequently stated (six times) descending minor triad, C-sharp minor (G♯-E-C♯ or vi in E major as in m. 2) marks a deceptive and therefore ambiguous resolution. For most of the song Bernstein plays on our expectation that the B major dominant seventh implied in the first motive, which corresponds to the "place" for Tony and Maria, should be followed by the tonic chord, E major. Like many nineteenth-century composers, however, Bernstein does not allow his song to actually arrive on the tonic E until the final measures. It is tempting to make a connection between these deceptive cadences and Wagner's Prelude to *Tristan und Isolde*, where harmonic resolutions are similarly denied to make the dramatic point that nowhere on earth will there be a place to rest for Wagner's star-crossed lovers.

The minor seventh melodic interval of the first motive ("There's a place") and the dotted rhythm signature of the triadic second motive ("place for us") also permeates the orchestral underpinning of "Somewhere."[69] After the offstage "Girl" introduces the first motive vocally, the orchestra will repeat it until interrupted by the first appearance of the third (or "Somewhere") motive (*c1*) at measure 8. The "place for us" motive gains in orchestral as well as vocal prominence after measure 8 as it frequently answers its vocal statements, occasionally straddling measures in the process.[70]

After its solitary appearance during the course of the first two A sections, the third "Somewhere" motive will emerge in the second half of the song as the principal rhythmic motive (with no less than eight statements). Bernstein introduces this third motive with a descending half-step (E to D♯); thereafter the most emphasized melodic interval will be an ascending whole-step (*c2*) to mark the modulation to C major on the words "Some day! Somewhere" (mm. 17 and 18). On three other occasions, "living," "–giving," and "Somewhere" (mm. 20, 22, and 23, respectively) he changes the third motive more drastically with a descending perfect fifth (*c3*). All three melodic versions of this third "Somewhere" motive share the same defining rhythmic identity.

At the outset of *Romeo and Juliet* the character known as the Chorus informs Shakespeare's audience of the destiny soon to befall the doomed lovers.[71] The characters themselves, of course, are not allowed to know this. Similarly, Romeo's dreams prepare audiences for the forthcoming tragedy, but Romeo himself does not fully grasp their significance until after the fact.

Bernstein borrows the theatrical device of foreshadowing when he successively anticipates the three "Somewhere" motives in "Tonight," Tony and Maria's impassioned love duet on the fire escape (Shakespeare's Veronese balcony) within minutes of their first meeting at the gym dance.[72] As in Wagner's music dramas, the orchestra gives an alert audience classified information to which the principals are not privy. At the end of Wagner's *Das Rheingold*, for example, the first opera in the *Ring* tetralogy, when the gods enter the newly constructed fortress Valhalla as the trumpet plays a new motive that will be identified one opera later in the cycle, *Die Walküre*, when Sieglinde tells Siegmund about the sword. At the conclusion of "Tonight" the idealistic lovers show their oneness by singing in unison and the celestial heights of youthful optimistic love by singing and holding high A♭'s. Meanwhile, back on earth, the omniscient orchestra warns audiences of their imminent doom (Example 13.5). Upon future hearings, audiences come to realize that the death associated with "Somewhere" is already present at the moment of greatest bliss in "Tonight." As with Wagner's *Tristan und Isolde*, another *Romeo and Juliet* prototype, love and death, like love and hate, are inextricably entwined.

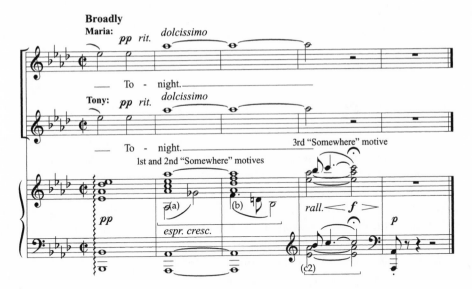

Example 13.5. Orchestral foreshadowing of "Somewhere" at the conclusion of the Balcony Scene ("Tonight")

A second prominent foreshadowing of "Somewhere" occurs minutes later during the dance between choruses of "Cool," when the Jets make an energetic but ultimately fruitless attempt to achieve a calm before the rumble. Here Bernstein uses the first "Somewhere" motive (without its usual second-motive continuation) as the first three notes of the fugue subject that introduces the "Cool" fugue, danced rather than sung by the Jets (Example 13.6a). Several measures later a slightly

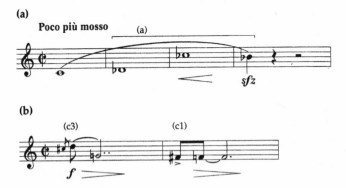

Example 13.6. "Somewhere" motives in "Cool" fugue
 (a) first "Somewhere" motive (motive *a*)
 (b) third "Somewhere" motive (motive *c*)

transformed version of the third "Somewhere" motive (Example 13.6b, *c3* and *c1*) can also be heard.[73] Like the use of the three "Somewhere" motives presented in succession at the conclusion of the "Tonight" duet, the idea here is an orchestral one that can be interpreted as a foreshadowing of death, much in the way the orchestra at the conclusion of Wagner's *Das Rheingold* informs the audience, but not Wotan, of Siegfried's sword.[74]

Ingeniously, Bernstein finds a new use for the "There's a place" motive when Maria and Anita reconcile their anger and pain in "I have a love," the song that follows the "Somewhere" dream ballet. In this climactic scene the composer transforms the first "Somewhere" motive into a new context. As shown in Example 13.7, Bernstein preserves the melody but alters the rhythm to fit a new declamation on the words, "I love him, I'm his" and "I love him, we're one" sung by Maria to Anita, and in harmony with her friend on the words, "When love comes so strong."[75]

The "Procession and Nightmare" introduces a new important motive shown in Example 13.8a, a motive that will return to conclude the musical in the Finale. In contrast to the three "Somewhere" motives, the "Procession" motive is not foreshadowed in earlier portions of the work. Rather, this "Procession" motive itself foreshadows a new principal theme, set to "I have a love, and it's all that I have" and "I have a love and it's all that I need" (the opening is shown in Example 13.8b), where it alternates with a rhythmic transformation of the first "Somewhere" motive (compare Examples 13.4a and 13.7).[76] The "I have a love" motive also retains its symbiotic relationship with the three "Somewhere" motives, since it will either adjoin or occur simultaneously with one or more of these "Somewhere" motives whenever it is heard. The "Procession" motive also bears an uncanny and perhaps intended melodic, rhythmic, and symbolic connection with Wagner's "redemption" theme (Example 13.8c) first sung by Sieglinde in *Die Walküre* and later by Brünnhilde during the Immolation Scene that concludes *Die Götterdämmerung*.[77]

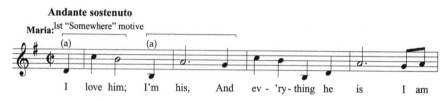

Example 13.7. "Somewhere" motive in "I Have a Love"

"Somewhere" and "Procession and Nightmare," with their foreshadowings and symbolic apotheoses, musically convey the principal dramatic message of *West Side Story*. But Bernstein also uses musical materials more directly by taking advantage of music's power to depict psychological states and by assigning appropriate musical equivalents to the driving emotions of passionate youthful hate and its counterpart in youthful love. Bernstein's principal musical accomplice to make this possible is the tritone or augmented fourth, a highly charged dissonant interval that figures prominently in the motive associated with the hate-filled gangs (Example 13.9a, F-B). It may not be coincidental that the pervasive use of the intervals formed by these notes C-F-B (a rising fourth followed by a rising tritone) as a central motive in *West Side Story*) employs the same three-note sequence of notes heard as the opening and central motive of Alban Berg's youthful late-Romantic early-modernist Piano Sonata, op. 1 (1907–1908), well known in Bernstein's circle (Example 13.9b, G-C-F♯). With its short upbeat, its disproportionately long second note, and the short final note on the tritone, to mark the second note of the tritone, the hate motive relates even more closely rhythmically as well in approximate pitch to the principal motive sounded by the Shofar (the latter not always easily determined on this instrument), the ancient ram's horn that announces Rosh Hashanah, the Jewish New Year, a sound that Bernstein knew well.

In any event, Bernstein's motive clearly serves as a central unifying element. Although no one has speculated on its possible connection with Berg's sonata, its appearance (in nearly every musical number of the show) was recognized as early as Jack Gottlieb's 1964 dissertation; the motive has been discussed in varying detail since then by Peter Gradenwitz, Larry Stempel, and Swain.[78] Gottlieb prefaces his discussion of the "hate" motive with the following statement:

> It was in WEST SIDE STORY that the fullest expression of the interval as a progenitor of musical development came into effect. Unlike WONDERFUL TOWN (perfect fifth)[79] and CANDIDE (minor seventh),[80] the interval here was not used for melodic purposes only, but as a harmonic force also. The interval in question is the tritone (augmented fourth), the famous *Diabolus in Musica*, certainly an appropriate symbolism for this tragic musical drama.[81]

A summary of how Bernstein uses the "hate" motive for dramatic purposes follows.

Example 13.8. "Procession" motive in "I Have a Love" and Wagner's *Ring*
(a) "Procession" motive
(b) "I Have a Love" ("Procession" motive)
(c) Redemption motive in Wagner's *Die Walküre*

Bernstein introduces the definitive form of the "hate" motive in the Prologue shortly after the stage directions "Bernardo enters."[82] Once Bernstein
associates his unresolved tritone motive with the hate-filled Jets, he positions
himself to convey dramatic meanings through its resolution or attempted
resolution. An example of the latter occurs in Promenade, when the social
worker Glad Hand attempts to get the Sharks and Jets to mix amiably at the

Settlement dance. Here the accented tritone dissonances in the bass (now spelled C-G♭), symbolically demonstrate the underlying tensions and resulting futility of attempts to resolve the animosity between the gangs. The drama reinforces this musical point when Promenade is interrupted by the Mambo, and Bernardo and Riff circumvent their intended partners and heed Anita's subsequent dictum to associate exclusively with "their own kind."

As the song instructs, the Jets in "Cool" attempt to achieve a degree of calm prior to The Rumble (or after The Rumble in the film version).[83] The main tune of "Cool" consists of a tritone (spelled C-F♯) followed almost invariably by its upward resolution to the perfect fifth (G) (Example 13.9c). Underneath the main tune the definitive "hate" (or "gang") motive appears as an accompaniment, and tritones also provide a harmonic foundation. One might interpret the upward resolution as an easing of tension, a perfect fifth as a metaphor for a more perfect world. If so, the Jets' attempt to compose themselves in this song, like their attempts to mix at the Settlement dance,

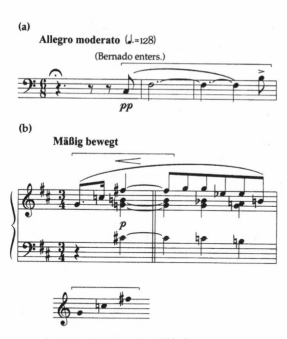

Example 13.9. "Hate" in *West Side Story*
  (a) "Hate" motive (Prologue)
  (b) "Hate" motive in Berg's Piano Sonata
  (c) "Hate" motive in "Cool" (attempted resolution)
  (d) Resolution of the "Hate" motive in "Something's Coming"
  (e) Tony's resolution of the tritone and Maria's name as resolution of the
    "Hate" motive in The Dance at the Gym

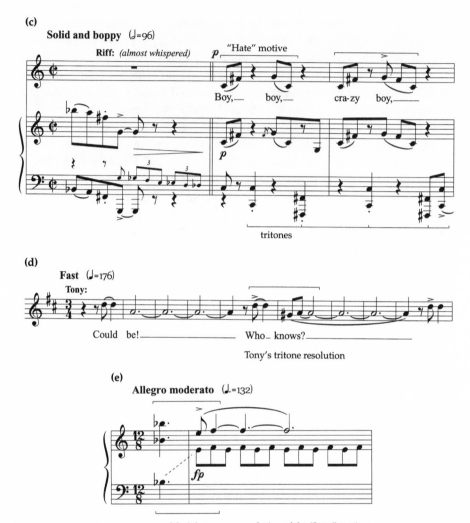

Example 13.9. Continued

are also destined for musical failure, a failure borne out dramatically by the subsequent deaths of Riff and Bernardo.

Only the characters who represent the triumph of love over hate, Tony and Maria, can unambiguously and convincingly resolve the tritone tension embodied in the gang's signature motive. This happens as early as Tony's first song, "Something's Coming" (Example 13.9d). Tony's first words, "Could be!," outline a perfect descending fourth (D-A), and his next question, "Who knows?," establishes a second perfect fourth after an eighth-note digression to the tritone (D-G♯-A). By this immediate resolution Bernstein lets his audiences know, at least subliminally, that Tony, an ex-Jet, is a man capable of assuaging the tensions of his former gang as his musical line resolves its tritones. Throughout the entire first portion of "Something's Coming," the orchestral accompaniment, which consists entirely of perfect fourths—in contrast to the alternating perfect fourths and tritones in the bass of Promenade—supports this important dramatic point: that Tony is a man who wants peace.

It is crucially significant that Maria's name (Example 13.2b) resolves the tritone and thus simply but powerfully embodies the musical antithesis of the unresolved "hate" motive, a "love" theme. As with the first and third "Somewhere" motives, Bernstein foreshadows Maria's motive orchestrally before fully establishing her identity vocally. Reasonably attentive listeners can hear her motive for the first time at the outset of "The Dance at the Gym" (the introduction to Blues) following Maria's explanation to her brother that "tonight" marks her debut "as a young lady of America!," where its upward resolution appears simultaneously with Tony's downward tritone (Example 13.9e). More obviously, Bernstein foreshadows the entire Maria tune in the Cha-Cha and brings it back appropriately as underscoring for her Meeting Scene with Tony. The first ascending three notes of the song "Cool" are the same as "Maria" (a tritone followed by a minor second), but instead of lingering on the tritone resolution, "Cool" focuses on the tritone, for example the tritone ascent on "crazy" followed by a tritone descent on "Boy." (The "cool fugue" dance after the song alternates between statement of the hate motive in its pure Jet gang form and the first three notes of "Somewhere" ["There's a place"] with interjections from the two-note "someday, somewhere" motive.)

The Maria motive or "love motive" of course dominates the song "Maria," where each repetition of the heroine's name conveys the message that Maria, to an even greater extent than her romantic counterpart, can resolve dramatic tensions. Maria's motive returns at other timely occasions during the remainder of the musical: throughout the orchestral underscoring that introduces the Balcony Scene that encompasses "Tonight"; in "Under Dialogue" as a cha-cha (a rare omission in Bernstein's "complete" 1985 recording); in the underscoring that marks the moment Tony and Maria declare themselves married directly prior to "One Hand, One Heart"; and at various other places in the orchestral accompaniment to this last-mentioned song and the Ballet Sequence. Thereafter, the full three-note Maria motive becomes displaced by its dramatic (and musical) associate, the third "Somewhere" motive ($c3$ in Example 13.4), which presents a readily apparent rhythmic association with the last two syllables of Maria's name.

The drama concludes with a "real" death procession (in contrast to the dream procession earlier in the Ballet Sequence of the second act). In the final moments Bernstein presents three statements of the third "Somewhere" motive (*c2*) with its customary rising whole-step (Example 13.10a). In the first two statements the bass answer to this C-major triadic resolution in the melody (C-E-G) is none other than the note that will complete the sinister tritone against C (F♯) for two statements. In the third and final statement, Bernstein allows an undiluted C major to stand alone.[84] Certainly it is possible to interpret the absence of a third F♯ as an optimistic ending, or at least more positive than if Bernstein had chosen to state the tritone the third time as well.

The screen version of *West Side Story* adds a *third* tritone to accompany the end credits. The original movie soundtrack album, however, departs both from the Broadway and the film ending in its musical resolution of the drama. As shown in Example 13.10b it abandons tritones altogether for all three statements of the "Somewhere" motive.[85] Why did the soundtrack do this? Here is one possible explanation. Despite the fact that the film omitted the Dream Ballet Sequence (based on "Somewhere"), except as underscoring at the beginning of act II, scene 3, the producers of the soundtrack wanted to find a place for the song "Somewhere." When first released, the soundtrack therefore used the dream version of this song, but now sung by the principals rather than an off-screen "Girl," to conclude the recording. For this reason the original soundtrack concluded with an unambiguously positive major ending that avoids tritones entirely.[86]

Example 13.10. "Finale" and "Procession and Nightmare" (conclusions)
(a) Broadway ending ("Finale")
(b) Conclusion of "Procession and Nightmare" and the film soundtrack

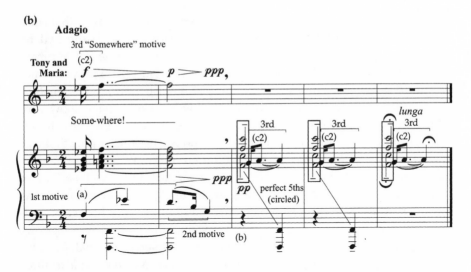

Example 13.10. Continued

   To better depict an age when gang warfare is still rampant and exponentially more violent than it was on the West Side in 1957 or 1961, Bernstein,
in his operatic recorded reinterpretation of the score he conducted in 1985,
departs from his Broadway ending. This time he has the orchestra follow
the third statement of the "Somewhere" motive with a third tritone as in
the "End Credits" that followed the drama in the film. But even in the 1985
recording Bernstein allows a hopeful glimmer of C major to sound when he
instructs the orchestra to quickly release the third tritone.
   Maria lives, but Bernstein, despite numerous attempts, was unable to
create an operatic aria for her that rang true. Thus in her most Wagnerian
moment Maria does not sing. In an opera, Maria, albeit "skinny—but pretty"
and "delicate-boned" in contrast to the "fat lady" of operatic legend, would
have no choice but to sing in order to inform audiences that the evening
was over. Despite this conspicuous departure from operatic expectations,
even requirements, *West Side Story* has been said to achieve genuine tragedy because "for the first time in a musical the hero sings while dying."[87]
Perhaps more significantly, when Tony is carried off, the music of *West Side
Story* has, metaphorically speaking, the last word. Audiences unaware of
the musical relationships between death ("Procession") and love ("I Have a
Love") and their mutual source in Wagner's "redemption" motive (Example
13.8a–c) nevertheless cannot fail to understand that the love of Tony and
Maria, like that of Siegmund and Sieglinde, Brünnhilde and Siegfried, and
of course Romeo and Juliet, has redeemed the tragedy of youthful death.

After *West Side Story* Bernstein failed to succeed on Broadway with a completely new musical, but a considerably revamped *Candide* directed by Hal Prince (which included Sondheim's newly created "Life Is Happiness Indeed," a reworded "Venice Gavotte"), triumphed in 1974. Two years later Bernstein produced a musical with librettist-lyricist Alan Jay Lerner, *1600 Pennsylvania Avenue*. Although this promising but problematic show vanished after only seven Broadway performances, Bernstein managed to salvage portions of its score in his last compositions, and after his death it was reworked by Charlie Harmon and Sid Ramin into *A White House Cantata: Scenes from 1600 Pennsylvania Avenue*. One song, the anthem "Take Care of This House" (originally sung by Abigail Adams in the White House), has since served as a talisman to protect many buildings, from houses of worship to the Kennedy Center. In 1983, Bernstein, who by then was focusing most of his creative energies on conducting, completed his final work for the musical stage, the opera *A Quiet Place*. A sequel to *Trouble in Tahiti* three decades later, *A Quiet Place* also recycled the former work (as a flashback) for a middle act.

Two years after *West Side Story*, Robbins, Laurents, and Sondheim would again collaborate successfully on a new musical, *Gypsy*, with music by Styne. Without Robbins, Laurents and Sondheim worked together on two unsuccessful musicals in the next decade before they went on to work with other partners: *Anyone Can Whistle* (1964), a show without a literary source, and *Do I Hear a Waltz?* (1965), an adaptation of Laurents's own *The Time of the Cuckoo* (an unhappy collaboration with Rodgers). Meanwhile, Robbins and his new creative associates, lyricist Sheldon Harnick and composer Jerry Bock, would direct and choreograph his greatest popular triumph, *Fiddler on the Roof*, in 1964. After *Fiddler*, Robbins virtually abandoned commercial theater. Laurents, without Sondheim, returned to Broadway in subsequent decades to direct Harold Rome's *I Can Get It for You Wholesale* (1962), a Tony-nominated *Gypsy* (1975), the Harvey Fierstein–Jerry Herman Tony Award–winning *La Cage aux Folles* (1983), and new Broadway productions of *Gypsy* (2008) and *West Side Story* (2009). Without Laurents in the 1970s, '80s, and '90s, Sondheim, the subject of another chapter in this survey, would, like the descendant of painter Georges Seurat in act II of *Sunday in the Park with George*, continue to "move on" and in the process launch a new era in the Broadway musical.

CHAPTER FOURTEEN

STAGE VERSUS SCREEN (2)

After Oklahoma!

Adapting to Broadway

In contrast to most of the films discussed in "Stage versus Screen (1)," the five films explored in this chapter—*Carousel* (1956), *Kiss Me, Kate* (1953), *Guys and Dolls* (1955), *My Fair Lady* (1964), and *West Side Story* (1961)—are widely known. All are accessible on DVDs that contain absorbing "Bonus" or "Special" Features that include one or more of the following: interviews with the creators of the show, interviews with members of the film cast, commentaries by various experts, documentaries about the making of the film, documentaries on film restoration, behind the scene notes, alternate vocal versions, a deleted scene or song, vintage featurettes and archival footage, historical background, storyboards, original intermission music, and trailers. Most of these films were popular in their time and several remain so in ours. Most made money. Within a three-year span of time *West Side Story* and *My Fair Lady* took home the big Academy Award prize for Best Picture, among numerous other awards.

Compared with the films of "Stage versus Screen (1)," these five films are for the most part far more faithful to their stage sources than the films we looked at in act I (the exception is Trevor Nunn's virtually complete televised 1993 film of *Porgy and Bess*). Also in contrast to the earlier films, three of the films discussed in this chapter even approximate the amount of stage time offered by their predecessors. None follow their stage sources to the letter, however. In fact, only George Cukor's *My Fair Lady* comes close to what was seen and heard on Broadway. Robert Wise's relatively faithful and relatively complete *West Side Story* takes significant liberties with song order and removes the second act ballet. Samuel Goldwyn and Joseph L. Mankiewicz's *Guys and Dolls* and George Sidney's *Kiss Me, Kate* subtract and add songs, but in the former the songs were newly written by the composer-lyricist Frank Loesser especially for the film and in the latter the new song was written by the show's rightful creative owner, Cole Porter. Henry King's *Carousel* film deletes but does not add songs.

Despite their commercial successes (the exception here is *Carousel*), the film versions of the musicals treated in act II have generated controversies over their artistic success as adaptations. Critics have taken issue with their direction, scenic design, and cinematography, and perhaps most vociferously over casting issues and the pros and cons of vocal dubbing. Two of the films, *Carousel* and *Kiss Me, Kate*, feature mainly singers. *Guys and Dolls* combines singers and non-singers but even the latter sang for themselves. In contrast, most of the principals in the *My Fair Lady* and *West Side Story* adaptations are dubbed by professional singers. Even Rita Moreno, herself an accomplished professional singer and recording artist, had her voice replaced.[1] Less obvious but arguably even more radical aspects of sonic technological change—orchestral augmentations, selective mixing via multiple-track recording, combining alternate takes via editing, the effects of microphone placement—have slipped past underneath most critics' notice. For those who have grown accustomed in recent years to the expectation that voices we hear on the soundtrack belong to the faces of those we see in the picture (e.g., *Chicago*, *Dreamgirls*, *Hairspray*, *Rent*, *The Phantom of the Opera*, and *Sweeney Todd*), the knowledge that Marni Nixon is the voice of Audrey Hepburn *and* Natalie Wood might be disconcerting. These musical adaptations may come across today as faithful to their theatrical origins to the point of being labored and unfaithful to their new medium. At the same time they allow us to imagine their stage counterparts and for the most part will satisfactorily see us through until something better comes along, such as a new Broadway revival or a community theater or high school production.

Carousel *(1956)*

Not long after the release of *Oklahoma!* in October 1955, *The King and I* and *Carousel* followed in quick succession in February and March of the next year. Unlike the popular successes of *Oklahoma!* and *The King and I*, the third Rodgers and Hammerstein film adaptation to appear within six months,

Carousel, 1956 film. Carrie Pipperidge (Barbara Ruick) and Julie Jordan (Shirley Jones) (foreground left) watch Billy Bigelow (Gordon MacRae) (right) at The carousel.

Carousel failed at the box office in its own time and has not enjoyed much critical approbation in the decades since its debut—even though it brought back from *Oklahoma!* the winning partnership of Gordon MacRae and Shirley Jones. Although spared the acrimony heaved at Joshua Logan and those disturbing colored filters he will always be blamed for in the next 20th Century-Fox Rodgers and Hammerstein film adaptation, *South Pacific* in 1958—which Gerald Mast found almost unrivaled "for sheer bad taste"—for Mast and many others *Carousel* remains unequivocally "the worst of the lot."[2]

Only two songs from the stage version were cut, however, "Geraniums in the Winder" (also missing from the original Broadway cast album) and "The Highest Judge of All." The screenplay also retains much of Hammerstein's libretto. Nevertheless, Thomas Hischak, who normally demonstrates equanimity in his assessments of film adaptations in *Through the Screen Door*, describes the *Carousel* adaptation, directed by Henry King, as "unfaithful, incompetent, and certainly uninspired" and "the most unsatisfying film treatment of a Rodgers and Hammerstein musical."[3] For a minority report one can turn to an essay by Bruce Babington and Peter William Evans in which the authors describe the dream ballets of *Carousel* as well as *Oklahoma!* as works in which "the greater surrealist possibilities of the cinema [are] used to their fullest advantage" and other "ways in which the film is as moving today as when it was made."[4]

One of the many ways in which the staged *Carousel* stands out from conventional musical theater fare is that the main character takes his own life. In *Oklahoma!* the villain (Jud Fry) kills himself accidentally while in the process of trying to kill the male protagonist (Curly), and film audiences who were seeing the Rodgers and Hammerstein shows in their filmed order had also recently witnessed the death of the King of Siam. Despite this sad eventual turn in the plot, perhaps in an effort to prepare younger viewers and those new to the show for Billy's death and to reassure them that he was still alive on screen, although technically dead, the film opens in heaven fifteen heavenly minutes later (the equivalent of fifteen years on earth) where Billy tells the story of *Carousel*, including his death, as if it were a flashback. For those viewers who might view Billy's suicide as a sin comparable to his decision to commit a robbery in order to get enough money to support the as yet unborn daughter he imagined in "Soliloquy," the suicide of the stage version was changed to an accidental death. By the end of the film Billy will take advantage of the opportunity to return to earth in order to rectify some of the emotional damage he inflicted on his daughter, Louise, now fifteen earth years old. At the end of the play he succeeds in comforting his troubled daughter at her high school graduation, and when he does, the strains of "You'll Never Walk Alone" can move even modern-day cynics to request some tissues.

Even if the film proves disappointing on many levels, it offers the opportunity to get a sense of what audiences saw onstage, including Louise's dream ballet with choreography pilfered from Agnes de Mille (who had to sue to be properly credited) as well as most of the songs and a large helping of the original stage dialogue. Looking at the scene we focused on in the *Carousel* chapter, we see that much has been retained. It begins about seven minutes into the film, after the first scene in heaven. Some of "The Carousel Waltz" was heard over the credits—significantly shorn of its dissonant and mysterious opening, which will be heard later with new associations—but a more substantial statement of the waltz, starting with the first main waltz after the introduction, occurs in the transformation from Heaven to Earth. Despite a few cuts here and there, most of the waltz returns when the scene shifts to the amusement park. There it supports the pantomimed prologue that tells us so much about how Billy regards Julie as special and how the carousel proprietress Mrs. Mullin jealously senses an undeniable romance in bloom. With a few small additions and deletions, most of the non-underscored dialogue with Carrie, Julie, Mrs. Mullin, and Billy that opens act I, scene 2, is preserved.[5] All this takes a little over five minutes.

The opening of the Julie and Carrie sequence that precedes "Mr. Snow," however, with its rhythmic recitative merging into the Julie Jordan tune and the "Mill Theme" is entirely removed from the film.[6] As a result, "Mr. Snow" appears after only thirty seconds of underscored dialogue (a little more than 15 minutes into the film), the conversation in which the stage Carrie assumes her friend now has "a feller of yer [your] own." Now that Julie has Billy, more an intuitive assumption than a reality at this stage in the relationship, Carrie can sing about her feller. Instead of the Julie Jordan music that underscores this conversation in the stage version, when we hear the "Mill Theme" for the first time in the film, it is impossible to understand its significance. By the end of the brief exchange, however, the underscoring will match the musical phrase indicated in the score (this is the musical passage of dotted rhythms and leaps in the deleted sequence illustrated in chapter 9), but now employed with equal meaninglessness. As a result of these liberties, the proof substantiating Carrie's presumption that Julie has a feller, so clearly explained in their musical exchange onstage but now deleted, creates an abrupt and less convincing transition to Carrie's song about her feller, "Mr. Snow."

Billy's long "Soliloquy" appears boldly without cuts and lasts nearly eight minutes, and earlier "June Is Bustin' Out All Over" continues with an elaborate and athletic dance of New Englanders that lasts nearly six minutes.[7] On the other hand, portions of "A Real Nice Clambake" and "When the Children Are Asleep," including their verses, were cut, and the latter is placed considerably later than in the stage version. In its new context, this song now takes place on a boat Carrie and Mr. Snow are sharing with Julie and Billy on the way to the clambake. Since they are now overheard by the more troubled partners, the contrast between Julie and Billy's turbulent relationship and the more placid one of Carrie and Enoch is more pronounced. In another departure, the distinctive dissonant chords that open the stage show were removed from the opening film credits and opening of the "Carousel Waltz." They return, however, in the film with a new meaning on two occasions to underscore the darker menacing presence of Mrs. Mullin a few minutes before the "Soliloquy" and again shortly after Billy's death, and a third time to announce the carnival troupe during Louise's ballet.

In the end, the mixture of fantasy and realism that worked so well onstage fails to persuade. Mast, the film critic who pronounced this Rodgers and Hammerstein adaptation "the worst of the lot," finds fault with nearly every aspect but saves his sharpest comments for the director: "Henry King's direction captures a styleless visual void—from a *papier maché* forest beside a backlot…to a tacky electric-blue heaven strung with plastic Stars of Bethlehem; to a real beach where a soliloquizing Billy wanders in thought (but never picks up a pebble, sifts some sand, or touches a rock)."[8]

It is possible that the musical film *Carousel* has negatively prejudiced many viewers against the show. In any event, of all the films from the Rodgers and Hammerstein era, *Carousel* is perhaps most in need of a film remake. This might happen. In 2006, an article in FirstShowing.net announced that the popular Australian movie and stage actor Hugh Jackman, who success-fully portrayed Curly in the film adaptation of Trevor Nunn's London stage revival of *Oklahoma!*, had acquired the rights for *Carousel* and is looking for a director and a screenwriter.[9] Once everyone recovers from the financial debacle of Baz Luhrmann's *Australia* (2008), Jackman's most recent star vehi-cle, it may be time to welcome a new turn on the carousel.

Kiss me, Kate *(1953)*

In the light of its MGM predecessors *On the Town*, which butchered Bern-stein's great 1944 score in its screen version of 1949, and the remake of *Show Boat* in 1951, which cut many songs and played havoc with both the script and spirit of its original, the film adaptation of *Kiss Me, Kate,* directed by

Kiss Me, Kate, 1953 film. Cole Porter (Ron Randell), Lilli Vanessi (Kathryn Grayson), Lois Lane (Ann Miller), and Fred Graham (Howard Keel) in Fred's apartment after a run-through of "So In Love."

Kiss Me, Kate, 1953 film. Petruchio (Keel) gives his new fiancée Katharine (Grayson) an unscripted paddling to conclude the first act of "Taming of the Shrew."

Show Boat alumnus George Sidney and starring *Show Boat* film alumni Kathryn Grayson and Howard Keel, was remarkably faithful. By later standards, however, the film adaptation has a long way to go in terms of fidelity to its increasingly respected source, the Broadway version. Sidney begins by taking a major structural liberty in his decision to open the film in Fred's apartment a month or so earlier than the first rehearsal rather than beginning with the stage show's opening rehearsal number, "Another Opnin,' Another Show." In addition to "Another Opnin,'" another song gone from the film was "Bianca," which Porter wrote for the character Bill Calhoun under duress when the actor who played him, Harold Lang, insisted he was contractually entitled to a song. In the chapter on *Kiss Me*, Kate (chapter 10), we noted Porter's erroneous belief that the song's banality would preclude its use.

Also absent from the film was the choral number, "I Sing of Love," which those familiar with the cast album also never got to hear, and most of the two parallel finales in which the vitriol and the martial nature of the former is replaced by the tender words and musically lyrical qualities of the latter. Partially compensating for these quasi-operatic omissions is the insertion of a dazzlingly jazzy song and dance number originally composed for Porter's

Out of this World, for Lois (Miller), her suitor (Tommy Rall), her former suitors (Bobby Van and Bob Fosse), and their new girlfriends (Carol Haney and Jeanne Coyne). In marked contrast to the *Pal Joey* and Kurt Weill films we looked at in act I, the *Kiss Me, Kate* screenplay, greatly shortened in the transition from stage to film, effectively creates a sequence of songs occasionally interrupted by five minutes or less of dialogue.

The show's principal ballad is the first of two songs to undergo a new context. Although the final A section of "So in Love" will eventually be heard in its rightful position as a reprise, sung by Lilli in her dressing room before the show moves to its Padua phase and "We Open in Venice," its main dramatic purpose in the film occurs in its new context as an audition number in Fred's apartment, a song performed by Fred to interest the prospective dramatic lead Lilli in the show. The character impersonating Cole Porter (Ron Randell), a depiction only slightly more believable than the casting of Cary Grant in *Night and Day* (1946), sits down at the piano (later joined by an invisible orchestra), and Fred starts the love song. Even before the second A section Lilli joins in, and immediately making the song her own, sings the second A by herself. Fred starts the B and is answered by Lilli, a process repeated in the final A before both Fred and Lilli conclude the song in glorious harmony and ardent glances. In the stage version Lilli sings the song alone in the dressing room unheard by Fred, and Fred sings a reprise in act II unheard by Lilli.

In contrast to the gradual unfolding of Fred and Lilli's love onstage, before seven minutes have gone by in the film, viewers in this medium hear and see that they are deeply in love. Fred may be infatuated with the sexy Lois (Bianca), but the flirtation is fundamentally innocent, or at least superficial. In any event, Fred's attentions are not seriously reciprocated by Lois, who is using Fred to further her show business career and that of her boyfriend Bill Calhoun (Lucentio). Despite its fundamental meaninglessness, the dalliance between Lois and Fred leads to an incriminating note intended for Lois but mistakenly delivered, with a bouquet of flowers, to Lilli, who imprudently reads the note onstage, thus provoking genuine rather than acted stage violence against Fred as Petruchio. Had Fred not included the note, it is likely that the onstage conflicts would not be mirrored by offstage fireworks but by reconciliation, which would spoil the fun (and not incidentally end the show prematurely). The flowers serve their purpose, helping Lilli to realize that she is still in love with Fred. Although she is engaged to the rich and powerful cattle baron Tex, a man incapable of song—in the stage version her fiancé is the Washington diplomat Harrison Howell, also without a song—tellingly we observe her remove the engagement ring in her dressing room before she finishes the reprise of "So in Love."

The re-connection Lilli and Fred make at the end of the "So in Love" duet in Fred's apartment is immediately interrupted by the whirlwind entrance of Lois, who is clearly familiar with the surroundings. Lois (Ann Miller) then proceeds to sing and dance a sexually charged and energetic song and tap dance number, which she hopes will go into the show. Those who find "Too Darn Hot," an entertaining but somewhat gratuitous act II opener may appreciate its new context as a diegetic show-within-show. In fact, when she is finished she learns that the song will be taken out because there's no place to put it— art imitating life evaluating art. In the absence of a second act subdivision, a luxury offered to all stage works but only to a few of their longest film adaptations (e.g., *My Fair Lady, West Side Story, Fiddler on the Roof*), where could such a song go? The answer: as an audition number in the director's apartment.

In order to guide film viewers who presumably are less familiar than stage audiences with the plot of *The Taming of the Shrew*, the *Shrew* performance in the film offers a narrative in which Petruchio explicitly introduces the main characters and situation. The film is also clearer than the stage version about such matters as the fact that Lilli reads Fred's note to Lois (at the end of "Were Thine That Special Face"), which explains why her violence toward Fred goes considerably beyond what is called for in the script. The film also clarifies the connection between Fred's removal of food from the hungry Lilli in the dressing room scene and when Petruchio deprives Kate of food in his later efforts to tame her. The cuts in the libretto deprive film audiences of some of the Spewacks' and even more of Shakespeare's lively dialogue, but when films were expected to run less than two hours, even great material had to go.

One of the more unfortunate aspects of this often successful film adaptation is that even nearly twenty years after the first film version of *Anything Goes* (see chapter 8), Porter's lyrics still required considerable cinematic expurgation. We might expect that the script would replace "bastard" with "louse," but changes in the lyrics amount to a censorship that is collectively depressing. What follows is a generous, if not exhaustive, sample:

- "Too Darn Hot"
  "According to the Kinsey report" is replaced by "according to the latest report" and instead of indulging his favorite sport, man prefers taking the lyrically cumbersome "lovey-dovey to court."
- "Tom, Dick, or Harry"
  "God-damned nose" is replaced by "Doggone nose" and "in the dark they [women] are all the same" is replaced by "in a brawl they are all the same."

- "I Hate Men"
  "Maiden" replaces "virgin" and instead of Mother having
  to marry Father, she now "deigns to marry Father." The film
  version goes on to make several other unfortunate deletions
  and additions in this song.
- "Where Is the Life that Late I Led?"
  Since "puberty" is suggestive and provocative, "the charming
  age of puberty" becomes the first awareness of "masculinity."
  Later in the song the mandatory removal of "hell" (also
  removed later in "Always True to You in My Fashion" and in
  "Brush Up Your Shakespeare") necessitates the replacement of
  the rhyme "well / hell" with "pain / Cain," as in raising a bit of.
- "Brush Up Your Shakespeare"
  The suggestive failure of a woman to defend her virtue (*All's
  Well That Ends Well*) is replaced by the infelicitous woman
  "shocked she pretends well."
- "I Am Ashamed That Women Are So Simple"
  Perhaps the title of this song should have been altered to
  something like "I Am Ashamed to Sing a Sexist Song about
  Women Being Simple." In any event, Kate replaces the
  music to this beautiful song with a recitation (with a little
  underscoring of "So in Love"), fortunately unexpurgated, of
  Shakespeare, who wrote the lyrics.[10]

While Porter's reputation will survive the changes made to his lyrics in the film, it is not enhanced by them. Yet all things considered, the film adaptation of *Kiss Me, Kate*, is not only relatively faithful to its stage version (when compared with its predecessors) but boasts full-throated but not overdone singing by Keel and Grayson, and exuberant singing and dancing by Miller. The ensemble dancing of Miller, Rall, Van, Haney, Coyne, and Fosse, choreographed by Fosse in the angular signature style that he would develop further in the 1960s and 1970s, is outstanding as well as historic, and the supporting roles, especially Keenan Wynn and James Whitmore as the two gunmen, add to the film's quality. Even the interpolated "From This Moment On," is arguably no more extraneous than "Too Darn Hot" was in its original place as the opening of act II. The film, shot and released in 3D, in its day a novelty and today a distraction, does not undermine the film's enjoyment, but it is probably good to know about it in advance.

The large and impressive oil painting of Laurence Olivier as Hamlet in Fred's apartment is clearly visible as a backdrop to Miller's "Too Darn Hot" and other scenes. The character of Hamlet not only demonstrates a Shakespearean connection but likely also alludes to the fact that producer Jack Cummings tried unsuccessfully to engage the non-singing Olivier for this role. It is difficult to imagine what would have happened if this had come to pass, since the demands of the role require a trained singer with a strong high G. The film also introduces a few touches that enhance the dramatic verisimilitude and topicality, such as when Fred, who thinks that Lilli has left the show, says in a stage whisper to a question about her whereabouts that she is probably at that moment flying over Newark. One charming musical touch that deserves honorable mention occurs during the duet in "Wunderbar" when Lilli sings the main melody of the overture and act II finale to Johann Strauss Jr.'s *Die Fledermaus* (one of the many operettas Fred and Lilli have doubtless sung together in various small towns) as a counterpoint to the main tune of Porter's song.

Guys and Dolls *(1955)*

The starting point for the Samuel Goldwyn (1879–1974) film adaptation of *Guys and Dolls* was Goldwyn himself who, in the words of his biographer A. Scott Berg, "grew determined to produce *Guys and Dolls* as the ultimate

Guys and Dolls, 1955 film. Sky Masterson (Marlon Brando) and Sarah Brown (Jean Simmons) dancing in Havana.

film musical, an epic" and in the end "spent $5.5 million overproducing the movie."[11] Interestingly, in a career that goes back to the 1910s and includes such memorable films as *Wuthering Heights* (1939) and *The Best Years of Our Lives* (1946), *Guys and Dolls* would be only the second in a group of musical films that concluded his body of work. The first film of this trilogy brought Goldwyn in contact with Frank Loesser on the successful original film musical *Hans Christian Andersen*, starring Danny Kaye, three years earlier. The second musical, *Guys and Dolls*, would also prove to be the penultimate product of Goldwyn's long career, his seventy-ninth feature film. Four years after *Guys and Dolls*, a huge box office success with the highest earnings of any film in 1956 (more than $13 million in the United States alone), Goldwyn finished his career with his third musical, the commercial and artistic failure, *Porgy and Bess* (discussed in chapter 8).

Goldwyn was famous for discovering and signing talent. In the case of *Guys and Dolls* it was mostly the latter. To complement Loesser and his great hit, Goldwyn turned to Joseph L. Mankiewicz (1909–1993), who not long before had gained distinction as the first to win a double pair of Academy Awards for both directing and screenwriting in two successive years *A Letter to Three Wives* (1949) and *All About Eve* (1950). Mankiewicz, who had never directed or written a musical, wanted to convert Abe Burrows's libretto into more of a play. In preparation for the transfer from stage to film Mankiewicz even wrote a new script that could stand alone without music. He made his goals and intentions clear in a letter to Goldwyn: "My primary, almost only, objective in this writing has been to tell the story as warmly and humanly as possible—and to characterize our four principals as fully as if their story were going to be told in purely dramatic terms."[12] Although Mankiewicz tried to flesh out Sarah Brown's character, especially in the extended scene in Havana, Cuba, the movie ultimately falls short because the experienced screenwriter, but musical theater novice, failed to grasp how the subtleties of music, at least in Loesser's songs, effectively removed the need to transform a musical into a play. Joseph Kerman's famous principle that "the music is the drama" was not a concept that Mankiewicz believed or understood.

When Gene Kelly proved unavailable, Mankiewicz and Goldwyn turned to *a*, or perhaps *the*, major film star of the day, Marlon Brando (1924–2004), who like Mankiewicz had never participated in a musical. Within a few years after his powerful stage performance in Tennessee Williams's *A Streetcar Named Desire* in 1947, Brando had earned a string of four Best Actor nominations, including one for the film adaptation of *Streetcar* (1951) and one for the role of Mark Anthony in a film version of *Julius Caesar* (1953), directed and adapted for the screen by Mankiewicz. One year before *Guys and Dolls*, Brando won the award for *On the Waterfront*. Although *Guys and*

Dolls proved to be Brando's last as well as first foray into musical film, he worked diligently under Loesser's coaching and performed the songs creditably. He even managed to master the basic dance steps of the Cuba interlude with some grace. For his leading lady, Goldwyn tried unsuccessfully to acquire Grace Kelly, another recent Academy Award-winning star. The third choice for Sarah Brown, after Kelly and Deborah Kerr, Jean Simmons (b. 1929), yet another star with no experience in musicals, proved to be surprisingly effective, both as a singer and as an actress.[13] Unlike Brando, Simmons returned to musical theater when in 1975 she played the lead in the London production of *A Little Night Music*.

In addition to these newcomers to musicals, Goldwyn and Mankiewicz brought back several key figures associated with the Broadway production, even if the original Adelaide, Vivian Blaine, was another second choice after Betty Grable declined the role. Another notable singer actor reassigned to the film was Stubby Kaye, who played a major role in the success of the stage versions as Nicely-Nicely Johnson. According to the young Stephen (or in this early case, Steve) Sondheim, who reviewed the Goldwyn extravaganza in 1955 for *Films in Review*, Kaye was "the real hero of the picture," who helped make "Sit Down, You're Rockin' the Boat" "one of the most memorable numbers in musical-comedy history."[14] For Sondheim, Kaye "sets the tone of every scene in which he appears: when he is singing 'Fugue for Tinhorns' and 'Guys and Dolls' he does more to create the atmosphere of Runyon's New York than all the scenery lumped together (which it often seems to be)."[15]

A major benefit of the film version of *Guys and Dolls* is the opportunity to see the original athletic and amusing choreography of Michael Kidd (1919–2007), who recreated the impressive original Runyonland opening and the sewer dance scene to the music of "Luck Be a Lady" much as audiences had seen these numbers onstage five years earlier. Many critics, including Sondheim, lamented scene designer Oliver Smith's sets in which realism and stylization clashed infelicitously, but Kidd created a convincing ambiance through the movements of his eccentric and cartoonish but developed characters, both major and minor. Kaye leading the trio of tinhorns in "Fugue for Tinhorns" near the beginning of the film and the gambling sinners in his rendition of "Sit Down, You're Rockin' the Boat" near the end are indeed two of the great translations from Broadway to film. Although Vivian Blaine's dramatic stage delivery is less suitable than Kaye's for the more intimate framework of film, it is still a treat to hear her repeat her stage performance of "Adelaide's Lament" (with the sole visual addition of a medicine cabinet). In addition to its entertainment value, the recreation of Kidd's choreography and the roles of Nicely-Nicely and Adelaide make the film an invaluable historical document.

On the debit side, although the three new songs added to the film are all by Loesser, they do not make up in either quality or quantity for the five songs deleted from the show. The first new song, "Pet Me Poppa," replaced "A Bushel and a Peck" for Adelaide and the Hot Box Girls for the simple reason that Goldwyn didn't like it. Seeing dancers precociously impersonating cats nearly thirty years before Lloyd Webber made this a must-see musical theater experience does not make up for the song switch. The second new song was written to give Frank Sinatra, then at the peak of his stardom as a recording artist and fresh from winning the best supporting actor Oscar for *From Here to Eternity* (1953), an expanded singing role as Nathan Detroit. We may recall from chapter 11 that his non-singing stage predecessor Sam Levene gradually observed his singing requirements dwindle down to a line or two in the verse of "Oldest Established" in act I and a few more lines in his duet with Adelaide, "Sue Me," in act II. In what corresponds to act I in the film Nathan gets more to sing in "Oldest Established" in the opening scene and replaces one of the tinhorns in the title song about an hour into the film. Another fifteen minutes later he sings a new song expressly written for Sinatra, "Adelaide," a song that Nathan sings to Lieutenant Brannigan to convince him that the gamblers are holding an engagement party rather than a meeting to decide where to hold the floating crap game.

The third and final new song, the lyrical "A Woman in Love" arguably receives more air time than any song in the film. Introduced after the title song in the Overture, the song dominates the musical ambiance of the dinner date in Havana, Cuba, where Sky has taken Sarah on a bet. For twelve minutes of movie time (roughly from 77 to 89 minutes into the film), we hear it as a serenade in the café, as background music in the restaurant, and finally sung over a Latin accompaniment over dinner. After Sarah sings "If I Were a Bell" in a state of drunkenness and the couple returns to New York, "My Time of Day," the song in which Sky bares his soul and reveals his biblical name (Obediah), is reduced to underscoring. Instead he sings a reprise of "A Woman in Love."

"Pet Me Poppa" was a matter of one Hot Box Tune replacing another, but the deletion of "My Time of Day" seriously defeats Mankiewicz's stated purpose of character development. In contrast to "Adelaide's Lament," which reveals so much about this character, the song "Adelaide" may be an opportunity for Sinatra but does little to enhance Nathan's character or the dramatic situation. Before the film is over, three more songs from the show would disappear. The first is "I've Never Been in Love Before," a genuine love duet between Sky and Sarah directly following Sky's intimate revelations in "My Time of Day," and arguably the great ballad of a rich theater score. The second casualty is "More I Cannot Wish You," another of Loesser's most lyrical ballads and the only chance Arvide Abernathy, Sarah's gentle Salvation Army mentor, gets to sing in the show. The last song to end up on the cutting room floor is the cynical duet between Sarah and Adelaide in which they each share their goal to "Marry the Man Today" "and change his ways tomorrow." The song was honest in its day, but its message would cast pallor on the romantic double wedding that ends the film and is the least missed of the five discarded numbers.

My Fair Lady *(1964)*

Not only did the film version of *My Fair Lady*, which arrived two years after the show completed its unsurpassed six-year Broadway run, present all the songs from its stage source, it also retained nearly all of the dialogue and most of the original running order. At nearly three hours, *Lady* is the most faithful adaptation in our group of films. As an added bonus, film audiences got a chance to see stage stars Rex Harrison as Henry Higgins and Stanley Holloway as Alfred P. Doolittle repeating their roles. Cecil Beaton returned as costume and set designer.[16]

My Fair Lady, 1964 film. Eliza Doolittle (Audrey Hepburn) and Henry Higgins (Rex Harrison) ("In Hertford, Hereford, and Hampshire, hurricanes hardly ever happen.") For a stage photo of this scene see p. 271.

My Fair Lady on film enjoyed some financial success, despite its then stratospheric production costs of $17 million. It also received more than its share of critical acclaim. Nominated for twelve Oscars, it won in no less than eight categories: cinematography (Harry Stradling), sound (George R. Groves), musical scoring (André Previn), art direction (Gene Allen, Cecil Beaton, and George James Hopkins), costume design (Beaton), and major awards for Best Actor (Harrison), Director (George Cukor), and Best Picture. The film also received Golden Globe awards in these last three categories. In the American Film Institute rankings of the Top Twenty-Five Movie Musicals of All Time created in 2006, *My Fair Lady* placed eighth, the fourth highest ranking among adaptations of Broadway musicals (the others in the top eight are original musical films).

We have noted that between the mid-1950s and early 1970s, roughly between *The King and I* and *Carousel* films of 1956 and *Fiddler on the Roof* in 1972, film musical adaptations of Broadway shows tended to be far more faithful and more complete than the films we have looked at between *Show Boat* and *Guys and Dolls* (with *Pal Joey* from 1957 and *Porgy and Bess* from 1959, not coincidentally shows created between 1935 and 1940, proving the exceptions). While some cuts, additions, and other changes can be expected, the film adaptations of Broadway musicals that debuted in the 1940s and 1950s more often than not attempted to recapture the spirit and more than occasionally the letter of their stage sources. Before the 1950s producers and studios ruled the roost. After that the creators took over. As producers, Rodgers and Hammerstein had acquired the control of their own films; Lerner and Loewe did the same for *Gigi*. After decades of Broadway films redesigned to serve the needs and values of Hollywood, *Gigi* (1958), an original musical film made by Broadway creators, served a new master. In Mast's astute epiphany, *Gigi*, which won an Academy Award for best picture, "is the best Broadway musical ever written for the screen."[17]

Countering the predilection toward greater fidelity to Broadway sources, Hollywood values, in particular the desire to sign movie stars with strong box office appeal, gradually led to casting decisions based more on popular appeal than on singing experience and talent. But even those first cast on Broadway as the King in *The King and I* (Yul Brynner) and Higgins in *My Fair Lady* (Harrison) were in roles conceived for dramatic actors without vocal credentials. Interestingly, there was an attempt to bypass Harrison in favor of a bigger film star—Cary Grant turned down the role and Peter O'Toole demanded unreasonably high contractual terms—but after Harrison was chosen there was no need to replace his voice with that of a more polished singer. Goldwyn, too, in casting *Guys and Dolls*, also wanted to attract big box office draws such as Gene Kelly and (no relation) Grace Kelly for Sky and Sarah, and his final choices, Brando and Simmons, fit this profile. Once cast, however, Brando and Simmons were expected to lend their own voices to the film and both proved adequate (or better) as singers.

Soon this would change. The film adaptation of *The Music Man* took a chance that paid off in casting the original stage lead, Robert Preston, who had little proven box office traction, but Jack Warner and Cukor were not eager to take a similar chance and allow Julie Andrews to repeat her stage role as Eliza Doolittle. In replacing Andrews, the goal was to find a star more likely to help Warner recoup the $5.5 million dollars he paid for the screen rights. The gorgeous and glamorous Audrey Hepburn, a box office tested movie star, fit this description, while Andrews, the luminous star of *My Fair Lady* on the stage but as yet an untested movie personality, did not.[18] Working under the assumption that she would be the voice of Eliza in the film, Hepburn made demos of at least two songs, "Wouldn't It Be Loverly?" and "Show Me," both of which can be seen and heard as a special feature in the two-disc DVD Special Edition. There is little question that Hepburn did not possess the voice quality either of Andrews, whom she replaced, or of Hepburn's vocal double Marni Nixon, who had dubbed the role of Anna Leonowens for Deborah Kerr in *The King and I*.

On the other hand, the demos reveal a voice roughly comparable in quality to that of Jean Simmons. By this standard, Hepburn arguably made a plausible candidate to sing her role, especially when playing a character who was more guttersnipe than lady. In his autobiography, Lerner praises Leslie Caron (*Gigi*) for her dancing and acting but thought her singing abilities were "not up to scratch, or, if you will, too much up to scratch."[19] Later in the same paragraph he places Hepburn in the same category as an actress with "the gift for auditory illusion" who when hearing her "sadly inadequate singing voice" in a control room imagines that she is hearing Joan Sutherland.[20] The fact that Harrison only sings a fraction of the actual notes in "You Did It" and about the same amount of "Hymn to Him" shows that double standards were alive and well when it came to casting Higgins and Eliza. Considering the widespread criticism Hepburn received for lacking the coarseness necessary to capture the guttersnipe Eliza before she became a lady, it seems a shame that Hepburn was not allowed to sing the songs her character sings prior to her transformation in order to create a vocal transformation to match the social one. To its credit, however, in its released version, just as we see the beauty of Hepburn underneath the dirt, thanks to the subterfuge of Marni Nixon we hear her beauty long before she emerges triumphant at the Embassy Ball.

Despite its fidelity, the film did make a few changes worth noting. "With a Little Bit of Luck" is delayed from act I, scene 2, to scene 4, where it had been reprised onstage. Now the song is both introduced and reprised in the same scene. Also in act I, scenes 6 and 7 are reversed and some dialogue of the former moved to the latter after the "Ascot Gavotte." The film contains other reordering and some new dialogue here and there that does not effect the placement of songs. The brief exchange between Higgins and his mother that follows Ascot, for example, is new in the film. Between what corresponds to act I, scenes 8 and 9, the film also offers a short scene in which Pickering cancels his bet six weeks before the Embassy Ball.

When Eliza returns to Covent Garden after leaving Higgins, her reprise of "Wouldn't It Be Loverly?" is sung as both a voice-over and a flashback. Not only are these techniques cinematically useful, but they also effectively demonstrate the extent of Eliza's transformation. Perhaps now that she is a lady she doesn't want to wake up her former neighbors so early in the morning. For the most part, however, the film does not take advantage of the possibilities cinema offers to "open up" the show onto a wider "stage" via quick-yet-elaborate scene changes and location settings. One modest exception is the short scene in which we discreetly observe the undressing and bathing of Eliza by Mrs. Pearce and other servants, an offstage event in the theater. The most obvious lost opportunity for cinematic extravagance is the "theatrical" Ascot scene. Although visually interesting with its suitably colorless black and white costuming for the rigid and lifeless upper crust of society—Eliza gets a conspicuous touch of red in her hat to match her inappropriate but refreshing enthusiasm for the event—we hear but do not see the horses actually racing. Perhaps we might conclude that the film adaptation works so well *because* of moments like this one, where cinematic excess is avoided in favor of a consistent, theatrical focus on the principal players and their interactions. At this and many other moments, we are reminded that we are seeing a film of a play rather than an original film— and this is a good thing.

In an effective cinematic juxtaposition, the shot of Higgins's laughter at the ball when he hears about Karpathy's erroneous conclusion regarding Eliza's national identity merges seamlessly with the continuation of this same laughter now shot in Higgins's study after the ball. When it ran in theaters the film included an intermission after the stunningly beautiful Hepburn descends the staircase in Higgins's apartment before they leave for the ball (about 100 minutes into the film). On Broadway, the act I curtain closes at the Embassy Ball with the suspense of whether Eliza will be able to fool the wily Karpathy. Theater audiences would have to wait to learn whether

Higgins's former student would expose Eliza's lowly origins. Since the film intermission had taken place *before* the ball, Higgins's laughter provides a welcome linkage between Eliza's triumph at the ball and "You Did It," in which Higgins and Pickering insensitively and undeservedly appropriate all the credit for her achievement.

Despite the iconic stature of Cukor's *My Fair Lady*, Comingsoon.net announced in 2008 that Duncan Kenworthy, who "has produced three of the most successful British films of all time, *Four Weddings and a Funeral, Notting Hill*, and *Love Actually*," all starring Hugh Grant, together with Cameron Mackintosh, the phenomenally successful stage producer who brought *Les Misérables, Miss Saigon*, and *The Phantom of the Opera* from London to New York, have cleared the rights with Columbia Pictures and CBS Films to produce a new version of Lerner and Loewe's classic. Discussions have begun with their chosen lady, the very fair Keira Knightly, in significant contrast to the casting process in both the stage and earlier film versions, in which the starting point was Higgins. While respectful of Cukor's treatment, Kenworthy and Mackintosh are confident they can improve on the 1964 original by shooting on location. In their press release Doug Belgrad, a president of Columbia Pictures, espoused the view that "by drawing additional material from *Pygmalion*" Mackintosh would create an updated version that "will preserve the magic of the musical while fleshing out the characters and bringing 1912 London to life in an authentic and exciting way for contemporary audiences."[21] To reach this lofty prediction Mackintosh will need more than just a little bit of luck.

West Side Story *(1961)*

Writers on *West Side Story* seldom neglect to mention that it was the film rather than the stage version that catapulted the show into universal popular consciousness. Indeed, the film, produced by Mirisch Pictures, won ten out of its eleven Academy Award nominations, including Best Picture and Best Direction (Robert Wise and Jerome Robbins). The other awards were for Best Supporting Actor and Actress (George Chakiris as Bernardo and Rita Moreno as Anita), Best Art Direction, Cinematography, Costumes, Film Editing, Scoring, and Sound Mixing.[22] With graceful irony, the Academy even presented a Special Award to Robbins, who had been fired from the film after directing the Prologue for falling behind the production schedule. The only nomination that did not result in an award was Ernest Lehman's for Best Screenplay. Lehman did, however, receive an equivalent award from the Writers Guild of America.

West Side Story, 1961 film. Tony (Richard Beymer) and Maria (Natalie Wood) meet at the Gym and fall in love at first sight.

In the early 1960s, most movie theaters continued the then-common practice of offering two films for one admission price, a feature presentation and a B-movie. Longer films appeared as a single feature with an intermission, a break in the action that presented an opportunity for audiences to purchase refreshments. At 152 minutes, *West Side Story* merited an intermission. Theoretically, it was possible to divide the film at the end of act I directly after the Rumble and begin the second act with "I Feel Pretty." Instead, director Robert Wise revamped the scenario and moved the Rumble closer to the end of the story where it was followed rather than preceded by "Cool."

Despite such adjustments, in marked contrast to the pillaged film version of Bernstein's *On the Town* and even such relatively faithful film adaptations as Rodgers and Hammerstein's *Oklahoma!*, all the *West Side Story* songs are present and accounted for. This may be a first (to be followed by *My Fair Lady*'s film adaptation three years later). Also in marked contrast to *On the Town* and numerous other Hollywood adaptations from the 1930s and 1940s, no songs were added by studio composers on contract or even by Bernstein, although Sondheim was called upon to add and rework his lyrics for "America" in response to the new gender mix. The film also reinstated an overture, which had been deleted from the stage version. It can be heard under the static abstract graphic design with changing colors that will metamorphose into an overhead realistic cinematic view of the southern tip of Manhattan before the camera makes its leisurely way to the West side, where it zooms in on the Jets protecting their little corner of the island. After diligently observing the musical order from the Prologue to "Maria" (Prologue, "Jet Song," "Something's Coming," "The Dance at the Gym," and "Maria"), however, the film made changes both large and small to the order of the next nine songs before returning to the stage order for the final songs, "A Boy Like That / I Have a Love," "Taunting," and Finale (see the online website for a list of the songs in the stage version).

It might seem strange at first to dwell on the ordering of songs. But consider how important the steps in a story's telling can be, even a story we know well like *Romeo and Juliet*. Try telling a friend the story in your own words, then compare its impact to Shakespeare's language. Similarly, the collaborators on the film version of *West Side Story* made a variety of creative decisions about how to re-tell the musical/dramatic story of the show, with the many differences between live theater and film techniques always in mind. Even though the film includes all the songs from the stage version, the sequence in which those songs are presented exerts a strong effect on how we understand the show.

We left off with "Maria." Onstage, after singing the song based on the name of his new love, Tony continues to call her name until he finds her on her tenement balcony. They then converse and sing "Tonight." The film follows "Maria" with a scene in Maria's apartment between Maria, Bernardo, and Anita, during which they move to the rooftop to join the rest of the Shark men and women for "America." In the film version of this song, the men, absent from the stage version, contrast the women's positive view of their newly adopted country with sarcastic new lyrics. Only after "America" does Tony reappear in the film and the lovers sing "Tonight."

More radically, "Cool," the song that follows "America" in the stage version, is replaced by "Gee, Officer Krupke" and will not be heard until late in the movie, where it directly follows the much-delayed Rumble. Since Riff led the "Cool" song onstage, his absence, as he is dead by this point in the show, necessitated the elevation of Ice (the character Diesel onstage) to lead both the Jets and the song. In the remarks about the show's genesis we pointed out that in its position in the film, "Gee, Officer Krupke" no longer functions as comic relief after the tragic events of the Rumble, a brief respite between the "Procession and Nightmare" that concludes the Ballet Sequence and the dramatically intense "A Boy Like That / I Have a Love."

The next change in song order occurs with the earlier appearance of "I Feel Pretty" in the film—in fact, right after "Gee, Officer Krupke!" Onstage, this song, which in the story occurs almost at the same moment as the

Rumble that ended act I (but presented consecutively rather than simultaneously to avoid modernist chaos), opens the second act with a moment of deeply ironic levity. By placing "I Feel Pretty" *before* the Rumble, the irony is lost. In its new position, the song serves as a prelude to the mock, but non-ironic, wedding depicted in the next song in the film, "One Hand, One Heart," which onstage had occurred after "Cool." "I Feel Pretty" is notable for the energy of its fast waltz tempo and Maria's lilting words full of inner rhymes ("it's alarming how charming I feel"). At every opportunity Sondheim has expressed his dissatisfaction with these lyrics and relates how he tried to remove the inner rhymes but was outvoted. From then until now he has criticized Maria's lyric as too urbane for a gritty inner-city character.[23] There is some truth to this. But in its new position, "I Feel Pretty" is arguably more in character than it was onstage. The following grim confrontations of the Rumble scene are perhaps more dramatic (or perhaps more cinematic) as a result—even if the complex irony of the stage version is lost.

In another departure of major significance, the offstage voice singing "Somewhere" in the second act Ballet Sequence is replaced in the film by a more realistic and conventional "Somewhere" duet between Tony and Maria. The removal of a dream ballet is typical of other transfers from stage to screen in the early 1960s, where audience expectations called for more apparent realism. Balancing the deletion of this major dance section, several other dances, including the Prologue, The Dance at the Gym, and the now mixed gendered "America" (in the film men as well as women sing and dance this number) are extended.

Realism as a vital component of the Hollywood film aesthetic and the likely motive for removing the surrealistic Ballet Sequence, is considerably challenged, however, by the presence of gang toughs snapping their fingers (painfully with their thumbs and first fingers at Robbins's insistence) and their balletic and acrobatic dancing up and down a real Manhattan. To better prepare film audiences for this incongruity, Robbins greatly expanded the Prologue, which itself followed an overture in contrast to the stage version. After the abstract drawing of Manhattan seen throughout the overture metamorphoses into realistic aerial footage that ends up on a West side playground and surrounding tenements, the lengthened Prologue allows the Jets to ease more naturally into dance through a series of incremental movements from natural to stylized movements, much in the same way spoken dialogue moves into a talky song verse before emerging as a great tune. Here, as at the Ascot races, a stage convention—the autonomy of dance as an expressive art form—is valued over conventional filmic naturalism. Shot on location in New York City using the fastest color film stocks and most advanced compact sound and camera equipment of the day, artistically executed mostly by New Yorkers, *West Side Story* was both grittier and artier than almost any contemporary Hollywood film made in beautiful sunny California.

In his eloquent memoir *Original Story By*, Laurents, writing about the stage version of *West Side Story*, concludes without false modesty, that this show was richer in content and quality than innovation:

> As for those inflated claims, if *West Side Story* influenced the musi-
> cal theatre, it was in content, not form. Serious subjects—bigotry,
> race, rape, murder, death—were dealt with for the first time in a
> musical and as seriously as they would be in a play. That was inno-
> vative; style and technique were not. They had all been used piece-
> meal in one way or another before....The music for the dances
> is extraordinarily exciting; that music and the basic story are the
> lasting strengths of the show. The difference between the music of
> *West Side Story* and other shows, however, is in quality, not in pur-
> pose....What we really did stylistically with *West Side Story* was
> take every musical theatre technique as far as it could be taken.
> Scene, song and dance were integrated seamlessly; we did it all
> better than anyone ever had before. We were not the innovators we
> were called but what we did achieve was more than enough to be
> proud of.[24]

While the musical and dramatic techniques of *West Side Story* may have been nothing new, the thought, complexity, and seriousness with which they were employed were exceptional. It was in the domain of overall quality that the show was innovative—it raised the bar (and the barre) for what a musical could be, beyond even the ambitious standards of Rodgers and Hammerstein's collaborations of the 1940s and early '50s. Their new post–*West Side Story* shows such as *Flower Drum Song* and *The Sound of Music* began to look a little artificial in comparison to Wise's film version of *West Side Story* in 1961 (but not the film version of *The Sound of Music*, which Wise also directed).

Although the movie may exert less appeal today in the context of the similarly accomplished and even grittier *Chicago* and *Sweeney Todd* adaptations, Wise's (and Robbins's) *West Side Story*—with its contemporary urban setting, ubiquitous and stunning dancing, and careful use of recurring sung and orchestral musical motives creatively augmented by location photography on the streets of New York—remains still something of a rarity in musical films where control over the soundtrack was typically facilitated by working on indoor stage sets. Anyone who has seen the opening of the film, with its unforgettable bird's-eye view of Manhattan office towers and slums, brings that memory with them to even the best staged revival of the show. Wise brought taste and sophistication to his direction. Although he changed the show quite a bit, he brought it enduring fame and introduced the realistic, contemporary musical to a much broader audience, first across the United States, then around the globe. On September 3, 2006, the American Film Institute placed *West Side Story* behind only *Singin' in the Rain* (1952) as the Greatest Film Musical of all time.[25]

Epilogue: The Age of Sondheim and Lloyd Webber

CHAPTER FIFTEEN

SWEENEY TODD AND *SUNDAY IN THE PARK WITH GEORGE*

Happily Ever After West Side Story *with Sondheim*

Sondheim and His Mentors

Within two years after creating the lyrics for *West Side Story* (1957) to music by Leonard Bernstein, Sondheim, who wanted to be a Broadway composer-lyricist, reluctantly but again successfully wrote the lyrics only for a show to Jule Styne's music for the canonic *Gypsy* (1959), also directed by Jerome Robbins. Sondheim's second foray into Broadway lyric writing brought him into direct contact for the first time with a major star, Ethel Merman, and Sondheim contributed greatly to the creation of her character, Rose. Merman's role in *Gypsy* capped a long career studded with star vehicles dating back to *Girl Crazy* (1930).[1] Sondheim's next show, the wacky but well-crafted farce, *A Funny Thing Happened on the Way to the Forum* (1962), marked his long-awaited Broadway debut as a lyricist *and* composer at the age of thirty-two. *Forum* won the Tony Award for best musical, and at 964 performances enjoyed a longer run (200 performances longer) than any future Sondheim show. Even during these early associations with acclaim and popularity, Sondheim was generally relegated to the background, barely mentioned in the reviews of *West Side Story* and *Gypsy* and bypassed as a nominee for his work on *Forum*.

Perhaps the major achievement of his next musical, *Anyone Can Whistle* (1964), again with a libretto by *West Side Story* and *Gypsy* author Arthur Laurents, was that despite the show's disappointing run of nine performances,

Stephen Sondheim in 2007.

Goddard Lieberson of Columbia Records had the foresight to produce a commercial original cast recording. One year later Sondheim completed his trilogy of collaborations with composer legends begun with Bernstein and Styne when, against his better judgment, he wrote the lyrics for Richard Rodger's *Do I Hear a Waltz?* (the fourth and probably final Laurents libretto that Sondheim set), an unpleasant and increasingly acrimonious experience for all concerned. The result was a quickly forgotten and subsequently neglected musical that despite its troubled genesis deserves to be heard and seen more often.[2]

After two hits (as a lyricist), one hit as a composer-lyricist, a flop, a disappointing run, and five fallow years Sondheim, in tandem with Harold Prince, erupted on Broadway between 1970 and 1973 with a creative explosion: *Company* (1970), *Follies* (1971), and *A Little Night Music* (1973). From this trilogy *Company* has been most frequently singled out for its historic and artistic significance as a pioneering exponent of the so-called concept musical. Not atypical is the assessment by Thomas P. Adler in the *Journal of Popular Culture* that *Company* was "every bit as much a landmark musical as *Oklahoma!*"[3] Eugene K. Bristow and J. Kevin Butler conclude their essay on *Company* in *American Music* with a similar epiphany: "As *Oklahoma!* was the landmark, model, and inspiration for almost all musicals during the three decades that followed its opening, *Company* became the vantage point, prototype, and stimulus for new directions in musical theater of the seventies and eighties."[4]

By 1973 Sondheim, now forty-three, had composed the lyrics to two of the most critically acclaimed shows of Broadway's Golden Age and music and lyrics for another five shows, including a trilogy that inaugurated a new age. Over the next twenty years Sondheim's next seven shows (three with director Prince, three with librettist-director James Lapine, and one with director Jerry Zaks) would provide Broadway with some of the most compelling, innovative, thought-provoking, and often emotionally affecting musicals of their, or any, time. Sondheim, although arguably a central figure in these collaborations, was not entirely responsible for all the remarkable qualities audiences and critics appreciate in these shows. In fact, the only show he initiated himself was *Sweeney Todd*.

Sondheim's shows have lacked in immediately popular appeal, but they are everywhere lavished with deep and lasting critical praise. In the long run, most of his works have acquired a consequential audience of lovers and aesthetes, year after year. The relatively short initial runs of even his most successful shows as composer-lyricist or their revivals therefore do not accurately reflect the influence and popularity of his work within the musical theater community. Here are the first performance runs of the twelve shows between 1962 and 1994 for which Sondheim wrote both music and lyrics, in numerical rather than chronological order:

Forum (1962)	964
Into the Woods (1987)	764
Company (1970)	706
Sunday in the Park with George (1984)	604
A Little Night Music (1973)	601
Sweeney Todd (1979)	558
Follies (1971)	522
Passion (1994)	280
Pacific Overtures (1976)	193
Assassins (Off-Off Broadway) (1991)	72
Merrily We Roll Along (1981)	16
Anyone Can Whistle (1964)	9

Obviously, Sondheim's towering reputation must be based on other factors, including critical esteem and widely available excellent audio and video recordings. Despite these relatively modest, and sometimes even less than modest runs, with the exception of *Passion* and the two-month workshop of *Bounce* (formerly *Gold* and *Wise Guys*) in 1999 and its brief return for a two-month New York Off-Broadway engagement in 2008 as *Road Show*, every Sondheim show has also received a major New York revival of some sort—Broadway, Off-Broadway, Staged Reading, New York City Opera—and innumerable productions in regional and community theaters, colleges, and high schools throughout the United States, and in opera houses throughout the world. After a popular *Forum* revival in 1996 (715 performances) starring Nathan Lane, then Whoopi Goldberg as the slave Pseudolus, the short twenty-first century has already witnessed a Sondheim Broadway revival nearly every year: *Follies* (2001), *Into the Woods* (2002), *Assassins* (2004), *Sweeney Todd* (2005), *Company* (2006), and *Sunday in the Park with George* (2008), and as a lyricist *Gypsy* (2003 and 2008) and *West Side Story* (2009). Sondheim's work, while lacking in initial popularity, appears to be gaining longevity and ubiquity.

What Sondheim Learned from Hammerstein

Sondheim, a native New Yorker whose father could play harmonized show tunes by ear after hearing them once or twice, was the beneficiary of a precocious, suitably specialized musical education. While still a teenager and shortly after the premiere of *Carousel*, Sondheim had the opportunity to be critiqued at length by the legendary Hammerstein, who, by a fortuitous coincidence that would be the envy of *Show Boat*'s second act, happened to be a neighbor and the father of Sondheim's friend and contemporary, James Hammerstein. Sondheim's unique apprenticeship with the first of his three great mentors, Oscar Hammerstein 2nd, one of the giants of the Broadway musical from the 1920s until long after his death in 1960 (see the chapters on *Show Boat* and *Carousel*), might serve as a Hegelian metaphor for Sondheim's thesis, antithesis, and synthesis of modernism and traditionalism, high-brow and low-brow. His great aesthetic achievements have been as a loyal revolutionary (not unlike Beethoven) who thoroughly engaged with—rather than rejected—Broadway's richest traditions. Before his collaborations with three major composers in this tradition as well as Robbins and Laurents and Merman, Sondheim was able to learn invaluable lessons about the craft of Broadway from one of its greatest pioneers. Sondheim never forgot Hammerstein's priceless lessons in how to write and how not to write a musical. To help his student develop his craft and discover his own voice, Hammerstein suggested that Sondheim write four kinds of musicals to develop his craft.[5] For the next six years Sondheim would attempt to follow this advice.

Some of what Sondheim learned about lyric writing and dramatic structure from the master soon became available to musical theater aficionados when Hammerstein published a seminal essay on the subject in 1949.[6] One central premise stated early in the essay is Hammerstein's conviction that "a song is a wedding of two crafts."[7] Later, Hammerstein articulates the importance of "very close collaboration during the planning of a song and the story that contains the song" and espouses the view that "the musician is just as much an author as the man who writes the words."[8] The resulting marriage of music and words, the welding of two crafts and talents "into a single expression" is for Hammerstein "the great secret of the well-integrated musical play."[9] Unlike Hammerstein, Sondheim would assume two mantles, author and musician—although, unlike his mentor, Sondheim did not write the librettos for any of his Broadway shows.

Throughout the course of his essay Hammerstein explores a number of issues and ideas about theatrical songwriting that did not go unnoticed by his student and neighbor. For example, Hammerstein advocates what we might call a non-operatic approach to the musical that maintains clear and sharp distinctions between spoken dialogue and song. With few exceptions, and in marked contrast to his popular contemporary Lloyd Webber, Sondheim has followed this approach ever since. Hammerstein also never wavered from his conviction "that the song is the servant of the play" and "that it is wrong to write first what you think is an attractive song and then try to wedge it into a story."[10] His protégé would follow this advice as well, in fact unwaveringly for the next forty years.

Hammerstein goes on to share his ideas about the craft of lyric writing. Here are some of the highlights:

- Hammerstein on rhyming: "If one has fundamental things to say in a song, the rhyming becomes a question of deft balancing. A rhyme should be unassertive, never standing out too noticeably.... There should not be too many rhymes. In fact, a rhyme should appear only where it is absolutely demanded to keep the pattern of the music. If a listener is made rhyme-conscious, his interest may be diverted from the story of the song. If, on the other hand you keep him waiting for a rhyme, he is more likely to listen to the meaning of the words."[11] As an example of the latter technique, Hammerstein points out the delay of the "cotton" and "forgotten" rhyme in *Show Boat*'s "Ol' Man River," a delay that focuses the rhymes on the most crucial words when additional and possible rhymes would detract from their power. Interestingly, Hammerstein considers the exuberant mood of "A Wonderful Guy" from *South Pacific* an opportunity for "interior rhymes, undemanded rhymes and light-hearted similes." These were techniques that Sondheim became justly critically famous for, but would generally avoid in later years, especially when setting lyrics for less educated characters. Opting for character over craft ("song" as "servant of the play"), Sondheim criticized his own brilliant lyrics for Maria's exuberant number in *West Side Story*, "I Feel Pretty," for their lack of verisimilitude.[12]

- Hammerstein on phonetics: "The job of the poet is to find the right word in the right place, the word with the exact meaning and the highest quality of beauty or power. The lyric writer must find this word too, but it must be also a word that is clear when sung and not too difficult for the singer to sing on that note which he hits when he sings."[13] Although Hammerstein points out a number of successful song conclusions that follow this principle, most of which end on a vowel (e.g., "Oh, what a beautiful *day*"), the self-critical lyricist chose to dwell on what he felt was one failed ending, the consonant that concludes "What's the Use of Wond'rin'" in *Carousel* ("all the rest is talk").

- Hammerstein on sincerity: "The most important ingredient of a good song is sincerity. Let the song be yours and yours alone. However important, however trivial, believe it. Mean it from the bottom of your heart, and say what is on your mind as carefully, as clearly, as beautifully as you can."[14]

A quarter of a century later Sondheim published some of his own thoughts about lyric writing adapted from a talk he simply called "Theater Lyrics" first given to the Dramatists Guild and then later published in a slightly altered form in the collection *Playwrights, Lyricists, Composers, on Theatre*. On the first page of this talk in its published form Sondheim informs his audience and readers that most of what he knows he learned from Hammerstein, his first mentor (although he also acknowledges the example of other lyricists, including Cole Porter). Sondheim recalls that the mentorship officially began when Hammerstein critiqued a draft of a musical called *By George*, a musical à clef about the preparatory school where the young protégé was then a junior.[15]

What Hammerstein taught the novice at their historic first session not only encompassed lyric writing but also addressed larger dramatic issues. This is how Sondheim recalled his lesson nearly thirty years later: "Detail by detail, he told me how to structure songs, how to build them with a beginning and a development and an ending, according to his own principles, how to introduce character, what relates a song to character, etc. etc. It was four hours of the most *packed* information. I dare say, at the risk of hyperbole, that I learned in that afternoon more than most people learn about song writing in a lifetime."[16] Some of what his teacher told him (e.g., the remarks on rhyming, phonetics, and sincerity quoted earlier) appeared a few years later in Hammerstein's essay. Over the years Sondheim also often repeated Hammerstein's anecdote about the importance of detail, which was inspired by his mentor's astonishment when he learned that the sculptor of the Statue of Liberty carefully detailed the top of Lady Liberty's head long before it was possible to anticipate the popularity of photographs of the iconic image from above.[17]

The first of the four apprentice musicals assigned by Hammerstein was to be a musical based on a play he admired, the second a musical based on a play he found flawed and felt he could improve, a third based on a novel or a short story, and for the finale an original musical. In the end only the first, *Beggar on Horseback*, based on a play by George S. Kaufman and Marc Connelly, was completed and performed (at Williams College in March 1949 at the end of Sondheim's junior year). Sondheim continued to work on the second, *Climb High*, based on Maxwell Anderson's *High Tor*, for several years after he graduated and made substantial progress on the third show, based on the Mary Poppins stories.[18] At the end of his sophomore year a fifth non-pedagogical show, a spoof on Williams College life called *Phinney's Rainbow*, was staged there and Hammerstein came up to Massachusetts to see it.[19] The final original musical was the post-collegiate *Saturday Night*. Abandoned after the unexpected death of its producer Lemuel Ayers in 1955, shortly before Sondheim was asked to join the *West Side Story* team, *Saturday Night* would not receive its first professional reading for another forty years.[20]

In "Theater Lyrics" Sondheim encapsulates the craft of lyric writing from two seemingly straightforward but potentially profound central principles: (1) "Lyrics exist in time" and (2) "Lyrics go with music." Both principles possess far-reaching artistic consequences for Sondheim's future in musical theater and both take as a given the wedding of music and lyrics that Hammerstein emphasized in his essay a quarter of a century earlier. The lyric writer must take into account not only the fact that "music is a relentless engine and keeps lyrics going," but that lyrics need to be "underwritten" and "simple in essence." In addition, a lyric writer must learn the difficult lesson of the fundamental difference between serious poetry and lyric writing. Sondheim begins with his "favorite example," Rodgers and Hammerstein's "Oh, what a beautiful mornin' / Oh, what a beautiful day" from *Oklahoma!* (a lyric that seemed simplistic on paper but came to life when sung) to demonstrate this last point: "I would be ashamed to put it down on paper, it would look silly. What Hammerstein knew was that set to music it was going to have an enormous richness. It did, it's a *beautiful* lyric—but not on paper."[21]

Another great Hammerstein lesson was a variation on the theme of sincerity Hammerstein espoused in his published essay on lyrics: the importance of expressing your own lyric voice (to "Say what you feel, not what other song writers feel"). Sondheim's view of the world was by no means the same as his mentor's. Nevertheless, for the rest of his career Sondheim would live by Hammerstein's example, which is eloquently captured in the advice Dot gives to her great-grandson in the song "Move On": "Anything you do, / Let it come from you." In addition to what he was able to impart about lyric writing and dramatic construction, Hammerstein played a major advisory role when he encouraged the aspiring *composer*-lyricist to accept seemingly less ambitious opportunities and agree to work exclusively as a lyricist with such talented and experienced composers as Bernstein, Styne, and Rodgers, a major star such as Merman, and a director-choreographer of Robbins's talent and stature.

Other Lessons Learned

Burt Shevelove, who co-authored the book for *Forum*, and Arthur Laurents, the librettist for the other four Sondheim shows staged between 1957 and 1965, also gave Sondheim lessons that would last long after he moved on to other creative partnerships. From Shevelove, Sondheim learned "that clarity of language was as important as well as clarity of thought" and to "never sacrifice smoothness for cleverness."[22] In a remark that might be considered dismissive of such musicals as *Carousel, South Pacific*, and *The King and I* Sondheim credits Laurents as someone who taught "playwriting principles about lyrics, much deeper and subtler than Oscar because Arthur writes deeper and subtler plays than Oscar."[23] This brings Sondheim to the major lesson he learned from Laurents, "the notion of sub-text":

> Now this is a word I had heard tossed around by Actors Studio types for a long time and really rather sneered at: but what it means simply is, give the actor something to act. I think this is a real secret; if I had to sell secrets about lyric writing I would sell this secret about sub-text. Watch how even some Broadway lyrics that you admire just sit there, with nothing for the actor to play. They just play the next logical step. A playwright when he writes a scene always gives some sub-text, or it's a very shallow scene. Well, that

happens with lyrics. They may be very good, but if they're just on the surface, if there's not pull, there's a kind of deadness on the stage.[24]

Sondheim's unstated parallel between subtext in a play and subtext in a song is a telling one. A few years before Sondheim's tutorial as an adolescent, Hammerstein wrote that songs "must help tell our story and delineate characters, supplementing the dialogue and seeming to be, as much as possible, a continuation of dialogue"—in short, to exhibit the characteristics of a well-made play.[25] Through a conscious use of subtext, Sondheim goes further when he takes the strengths of a well-made play and applies them to a well-made song. The result is a song that expands into its own miniature play.

Among the examples that Sondheim uses to illustrate subtext is "In Buddy's Eyes" from *Follies*. In this poignant and touching song, Sally Plummer tells her former and inextinguishable flame, the seemingly self-confident but ultimately pathetic Benjamin Stone (described by Sondheim as "ripped to shreds internally"), about how her husband, the devoted but philandering Buddy, sees what Sally herself cannot see:

> In Buddy's eyes,
> I'm young, I'm beautiful.
> In Buddy's arms,
> On Buddy's shoulder,
> I won't get older.
> Nothing dies.

In contrast to a sophisticated and pyrotechnically verbal character such as the lawyer Fredrik Egerman in *A Little Night Music*, the emotionally transparent Sally sings deliberately, repeats words, and utters mostly simple one-syllable rhymes. Like her husband, Buddy, who is fated to love a woman who cannot return his love, Sally continues to carry the torch—and sing torch songs—for the unhappily married and emotionally unattainable Ben, who discarded her thirty years ago and will take advantage of her vulnerabilities at their reunion. Sondheim's words have often been celebrated for intellect and intricacy. Here is a clear example of his own early preference for simplicity and emotional directness in lyrics and, as we will soon see, music as well.

In the central chorus of her song, Sondheim gives Sally an identical four-note melodic figure each of the six times she sings "in Buddy's eyes" (the last up an octave) and the one time she sings "in Buddy's arms." The music sets the lyrics simply and syllabically (rather than melismatically, with more than one note per syllable). The figure turns on itself, down from and back to F via D and E♭, above a static harmony that reflects Sally's sincere simplicity, Buddy's stoic solidity, and perhaps also Sally's boredom with Buddy's constant admiration. Significantly, the music Sondheim gives Sally to sing for this mantra, "in Buddy's eyes" (or "arms"), is the only music that fits the underlying static harmony. It is also significant, perhaps a sign of her lack of self-awareness and desire to avoid the psychological root of her problems (symbolically represented as the harmonic root of her song), that when Sally moves from the third to the fifth of the tonic triad, she conspicuously avoids singing the root note of this chord, so relentlessly repeated in the bass.

In "Theater Lyrics" Sondheim describes this song as a "woman's lie to her former lover" (Ben), but it may also be interpreted as her lie to the man she married (Buddy), a man who loves her deeply and who provides a steady but boring static grounding, both psychological and harmonic. For Sondheim, the song's subtext is Sally's anger at being rejected by Ben many years ago, a subtext that is not found explicitly in either the lyrics or implied by the melody or harmony. Sondheim credits and praises Jonathan Tunick, his principal orchestrator for more than the thirty years between *Company* and *Road Show*, who demonstrated his understanding of the subtext of this song by assigning the "dry" woodwinds to Sally's wry references about Buddy, and warm strings for the self-referential parts of the text, Sondheim perhaps gives too much credit to Tunick. Even without this orchestral subtlety, which Sondheim describes as analogous to the details in the head of the Statue of Liberty that so impressed Hammerstein, it is arguable that Sondheim's own subtle musical distinctions between the harmonically synchronized repetitive rhythmic pattern that accompanies the melodic mantra "in Buddy's eyes" and the more varied contrasting musical phrases when she refers to herself (but still in Buddy's eyes) would emerge with comparable clarity even in a piano-vocal reduction.

One last mentor, one not cited in "Theater Lyrics," needs to be mentioned: the composer and mathematician Milton Babbitt. Babbitt's mentoring began several years after Hammerstein's initial tutelage when Sondheim, who had majored in mathematics as well as music at Williams College, elected to use his Hutchinson Prize money to study principles of composition and analyze popular songs such as Jerome Kern's "All the Things You Are" with the illustrious Princeton music theory and composition professor and avant-garde composer, who also was knowledgeable about jazz and loved musicals (he even tried his hand at writing a musical score once and published some of the resulting theater songs).[26] At the same time he was teaching Sondheim traditional classical and popular musical forms, Babbitt was pioneering a new composition technique widely known as "total serialization" as well as complex electronic works. Babbitt has stated that he did not ask Sondheim to work within this modernist idiom because he did not consider it appropriate to his student's aesthetic aims. But is it not possible that Sondheim chose Babbitt as a postgraduate compositional mentor at least partly because of his gathering reputation as a mathematically adept modernist? While thirty years earlier Schoenberg systematically arranged pitch according to various permutations of a twelve-tone series in his quest to systematically avoid a tonal center, Babbitt less systemically serialized other parameters as well, including rhythm and tone color.

Stephen Sondheim. © AL HIRSCHFELD. Reproduced by arrangement with Hirschfeld's exclusive representative, the MARGO FEIDEN GALLERIES LTD., NEW YORK. WWW. ALHIRSCHFELD.COM

It is possible to make the analogy between Babbitt's allegedly "total" serialization and Sondheim's allegedly "modernist" musicals, aided and abetted by extraordinarily thoughtful and creative choreographers, directors, scene designers, and orchestrators, which really expand upon, rather than discard, the traditions established by earlier acknowledged masterpieces. Like Babbitt, who only seemed to break with the past while really extending Schoenberg's aesthetics as well as his methods, Sondheim expanded on the insights and achievement of Hammerstein and other predecessors in what had become, by the 1950s, a great American musical tradition. Following the example of his theatrical mentors, Hammerstein, Shevelove, and Laurents, the revolutionary traditionalist Sondheim would continue to probe into the nuances of his complex characters and the meaning of his dramatic subjects, achieving moments of moving emotional directness as well as dazzling verbal and artistic pyrotechnics.

The Prince Years (1970–1981): Sweeney Todd

While the so-called integrated musical remained very much alive after *West Side Story*, the next step in dramatic organicism, the so-called concept musical, where "all elements of the musical, thematic and presentational, are integrated to suggest a central theatrical image or idea," began to receive notoriety in the 1960s and 1970s.[27] Sondheim and his collaborators, especially Jerome Robbins, Michael Bennett, Harold Prince, Boris Aronson, who designed the first four Prince-Sondheim collaborations with striking originality, and several excellent librettists (George Furth, James Goldman, John Weidman, and Hugh Wheeler), were in the forefront of this development. Musicals based more on themes than on narrative action were no more new in the 1960s than the integrated musicals were in the 1940s. Nevertheless, earlier concept musicals, for example, the revue *As Thousands Cheer* in 1933 (arguably all revues are concept musicals), book musicals such as Rodgers and Hammerstein's *Allegro* (1947), or Kurt Weill and Alan Jay Lerner's *Love Life* (1948)—like the precociously integrated *Show Boat* and *Porgy and Bess* explored in the present survey—deviate from what Max Weber or Carl Dahlhaus would call an "ideal type."[28] In any event, the pioneering concept musicals of the late 1940s, *Allegro* and *Love Life*, failed to inspire a flock of popularly successful followers. In the 1970s, Sondheim and his collaborators were clearly critically central Broadway figures, even though they garnered only relatively limited live audiences, while more popular artists such as Andrew Lloyd Webber or Stephen Schwartz were marginalized and criticized, probably unfairly, for their alleged aesthetic vacuities.

Perhaps more than any single individual, the inspiration in the move toward the concept musical ideal was Robbins, who early in his career had established thematic meaning through movement and dance as the choreographer of *The King and I* (1951) and as the director-choreographer for Sondheim's first Broadway efforts, *West Side Story* and *Gypsy*. Robbins was notorious for relentlessly asking, "What is this show about?," a question that led to the late (and uncredited) insertion of "Comedy Tonight" in *Forum* to inform audiences and prepare them for what they might expect in the course of the evening. Robbins's insistence on getting an answer to this probing question soon led to the show-opener "Tradition" in *Fiddler on the Roof* (1964), a song that embodied an overriding idea (rather than an action) that could unify and conceptualize a show.

After *Fiddler*, the concept musical was principally championed by Prince (b. 1928–), who had co-produced two of the above-mentioned Robbins shows (*West Side Story* and *Fiddler*). Prince also directed and produced John Kander and Fred Ebb's *Cabaret, Zorbá*, the considerably altered 1974 hit revival of Bernstein's *Candide*, and produced the first four of the six Sondheim shows he directed from *Company* in 1970 to *Merrily We Roll Along* in 1981.[29] While producing or co-producing such major hits as *The Pajama Game, Damn Yan-kees, West Side Story, Fiorello!*, and, with Sondheim, *A Funny Thing Happened on the Way to the Forum* (with Sondheim), and *Fiddler on the Roof* between 1953 and 1964, Prince came into his own as a producer-director with Jerry Bock and Sheldon Harnick's *She Loves Me* (1963). The use of a German cabaret as a metaphor for pre–World War II German decadence in *Cabaret* exemplifies Prince's continuation of the concept idea developed by Robbins.

Arguably, the Sondheim-Prince standard of the concept musical—in the absence of a more meaningful term—throughout the 1970s, with the non-linear *Company* as its iconic exemplar, was in the end, like most of Sondheim's work with other collaborators, less a revolution than a reinterpretation of the integrated musical.[30] In line with high-modernist aestheticism, narrative structures became more avowedly experimental in the Robbins-Sondheim-Prince "concept" era, and ambitious attempts to expand the expressive scope of the musical were also in vogue. Open appeals to a broad audience Lloyd Webber-Schwartz style, perhaps borrowed from rock, were as critically suspect as a pop song by Babbitt might have been in the same era. Nevertheless, at least one influential director, Prince, managed to navigate through the treacherous shores of the Broadway aesthetic divide.

During the Sondheim years Prince also collaborated with the man this volume has singled out in its Epilogue as the *other* major Broadway composer who flourished from the early 1970s to the mid-1990s, Lloyd Webber (see chapter 16). In a dazzling display of Prince's versatility, the Lloyd

Webber-Prince collaboration, *Evita*, appeared only a few months after *Sweeney*. In addition to his work with Sondheim, Bernstein, Kander and Ebb, and Lloyd Webber, Prince during these years managed to direct *On the Twentieth Century* with yet another composer, Cy Coleman (with the legendary librettist-lyricists Comden and Green). Coleman was another distinguished composer with a long career that flourished during the Sondheim-Lloyd Webber era in musicals from *Wildcat* and *Sweet Charity* in the 1960s to *City of Angels, Will Rogers Follies*, and *The Life* in the late 1980s and 1990s. By the later 1990s, Prince had received more Tony Awards, twenty-one, than anyone since the awards were established in the later 1940s. Of these, no less than eight were bestowed in his capacity as director: *Cabaret, Company, Follies* (shared with Michael Bennett), the *Candide* revival of 1974, *Sweeney Todd, Evita, Phantom of the Opera*, and the *Show Boat* revival of 1994. The quantity and range of Prince's achievement is nothing short of staggering. This chapter will focus on selected moments in the historic collaboration between Prince and Sondheim.

Although Prince and Sondheim had been friends since 1949—according to Prince's recollection they met on the opening night of *South Pacific*—and Prince had co-produced *West Side Story* and produced *Forum, Company* was the first of the six Sondheim productions he either directed, or in the case of *Follies*, co-directed (with Bennett). These six shows, *Company, Follies, A Little Night Music, Pacific Overtures, Sweeney Todd*, and *Merrily We Roll Along*, form a remarkable group. We have already noted the historical and artistic significance assigned to *Company* and an example of subtext in *Follies*.

Each musical in the first trilogy of Sondheim-Prince shows, *Company, Follies*, and *A Little Night Music*, earned Sondheim Tony and Drama Critics Circle Awards for best score. This was a major critical achievement, if not always a financial one. *Company* and *Night Music* earned some profit despite relatively modest runs, 706 and 601 performances and profits of $56,000 and $97,500 respectively, while the more lavish *Follies* lost $665,000 of its $700,000 investment during its 522 performance run.[31] As a tie-in with the "nostalgia" revival along with the more successful revival of Vincent Youmans's *No, No, Nanette* (1925) in 1971, *Follies* even appeared on the cover of *Time* magazine.[32] Only *Night Music*, however, was spared the criticism that Sondheim was destined to share with another early twentieth-century modernist, Igor Stravinsky, who was also, unfairly, accused of cynicism, coldness, and "bloodlessness." In the waning days of high modernism, Sondheim was neither high nor low, but somewhere in between. Thus he suffered from some critics' binary high/low expectations. Like Stravinsky in his early Ballet Russe period (*Firebird, Petrushka, Rite of Spring*), Sondheim was delightfully novel for some in the audience, and yet still not too cerebral and difficult (at least some of the time) for the mass of musical theatergoers with more traditional expectations of a diverting night out with a happy ending.

The career of Sondheim marks, perhaps for the first time, not only the consistent failure of a composer of the most highly regarded musicals of his generation to produce blockbusters on Broadway, but even major song hits (*Night Music*'s "Send in the Clowns" is the exception that proves the rule).[33] *Pacific Overtures*, competing in the same season as *A Chorus Line* and *Chicago*, lost its entire investment as well as most of the Tonys. *Sweeney Todd*, which lost about half of its million dollar investment, received more than half of the major Tony awards, including those for best actor (Len Cariou), actress (Angela Lansbury), director (Prince), scenic design (Eugene Lee), costume design (Franne Lee), book (Wheeler), best score (Sondheim), and best show.

Sweeney Todd *as Melodrama and as Opera*

Within a short time *Sweeney Todd* also earned classic status among critics and cognoscenti as perhaps Sondheim and Prince's finest effort. Even those who prefer other Sondheim shows regard this score as one of the composer's richest. In 2007, *Sweeney Todd* gained hordes of new converts via its acclaimed and reasonably popular (by Hollywood standards) transfer to film by director Tim Burton starring Johnny Depp. While many regard the work as one of the great musicals of the post–Rodgers and Hammerstein generation, others consider it to be one of the greatest operas composed by an American. It will be helpful to try to understand what genre *Sweeney Todd* represents and what is at stake in the formulation.

With the exception of national comic opera traditions, which alternate between spoken dialogue and songs (the latter known in operas as arias)—the *Singspiel* in Germany and Austria (*The Magic Flute*), the *opéra comique* in France (*Carmen* in its original form), the ballad opera in England (*The Beggar's Opera*)—opera in the European classical tradition tends to be through-sung (i.e., sung throughout without spoken dialogue). In the eighteenth and early nineteenth centuries, composers presented a strong contrast between arias and sung speech (recitative). Although less so for Verdi and Puccini than for Wagner and Strauss, as the nineteenth century progressed and moved into the twentieth, recitative often became more like arias and the arias more like recitative. For the most part—we have already looked at two such exceptions, *Porgy and Bess* and *The Most Happy Fella*—Broadway musicals adopted the national comic traditions that go back to *Beggar's Opera* in the eighteenth century and Gilbert and Sullivan in the nineteenth: spoken dialogue interrupted by song, or vice versa, depending on your point of view.

In distinguishing between operas and musicals, what is arguably more important than measuring amounts of song and speech is asking whether *significant* dramatic moments are sung or spoken. After the death of Tristan, his beloved Isolde must sing, and sing she does. Until a late stage in the creative process, Maria was going to sing, and Bernstein remained hopeful that he would be able to come up with effective love-death music to serve the dramatic moment after the death of Tony. For Bernstein, spoken dialogue for Maria was an option. If *West Side Story* were unequivocally an opera, Maria, like Isolde, would have no choice. She would sing.

The fact that by Sondheim's estimation 80 percent of the first act of *Sweeney Todd* is through-sung seems to locate the work more in the direction of opera.[34] Furthermore, much of the dialogue (the other 20%) is delivered over an orchestral backdrop. Dialogue over underscoring in fact is a key component in the traditional definition of melodrama, a word frequently used to describe *Sweeney Todd*—and used by Sondheim. Melodramatic story lines also are expected to be "thrilling," with the audience in on violence to come (while the characters on stage are unaware) and occasionally moved to yell remarks such as "*Don't* open the door" at evidently clueless players. Well-known operatic examples of early nineteenth-century melodrama include portions of Beethoven's *Fidelio* and Carl Maria von Weber's (not Lloyd Webber's) *Der Freischütz*. Schoenberg adapted the technique to create a spooky heightened speech known as *Sprechstimme* in his chamber song cycle *Pierrot Lunaire* in 1912.

Sondheim loved melodrama. In fact, he found not only the inspiration but the source for his own version of *Sweeney Todd* when he attended a telling of the tale in an exceptionally artful melodramatic play by Christopher Bond at a theater known for putting on the genre in London. Perhaps idiosyncratically, Sondheim also considered the melodrama compatible with high art. At the same time, he acknowledges that in calling *Sweeney Todd* a musical thriller instead of a musical melodrama, he could circumvent some of the genre's negative connotations, including its extravagant theatricality, the emphasis of plot over characters who are prone to be one-dimensional, and the sensationalism of the form. For Sondheim, "Melodrama is theater that is larger than life—in emotion, in subject, and in complication of plot."[35] *Sweeney Todd* admirably fits this description.

Early in their collaborative process Sondheim and his librettist Hugh Wheeler "wanted to make a melodrama but with a twentieth-century sensibility," and they wanted audiences to take the subject as seriously as audiences took nineteenth-century versions.[36] Sondheim wanted both the story and the music "to scare an audience out of its wits," but not with cheap theatrical thrills.[37] In Sondheim's view, "The true terror of melodrama comes from its revelations about the frightening power of what is inside human beings."[38] He also expressed his intention to achieve in a musical what Christopher Bond achieved in the play that inspired Sondheim, "which is to make Sweeney a tragic hero instead of a villain, because there is something of Sweeney in all of us," even if most of us elect not to become serial killers.[39]

Sondheim's interpretation of what *Sweeney Todd* is all about differed from Prince's initial concept. Prince wanted the show to be about "how society makes you impotent, and impotence leads to rage, and rage leads to murder—and in fact, to the breaking down of society."[40] Sondheim credits Prince with developing this socially critical perspective in his setting of the story but does not identify with it. Instead, Sondheim interprets *Sweeney Todd* as a musical about an individual's psychological obsession, an obsession that leads to revenge and murder.

Bernstein was not alone in his inability to find a musical solution for a major dramatic moment, in his case a final aria for Maria. Sondheim too has acknowledged that he was originally unable to determine how to musicalize eight scenes of *Sweeney Todd*, five of which he found solutions for after the fact: "I sort of figured the five, but I've never gotten around to doing them. I thought I would do them for the National Theatre production in London [1993], but Julia McKenzie said: 'Oh, please don't give me anything new to learn. *Please* don't give me anything new to learn.' That was all the incentive I needed not to work, so I didn't do it."[41] Sondheim specifically identifies one of these scenes as "the trio in the second act, which I'd always wanted to do, where Mrs. Lovett tries to poison the Beadle."[42] Bernstein faced a creative impasse and Sondheim a time crunch and, as a result, dramatic moments in *West Side Story* and *Sweeney* are today spoken rather than sung.

Some critics consider the absence of music for such important moments a dramatic flaw or a lost opportunity, especially the final moments of *Sweeney*, which are occupied by a speaking rather than a singing Tobias. Sondheim scholar Stephen Banfield considers the brighter side of the musical respite: "Sondheim says that there are five spoken sections of the show that he would like to set to music one day. One of them is the ending. The last three minutes of plot involve very little music: after Todd has sung his last word, even the underscoring peters out and leaves the stage to Tobias's last speech and still more to the silence of mime. It remained unsung and unplayed simply because Sondheim did not have time to add music before the production opened." And yet: "*Sweeney Todd*, even if by authorial default at this point, demonstrates the dramatic potency and rightness of music's self-denial in this genre that is not opera, just as Maria's final speech does in *West Side Story*."[43]

Bernstein's lack of inspiration and Sondheim's lack of time may have played a role in the musical silence of Maria and Tobias, and some may continue to lament the absence of music within the finales of each show. It is also worth mentioning that in its present form Tobias may have the last words but Sweeney has the last *musical* word (in *West Side Story* Maria's speech is similarly followed by a moving musical death procession). When Sweeney dies, so does the music. Only in the epilogue do the characters (including Sweeney) return to sing "The Ballad of Sweeney Todd" one last time. On stage, Tobias needs to kill Sweeney, but he does not need to sing. In the film version, his final speech is also removed. As with Maria and *West Side Story*, if *Sweeney Todd* were an opera, neither Tobias nor Sondheim would have a choice; everything would be sung.

Banfield insightfully captures a crucial distinction between opera and musicals that gets lost in the shuffle when brooding critics focus with Sweeney Todd-like obsession on how much is sung and whether trained opera singers or singing actors are best equipped to handle the demands of the latter genre:

> Yet we must again stress that Sondheim's way of privileging music within melodrama is not opera's way. The pacing of his sung verbal language remains that of spoken drama, rather than being, as in opera, subservient to the slower and longer-spanned emotional arcs of music. Thus, unlike most opera composers, he does not draw out syllables to unnaturalistic length, nor does he repeat verbal phrases except in a refrain context; the book of *Sweeney Todd* is consequently a good deal fatter than a printed opera libretto. Coupled with this verbal fecundity, he retains wit, colloquialism, and (taking the word in a neutral sense, as building action into the delivery) pantomime as governing *Affekts* in his songs, whose verbal values thereby remain those of the musical theater.[44]

In the case of *Sweeney Todd*, Angela Lansbury in the role of Mrs. Lovett was an actor who could also sing, but other roles could profit from a singing actor who also possessed a trained voice. It is not the voice that defines the work as an opera or musical but how the work weighs the balance between words and music.

In an interview with David Savran about a decade after *Sweeney Todd* Sondheim expressed his lingering distaste for opera: "I've never liked opera and I've never understood it. Most opera doesn't make theatrical sense to me. Things go on forever. I'm not a huge fan of the human voice. I like song, dramatic song. I like music and lyrics together, telling a story."[45] Despite this fundamental antipathy, Sondheim has also readily acknowledged that after seeing a production of Bond's transformation of George Dibdin Pitt's

Sweeney Todd play of 1847 his original intention was to make an opera out of Bond's entire script rather than a more traditional cut-down libretto version of the play. When Sondheim had reached only page five of Bond's text after twenty minutes of music, however, he turned to *Night Music* librettist Wheeler and director Prince to convert the work into a musical, but a musical with a lot of through-singing (almost like an opera).

Bernard Herrmann and the Dies Irae (Day of Wrath)

The sheer amount of music—nearly four hundred pages in the published vocal score—as well as its continuity was also greatly influenced by another subgenre, the musical film score. Sondheim has often referred to his intense enjoyment of *Hangover Square* (1945), a thriller about a composer who becomes deranged when he hears certain high pitches and, in a stupor induced by these sounds, unwittingly murders people. At the end of the film the composer-serial killer, played by the legendary film noir star Laird Cregar, collapses while performing the piano concerto he was composing during his saner moments. The film score, including the concerto, was composed by Bernard Herrmann, who during this period was also creating masterful scores for director Orson Welles's masterpiece *Citizen Kane* and several suspense thrillers in the 1950s and 60s directed by Alfred Hitchcock, including *Vertigo*, *North by Northwest*, and *Psycho*. The film, and especially Herrmann's score, had a powerful effect on the fifteen-year-old Sondheim, and since that time he had "always wanted to [write] an answer to *Hangover Square*."[46] In the end, the "Musical Thriller" *Sweeney Todd*, the first show idea generated by Sondheim himself, offered its rich and often continuous score, not to emulate opera, but to emulate film:

> "What I wanted to write," Sondheim says, "was a horror movie. The whole point of the thing is that it's a background score for a horror film, which is what I intended to do and what it is. All those chords, and that whole kind of harmonic structure...the use of electronic sounds and the loud crashing organ had a wonderful Gothic feeling. It had to be unsettling, scary, and very romantic. In fact, there's a chord I kept using throughout, which is sort of a personal joke, because it's a chord that occurred in every Bernard Herrmann score."[47]

In a later interview Sondheim elaborates on the connections between Hermann's score for *Hangover Square* and the musical requirements for a "musical thriller." His remarks reinforce the position that the plentiful score of *Sweeney Todd* was due more to the requirements of mid-twentieth-century American horror film scoring and harmony than the demands of nineteenth-century European opera:

> I wanted to pay homage to him [Herrmann] with this show, because I had realized that in order to scare people, which [is] what *Sweeney Todd* is about, the only way to you can do it, considering that the horrors out on the street are so much greater than anything you can do on the stage, is to keep music going all the time. That's the principle of suspense sequences in movies, and Bernard Hermann was a master in that field. So *Sweeney Todd* not only has a lot of singing, it has a lot of underscoring. It's *infused* with music, to keep the audience in a state of tension, to make them forget they're in a theater and to prevent them from separating themselves from the action. I based a lot of the score on a specific chord that Herrmann uses in almost all his film work, and spun it out from that. That and the "Dies Irae," which is one of my favorite tunes, and is full of menace.[48]

Like *West Side Story*, the score of *Sweeney Todd* demonstrates impressively intricate musical connections that are dramatically meaningful. Although he acknowledged some indecision about the conclusion of the work, the idea that major characters would be given distinctive themes and the decision to have these themes "collide in the end" was present almost from conception. This is how Sondheim explained his procedure: "I determined that it would be fun for *Sweeney Todd* to start each character with a specific musical theme and develop all that character's music out of that theme, so that each song would depend in the true sense of the word on the last one. Sweeney's opening scene dictates his next song, and so on. It's a handy compositional principle, and it seemed to me that it would pay off very nicely at the end."[49]

In order to understand how this compositional principle works it is necessary to introduce the Gregorian chant *Dies irae* (literally the Latin for "Day of Wrath" and more conventionally Judgment Day), a thirteenth-century text and melody that became officially incorporated into the Catholic Requiem Mass, the mass for the dead, by the sixteenth century. It is this chant that Sondheim chose as the starting point for Sweeney's theme and for the opening choral number, "The Ballad of Sweeney Todd," sung by a chorus to help the audience "attend the tale of Sweeney Todd" and reprised to introduce various episodes throughout the story. With its connections to death and the

Last Judgment and its musical resonances, the theme has been especially favored in the last two hundred years from Berlioz to Rachmaninoff. It was an inspired choice to serve as the embodiment of a character who by the end of the first act "Epiphany" will take it upon himself to impart his demented vengeful judgment on the world. On the stage, "Epiphany" provided an opportunity for Sweeney to break the fourth wall and invites the audience to "Come and visit your good friend Sweeney" and to get a shave and "welcome to the grave." The Sweeney in Burton's film extends this idea and, in a fantasy sequence, leaves his shop, roams the streets like a ghost visible only to the audience, and invites unaware passersby to get their shaves and his vengeance.

Sondheim explained why he chose the chant and offers information about how he used it: "I always found the Dies Irae moving and scary at the same time," says Sondheim. "One song, 'My Friends,' was influenced by it...it was the inversion of the opening of the Dies Irae. And although it was never actually quoted in the show, the first release of 'The Ballad of Sweeney Todd' was a sequence of the Dies Irae—up a third, which changed the harmonic relationship of the melodic notes to each other."[50]

The following set of examples (see Example 15.1 on the next page) begins with the opening of the *Dies irae* chant, continues with various transformations of the chant's opening in *Sweeney Todd* (mainly its first seven notes), and concludes with a famous use of the work in the classical literature and a possible earlier allusion by Sondheim himself.

Although Sondheim states he did not quote *Dies irae* (15.1a) literally in *Sweeney Todd*, the published score offers just such a quotation on its second page in the Prelude (15.1b).[51] Probably the most prominent and most recurring reference to *Dies irae* is the paraphrase of the chant that marks the opening of "The Ballad of Sweeney Todd," which includes notes 2–7 of the chant (15.1c). Interestingly, the jig-like rhythm of this paraphrase is reminiscent of the melodically more literal rhythmic and major mode transformation of the chant in the "Dream of the Witches Sabbath" movement of Berlioz's famous *Symphonie fantastique* of 1830 (15.1h). The longer and more chant-like notes (the first five notes) at the portion of "The Ballad" shown in Example 15.1d described by Sondheim are offset by some pitch alterations to create another major mode variation on the tune. Anthony's paraphrase of the tune (including some changes in the note order in the first four notes of the chant) in "No Place Like London" (15.1e) adds harmonic density by placing the *Dies irae* in F minor against E♭ in the bass (plus two non-chord tones B♭ and D), to create an enriched variant of the "Sweeney Todd" chord (a minor seventh with the seventh in the bass or in this case E♭-F-A♭-C).

(a)

Original Gregorian chant:

(b)

(c)

(d)

Example 15.1. *Dies irae* and *Sweeney Todd*

(a) *Dies irae* original chant (beginning)

(b) First reference of the *Dies irae* in *Sweeney Todd* Prelude (first seven chant notes)

(c) *Dies irae* paraphrased in the opening of "The Ballad of Sweeney Todd" (notes 2 through 7 of the chant)

(d) "Sequence of the Dies Irae—up a third" described by Sondheim in "The Ballad of Sweeney Todd" (first five chant notes)

(e) *Dies irae* paraphrased in "No Place Like London (first four chant notes rearranged as notes 4, 2, 1, and 3 with notes 5-7 in original order and all seven notes harmonized with the "Sweeney Todd" chord)

(f) Fleeting allusion to *Dies irae* in "The Worst Pies in London" (first five chant notes)

(g) *Dies irae* in "My Friends" (first four chant notes first inverted and then in their original order)

(h) *Dies irae* in Berlioz's *Symphonie fantastique* (quotation and transformation, first seven chant notes)

(i) Possible allusion to *Dies irae* in the "The Miller's Son" from *A Little Night Music* (first five chant notes with an added note between notes 4 and 5)

Example 15.1. Continued

357

The *Dies irae* does not appear directly in the music of the Beggar Woman (Sweeney's wife Lucy) but nevertheless provides its foundation. In particular, the half step descent on the first two notes of the chant appears prominently in her recurring lament ("Alms...alms...for a mis'rable woman"). In "Epiphany" the descending half step will launch a scalar series of four notes starting with the musical phrase that begins "never see Johanna" and repeated obsessively with new words for the rest of the song. It is possible Sondheim realized that the descending four-note scalar figure, a ubiquitous motive that goes back at least as far as John Dowland's song "Flow My Tears" in the early seventeenth century, has become a traditional musical sign of lament and mourning. In any case, this is how Sondheim used this simple but powerful figure in "Epiphany" and later when Sweeney mourns his Lucy's death in the Final Scene. Although the musical connection between the *Dies irae* with Mrs. Lovett is present (in the midst of "The Worst Pies in London" for the first notes of the chant), the chant reference occurs so fleetingly it is barely audible and may be more imagined than real (15.1f).

Example 15.1g shows how the first four notes of "My Friends" inverts the opening notes of *Dies irae* as Sondheim noted when describing his use of the chant (in the second phrase of the song, the first four notes of the chant appear in their original order). The remaining excerpts demonstrate how Berlioz famously reused the *Dies irae* in his *Symphonie fantastique* (15.1h) and how Sondheim might have previously incorporated the chant in the music he gave Petra to sing in the defiant recurring faster section of *Night Music*'s "The Miller's Son" (15.1i). If the allusion is intentional in the earlier musical, the point might be considered ironic in that this young sensual character seems so non-judgmental and full of life. On the other hand, the irony is tempered by the fact that Petra points out in her song that life is brief and moments of joy are fleeting.

Reprise Redux

The reprise or return of a song, usually the return of a song from the first act in the second, is a tested, ubiquitous, and perhaps even invariable feature of the Broadway musical. In a previous chapter we have observed the replacement of "Buddie Beware" in favor of a reprise of "I Get a Kick Out of You" in *Anything Goes* in deference to Ethel Merman's wishes. In another chapter we noted that *Kiss Me, Kate*, a show written by Cole Porter during the heyday of Rodgers and Hammerstein, implausibly reprised a song "So in Love" by a character who had no discernible opportunity to have heard it. We have also seen that the change of a word "*how* I loved you" instead of "*if* I loved you" was momentous when it was reprised in *Carousel*. The next chapter will look at the frequent, systemic reprises of Lloyd Webber.

In his essay, "The Musical Theater," Sondheim voices his skepticism about the effectiveness of reprises.[52] For Sondheim, the fact that most characters change throughout the play necessitates at least a change in the lyric of a reprised song. Throughout his career Sondheim has found welcome opportunities to reprise the melody of a song, but never a situation where it was possible to reprise its lyric. This is why he objected to Rodgers's desire to reprise "Take the Moment" in *Do I Hear a Waltz?* simply because the composer wanted the audience to hear the tune again (as was Merman's rationale for reprising "I Get a Kick Out of You" thirty years earlier).[53]

In a double interview with Prince and Sondheim, "Author and Director," the "author" commends the "director" who initiated the idea to reprise all the songs at the end of *Night Music*.[54] Although in the end they were able to reprise only five songs ("Soon," "You Must Meet My Wife," "A Weekend in the Country," "Every Day a Little Death," and "Send in the Clowns," plus significant underscoring of "Liaisons"), Sondheim found this device movie-like and "very effective." With *Sweeney Todd*, Sondheim credits Wheeler with the suggestion that he could base the final twenty minutes of the show on "little modules" of reprised melody. Although Sondheim may not have completed some of the unmusical portions of these twenty minutes to his full satisfaction, the conclusion of *Sweeney Todd* demonstrates an impressive use of earlier songs, mostly from the first act, whether as fragments or relatively extended segments, underscoring, or in combination with other modules.

The Final Sequence (Vocal Score No. 25-No. 29B), framed by "The Ballad of Sweeney Todd," includes one brief interjection of the Ballad's refrain after Sweeney's failed attempt to kill Johanna at the end of No. 28. According to the stage direction, following a chorus of the Ballad (No. 25), the Company "transform themselves into the inmates of Fogg's Asylum, which is now revealed." In the early portion of the sequence these lunatics on the loose use and repeat the frantic new "City on Fire!" music no less than four times.[55] In addition to the "Ballad," Sondheim inserts significant returns of no less than eleven songs listed below (see "Thematic Reminiscences in *Sweeney Todd*" in the online website for a more detailed outline of thematic returns during this exciting finale).[56]

ACT I: "No Place like London" (including Beggar Woman's music), "Poor Thing," "My Friends," "Ah, Miss," "Johanna" (Judge's version), "Kiss Me," "Pretty Women," "Epiphany," "A Little Priest"

ACT II: "By the Sea," "Not While I'm Around"

Each one of these reprises contains significant dramatic meaning and contributes to the propulsion of the final scene toward its tragic conclusion while at the same time sonically summing up what has come before. For those who have not already perceived the musical connections between the Beggar Woman's music ("Alms") and "Epiphany," in the final moments her identity as Sweeney's beloved Lucy is unmistakably revealed. The main musical connection is the pronounced half step shared by both musical lines, both of which are ultimately connected with the *Dies irae*. The connection is especially pronounced in the orchestral passage that follows the death of the Beggar Woman with the return of the opening of "Epiphany" and the return of the half steps on the word "Lucy" (Vocal Score, p. 352) when Todd realizes the enormity of his action. As Todd acquires this tragic understanding, the audience can see his potential as a tragic figure, if not necessarily a sympathetic one. The collision of themes Sondheim referred to in his initial plan then returns in full force as Mrs. Lovett sings "Poor Thing" against Todd's latest (and last) "Epiphany." Most strikingly, just before the reprise of "A Little Priest"—and her own death at the hands of Sweeney— Mrs. Lovett herself starts singing a fragment of "Epiphany" in counterpoint to the demon barber of Fleet Street.

The Film

Sondheim, discussing *Sweeney Todd* with Mark Horowitz in 1997, spoke of possible plans for a film of this show directed by Tim Burton, who "fell in love with the show when he was in London in 1981 and saw it ten times."[57] Not only did the composer agree when Horowitz summarized Sondheim's often stated position that "film musicals usually don't work," he commented specifically with the pessimistic prediction that a film of *Sweeney* wouldn't "work for two seconds."[58]

Despite his lifelong love for film, Sondheim admires very few film *musicals*; of those which he does like, none are adaptations.[59] Unfortunately, among the adaptations he found unsatisfying were the four films based on his own shows, *West Side Story*, *Gypsy*, *A Funny Thing Happened on the Way to the Forum*, and *A Little Night Music*. In Sondheim's view, the action in a film must "move forward constantly," and this does not happen in these adaptations. For Sondheim, the theatrical convention of stationary singers, such as Tony and Maria singing "Tonight," does not translate well into film. He also expressed some skepticism about whether a *Sweeney Todd* film would happen before the year 2099 since Burton needed time to finish *Superman Twelve*. Although it took another ten years (twenty-six you start from Burton's initial binge on the London stage version), the musical film of *Sweeney Todd*

Sweeney Todd, 2007 film. Mrs. Lovett (Helena Bonham Carter) and Sweeney Todd (Johnny Depp) at the bloody conclusion of the film.

finally appeared shortly before Christmas 2007. It was directed by Burton and starred Johnny Depp.[60]

Like most of the musical films discussed in acts I and II beginning with the *Show Boat* adaptation of 1936, *Sweeney Todd*, and like most of the films with the exception of *My Fair Lady* and to a lesser extent *West Side Story*, the musical film *Sweeney Todd* does not attempt to present a faithful and complete version of its stage sources. In addition, for the most part, stage musicals exceed "the two hours' traffic" announced by Chorus at the outset of *Romeo and Juliet*. *Sweeney*'s stage traffic is about three hours. Film musicals, whether original or adaptations from the musical stage, generally take Shakespeare's estimated performance time more seriously. Burton's film realization of *Sweeney Todd* contains even less than two hours of traffic congestion, 116 minutes to be exact.

In order to perform *Sweeney Todd* so succinctly, some material had to be cut, including some of the 80 percent that was taken up by music. Sondheim thus went into the *Sweeney Todd* project knowing that some songs would have to go, especially those songs that did not keep the action moving. For example, the Beadle's "Parlor Songs" served the dual purpose of creating a diversion to keep this character from inspecting Todd's basement and giving a tenor something substantial to sing in the course of an evening, but it slowed the action and could be slashed with impunity in order to "shave" close to four minutes. Since the lyrical middle section of "Ladies in Their Sensitivities" was also removed, the Beadle's vocal contribution to the film is greatly reduced. We have earlier remarked that Sondheim for a long time regretted not *adding* music for this scene with Mrs. Lovett in the scene with the Beadle.

Another cut was Anthony's "Ah, Miss," which appeared on stage between Johanna's solo song "Green Finch and Linnet Bird" and Anthony's "Johanna," the show's great love ballad. To create greater plausibility as well as a few minutes of film time, the Beggar Woman and her "Alms" music no longer welcome Sweeney and Anthony when they get off the boat in the first scene. Instead she sings her "Alms" when she stumbles upon Anthony in front of Johanna's house (a more logical place for her mother to hover, although we do not yet know her identity). In some newly inserted dialogue after the "Alms" music Anthony gives her some money and the Beggar Woman in return informs the young man, who has seen Johanna in the upstairs window and is clearly smitten, that Judge Turpin is the owner of the house and that the young woman Johanna is his ward. She then warns Anthony of dire consequences should he pursue the beautiful ward in the window.[61]

Before Rodgers and Hammerstein acquired control of their own film adaptations, stage properties were at the mercy of producers and directors who simply did not believe in the material and were given carte blanche not only to cut mercilessly but to add songs by studio composers. Sondheim's contract allowed him the authority to approve or reject the proposed changes. Since he agreed with the premise that cuts would be needed whenever the music held up the action and that the film should be primarily cinematic rather than theatrical, Sondheim himself assumed the major role in the decisions of what to include, delete, or rework.

One of the deleted songs in the film, the Judge's version of "Johanna"—a completely different song from Anthony's "Johanna"—was also deleted in the stage version of the show and relegated to the Appendix of the published vocal score (although it appears on the cast recording and in the revised vocal score in its originally intended position). Prince either found the song offensive or thought others would object to the depiction of masochism and self-flagellation in the song and urged Sondheim to take it out. A few years later, however, Sondheim persuaded Prince to reinstate the Judge's "Johanna" in the New York City Opera production (1984) and has continued to advocate its inclusion in future productions.[62] In the film, the Judge's perverted nature could be observed more directly in the privacy of his room where screen audiences watch as he fondles his leather-bound volumes of pornography and spies on Johanna through a peephole in the wall. Within a few seconds the film captures what it takes the Judge nearly four minutes to sing, and although the Judge now has nothing of his own to sing, this is less of an expectation for a major character in a movie than on a stage.

Much of the material involving the chorus also vanished from the screen version, although some of this music, so important to the stage effect, found its way into orchestral underscoring. The most audible example of this non-vocal use occurs over the extensive Opening Title sequence in which "The Ballad of Sweeney Todd" can be heard without either words or voices (there are, however, some chorus-like synthesized vocals during an orchestral climax). The orchestral vamp from the "Ballad" recurs throughout the film and contributes greatly to the melodramatic atmosphere. Other ensembles, including "The Letter" quintet, the "City on Fire!" chorus of Fogg Asylum lunatics, and a good slice of the "God, That's Good!" pie, join the discarded "Parlor Songs" among the major deletions of act II.

In his interview with Jesse Green in the *New York Times*, Sondheim estimated that about 20 percent of the remaining songs were trimmed and "in all fewer than 10 of the stage show's 25 major numbers survived substantially intact."[63] Add up all the time saved and the result is a leaner and meaner *Sweeney* approximately one-third shorter than its staged predecessor. When interviewed for a special feature of the DVD, Sondheim extends the 80 percent–20 percent ratio he offered for the first act twenty years earlier in "Author and Director" to encompass the entire show: "There are very few moments of silence from the orchestra pit in the show. I'd say the show is probably about 80% sung, 20% talk, but even the talk, about half of that, is underscored, and it's the way to keep the audience in a state of tension, because if they ever get out of the fantasy, they're looking at, you know, a ridiculous story with a lot of stage blood."[64]

Burton's *Sweeney Todd* gathered a lot of critical attention and audience appeal for casting the popular Depp, an enormously talented and versatile actor who had worked with the director on six previous films (e.g., *Edward Scissorhands* and *Ed Wood*) but had never sung anything other than backup vocals in a rock band. Fortunately, thanks to the wonders of film technology, it was not necessary for Depp—or Helena Bonham Carter, who had never sung at all, in the arguably more demanding role of Mrs. Lovett—to be able to project in a theater or even to have to sing all the notes of a song consecutively with the correct rhythms and pitches.

The recording process went through several stages. First, music supervisor Mike Higham created a backing track without voices. Then, after rehearsing with Sondheim, the cast recorded their solos and duets (the only exception was Laura Michelle Kelly in the role of the Beggar Woman and Lucy who sang live on the film set). Each member of the cast was recorded on a separate track. The solitary sounds could then be refined, retuned, and mediated sufficiently that a sung whisper could be heard over a mighty orchestra. Finally, this orchestra of sixty-four musicians, more than double the number that squeezed into the Uris Theater in 1979, recorded the voiceless backing track audiences hear in the film.

In borrowing a major production technique from MTV and rock videos, Burton's *Sweeney* departed from two generations of traditional film practice, in which the actors in the film or the singers who dub the actors in the film lip-synch to a finished *visual* product. Burton's *Sweeney* reversed the process (with the professional singer Kelly again the sole exception). The recordings came first. After the recordings, the actors, none of them dubbed, lip-synched to the pre-recorded *sounds*, which included the sixty-four piece orchestra and any duet partnerships in a given song. Lip-synching to prerecorded sound, the norm in MTV and rock videos, was rare, if not unprecedented in the production of a film musical. The process seemed to help produce a natural and intimate look to the singing without any operatic signs of strain in the final product.

At every turn Burton applies cinematic techniques, some of which would be difficult to capture in the theater. They appear most often in the narrative songs, "Poor Thing," where Mrs. Lovett's tale of the Barber and his Wife is shown in vivid flashback; "A Little Priest," in which the camera zooms in from Mrs. Lovett's window on people who represent the various occupations of potential victims described in the song; and "By the Sea," in which Mrs. Lovett and Sweeney are placed in the locations and situations described in the song. These songs are also set off by adding splashes of color to the grayish tint that pervades the film (other color splashes would appear from time to time such as Pirelli's garish blue outfit and Sweeney's specially constructed red barber's chair). This kind of filmic enhancement of text and story has become more common in recent years, for example, the visual realization of thoughts in Rob Marshall's award-winning *Chicago* in 2002). A rare early example of the practice can be seen in the visual images that capture the bridge of "Ol' Man River" in the 1936 *Show Boat* (starting with images of stevedores sweating and straining and Joe, played by Paul Robeson ending up in jail looking up at a distorted camera angle). It seems surprising how seldom directors have taken advantage of this cinematic opportunity to tell a story.[65] Perhaps the success of Burton's *Sweeney* will influence future directors.

In a DVD special feature and in other public interviews, Sondheim makes the case that Burton's *Sweeney Todd* is not only different from the stage *Sweeney* but is different from other film adaptations. He offers this advice to audiences who may be disappointed in this difference: "I'm going to urge them as much as possible to leave their memory of the stage show outside the door, because, as I say, unlike all other movies of musicals that I know, this really is an attempt to take the material of the stage musical and completely transform it into a movie. This is not a movie of a stage show, this is a movie based on a stage show."[66] In a public conversation with former *New York Times* theater critic and current political affairs editorialist Frank Rich that took place in Portland, Oregon, on March 11, 2008, a few months after Burton's *Sweeney Todd* opened nationally and one month before its release on DVD, Sondheim went as far as to say that Burton's transformation was the "most satisfying version of a stage piece I've ever seen."

The Lapine Years (1984–1994): Sunday in the Park with George

After *Sweeney Todd* and *Merrily We Roll Along*, Sondheim joined forces with a new, younger creative partner, James Lapine (b. 1949). During the next ten years, Lapine became arguably as important and innovative a collaborator as Prince and his generational peers were in the previous decade and exerted an influence in Sondheim's post-Prince development comparable to that of earlier collaborators such as Bernstein, Robbins, Styne, and Laurents before the Prince years.

Sondheim's first show with Lapine was about the art of making art. The first act of *Sunday in the Park with George* focuses on the painter Georges Seurat, and the creation of the painting lent its title to Sondheim's musical. The first act also creates the imagined lives of his imagined mistress Dot among others who have become immobilized and immortalized in this famous painting in its permanent residence at the Art Institute of Chicago. In contrast to Franklin Shepard, the fictional composer in *Merrily We Roll Along*, Seurat was not only an actual historical figure but one of the least compromising artists in any field of art. In this landmark Pulitzer Prize–winning show, Sondheim and Lapine, who wrote the book and directed, explore the relationship between artistic and procreative legacies as embodied in the contrast between the ephemeral cream pies of Louis the baker versus the timelessness of an artistic masterpiece, and the contrasting legacies of children and art.[67] In his dedication to art Seurat has foresworn his relationship with Dot, although through her he will leave a human legacy in their daughter Marie and, two generations later, in another artist named George (without the "s"), Marie's grandson, whom we will meet one hundred years later in act II.

In the song "No Life," Sondheim creates more characters who voice criticisms that Sondheim himself has been subjected to throughout much of his career. When viewing a *tableau vivant* of Seurat's recently completed *Bathing at Asnières*, his rival, Jules, and Jules's wife, Yvonne, decry the passionless, lifeless, unlyrical, and inappropriate subject matter of Seurat's paintings.

Yvonne ridicules Seurat for painting "boys with their clothes off," and Jules responds mockingly that *he* "must paint a factory next." Similarly, Sondheim has frequently been indicted for writing about cold, neurotic, and frequently unlikable people and for confronting unpalatable subjects ranging from marital infidelity (e.g., *Company, Follies, A Little Night Music, Sunday in the Park, Into the Woods*), the loss of youthful dreams (*Follies, Merrily We Roll Along, Woods*), murder (*Pacific Overtures, Woods, Assassins*), and even serial murder (*Sweeney Todd*).

The contrast between accessible and difficult art is powerfully delineated in Dot's song, "Everybody Loves Louis." Louis the baker, a man who neither fathers a child nor sings a song in the show, is willing to take Dot and her child by Seurat to America, where the baker can cater to the whims of a wealthy and boorish Texas businessman. In vivid contrast to the unlovable, unpopular, and overly intellectual painter, Louis is lovable, popular, and "bakes from the heart." "Louis' thoughts are not hard to follow," his "art is not hard to swallow," and, unlike George, the baker is "not afraid to be gooey." Also in contrast to George, Louis "sells what he makes." In return, Louis, like his pastries, will perish without producing either art or (in a plot twist) children of his own. Louis also has the potential to become a better father than George, as well as a better provider and companion.

Putting It Together

In the final scene of act I, the uncompromising Seurat completes his great painting *Sunday Afternoon on La Grande Jatte* after two years and many months of Sundays, an act marked musically by the completion of the opening horn melody that represents Seurat's blank canvas (Example 15.2a) and its transformation into the song, "Sunday" (Example 15.2b).

Act II centers on a contemporary artist, still confronting old dilemmas of popular versus personal, more "sincere" art (remember Hammerstein's emphasis on this quality in a song's genesis). But this new George is a lot more like Louis in some respects. In stark contrast to the painter's exceptional meticulousness, his great-grandson is rapidly turning out a series of similar and risk-free high-tech sculptures known as Chromolumes. The new George also shares with his forefather an inability to connect the dots of human relationships (a central task for both artists), but unlike Seurat, the modern George has managed to successfully negotiate the politics of art and has gained all the trappings of success, including the profit and fame denied the greater artist. Nevertheless, he is deeply dissatisfied with his own work.

Like the characters in *Lady in the Dark* who appear metaphorically in Liza Elliott's dreams, many characters in Seurat's life and painting reappear in

Example 15.2. *Sunday in the Park with George*
(a) Opening horn melody
(b) Opening of "Sunday" based on the opening horn melody

the life of the present-day George. Seurat's mistress, Dot, lives on as her daughter, the aged Marie. Seurat's unsympathetic rival, Jules, metamorphoses into Bob Greenberg, the director of the museum that now houses Chromolume #7. Perhaps most tellingly, the Old Lady who turns out to be Seurat's hypercritical but supportive mother in act I returns in act II as the perceptive art critic Blair Daniels, who, like Seurat's mother, is able to see

Sunday in the Park with George, 1986 film of the Broadway show. George, the painter based on Georges Seurat (Mandy Patinkin) (left), finishing his painting, "A Sunday Afternoon on the Island of La Grande Jatte," at the end of act I.

that the emperor has no clothes, but also like her act I counterpart believes in George's talent and promise.

The connections between act I and act II are also musical ones, in which key musical material develops character and plot through dramatically meaningful thematic melodic reprises and transformations. One of the most audible examples is the music Seurat uses in the act of painting his master-piece ("Color and Light") in act I, which returns in an electrified version that marks the Chromolume music in act II. When the ghost of Dot returns at the end of act II to resolve her personal issues with George and to help the modern George "Move On" artistically, her music shares several prominent motives heard in "We Do Not Belong Together" that Dot sang in act I when she left the great artist in order to start a new life in America with Louis. To cite but one prominent example, "Stop worrying where you're going" is set to the same music as the title and opening phrase, "We do not belong together." The gossips in the museum in act II sing the same "I'm not surprised" motive in discussing the Chromolumes ("Putting It Together," Part II) as Seurat's contemporaries in act I ("Gossip Sequence"). The textual and musical phrase that George uses to express his discomfort at the heat in his studio in "Color and Light" becomes the foundation for the song the characters, now

Sunday in the Park with George, 1986 film of the Broadway show. The picture frame descends to enclose the finished painting, "A Sunday Afternoon on the Island of La Grande Jatte," at the end of act I.

imprisoned and frozen forever at the Art Institute of Chicago, sing to open act II, "It's Hot Up Here." The obsessively repeated musical motive of "Putting It Together" (Example 15.3a) can be traced to the music associated with the phrase "Finishing the Hat" in the song of that name (Example 15.3b), and at the end of act I with its one note extension—from four shorts and a long to four shorts and two longs—as Seurat completes his canvas before the characters in the painting start to sing "Sunday" (Example 15.3c).[68] These examples are only the most prominent of a much longer list.[69]

Just as Seurat's mother evolves from a critical pose to an attitude of understanding and appreciation in act I, the childless Blair Daniels in act II—the act II George is both childless and divorced—rightly points out the meaninglessness and superficiality of recycling past successes and encourages the formerly vital artist to move on to something new. By the end of the evening, young George returns to La Grande Jatte and meets Dot, a deus ex machina figure introduced to help George change and grow as an artist and "move on." Like the sadder-but-wiser characters in *Into the Woods*, George learns that he too is not alone, but rather part of a great tradition that includes the artistry of his great-grandfather and the wisdom of his maternal ancestors.

Example 15.3. "Putting It Together" motive from *Sunday in the Park with George*
    (a) "Putting It Together" motive in "Putting It Together"
    (b) "Putting It Together" motive anticipated in "Finishing the Hat"
    (c) "Putting It Together" motive anticipated in "Sunday"

Most important, he learns that his duty as an artist is to grow and develop his art and his humanity. The modern George has thus escaped the fate of Franklin Shepard Inc., the composer anti-hero of *Merrily We Roll Along*.

    It is crucial to emphasize that despite the seemingly endless critical statements about its redundancy, a second act is necessary for George to learn this great lesson. At the end of the first act the painter has completed his great painting and connected fully with his art. Indeed, the completion of the painting (see pages 366 and 367) is a breathtaking conclusion to act I, one of the most stunning visual wonders in Broadway history. But Seurat has not yet connected with his life and the people in it. We know that although Sondheim and Lapine struggled with the second act, the issue was *how* to follow up act I, not whether this needed to be done.

    Increasingly for audiences and critics—although Frank Rich boldly and repeatedly championed the work in the *New York Times* when it was new— the story of *Sunday in the Park with George* is not simply the completion of the painting. It is the completion of the artist as a human being. Sondheim clearly states his personal interpretation of the work in his interview with Savran: "He takes the trip. It's all about how he connects with the past and with the continuum of humanity. The spirit of Dot in the painting is exactly what makes him do it. But he's the one who comes to a recognition at the end. If you don't connect with the past, you can't go on. People who say the second act's not necessary misunderstand the play. The second act is what it's about. The first act's the set-up."[70]

A Few Words on Into the Woods

For their next show, Sondheim and Lapine continued to explore the topics of personal growth and maturation in another musical with two quite different, but complementary, acts. They decided to explore the deeper psychological properties of such popular fairy tales as Jack and the Beanstalk, Rapunzel, and Cinderella, among others, combined with several new fairy tales of their own, most notably a story about the Baker and his Wife. In the first act, the characters, each with a wish, intersect in complicated ways and everyone gets what they wish for. In act II, the characters—in this case the same characters in each act—face the often unethical and unsavory paths they have taken to fulfill their wishes and the negative consequences of attaining them, problems that their original fairy tale counterparts did not have to confront. The intricate and interactive dramatic connections among the characters from many tales demonstrate the aptness of John Dunne's *Meditation XVII*: "No man is an island, entire of itself." Eventually, after deflecting responsibility for their predicament to each other in the song "Your Fault," they realize that if they work together they can resolve their collective crisis and grow, both individually and as a group. Sondheim acknowledges his connection to Dunne's message in an interview with Michiko Kakutani:

> I think the final step in maturity is feeling responsible for everybody. If I could have written "no man is an island," I would have. But that's what "No One Is Alone" is about. What I like about the title is it says two things. It says: no one is lonely, you're not alone— I'm on your side and I love you. And the other thing is: no one is alone—you have to be careful what you do to other people. You can't just go stealing gold and selling cows for more than they are worth, because it affects everybody else.[71]

Not surprisingly, Sondheim came up with a musical idea that not only metaphorically but literally realizes the dramatic implications of the idea that

(a)

(b)

Example 15.4. The Bean Theme from *Into the Woods*
    (a) The Bean Theme
       "Baker drops five beans in Jack's hand" followed by the Bean theme as
       an accompaniment figure to "I Guess This Is Goodbye"
    (b) Rapunzel's theme (based on the Bean theme)

we are connected and not alone. Put simply, he links the themes with an *Ur*
theme ultimately common to all, the theme which the characters identify
early in the story as the Bean Theme.

Although we hear the Bean Theme for the first time when the Witch mentions her garden (where the beans grow), a clearer example to open our discussion is the significant moment a little later when the Baker gives Jack
five beans ("keeping the sixth for his own pocket") in exchange for his cow
(Example 15.4a). The isolated xylophone that clearly sounds out one note for
each of the five beans makes the connection between the Bean Theme and
the beans themselves memorable and unmistakable. In the next measure the
Bean Theme is then used as the main melodic material for a lyrical vamp
that accompanies Jack's poignant farewell to his cow, "I Guess This Is Good-
bye." One of the central manifestations of the Bean Theme is embodied in
Rapunzel, who as the Witch's daughter—but audiences won't find this out
for some time—is naturally a direct outgrowth of the beans. Throughout the

story we will hear her singing a lyrical extended and unchanging version of the Bean Theme offstage and without words (Example 15.4b).

Space does not permit a full-scale description of how the Bean Theme evolves from here. A few highlights from the first act must suffice. In "Maybe They're Magic," the orchestra underscores the music sung by the Baker and his Wife with the Bean Theme and follows the clever punch line ("If the end is right, it justifies the beans") with an isolated statement of the five-note theme. A few songs later in "First Midnight," Rapunzel starts with the same five notes when she sings her elongated transformation of the Bean Theme. In fact, for the entire first act this is the only music Rapunzel sings; in the second act she does not sing at all, although we continue to hear her music. Audiences may not realize that Rapunzel's Theme and the Bean Theme are the same, but they know that Rapunzel is repeating her music ad nauseam. On the words "giants in the sky" Jack introduces the song of this title with the Bean Theme before it submerges as underscoring. Fittingly, when Rapunzel's Prince sings his "Agony about the unreachable woman in the tower with the long hair," he quotes her theme. Also fittingly, Rapunzel's mother, the Witch, uses her daughter's theme as the starting point for the song "Stay with Me."

Sondheim and the Broadway Tradition: *Two Follies*

Although Kern died before all the revisions were made, the 1946 revival of *Show Boat*—from then until the 1990s the only version regularly performed—gave Kern and Hammerstein an opportunity to rethink the work together in the light of a new present. Audiences accustomed to reworked versions of the pre–Rodgers and Hammerstein musical and to relatively fixed versions of musicals composed in the 1940s, '50s, and '60s may be surprised to discover that the sometimes extensive changes made in revivals of Sondheim shows parallel the revival histories of several musicals treated in the present survey, including *Show Boat*, *Porgy and Bess*, *Anything Goes*, and *On Your Toes*.

The 1985 La Jolla Playhouse revival of *Merrily*, for example, dropped "Rich and Happy," the high school scene, and the idea of casting adolescents. More radically, the 1987 London revival of *Follies* precipitated a revised book with a new ending and both new and discarded songs.[72] The *Follies* section in the online website encapsulates the genesis of the show from *The Girls Upstairs* in 1965 to the tryouts in 1971 and lists the songs of the 1987 London *Follies*.

The *Follies* revival in particular offers a striking modern example of a process that has much in common with the pre–Rodgers and Hammerstein musicals examined in the first part of this survey.[73] After a long gestation period that included the composition and production of *Company*, Sondheim & Co. were ready to return to a drastically revamped James Goldman script, *The Girls Upstairs*, originally drafted in 1965. According to Prince, the new *Follies*, begun in earnest 1970 after the completion of *Company*, could salvage only six of the songs from the earlier version.[74] Prince biographer Carol Ilson summarizes the radical metamorphosis from *The Girls Upstairs* to *Follies*:

> The realistic and naturalistic *The Girls Upstairs* became the sur-realistic *Follies*. Originally, Sondheim and Goldman wanted the show to be a backstage murder mystery with an attempted murder being planned. The idea was dropped. Prince, working with his collaborators, decided to use only the two couples that had been written to be the major characters, and to use the theatre locale. He encouraged the authors to utilize the younger selves of the leading characters. Four new cast members would represent the leading characters as they had been thirty years earlier.[75]

All involved agree that it was Prince's concept to mirror the younger unmarried versions of the two unhappily married couples, Phyllis and Benjamin Stone and Sally and Buddy Plummer (we have already met Sally and examined her act I ballad, "In Buddy's Eyes"). The collaborative minds of co-directors Prince (stage director) and Michael Bennett (musical director) led to many additional dramaturgical changes, including an unusually large number of nine song replacements during rehearsals.

An opening montage that consisted of a medley of five songs, one of which was dropped during rehearsals, was also abandoned, and two additional songs were replaced during tryouts.[76] The first of these songs, "I'm Still Here," was added because Yvonne De Carlo "couldn't do" the song originally intended for her, "Can That Boy Foxtrot!"[77] Out of this neces-sity Sondheim invented a song that more closely fit the evolving concept. De Carlo's character, *Carlo*tta Campion, like De *Carlo* herself, was an actress who stayed in show business for many years after her prime and endured the ravages of time. A clever musical conceit of Sondheim's in the song is to have her sing an ascending major triad nearly every time she sings "I'm Still Here" (E♭-G-B♭).[78]

The device of repeating a simple motive parallels torch songs such as "In Buddy's Eyes" and would occur in other obsessive situations in subse-quent Sondheim shows, for example, when Seurat sings about "Finishing the Hat." Sally's song expresses a defeatist attitude and a disconnection with reality, exemplified metaphorically by her inability to find a root or tonal center when she sings the oft-repeated "in Buddy's eyes" in her first song and her descending melodic phrase that matches "I think about you" in her second song. In bold contrast, Carlotta's mantra, a major triad invariably ends each time in ascending and affirmative melodic triumph on its fifth, like a bugle call. *Sweeney Todd* may be about obsession, but compared with Sally and later George in *Sunday in the Park with George*, Sweeney's *musical* obsessions are relatively tame.

Two songs were added to *Follies* late in the process. The first was Phyllis's folly number, "The Story of Lucy and Jessie," a song that replaced "Uptown, Downtown"; the second was Ben's folly song, "Live, Love, Laugh." Both were apparently composed and staged during a frenetic final week of rehearsals. In their published remarks Sondheim and Bennett disagree about why "Uptown, Downtown" was discarded. Sondheim remembers that he wrote it after he had worked out Ben's breakdown number and gave it to Bennett one day before the Boston try-outs. Sondheim also recalls that Bennett resented being rushed, "turned against it," and asked for a new number: "I don't think there's really any difference between the numbers, but because he had more time to think about it, I think he liked it better."[79] Bennett recalled the situation somewhat differently: "I quite honestly don't understand why Steve had to write 'Lucy and Jessie' for Alexis [Smith] to replace the other number. I like 'Uptown Downtown' so much better. It also lost me a phrase to hang her dance on. I was originally able to differentiate the character's two personalities by having half the phrase strutting up and the other half strutting down."[80]

In a view that lies between these contrasting recollections, Prince commented tersely that "Uptown, Downtown" was "the right idea" but that "The Story of Lucy and Jessie" was "a better number."[81] Jeffrey Lonoff's notes to *A Collector's Sondheim* offer a thoughtful comparison that places these disparate memories within a critical perspective: "In the show we see two Phyllises—the young, open, vibrant girl and the cool, distant woman she carefully molds herself into. Her song in the Loveland section was to reflect her schizoid personality. But 'Uptown, Downtown' presented Phyllis as a two-sided character whereas she was, as the show presented, really two separate people. It was dropped, and 'The Story of Lucy and Jessie' was written to better portray this."

Although Sondheim credits the influence of Cole Porter on "The Story of Lucy and Jessie," a more likely model might be Kurt Weill and Ira Gershwin's "The Saga of Jenny" from *Lady in the Dark*. Resemblances between the Sondheim and Weill songs go beyond their suggestively similar titles and subject matter—a woman responding to the accusation that she cannot make up her mind—and include such musical details as the nearly constant dotted rhythms and frequent descending minor triads, a predilection for flatted (blue) fifths, and a general jazz flavor.[82]

Earlier it was observed that the successful cast recording of *Pal Joey* led to a Broadway revival that surpassed its initial run. The abbreviated and what was generally perceived as an uncharacteristically poorly produced original 1971 cast album of *Follies* (albeit with a great cast) generated the need for a recording that was both more complete and more felicitously engineered. Unfortunately, in contrast to the pre-production *Pal Joey* recording that led to a full staged revival two years later, the new *Follies* album with its all-star cast issued in 1985 was not followed with a staged Broadway performance. Although a revised *Follies* made a successful appearance on the London stage two years later, it was not until a 1998 revival at the Paper Mill Playhouse in Millburn, New Jersey, that a staged version would return to the New York vicinity. A modestly staged production finally made it to Broadway for a short run in 2001.

James Goldman's original libretto for *Follies* was not only critically controversial, it provoked strenuous debate between the two visionary co-directors, Bennett and Prince. What mainly bothered Bennett was the absence of humor and the general heaviness of tone—in short, its lack of commercial appeal. When Prince vetoed the idea of bringing in Neil Simon, a master of the one-liner, Bennett gave Goldman a joke book.[83] Although he remained embittered by *Follies*'s disappointing box office returns, Bennett felt that his judgment of the book was vindicated by the show's box office failure.[84] Goldman agrees that the show might have had a long run, but that "at the same time we would have disemboweled it."[85] In retrospect, although Prince does not go as far as to say that he *likes* the book, he valued the book more highly than Bennett and clarifies that he did not "hate the book at all."[86] Sondheim thought the large number of pastiche numbers "hurt the book and subsequently hurt the show" and concluded that if they "had used fewer songs and had more book the show would have been more successful."[87]

For the 1985 concert performance, Herbert Ross, hired to stage the show, asked Sondheim to change the ending: "I never liked the kind of hopelessness of the show's finale....I think you never really believed that the death of the theater was a sort of symbol for the death of these people's lives. My view of it was that this was a celebration, and the original ending was too downbeat and not appropriate for this event."[88] Eventually Goldman himself had second thoughts about the ending of his 1971 *Follies*: "The final scene of the show has always bothered me, I must admit. There were all kinds of thoughts as to how we should have gone out at the end. I was pleased with the ending that Buddy and Sally had. I think it was honest and on target and about all you could do. I'm not so sure that if I had it to write over again that I would have had Ben and Phyllis together at the end."[89] Two years later Goldman *did* have it to write again when *Follies* was staged in London. This time, Goldman produced a new and even more upbeat book than the one implied in the 1985 concert performance.[90]

The principal deletions from the 1971 *Follies* (see the online website) are Ben Stone's philosophical "The Road You Didn't Take" and, perhaps significantly, the two latest additions to the earlier version, Phyllis's folly song, "The Story of Lucy and Jessie," and Ben's concluding folly song, "Live, Laugh, Love."[91] Sondheim also created a new "Loveland" to replace the 1971 song of the same name to open the quartet of follies (one each for Benjamin and Phyllis Stone and Buddy and Sally Plummer) that brought the earlier show to its depressing close. Perhaps not surprisingly, the superficially successful Ben, who ultimately emerges as the most pathetic of the quartet in 1971, underwent the most surgery in 1987.

The first discarded song, Ben's "The Road You Didn't Take," is replaced two songs later with "Country House," a duet between Ben and Phyllis. This new song, although it conveys their poor communication and half-hearted attempts to work out their problems, demonstrates a civil and resigned incompatibility rather than their earlier bitterness and hostility. Phyllis's new song, "Ah, but Underneath," like "Being Alive" in *Company*, provides another illustration of a final attempt to capture a difficult dramatic situation. It also marks a return to Phyllis's two-sided nature depicted in "Uptown, Downtown," discarded earlier from the 1971 *Follies* in favor of "Lucy and Jessie."

Ben's new folly song, like his new duet with Phyllis, constitutes the most radical change of tone between 1971 and 1987. Rather than breaking down as he did in "Live, Laugh, Love," with newly acquired equanimity Ben tells his 1987 audiences not "to disclose yourself" but to "compose yourself" as he sings "Make the Most of Your Music." Among the ironies of the song—and perhaps also its subtext—with its instructions to "Make the most of the music that is yours," is Sondheim's decision to begin Ben's song with a quotation from the opening of Edvard Grieg's Piano Concerto set to words in the vocal line (in the orchestra alone the related opening of Tchaikovsky's first Piano Concerto directly follows).[92] Ben initially considers himself "something big league" along with "Tchaikovsky and Grieg." Soon, however, he advises his admirers that even if they are unable to produce a work like Debussy's *Clair de Lune*, they can "make the most of the music that is yours" and eventually produce music that "soars." Whatever Sondheim is saying about the relative merits of Tchaikovsky, Grieg, and Debussy, Sondheim himself might be accused in this rare case of not practicing what his character preaches.

Although Sondheim's new songs were expressly composed for this revival rather than for other shows, the results are not dissimilar. In fact, the 1987 London *Follies*, with its rewritten book and deleted, reordered, and new songs, is clearly analogous to Porter's *Anything Goes* in its 1962 and 1987 reincarnations, and perhaps even more closely akin to the changes in *Show Boat* between 1927 and 1946. Just as the comic, even farcical, touches added to Bernstein's 1974 *Candide* (including Sondheim's own new lyric for "Life Is Happiness Indeed") no doubt contributed to its newfound success, perhaps at Voltaire's expense, the more upbeat 1987 *Follies* might eventually have found the audience it lost in 1971. But it did not. Despite its relative grimness, the original 1971 *Follies* soon replaced the 1987 book.[93]

In his conversations with Mark Horowitz, Sondheim explains that he went along with Goldman's and Cameron Mackintosh's ideas about changing *Follies* for London, but like Goldman and eventually even Mackintosh, he voiced his strong preference for the earlier version: "It might have turned out better. It didn't. And when it didn't, I said: I don't want this show ever shown in America, and I made it legally certain that the London version can never be shown here. I don't want it shown again in England either, but Cameron has the right to do it. But Cameron's given in now too, and there was just a production in Leicester last year, and it's the original."[94] As George says in *Sunday in the Park with George*'s "Putting It Together," "If no one gets to see it, it's as good as dead." This is a good description of the 1987 London *Follies*.

The Art of Compromise

By the end of Sondheim's *Company*, Robert, the bachelor protagonist, has learned that compromise is an essential feature of marriage. The ambiguity that three of Robert's married male friends feel toward their wives and their marriages, expressed relatively early in the evening in "Sorry-Grateful," culminates in Robert's final readiness to share their fate, "Being Alive." It is widely known that "Being Alive" was Sondheim's fourth attempt at a final song for Robert.[95] "Marry Me a Little," which expressed Robert's unwillingness to compromise, has found a secure place, albeit a new place, in the revised book of *Company*. The extraordinarily biting "Happily Ever After" described a marriage that ends "happily ever after in hell." The marriage envisioned in "Being Alive" is far from perfect, but advocates of marriage can take heart that Robert has come to realize that "alone is alone, not alive." In his autobiography, *Contradictions*, Prince voiced his continued dissatisfaction with this final song, which he felt "imposed a happy ending on a play which should have remained ambiguous." Otherwise, Prince concludes his chapter on *Company* by saying that this show "represents the first time I had worked without conscious compromise." The producer in Prince was doubly pleased with its profit, however small, since "that is what commercial theatre must ask of itself."[96]

Follies, which explores the compromise of ideals in the lives of two unfulfilled married couples, lost most of its backers' money because of its creators' refusal to compromise and offer a lighter touch. The characters in Sondheim's (and Prince's) next musical, *A Little Night Music*, may need to discover their true feelings and are subjected to humiliation in the process, but at least they do not have to compromise them. The compromises were artistic ones and occurred offstage, at least according to Prince, who wrote in his memoirs sardonically that "mostly *Night Music* was about having a hit."[97]

In *Pacific Overtures* (1976), generally perceived as a less compromising musical than *Night Music*, the formerly obedient feudal vassal Kayama forsakes ancient traditions in order to profit financially from his new Western trading partners. In act II, Kayama sports "A Bowler Hat" and a pocket watch, pours milk in his tea, and smokes American cigars. The eponymous anti-hero in *Sweeney Todd* (1979) and the infamous historical murderers and would-be murderers in *Assassins* (1991) relinquish their moral decency for the sake of revenge, notoriety, or other misguided ideals. *Into the Woods* (1987) concludes with abandoned, deceived, and disillusioned fairy-tale characters who have compromised their innocence but now understand that "No One Is Alone." Some, such as Martin Gottfried, find the moralizing tone of *Into the Woods* platitudinous, yet a critic as rigorous as Stephen Banfield assesses this show as "Sondheim's finest achievement yet."[98]

In his first two shows of the 1980s, *Merrily We Roll Along* and *Sunday in the Park with George*, Sondheim directly confronted the issue of artistic compromise in his own work, an issue previously faced more obliquely by several of Broadway's spiritual fathers surveyed in earlier chapters. *On Your Toes* addresses the dichotomy between art music and popular music and *The Cradle Will Rock* offers a devastating attack on compromising artists, but *Merrily* and *Sunday* may be unprecedented in the degree to which they explore the creative process and commercial pressures on artists. *Merrily* tells the disconcerting story of a Broadway composer, Franklin Shepard, who has sold out his ideals and his artistic soul, the road pointedly not taken by Sondheim. *Sunday* presents two portraits of artists. In act I we meet a fictionalized but nevertheless once-real artist in 1884, the uncompromising painter

Georges Seurat, who refused to sell out. In fact, Seurat reportedly never sold a painting in his lifetime. One hundred years later in act II, we meet his great-grandson, also an artist named George, a man who evolves from a compromising sculptor grubbing for grants and commissions to a genuine artist more like Seurat by the end of the evening.

Since *Merrily* is told in reverse, the disintegration of this Broadway Faust is all the more disturbing. When we first meet Franklin Shepard in 1980 as the graduation speaker of his former high school (a scene dropped from the 1985 revival), the once idealistic but now artistically sterile Broadway composer tells "young innocents a few realities" and introduces them to the two words that symbolize his abandoned ideals, "practical" and "compromise." The older Frank says "compromise is how you survive"; the younger Frank answers that compromise is "how you give up."

Twenty years earlier, but much later in the show, Franklin, his high school classmate and present collaborator Charley Kringas, and their mutual friend Mary Flynn, an aspiring novelist, sing "Opening Doors." Sondheim has acknowledged the autobiographical aspect to this song: "If there is one number that is really me writing about me, it is 'Opening Doors.' That was my life for a number of years. It is a totally personal number. Luckily it fits into the piece."[99] In this song Frank and Charley are creating their first show, auditioning the material, facing rejection and disappointment, and struggling to reject compromising alternatives. Charley is typing and Frank is composing "Good Thing Going," heard in its completed state earlier in the show when Frank and Charley sing it at a party in 1962. This is the party where Frank tells Mary, now a critic who has forsaken her dream to write a great American novel, that he has not composed the music for his own recent film. In fact, Frank has long since abandoned his creative partnership with Charley, who did not sell out, yet has become a distinguished playwright. Frank may be "Rich and Happy" in 1970, but he is also morally and artistically bankrupt and sad. By the end of Shepard's career, which real-life audiences witnessed with disappointment near the beginning of the show, the selling of an artistic soul is complete.

In the creation of "Opening Doors," Frank experiences considerable difficulty going beyond the opening phrase, which, not incidentally, is the phrase that most clearly resembles the idealistic anthem that he and Charley composed for their high school graduation (both at the opening and toward the close of the musical in its original production).[100] When Mary calls to tell Frank that she is about to abandon her principles and her novel by taking commercial writing jobs, she sings this same opening phrase. Later in the song Charley and Frank audition the first several phrases of their future hit song for a wary producer, Joe Josephson.

Even without Sondheim's admission, reaffirmed at the March 2008 public interview in Portland with Frank Rich, it would be difficult to overlook the autobiographical component of Josephson's criticism, so closely does it correspond to the critical reactions which the modernist Sondheim, a close contemporary of the fictional Mr. Shepard, had by then been facing for more than two decades. Ironically, however, when Josephson tells them that "There's not a tune you can hum.—/ There's not a tune you go bum-bum-bum-di-dum" or that he will let them "know when Stravinsky has a hit," he sings Frank's tune. After this initial rejection, Charley and Frank continue to pitch their song. Josephson then abruptly dismisses them and sings his own: "Write more, work hard,—/ Leave your name with the girl.—/ Less avant-garde."

At this moment the ghost of Rodgers and Hammerstein returns to haunt Sondheim as well as Franklin Shepard. The "plain old melodee dee dee dee dee dee" that Josephson desires is none other than the chestnut, "Some Enchanted Evening," from *South Pacific*. Characteristically, Josephson does not know the words to this familiar classic and apparently does not even realize that he is trying to hum a Rodgers and Hammerstein song. In addition to several conspicuously incorrect pitches, Josephson also sings its opening musical phrase completely outside of its proper metrical foundation (with an extra quarter-note within a measure of 4/4 time, one extra beat too many for the measure).

Sondheim is reinforcing what we all know: that in 1958 as well as in 1981 a Rodgers tune was and is the ideal Broadway theater song and the standard by which Shepard—and Sondheim—will be measured. In defiance of this expectation, Charley and Frank refuse to alter their work and write a Rodgers and Hammerstein-type song, and instead join with Mary to create something new and all their own, an original revue. Within a few years the rejected song becomes a hit song in Frank and Charley's new Broadway show, produced by Josephson. By the 1980s, people everywhere were beginning to hum Sondheim's songs, too, and by the 1990s and 2000s more and more could be heard out of their original stage contexts in cabaret theaters, recordings, and television.[101] And although few, if any, of his songs match the familiarity of "Send in the Clowns," and of course many songs by Rodgers, Sondheim's songs have belatedly begun to receive broader recognition. Paradoxically, what was uncommercial has become, to an extent, evergreen (and belatedly commercial as well).

The fin-de-siècle classical modernists are rarely accused of compromising their ideals, but they are, like Sondheim and Seurat, equally faulted for lacking artistic passion. Sondheim also shares with his modernist counterparts a profound awareness of his classic predecessors and self-consciously responds to his tradition in varied and profound ways. Just as the European modernists recreate the past in their own image, so Sondheim pays allegiance to and reinterprets his tradition and makes it his own. At the center of this tradition are the integrated musicals of Rodgers and Hammerstein, Sondheim's one-time collaborator and long-time mentor, respectively. Sondheim's shows depart from the Rodgers and Hammerstein models stylistically and dramaturgically, especially in their subject matter and in their use of time and space. But at least from *Company* on they preserve the concept of the integrated musical. As with Rodgers and Hammerstein, the more-than-occasionally compromising characters in a Sondheim musical sing lyrics and music that reveal their essences and nuances and move the drama, narrative or non-narrative, uncompromisingly forward.

Sondheim, like Seurat and his modernist musical counterparts, Debussy, Schoenberg, and Stravinsky, has long since demonstrated his ability to move on, to learn from the example of his mentor Hammerstein who wrote "You'll Never Walk Alone" and to give the Rodgers and Hammerstein tradition renewed life in "No One Is Alone." Throughout his more than fifty-year career on Broadway, Sondheim has successfully combined the musical trappings of musical modernism and created works that encompass an extremely broad dramatic range. Like Beethoven, who radically reinterpreted the classical style without abandoning its fundamental principles, in a larger sense Sondheim's modernism might also be construed as a reinterpretation rather than a revolution. Nevertheless, despite this allegiance to the innovative but traditional principles of Hammerstein and Robbins, Sondheim's music is more dissonant and less tonal than his predecessors'—with the possible exception of Bernstein's tritone-laden *West Side Story*—and his characters are usually more neurotic and even occasionally psychotic.

Like Seurat and the modern George, Sondheim is willing to rethink his theatrical legacy to say something new. The ingenious incorporation of past models in the pastiches of *Follies* would reappear in subsequent shows, most extensively and literally in *Assassins*.[102] In this respect, Sondheim's shows are very much analogous to *Show Boat, On Your Toes, The Cradle Will Rock*, and *West Side Story*, to name only the musicals discussed in the present survey that prominently display popular and classical allusions. Sondheim succeeded in moving the Broadway musical to a new phase through words and music supported by imaginative solutions to perennial dramatic problems. At the same time, Sondheim's approach to the musical can be placed firmly in the great tradition from *Show Boat* to *West Side Story*. The Broadway musical from the 1920s to the 1950s could hardly ask for a worthier heir or more enchanted evenings.

CHAPTER SIXTEEN

PHANTOM OF THE OPERA

The Reigning Champion
of Broadway

The Lloyd Webber Problem

The composer's career was thus marked by popular success and critical doubt; in the years since his death, these motifs have remained central to his musical and musicological reputation....For some time his works remained objects of contempt, and even when he was not openly derided, he was often conspicuous by his absence, failing to merit more than a cursory mention in many supposedly "comprehensive" studies of the American and British musical.[1]

The above panegyric, purposely misquoted, contains one important omission that should be cleared up without delay. In place of the anonymous "composer's career," the author of the passage, Alexandra Wilson, put forward a particular composer. The composer named by Wilson in her critical reception study *The Puccini Problem* is actually Giacomo Puccini (1858–1924), who composed operas rather than musicals and received little more than "cursory mention in many supposedly 'comprehensive' studies of twentieth-century music," rather than in "studies of the American and British musical" as misstated in the passage. Instead of the anonymous "composer's career," try to imagine the name Andrew Lloyd Webber (b. 1948) at the outset of the excerpt. Aside from the not unimportant fact that Lloyd Webber, at the time this second edition of *Enchanted Evenings* is written (2008), is only sixty years old and still quite active in the musical theater domain, the parallels in reception history between Lloyd Webber and Puccini are arguably present, perhaps uncannily so. The composer of *The Phantom of the Opera* has, in fact, like Puccini, so far endured an unresolved dissonance between high popularity and great wealth on the one hand and relatively low critical stature and recognition on the other. Before resuming our focus on the critical contradictions that surround the remarkable career of Lloyd Webber, it will be useful to review its well-known highlights.

While still a teenager, Andrew, the talented son of a prominent composer and teacher at the London College of Music, William Lloyd Webber, teamed up with Tim Rice to write a fifteen-minute staged cantata based on the biblical story of Joseph and many brothers for the students of a boys' school, Colet Court, in 1968. A slightly longer version was recorded and then expanded still further into a full-length musical that was performed in London in 1972 as *Joseph and the Amazing Technicolor Dreamcoat*. By that time, Lloyd Webber and Rice in 1970 had produced a two-record concept rock album based on another biblical theme, the last days of Christ told from the perspective of his betrayer Judas Iscariot. *Jesus Christ Superstar*, a stage realization of this album, significantly sung throughout, became a

Andrew Lloyd Webber in 2004.

modest hit in New York in 1971 and a major hit when it opened in London the following year.

After the failure of the first version of the more traditional *Jeeves* (1975; revised as *By Jeeves* in 1996) with the playwright Alan Ayckbourn, the following year Lloyd Webber and Rice produced another two-record concept album in a mixture of rock and Latin styles based on the stormy life and early death of Eva Peron, the controversial and charismatic wife of Argentina's authoritarian leader Juan Peron. Under the guidance of Harold Prince, *Evita*, first in London (1978) and the next year in New York, developed into another successful through-sung musical (i.e., with minimal spoken dialogue) on a provocative political theme. In retrospect, it is clear that *Evita*, the longest running imported musical until that time, was the true launching pad for the second British musical theater revolution (the first being the comparably earth-shaking arrival of Gilbert and Sullivan exactly one century earlier). By the time he was thirty, Lloyd Webber thus had created three significant works for the musical stage. The greatest successes would follow in the next decade.

The first of these was *Cats* in 1981, an unusual show that abandoned a traditional book and instead added a loose revue-like story line to T. S. Eliot's poetic collection *Old Possum's Book of Practical Cats* (1939). Unlike a traditional revue, *Cats* was told entirely through dance and song. The song "Memory," Trevor Nunn's reworking of another Eliot poem not part of *Practical Cats* called "Rhapsody on a Windy Night," surpassed in popularity even the big song hits of *Jesus Christ Superstar* ("I Don't Know How to Love Him") and *Evita* ("Don't Cry for Me, Argentina"). In his next show, *Starlight Express* (1984), with lyrics by Richard Stilgoe (who would contribute about 20 percent of the lyrics to *Phantom*), toy trains come to life, perform on roller skates, and sing a rock based score with a smattering of other popular vernacular styles (blues, spirituals, gospel, and country).

One year after *Starlight*, Lloyd Webber produced yet another album that would eventually lead to a staged show, this time a hit single and promotional music video of the title song of *The Phantom of the Opera* performed by his new bride Sarah Brightman and lead rock singer Steve Harley. That same year, July 1985, a rough rock-oriented version of act I was performed at Lloyd Webber's annual summer Sydmonton Festival, a performance that introduced his new and previously untested lyricist Charles Hart then only twenty-four. Not wanting to be influenced by a performance, however unpolished, Prince stayed away from Sydmonton but would soon join Lloyd Webber and Hart to shape the work into its present form.

Popularity...

It took some time for Sondheim to gain a wide following and critical respect as a composer-lyricist. I have duly noted allegations of coldness, a lack of melody, and, when discussing *Sunday in the Park with George*, even the absence of a second act. Despite enormous critical praise and scholarly attention, not one Sondheim show lasted as many as one thousand performances during its first Broadway run. Most lasted fewer, and some considerably fewer, than five hundred performances.

By contrast, from the early 1970s to the present, Lloyd Webber has enjoyed record-breaking success on both sides of the Atlantic. The facts are indisputable. Via immense popular and commercial success (with a few exceptions in New York), the British composer of *Jesus Christ Superstar* (New York, 1971; London, 1972), *Joseph and the Amazing Technicolor Dreamcoat* (London 1972; New York, 1981), *Evita* (London, 1978; New York, 1979), *Cats* (London, 1981; New York, 1982), *Starlight Express* (London, 1984; New York, 1987), *The Phantom of the Opera* (London, 1986; New York, 1988), *Aspects of Love* (London, 1989; New York, 1990), and *Sunset Boulevard* (London and Los Angeles, 1993; New York, 1994) has achieved unprecedented popular acclaim on Broadway and still greater popularity in London's West End.[2] With the two longest all-time Broadway runs (*Phantom, Cats*) and three of the top five West End runs (*Phantom, Cats, Starlight*), Lloyd Webber is simply the most popular Broadway composer of the post–Rodgers and Hammerstein era and probably of all time. Paul Prece and William Everett summarize the economic and geographic reach of the *Phantom*: "In January 2006, it was reported that *Phantom* alone had grossed more money than any other production on stage and screen (£1.7 billion/approximately $3.2 billion), surpassing huge money-making films such as *Star Wars, E.T.*, and *Titanic*. The show has been seen by over eighty million people."[3]

One unmistakable sign of success and critical acclaim is the number of major awards a show and its creators earn in a given year and over time. Comparing the awards to Lloyd Webber and Sondheim, the two dominant Broadway composers of the past several decades, and to the number of Tonys awarded to each for Best Score, Sondheim owns a distinct advantage. Between 1971 and 1994 Sondheim received six awards for Best Score (*Company, Follies, Night Music, Sweeney Todd, Into the Woods*, and *Passion*). Lloyd Webber received three between 1980 and 1995 (*Evita, Cats*, and *Sunset Boulevard*).[4] From this elite group all but *Follies* and *Into the Woods* also won the Tony Award for Best Show.

Since *Phantom* was nominated the same year as *Woods*, it would have been necessary for the shows to share the award for both to win. In some sense they did share the award in that *Phantom* received the award for Best Musical, Director (Prince), the three major design awards (Maria Björnson for both scenic and costume design and Andrew Bridge for lighting), principal actor (Michael Crawford as the Phantom), and actress in a featured role (Judy Kaye as the Prima Donna Carlotta Guidicelli), while *Into the Woods* took home the awards for Book (James Lapine), Score (Sondheim), and principal actress (Joanna Gleason as the Baker's Wife). Staging awards to *Phantom*, the writing awards to *Into the Woods*, and a split in acting awards (with the edge to *Phantom*).

In the years since *Into the Woods* (November 5, 1987) and shortly thereafter *Phantom* (January 26, 1988) first arrived on Broadway, the former show, with a solid but unremarkable 765 performances, has already experienced a seven-month revival in 2002 (18 previews and 279 performances). Meanwhile, *The Phantom of the Opera*, like Carlotta in *Follies*, is still here. Four years after the *Into the Woods* revival closed, on January 9, 2006, *Phantom* surpassed another Lloyd Webber musical, *Cats*, as Broadway's longest running show. At the time this is written *Phantom* has reached 8,771 performances, giving it the distinction of being the first to cross 8,000. *Cats* remains in second place at 7,485.

Among currently running shows only the revival of *Chicago* (5,088) or *The Lion King* (4,720) are in any position to overtake these two Lloyd Webber megamusical megahits, and these still have long way to go.[5] From the New York arrival of *Jesus Christ Superstar* in 1971 to the present, the sun has yet to set on the Lloyd Webber era either on Broadway or in the West End. As John Snelson writes, "in the West End, the opening of *Jesus Christ Superstar* in 1972 marked the start of a continuous presence of Lloyd Webber shows through to the time of writing [2004]; often during that span there have been four concurrent Lloyd Webber shows, and in both 1991 and 1997 six were playing simultaneously."[6]

...versus Critical Acclaim

Before the first edition of *Enchanted Evenings* was published in 1997, the only serious Lloyd Webber biography to appear was Michael Walsh's biographically thorough, generally sympathetic, non-technical *Andrew Lloyd Webber: His Life and Works* (1989, revised and enlarged 2nd ed., 1997).[7] In *The Broadway Musical* (1990; revised and expanded 2nd ed., 2002), Joseph P. Swain devoted a highly critical chapter to *Jesus Christ Superstar* and *Evita*.[8] Before the end of the 1990s serious Broadway scholarship was still the exception to the rule, but a number of books, dissertations, and journal articles on Sondheim had already appeared, including Stephen Banfield's comprehensive analytical study *Sondheim's Broadway Musicals* (1993). A journal devoted exclusively to Sondheim, *The Sondheim Review,* was launched in 1994. In recent years at least three full essay collections on Sondheim have appeared in addition to major scholarly and analytical attention to Sondheim in books, journals, courses and seminars, papers and even whole sessions of papers at musicological conferences, and substantial parts of more general books in the field. Readers have come to expect more than a "cursory mention" (see the quotation that opened this chapter) on Sondheim when they pick up a survey of the Broadway musical.

On the other hand, in a situation similar to the relatively sparse attention given Puccini in comparison with Verdi and Wagner, serious study of Lloyd Webber, including recent scholarship, "is conspicuous by its absence" (also quoted from the opening of the chapter). The second edition of Steven Suskin's *Show Tunes* (1991) included a section called "Notable Imported Shows." About half of the shows listed were shows with music by Lloyd Webber. In the Preface to the third edition Suskin justifies the omission of this section and the expunging of Lloyd Webber that resulted: "All of the British imports since the Second Edition have failed; thus, I have seen fit to excise the import section and concentrate on matters of more interest."[9] As a consequence of this executive decision, the most popular Broadway composer of the last thirty years and probably in history is now banished from a major reference book that purports to cover "The Songs, Shows, and Careers of Broadway's Major Composers." In his critical remarks on Maury Yeston's excellent version of *Phantom,* which was performed to some acclaim by Houston's Theater of the Stars in 1991, Suskin compares the work favorably with its vastly better known predecessor: "Yeston's score is actually far more tuneful than you-know-who's."[10] Even the identity of "you know who" remains securely hidden, a phantom of the musical theater.

Of the thirty-eight Broadway musicals explored in Raymond Knapp's two-volume survey of the American musical and musical film, seven feature shows by Sondheim and only one considers a show by Lloyd Webber (*Evita*).[11] Although Knapp notes that not everyone shares a negative view and offers dramatic reasons behind Lloyd Webber's reuse of melodic material, the disparity in emphasis nonetheless speaks for itself and reveals a stronger interest in Sondheim. Of the thirty-four shows discussed in Scott Miller's three volumes of essays, eight are devoted to works by Sondheim, only one by Lloyd Webber (the early *Jesus Christ Superstar*).[12] Ethan Mordden, who devotes from four to fourteen pages each to nearly every Sondheim show in his seven-volume survey, dismisses Lloyd Webber through sharp criticism but mainly through neglect. In fact, among all of Lloyd Webber's output, only *Jesus Christ*

Superstar, according to Mordden, demonstrates meaningful dramatic correlation between theme and characters (and consequently merits two pages).

Despite relative inattention in mainstream surveys, the past few years have witnessed serious studies on Lloyd Webber musicals that combine biographical, critical, and analytical commentary, especially John Snelson's *Andrew Lloyd Webber* (2004) and Jessica Sternfeld's *The Megamusical* (2006).[13] Both Snelson and Sternfeld are sympathetic to their subject and offer spirited defenses of Lloyd Webber against his many critics. For the most part, however, authors who devote some attention to Lloyd Webber characteristically treat significant elements of his shows, if not the composer himself, with undisguised disdain. Some of these studies minimize—they can't ignore—Lloyd Webber's achievement and attribute the staggeringly popular success of his shows, and other overblown megamusicals, merely to stagecraft and media hype.[14] Another commonly voiced criticism of Lloyd Webber shows, even in writings that are largely positive—for example, Stephen Citron's double study of Lloyd Webber and Sondheim in 2001—are aimed at what is perceived as generic and otherwise sub-par lyrics, especially those written by lyricists who have come after *Evita*, when Rice and Lloyd Webber parted ways.[15] On the whole, the overwhelming critical assessment of Lloyd Webber so far consists of high marks for stagecraft, spectacle, and popular success, and low marks for artistic craft, inspired originality, and general overall esteem.

Borrowing and the Organically Overgrown Megamusical

Two controversial issues have long haunted the musicals of Lloyd Webber: (1) his common practice of musical borrowing from other composers; and (2) allegations of excessive reuse of his own music within a musical. Neither issue is unique to Lloyd Webber. Virtually all composers, including Broadway composers, borrow from other musical sources. Composers in the classical tradition from Handel, Bach, and Mozart to Stravinsky and Ives have used previous music frequently and with great originality and craft for centuries, a force that prompted eighteenth-century theorist Johann Mattheson to pronounce that "borrowing is permissible, but one must return the object borrowed with interest."[16] The problem is that Lloyd Webber is often accused of borrowing without paying interest. Since the days of Sigmund Romberg it would be difficult to produce a Broadway composer who has so blatantly been accused of plagiarism, several steps beneath borrowing.[17] Similarly, in regard to the second controversy, all composers surveyed in this volume reuse material and reprise songs in their musicals. Here too, the issue is that Lloyd Webber, perhaps more than any major Broadway figure, is accused of indiscriminate or dramatically meaningless reuse.

Borrowing

This volume has shown that the composers of our featured shows occasionally quote or allude to the music of other composers. The most interesting borrowings are those that are dramatically purposeful and meaningful—for example, the use of Dvořák's "New World" Symphony as a source of the River Family in *Show Boat*, the use of Tchaikovsky's *Romeo and Juliet* and Wagner's "Redemption through Love" leitmotiv in *West Side Story*, and the "Dies irae" in *Sweeney Todd*. It has also been observed that a number of borrowings are seemingly less than meaningful to the work at hand (e.g., the Puccini allusions in *My Fair Lady* or the undisguised resemblances between Bernstein's "Maria" and Blitzstein's *Regina*).

Writers such as Stephen Citron, John Snelson, Jessica Sternfeld, and Michael Walsh who have discussed the music of Lloyd Webber's shows more often than not dismiss the borrowings as inconsequential. This chapter espouses the view that the sheer number of examples and their closeness to their borrowed sources suggest that students of musical theater should examine this phenomenon critically rather than ignore it. Lloyd Webber's first major hit, *Superstar*'s "I Don't Know How to Love Him" is the first of many examples that writers have noticed and commented on for its strong melodic and harmonic similarity to the second movement of Mendelssohn's Violin Concerto in E Minor, op. 64. Before he goes on to show what Lloyd Webber added to Mendelssohn, Snelson writes that "from a musical standpoint, the resemblance between the pop melody and the concerto is so obvious and continues through such an extended passage (some seven bars) that any claim to coincidence is untenable."[18]

In his chapter-length study of "musical reminiscences" in Lloyd Webber, Snelson describes the even closer connection between "On This Night of a Thousand Stars," sung by the nightclub singer Magaldi in *Evita*, and the popular Latin tune "Cherry Pink and Apple Blossom White," by the composer who wrote under the nom de plume Louiguy, as "self-evident."[19] He concludes that since the borrowing "sticks so closely to those features which create the character of the Louiguy number, the whole piece can even be seen as a vocal extemporization around 'Cherry Pink and Apple Blossom White' in the manner of an interpretation-in-performance of the original."[20] In short, Lloyd Webber's "Thousand Stars" has accomplished for the unknown Louigay what Romberg's *Blossom Time* earlier did for Schubert.

By way of comparison, Magnolia in *Show Boat* sings Charles K. Harris's "After the Ball" to evoke fin-de-siècle popular music. The published score, however, credits Harris (and not Kern) as the composer. The composers of much of "I Don't Know How to Love Him" and "On This Night of a Thousand Stars" receive no attribution. Before moving on to *Phantom* I would like to bring up another likely "musical reminiscence" that to my knowledge has gone unrecognized, at least in print. When I used to give an annual musical plagiarism lecture to non-music majors, I frequently asked students whether the melody and harmony of the opening of "I'd Be Surprisingly Good for You," also from *Evita*, reminded them of any other popular song they happened to know. Invariably several students would immediately volunteer the Beatles' "Yesterday."

The relationship between these songs is analogous, but not identical, to the bop practice of creating new tunes using harmonic progressions from older popular tunes (e.g., "Shaw Nuff" and "Cottontail," among others, employ the harmony of Gershwin's "I Got Rhythm"). Among music historians, the term of choice to describe this practice is *contrafacta* (the plural of *contrafactum*), a fancy name used to describe either the appropriation of harmony from one song to another or the recycling of melodies with new texts. "I'd Be Surprisingly Good for You" borrows more than a little from both the melody and harmony of "Yesterday," but unlike most contrafacta the borrowing does not continue throughout the entire song. The technique of contrafacta as more commonly practiced was widely used in the Renaissance and can be found later in multi-texted reharmonized chorale melodies in Bach's *St. Matthew Passion* and in popular songs recycled with texts, such as the conversions of "Anacreon in Heaven" into "The Star Spangled Banner" and "God Save the King" into "America." The technique ensures unity and musical integration and provides opportunities to create new dramatic meanings for previously heard musical themes.

Several borrowing possibilities in *Phantom* have been proposed, some by more than one author. Both Mark Grant and Michael Walsh, for example, suggest that the distinctive, powerful, and meaningfully employed descending instrumental chromatic figure that introduces *Phantom*'s overture, title song, and seven additional Phantom appearances in the score is noticeably derived from Ralph Vaughan William's Second (or "London") Symphony, the first version of which appeared in the years before World War I (see Example 16.1).[21]

No fewer than three borrowings have been offered for the opening phrase of "Music of the Night" alone: "Come to Me, Bend to Me" from *Brigadoon*, "School Days" from 1907 ("School days, school days / Dear old Golden Rule days"), and a phrase from "Recondite armonia" from Puccini's *Tosca*.[22] In each case only the first five notes, and in the first two examples the rhythms

Example 16.1. Descending chromatic motive in Vaughan Williams's Second ("London") Symphony

also, are the same. The "School Days" connection became a part of popular culture when the character played by Billy Crystal in the movie *Forget Paris* (1995) left a performance of *Phantom* with Debra Winger accusing "Music of the Night" of ripping off the old tune. To prove his claim, Crystal sang the opening phrase of the earlier melody.

The second phrase of the Phantom's serenade shares eight consecutive notes and the same rhythmic contour with another melody, this time by Puccini (see Example 16.2). Snelson acknowledges that this phrase in "Music of the Night" "is identical to the climactic section of Dick Johnson's declaration of love to Minnie at the conclusion of act I of *La fanciulla del West*." Although he does not claim a dramatic purpose in the borrowing, in Lloyd Webber's defense Snelson finds an *"emotional* [italics mine] link from one musical theater work to the other."[23]

Example 16.2. Dick Johnson's "Una gioia" from Puccini's *La fanciulla del West*

Walsh notes that the melody first sung by Christine when she describes the Phantom to Raoul on the rooftop of the opera house with the words "Yet in his eyes, all the sadness of the world," "is closely related to Liù's suicide music in the last act of Puccini's *Turandot*" (see Example 16.3).[24]

This is not the first time audiences heard this famous theme, however. It appeared earlier in the orchestra after the Phantom had cursed Christine for unmasking him in his lair and again in the orchestra when Raoul and Christine first arrive on the roof. The theme then reappears at two significant moments in the second act, once when Raoul asks Christine to sing the

Example 16.3. Liù's motive in Puccini's *Turandot*

Phantom's opera and later when Christine tells the Phantom in the final scene that "This haunted face holds no horror for me now." The melody is one of the most important in *Phantom*, as Liù's melody is in *Turandot*.

Surprisingly, neither Citron, Snelson, nor Sternfeld mentions the extraordinary melodic and rhythmic correspondence between this *Phantom* theme and Liù's comparably significant melody, heard relentlessly for nearly eight minutes in *Turandot*'s second act. Snelson, who alone among this trio acknowledges that scholars need to seriously consider the issue of Lloyd Webber's borrowing, provides numerous examples that he tries to explain or justify, but not this one. For the most part, Sternfeld's response to Lloyd Webber's accusers seems unwarrantedly dismissive: "When critics or historians do go hunting for actual stolen tunes, they rarely find any, and when they do, the results do not amount to much."[25]

Unless one is wearing a mask that covers the ears, however, I would argue that borrowings come to some of us unbidden and that they do add up to something significant. The amount Lloyd Webber borrows from *Fanciulla* in "The Music of the Night" and the *Turandot* borrowing in "Yet in his eyes" and "This haunted face" is approximately the same as Bernstein's appropriation of Wagner's "Redemption through love" motive in "I Have a Love" and the death processional in *West Side Story*. The issue is not the fact of borrowing or even how much is borrowed. The problem lies in the gratuitousness and apparent arbitrariness of the borrowings. In another famous, more recent Puccini borrowing that occurs in *Rent*, Roger, the character doing the borrowing, informs the audience that he is trying to compose a love song that does not sound like "Musetta's Waltz" from Puccini's *La bohème*. Eventually Puccini's melody returns, but not before Roger has finished his own original love song, "Your Eyes," inspired, but not composed, by Puccini.

To a remarkable extent perhaps not seen since his British predecessor Handel, who is nonetheless generally credited for borrowing with interest, Lloyd Webber reuses music by other composers and does not acknowledge his sources. A typical Lloyd Webber show also contains more reprises and contrafacta than most previous and current successful Broadway shows. More significant than the number of reprises is the frequent absence of dramatic meaning. Lloyd Webber continues to receive criticism from many quarters for these practices and habits and audience approbation in spite of them. Either way, friends and foes alike perhaps might concede that the works he created for London and Broadway from *Joseph* to *Sunset Boulevard* amply support Lloyd Webber's claim as the reigning champion of Broadway.[26]

Musical Organicism

If Rodgers and Hammerstein did not invent what soon would become known as the "integrated" musical, their success with *Oklahoma!* and *Carousel* popularized this approach, gave it cachet, and arguably made it desirable, if not imperative, for others to follow in their path. The fundamental principles of the integrated musical, in contrast to the allegedly more frivolous fare of the 1920s and 1930s, are that the songs advance a plot, flow directly from the dialogue, and express the thoughts of the characters who sing them. In addition, the presence of dance serves to advance the plot and enhance the dramatic meaning of the songs that precede them, and the orchestra, through accompaniment and underscoring, parallels, complements, or advances the action.[27]

Despite increased attention to these basic principles of integration, which also involved greater attention to the integrity, coherence, and depth of the book, the principle of the integrated musical is to some extent undermined by the separation of dialogue and song.[28] The megamusicals of Lloyd Webber and Boublil-Schönberg from the late 1970s through the mid-1990s increased the possibility of integration by making their works through-sung. Even such a harsh detractor of the megamusical as Scott McMillin, who finds *Phantom* "pretentious and overblown," concedes that the through-sung musical, often composed in a rock style, surpasses the Rodgers and Hammerstein integrative model: "I can see the logic of claiming that the drive for integration has finally been achieved in Lloyd Webber. Perhaps *Phantom* should be celebrated for being a musical on the verge of becoming an opera."[29]

One of the problematic side effects of the integrated, through-sung megamusical is the potential for integration that lacks dramatic meaning. *Evita*, *Les Misérables*, and *Phantom* are musically integrated in the sense that they use a relatively small repertoire of motives and themes and recycle these melodies continuously, usually with new lyrics (i.e., contrafacta, a term used extensively in Joseph Swain's chapters on Lloyd Webber and Boublil-Schönberg).[30] When characters in musicals use each other's music and when the underscored passages appear without seeming regard for the appropriateness of the appropriation, the increased integration leads to decreased dramatic meaning. The reuse, or overuse, of contrafacta in the work of the composer at hand, according to Swain, "has become a rather careless infatuation with [Lloyd] Webber's not inconsiderable powers of melody."[31]

The reliance on contrafactum also frequently results in mismatched texts. Raymond Knapp discusses the implications of the problem: "Especially in its seemingly wanton recycling of music and inadequate attention to text setting, *Evita* is seen as lacking two perceived strengths of the more traditional Broadway stage: musical variety and an oft-demonstrated capacity for marrying words and music so intimately that neither seems sufficient without the other. According to this ideal, Lloyd Webber's use of the same music for quite different songs seems fundamentally inadequate."[32] The problem is not the reuse, or even the ubiquitous reuse of the material. The problem is the lack of discrimination in the recycling of melodic material. When used indiscriminately, the opportunities for increased dramatic meanings are squandered. Music can become just an attractive but subsidiary adjunct to the show rather than a conveyor of idiomatic meanings and moods. I will return to the use and reuse of themes in the section "Music and Meaning in *The Phantom of the Opera*."

The Phantom of the Opera: *The Novel and the Silent Film*

The story line of Andrew Lloyd Webber and Hal Prince's *The Phantom of the Opera* can be traced to two sources, the classic fairy tale about the Beauty and the Beast and George du Maurier's novel *Trilby* from 1894. The novel, in which the musical magician Svengali places the nonmusical ingénue Trilby in a trance during which she attains great operatic success, was a popular novel in both England and America in its day and was soon adapted into a popular play. Between September 1909 and January 1910, Gaston Leroux's new twist on this story, *Le Fantôme de l'Opéra*, appeared in serial form (in French); the English translation *The Phantom of the Opera* followed in 1911. More than seventy years later, three years after the phenomenon of *Cats* had begun its long-lived London run, Lloyd Webber found a copy of Leroux's gothic novel in a used book shop. The novel inspired the modern-day musical theater Svengali (Lloyd Webber), inspired by his Trilby and wife at the time (Sarah Brightman), to create a musical version that proved to be a greater phenomenon even than *Cats*, at least on Broadway, when *The Phantom of the Opera* opened in London (1986) and New York (1988).

The genesis of *Phantom* has been told often, and authoritative summaries of the novel and film and television adaptations can be found in George Perry's *The Complete "Phantom of the Opera."* Less explored are the creative choices Lloyd Webber and Prince—in collaboration with the Midas-touched producer of *Les Misérables* the previous year, Cameron Macintosh

(b. 1946)—made in their conversion of Leroux's novel and the comparably influential 1925 classic silent film directed by Rupert Julian and starring Lon Chaney as the Phantom, Marie Philbin as Christine, and Norman Kerry as Raoul.[33] Although the novel provided a broad structure and the film a more focused structure (in addition to providing a visual model for the opera house stage and majestic staircase), the Lloyd Webber-Prince version departed in significant ways from each.

The film had already accomplished some of Prince's work. Foster Hirsch credits Prince for removing the gruesome details of the Phantom's medical afflictions and early biography, the back story to Christine's relationship to her father (it was the father's prophecy of an angel-to-come that worked on Christine's susceptibility to the magical charms of the Angel of Music), and the childhood romance between Christine and Raoul.[34] All of this material, plus Leroux's detailed explanation of how the Phantom accomplished his supernatural tricks, had already vanished in the 1925 film. The character of the Persian, the man who knew the true story about Erik, the future Phantom, was retained from the novel but transformed in the film into a suspicious character often seen lurking about the same time film viewers witnessed actions attributed to the Phantom. In the early portions of the film it seemed possible that the Persian and the Phantom were the same. Deeper into the story, viewers learn that the Persian is working on behalf of the police to apprehend the Phantom.

As in the novel, the Persian, who sports an astrakhan hat, is the detective Ledoux (a name that sounds similar and is spelled suspiciously close to the novel's author Leroux) who tries to help Raoul escape harm in the vast and literally torturous underground of the Paris Opera as they pursue Christine and her abductor, the Phantom. To achieve what is often referred to as the "Abbott shorthand," in deference to the ability of director George Abbott, Prince's mentor, to capture the essence of a plot, both forms of the Persian, the Phantom's former acquaintance in the novel and the private investigator Ledoux from the silent film, entirely disappeared from the musical. To fill in for the absence of the Persian, another mysterious character, Madame Giry, served as a secret liaison between the Phantom and the other principals. No one felt the need to provide an alternative character to replace detective Ledoux.

The Lloyd Webber-Prince scenario added much to the novel and film to enhance the plot and alter its effect. By making the Phantom physically less deformed and musically more brilliant and seductive, he becomes for the first time a serious "romantic alternative" to Raoul.[35] Raoul, too, has become a more endearing figure, especially when compared to his depiction in the novel and film as a condescending, controlling character who possesses neither sympathy nor understanding for Christine's plight nor the heroism to withstand the Phantom's threats. In the novel and the 1925 silent film, the Phantom's spell inhibits Christine's judgment, and her fear of the Phantom causes her to put Raoul at arm's length. In a significant discrepancy, through-out much of the musical the Phantom is portrayed as a relatively benevolent figure who has entranced Christine into believing he is the Angel of Music as prophesied by Christine's father. Until "The Point of No Return" toward the end of the evening, audiences would probably not be too shocked if Christine decided to join her Phantom in the depths of the Paris Opera and leave Raoul behind.

Although film viewers see the Phantom at his organ and know that he is composing *Don Juan Triumphant*, inspired by his love for Christine, it is only in the stage musical that audiences witness and actually hear his trium-phant work. As a modernist decades ahead of his time compositionally, the Phantom, when he isn't serenading Christine with a lyrical lullaby ("Music of the Night"), composes music that tends to be dissonant and even vio-lent. It is filled with whole-tone scales and whole-tone harmonies, sounds that before long would be associated with the real-life French modernist Claude Debussy (with a touch of Vaughan Williams as the basis for a vamp in the title song in a rock style, see Example 16.1). Not only does the whole-tone scale pervade the phrase "Those who tangle with Don Juan" (which the traditionally trained and musically limited Piangi cannot master in the rehearsal [act II, scene 4]), but it also appropriately melodically and har-monically underlies the "I have brought you" verse to "Music of the Night" and, less explicably, when the same verse returns at the outset of "All I Ask of You."[36]

In the novel and the silent film, all the opera scenes—prior to the time when the opera scenes were granted the gift of sound in 1930—are taken from Charles Gounod's opera *Faust*, probably the most popular French opera between its premiere in 1859 and the appearance of the novel and silent film of *Phantom*. After the largely spoken Prologue told as a flashback, a framing device absent in both the novel and film, the story of *Phantom* in the musical begins with a rehearsal of *Hannibal*, clearly a parody of the once towering mid-nineteenth-century French composer Giacomo Meyerbeer. Later in the first act, Lloyd Webber offers a second operatic pastiche, *Il Muto*, this time in the late-eighteenth-century Italian style of Antonio Salieri, another largely forgotten composer. At the center of the second act, musical themes of the first act come together in the Phantom's creation, *Don Juan Triumphant*, which offers the dissonant sound of modernism, including whole-tone scales and harmonies, an appropriate musical language for a precociously avant-garde and vengeful composer.

The Musical Film

It took nearly twenty years from its London premiere before the musical film adaptation of *The Phantom of the Opera* arrived in 2004. The film was directed by Joel Schumacher, an American director who came on the scene in the 1980s with *St. Elmo's Fire* and *The Lost Boys*. In the 1990s he directed two films based on John Grisham novels, *The Client* and *A Time to Kill*, and replaced Tim Burton as the director of choice in the ongoing series of Batman films, *Batman Forever* and *Batman and Robin*. The film version of *Phantom*, which the composer had discussed with Schumacher in the late 1980s, was for the most part faithful in spirit and letter to the stage original. In contrast to Burton's *Sweeney Todd*, Schumacher's *Phantom* is also "a movie based on a stage show."[37] At a leisurely 143 minutes it is able to accommodate most of the original stage version, with a few minor (but not inconsequential cuts) and a few moments of cinematic and non-verbal leisure.[38]

The film, shot in a faded black and white tint, ranges backward in time from 1919 to 1870, the auction omits the Meyerbeer memorabilia auctioned in the stage version, and film viewers are introduced not only to the Vicomte

The Phantom of the Opera, 2004 film. Close-up of Christine Daaé (Emmy Rossum) and The Phantom (Gerard Butler).

The Phantom of the Opera, 2004 film. Christine Daaé (Rossum) and The
Phantom (Butler) performing in The Phantom's opera *Don Juan Triumphant*.

de Chagny, or Raoul (Patrick Wilson), but also to Madame Giry (Miranda
Richardson), whom he outbids for the monkey. The original stage version
begins in 1905 with a Prologue that takes place at an auction in which items
from a distant time are being auctioned off, a poster from the opera *Hannibal*,
"a wooden pistol and three human skulls from the 1831 production of *Robert
le Diable* by Meyerbeer" (an opera actually composed for the Paris Opéra by
the composer, unlike the fictitious Meyerbeer *Hannibal* parody), a papier-
mâché music box of a monkey in Persian robes clanging cymbals, and a
chandelier from the Opéra restored from a shattered state. The auctioneer
switches on the chandelier and the scene miraculously shifts to a rehearsal
of *Hannibal* at the Opéra Populaire in Paris 1861.

Prince never returns to the older Vicomte in the stage version to remind
audiences that they are watching a flashback, but Schumacher makes several
strategic returns to Raoul and the events of 1919 in the film, starting with
the scene in act I between Christine Daaé (Emmy Rossum) and the Phantom (Gerard Butler) in the Phantom's lair (about 47 minutes into the film).
The last of these flash-forwards occur at the film's conclusion when Raoul
is wheeled to the cemetery to place the papier-mâché monkey on a tomb.
The tomb inscription informs us that Raoul and Christine, the future Countess de Chagny (1854–1917), were married after the events of the story, that

she was only sixteen at the time the story takes place—Rossum herself was only seventeen at the time of filming—and died two years before the film begins. Film viewers also learn that history remembers her as a "Beloved Wife and Mother" and not as an opera star. Christine did not have it all. The final image of the film is a withered rose, just like the rose the Phantom gave to Christine after her first performance nearly fifty years earlier. In the stage version the Phantom disappeared at the end and stage audiences never learn whether he was alive or dead in 1905. In contrast, the film lets viewers know that the Phantom still lives (thus preparing for the possibility of a sequel) and that he has by no means forgotten the only woman who was able to love him.[39]

Whereas the stage version sustains much of the mystery until the end about the connections between Madame Giry and the Phantom, the film soon lets us know by silent visual clues that Madame understands what is happening. Later in the film, when Madame Giry explains to Raoul about the Phantom's early history, Schumacher assists her tale with vivid cinematic flashbacks. Film viewers learn from Giry and see the documentation, not only that the Phantom was deformed from birth but that he was abused and battered before lashing back by garroting his father with the Punjab lasso. Finally, film viewers see Giry smuggling the future Phantom safely into the opera house where he would establish a refuge for the rest of his life.

The film takes advantage of other opportunities to add clarity and remove mystery. Raoul is now identified in the first scene as a Count during the rehearsal instead of as a mysterious aristocrat who recognizes Christine from his box at a performance. Raoul does not notice Christine at the rehearsal, but she notices him and informs Meg (and film viewers) that he was a childhood sweetheart. When Christine travels by coach to the cemetery to visit her father's tomb, stage audiences might rightfully wonder how the Phantom found her there. Film viewers watch the Phantom as he overhears Christine tell a drunken stable hand she is going to the cemetery, easily knocks out the intended driver, and takes her there himself.

Madame Giry's explanation about the Phantom's origins gives film viewers a more sympathetic understanding of the childhood abuse that eventually created a pathetic murderer, albeit a genius. Not only does the Phantom's life acquire a context, he is also less loathsome physically than earlier Phantoms. Thus, when Christine unmasks the Phantom during the performance of his opera, viewers see a man with burn-like scars on the upper portion of one side of his face, but nowhere near the disfigurement that shocked film audiences in 1925 when Lon Chaney was revealed for the first time in the Phantom's lair. Even more than the stage Phantom, the film Phantom of 2004 was a dashing and credible romantic alternative. As Christine observes in the climactic scene, it is the Phantom's soul, not his face, where "the true distortion lies."

Lloyd Webber and Schumacher also found an imaginative way to add a new song. Since, as previously noted, musical film adaptations are encouraged to include at least one new song in order to become eligible for an academy award, an early plan was to give the Phantom a new solo song called "No One Would Listen." When the film's length became prohibitive and the song was viewed unnecessary (other than perhaps to secure an award nomination), Schumacher and Lloyd Webber took the song away from the Phantom and inserted its melody as underscoring when Raoul places the monkey on his wife's tomb at the end of the film. Immediately thereafter the song can be heard as the credits roll. The title has been changed to "Learn to Be Lonely" and the lyrics are also new. Since Raoul's "All I Ask of You" usurped portions of "The Music of the Night" and transformed other parts of this song into something new, it is fitting that the Phantom's song in its final context and associations with Raoul would retain the melody of a Phantom tune, another example of a contrafactum.[40]

The film takes various liberties in scene order, such as the placement of the cemetery scene (act II, scene 5) directly after Madame Giry's story about the Phantom's origins in scene 2, returning after the cemetery scene to portions of scenes 3 and 4. Another revealing example of Schumacher's desire to avoid continuity occurs between what was act I, scene 5 (the scene in the Phantom's lair where he sings "Music of the Night"), and the next morning when Christine unmasks the Phantom while he is playing the organ. After "Music of the Night" in the film, instead of the continuation of the scene between the Phantom and Christine that stage audiences experience, film viewers are shown some leisurely new footage of Meg Giry looking for Christine, her discovery of the mirror ("the mechanics of what seemed at first magic") and the passageway to the Phantom. The music of "I Have Brought You" grows louder as the shadow lurking ominously behind Meg turns out to be her mother reaching out in the darkness to place a hand on her inquisitive daughter's shoulder and lead her back to the safety of the dressing room. Only then does the film return to the Phantom's lair.

The next scene in the film corresponds to scene 7. Joseph Buquet, described at first meeting in the screenplay as a leering "sinister scene shifter in overalls" (a description that helps viewers adjust to his violent death later in the film), is explaining to the ballet girls about the Phantom and his magical lasso to their "horror and delight." Madame Giry appears and chastises him for this sacrilege. Both Buquet and Giry sing what I am calling the "I remember" motive, the music that becomes *Don Juan B*, previously unheard on stage since the Prologue. The next morning the monkey music box gently awakens Christine. The first music she sings is the "I remember" motive, which viewers have just heard Buquet and Madame Giry sing several times.[41] The next image is the Phantom at his organ, but unlike the stage version, film viewers do not hear him. Is he composing an important theme from his opera (e.g., "Tangled in the Winding Sheets!" or *Don Juan C*)? Film viewers will never know.

The film adaptations of both *My Fair Lady* and *West Side Story* included intermissions during their opening runs in movie theaters (although in neither case did the intermission in the film correspond precisely to the conclusion of act I in its stage counterparts). Had it been the 1950s or 1960s, it would have easily been possible in a musical film adaptation of *Phantom* to present an intermission break at the end of what was act I of *Phantom* on the stage. Forty years later, however, when single features had long been the rule, it was no longer necessary, or even a realistic option, to make a film with an intermission. This posed a problem for *Phantom* (only ten minutes shorter than the *West Side Story* film), since the first act contained such a dramatic and scenically dazzling climax: the freefall of the chandelier. Instead of the falling chandelier, the musical film thus fades forward to 1919 to reveal a shot of Raoul observing a young couple admiring the sumptuous jewels in the windows of a jewelry store. Finally, much closer to the end of the film, the Phantom launches the chandelier at the climax of his opera. Its fall creates a fire and in the chaos the Phantom is able to move Christine to the opera underground as the film moves to its dramatic conclusion.

The film, which cost somewhere between $60 and $70 million to produce, did well during its first month, but less well financially in the United States than either *The Incredibles* or *The SpongeBob SquarePants Movie*. It also failed to garner the critical acclaim lavished on the film versions of *Chicago* (2002) or later, *Sweeney Todd* (2007). Nevertheless, the $100 million it earned in world markets provided its makers with popular and financial vindication. Although lacking the transformative qualities of the *Chicago* and *Sweeney Todd* films, Schumacher's *Phantom* offers a scenically beautiful and admirably sung souvenir of Broadway's great stage hit.

Music and Meaning in The Phantom of the Opera

In earlier chapters, when comparing the relative dramatic meanings between the second act reprises of "If I Loved You" from *Carousel* and "So in Love" from *Kiss Me, Kate*, I suggested that the former was based on something Billy and Julie Jordan shared while the latter seemed more for the purpose of bringing back a great song.[42] While one might argue whether Fred's reprise of Lilli's song demonstrates a bond that transcends what audiences have experienced in the play, and it is certainly a priceless romantic song that audiences enjoy rehearing for its own sake, I concluded that an opportunity for dramatic meaning was lost. I also noted that even Puccini advocate Roger Parker acknowledged the lack of dramatic meaning when "E lucevan le stelle" returns in act III of *Tosca*, the opera that prompted Joseph Kerman's famously derogatory description of the popular work as a "shabby little shocker."[43]

Several scholars offer dramatic explanations for the reuse of Lloyd Webber's recurring themes in *Phantom*, and in some cases the explanations are plausible. As with Puccini's *Tosca*, however, other explanations are less persuasive. The problem lies not with the dramatic uses served by the seven big tunes in the show ("Think of Me," "Angel of Music," "The Phantom of the Opera," "The Music of the Night," "All I Ask of You," "Wishing You Were Somehow Here Again," and "The Point of No Return"), but with the dozen or more motives, many of which I argue are used indiscriminately. Ironically, the problem is too *much* integration.

A comparison between two complementary sections from *The Phantom of the Opera* reveals the extent to which Lloyd Webber has taken advantage of or thwarted the opportunities for musical meaning and dramatic effectiveness. The sections in question are the first scenes between the Phantom and Christine in his lair in act I, scenes 5 and 6, and the performance of the Phantom's opera in act II, scene 7 (the online website offers a detailed thematic outline of these scenes). The scenes share a considerable amount of musical material, and it is this sharing that can potentially lead either to increased or decreased meaning.

Some themes are used with consistency and effectiveness. The descending chromatic scale that figures so prominently in the title song, for example, first heard throughout the overture, firmly establishes a connection between the musical figure and the Phantom that will follow him wherever he goes. The fact that it may be derived from Vaughan Williams (Example 16.1) does not diminish its dramatic effectiveness in *Phantom*. The orchestra announces the Phantom's chromatic presence at the conclusion of "Prima Donna"; they play it when audiences see Buquet's dead body hanging from the stage, when the Phantom makes the chandelier fall at the end of act I, and finally when Christine publicly removes the Phantom's mask during the performance of *Don Juan Triumphant*. Another important motive that is effectively associated with the Phantom is first heard fittingly on the words "He's here, the Phantom of the opera." This occurs early in the work where it interrupts Carlotta's rendition of "Think of Me." Like the chromatic figure, the motive first associated with "He's here, the Phantom of the opera," will appear numerous times (at least eight), always in proximity with the Phantom—or the idea of the Phantom—and always serving a persuasive dramatic effect.

On several occasions Lloyd Webber also goes beyond thematic recurrence and creatively transforms his musical material. For example, the phrase often repeated by the lead tenor Piangi—who futilely attempts to sing the ascending whole-tone scale on the words, "Those who tang-"[without the "le"], in the rehearsal of *Don Juan Triumphant* in act II, scene 4— was fore-shadowed as violent orchestral underscoring when the Phantom curses Christine in act I, scene 6, for removing his mask. The "I remember" phrase that Christine sings at the beginning of this scene also returns in a loud and dissonant version in the orchestral introduction of *Don Juan Triumphant* and in a comparably dissonant choral version when the chorus begins the sung portion of the work on the words "Here the sire may serve the dam" (shown in the outlines of the online website).

All together, the first part of the "I remember" phrase appears no less than fourteen times in the opera, more than any other motive; the second part by itself appears on two other occasions.[44] It is the first music sung in the Pro-logue, the auction flashback which occurs forty-four years after the story's main action, and it is indeed possible that the aged Raoul remembers a major phrase he himself heard his beloved Christine sing at the climactic moment when she kisses the Phantom in his lair. But why do Buquet, Raoul, Madame Giry, and the Phantom sing this theme? Its transformation in *Don Juan Trium-phant* offers the possibility that the theme belongs to Christine and that she has served as a muse and inspiration for the Phantom's great and forward-looking operatic work. Unfortunately, this possibility goes unrealized.

In the film, but not the original London cast album, the "I remember" motive can be heard earlier, albeit softly, in the orchestra under the dialogue that followed the moment when the backdrop fell in front of Carlotta, inter-rupting her inappropriately operatic rendition of "Think of Me." It reappears in the film soon thereafter when viewers observe the Phantom stealthily lock the door to Christine's dressing room (an action not shown in the stage version). Placing the short scene with Buquet and Madame Giry *before* the continuation of the lair scene (the morning after) not only interrupts the con-tinuity of the scene between Christine and the Phantom, but it also deprives Christine of the opportunity to be the first to sing this motive in the main part of the story. If Christine was the first to sing the motive, it would be possible to imagine a scenario in which her music serves as the inspiration behind the Phantom's opera. It is not dramatically clear how Buquet and Madame Giry would have heard a theme from this as-yet-unwritten work. By placing this motive in the mouths of these characters, one must conclude that any-one involved with the Phantom would know the "I remember" theme and are free to use it in normal conversation. In this case, enhanced integration results in a reduction of dramatic meaning. The theme no longer belongs to Raoul and Christine. It belongs to anyone who knows the Phantom.

When audiences eventually hear *Don Juan Triumphant* they might realize (perhaps on a second or third hearing) that the music the Phantom played at his organ before Christine awoke to sing "I remember" functions in retrospect as the starting point of this work. Here too audiences can imagine the Phantom, inspired by Christine's presence, formulating the seeds of his masterpiece. Unfortunately, this possibility is removed when the orchestra inexplicably returns to this theme as Raoul and Christine escape to the roof toward the end of act I. It was noted previously that at the end of the Balcony Scene in *West Side Story* an omniscient and clairvoyant orchestra explained what the characters do not know (see Example 13.5). It is not clear in this case what dramatic purpose is served by using the Phantom's *Don Triumphant* theme to accompany the flight of Raoul and Christine. Instead, the indiscriminate recycling of a theme becomes a lost opportunity to achieve a meaningful dramatic association between theme and character.

The lair scene in act I contains other reminiscences of music previously heard and new music that will be reheard in act II. In the former category, the "I remember" motive and "Masquerade" appeared in the Prologue and "Angel of Music" had set up associations between Christine and the Phantom in Christine's duet with Meg "After the Gala" (scene 2) and in Christine's duet with the Phantom between the mirrors in "Christine's Dressing Room" (scene 3). The verse of "Music of the Night" ("I have brought you"), which was anticipated in the "Little Lotte" music, returns in the performance of *Don Juan Triumphant* as the verse for "The Point of No Return."[45] This latter return constitutes another meaningful and powerful connection between the Phantom and Christine that retains these associations when Christine employs its bridge and relates her visit to the Phantom's lair with Raoul in the final scene of act I, "The Roof of the Opera House" (scene 10). The Phantom himself recalls the music of "Stranger Than You Dreamt It" in the reprise of "Notes" in act II, scene 3, when he instructs the house to "Let my opera begin!" to launch the performance of *Don Juan Triumphant* (at the end of scene 6), and in the final confrontation with Raoul (scene 9).

The last important music introduced in the lair scene ("The Next Morning," act I, scene 6) is the instrumental music that followed Christine's unmasking and the Phantom's violent response. This is the theme that so closely resembles Liù's theme in *Turandot* (Example 16.3). On this first appearance it is heard and not sung. Snelson describes this melody as the "Sympathy" theme and Sternfeld labels it the "Yet in his eyes" phrase (I am tempted to call it Liù's theme). After the first unmasking in the lair, this

theme will return four times, the last three of which are sung in three different pairs of conversations: Christine to Raoul on the roof ("Yet in his eyes"),
Raoul to Christine shortly before *Don Juan Triumphant* ("You said yourself
he was nothing but a man"), and Christine to Phantom in his lair during the
final scene ("This haunted face holds no horror for me now"). It makes sense
why Christine, in describing the Phantom, would sing this music to Raoul
and why she would return to this phrase in the final scene. On the other
hand, the appropriation of the phrase by Raoul seems gratuitous. Although
audiences might understand how he would know this theme, it remains
unpersuasive why he would choose to sing it.

The next appropriation by Raoul of the Phantom's music is fully appropriate. It also demonstrates what is arguably the most ingenious transformation from one theme into another in the work and a transformation
that also makes a strong dramatic point. The appropriation occurs in the
opening phrase of "All I Ask of You," the love duet between Raoul and
Christine in the final scene of act I, scene 10.[46] Raoul's tune, later sung by
Christine as well, bears three subtle but collectively meaningful connections with Phantom's serenade to Christine in his lair in scene 5. Sung by
the Phantom as a solo, "The Music of the Night" possessed serenity and
a seductiveness that is never fully recaptured again when it is reprised.
Nevertheless, its initial power is sufficient to persuade audiences, and
Christine, that the Phantom, indeed for the first time in many adaptations, offers a viable romantic alternative to Raoul. After a gentle sustained D-flat major harmony for four measures, the harmony moves for
the first time to a second harmony on the words "Silently the senses" (this
is the phrase that borrows directly from Puccini's *Il Fanciulla* shown in
Example 16.2). The harmony selected, the subdominant (G-flat major) creates a hymn-like quality that returns on the note of the song (on the word
"night"), which can be identified as an enhanced plagal IV-I (or Amen)
cadence from G♭ to D♭. Similarly, Raoul's "All I Ask of You" opens with a
tonic pedal, also on D♭ for more than two full measures before it moves to
its second chord, which not coincidentally is also a IV chord on G♭ (on the
words "harm you").

The connections between "The Music of the Night" and "All I Ask of
You" are even more striking and recognizable, as both songs share an *identical* final phrase. Just as the verse of "Music of the Night" ("I have brought
you") returns to introduce the verse of "The Point of No Return" ("You
have come here"), the final phrase of "All I Ask of You" shares the same
music as the end of "The Music of the Night" (in each case incorporating the
words of the song's title, another fleeting contrafactum). But the openings of
each song are also remarkably intertwined, albeit subtly so. Snelson offers

a musical example in which he juxtaposes these openings and explains perceptively that "the opening phrase of one is pretty much a musical anagram of the other, for both melodies encompass the same pitches, A♭-D♭-E♭-F, and both are bounded by their dominant at lower and upper octaves."[47] Both openings also reach these lower and upper dominants the same way, by a two-note descent from F to A-flat (ironically on the syllable "sharpens" in "Music of the Night" and "darkness" in "All I Ask of You") and an eighth-note ascent, D♭-E♭-F, that arrives on A♭ at the end of the phrase in the second measure of each song. In singing this "duet" between the Phantom and Raoul, one could follow the first phrase of either song with the first phrase of the other without any loss of coherence.

Snelson offers a persuasive explanation as to why Raoul appropriates the Phantom's unheard theme:

> Both men are trying to lure their prey, initially one ostensibly for art and one for human love, but ultimately both for emotional and physical love; both are investing Christine with their own desires and aspirations; each represents a different potential within Christine.... The Phantom and Raoul are reflections of each other—each defining himself through his opposite number—yet they share a common purpose in the seduction of Christine; and so it is appropriate that their two big vocal gestures should have common features.[48]

More than any other factor, it is the song "Music of the Night" that persuades Christine (and the audience) that the Phantom should be taken seriously as a romantic alternative to Raoul. In "The Point of No Return," Raoul gains the trust and love of Christine by usurping the Phantom's music, making it his own, and thus breaking the spell. In the end, Lloyd Webber's Christine sings the music of the Sympathy (or Liù's) theme, "Yet in his eyes," and ultimately rejects the Phantom, the man who developed her potential as an artist. Instead, she chooses the soon-to-be-endangered Raoul, the man who offers a life of wealth and high society but who might not embrace Christine's professional career. It is crucial to the Lloyd Webber-Prince vision of the story that the reason Christine decides as she does is neither the Phantom's "haunted face" nor any lack of musical talent, but the Phantom's vengeful, murderous, and immoral soul. It is striking that Lloyd Webber gives Christine one of her most original and expressive melodies (and a melody that does not belong to anyone else) to express her conflict about whether to regard the Phantom as an angel or a monster ("Twisted every way what answer can I give?).[49]

In addition to borrowing and reuse issues, some may legitimately wonder why in a non-rock score the title song should contain such a prominent rock beat or why the Meyerbeer parody, *Il Muto*, which sets up for the most part a reasonable facsimile of mid-nineteenth-century French grand opera style, would include a generic pop song "Think of Me" that undermines the evocation of a historical style. In the film, servants insert ear plugs when Carlotta begins to sing in an overdone operatic manner and remove them when Christine continues with her lighter and more pop manner, modeling a nihilistic boredom with the opera tradition for a presumably appreciative audience—yet this is the same tradition Lloyd Webber draws on frequently (although relatively few in the audience know it).[50] Is it fair to ask "What would Sondheim do" or is popularity the final critical arbiter for these decisions?

Lloyd Webber may not be Sondheim, but his ability to reach audiences is impressive. *Phantom*, the show that Snelson and other authorities considers the Lloyd Webber show "most assured of a place in the canon," is a musical that authors of surveys on Broadway should take seriously for its stage-craft, theatrical polish, and memorable melodies.[51] Snelson admirably sums up the significance of this achievement: "His work has inspired a visceral response to be praised for itself, and the enjoyment in the dramatic moment or the phrase that catches the ear so effectively is not to be lightly dismissed. This, after all, is fundamental to the greatest of musicals composers and the most long-lived of shows."[52]

Although Lloyd Webber continued to grow musically in his next two musicals *Aspects of Love* (1989) and *Sunset Boulevard* (1993), he would not be able to capture the magic that placed Broadway audiences in raptures over *Cats* and *Phantom of the Opera* for so many years. *Aspects of Love* not only received a critical bashing, but it lasted less than a year on Broadway, and while *Sunset Boulevard* won the major Tony Awards and had a relatively long run, it managed to lose a record $25 million.[53] After *Sunset*, Lloyd Webber was unable to secure a Broadway venue for either of his next two shows, *Whistle Down the Wind* (1996) or *The Beautiful Game* (2000), and his next return to New York was as a producer (not a composer) for *Bombay Dreams* (2003), another failure. In fact, since *Sunset Boulevard* closed, only one new Lloyd Webber show, *The Woman in White*, managed a short New York engagement (108 performances) in 2004.

Just as Rodgers and Hammerstein musicals typically fared far better in New York than in London, Lloyd Webber's shows were more warmly received on his home turf with the exception of the initial run of *Joseph and the Amazing Technicolor Dreamcoat*.[54] The pattern continued with the shows that followed *Phantom*, although none were hits on the order of *Jesus Christ Superstar, Evita,*

Cats, Phantom, or *Starlight Express* (which failed in New York). The London *Aspects of Love* ran four years and *Sunset Boulevard* ran 1,529 performances (but still lost money). *Whistle Down the Wind,* which did not even make it to New York, ran a respectable 1,044 performances in London. Even in London, however, *The Beautiful Game,* another non-starter in New York, closed after only eleven months (and is currently being reworked as *The Boys in the Photograph*), and *The Woman in White* barely lasted 500 performances.

As of this writing Lloyd Webber's next show is on the verge of a production in London, if not New York, in 2009. Consistent with his longtime practice, Lloyd Webber's guests at Sydmonton were treated to a run-through of act I in July 2008. The show is a sequel to *The Phantom of the Opera,* currently called *Phantom: Love Never Dies,* and is based on Frederick Forsyth's 1999 novel *The Phantom of Manhattan.* According to press reports, the new *Phantom* takes place in Coney Island in 1906 where Erik has escaped to run a freak show. For those who feared that marriage to Raoul would thwart her career Christine is now a famous prima donna. Unfortunately, Raoul has turned into a dissolute version of Ravenal, not only broke but "a drunken wreck." *New York Post* reporter Michael Riedel provides another clue to the plot that leads to unanswered questions: "Christine has a child, Gustave, but is his father Raoul or the Phantom? I can't tell you because no one's seen the second act yet."[55]

I began this chapter with analogies between Puccini and Lloyd Webber, two phenomenally successful composers for the theatrical stage who are also burdened by a corresponding lack of critical esteem. One can defend or attack either Puccini or Lloyd Webber, and although probably less common, some might remain neutral or agnostic and simply report the parallel criticisms that have followed these perpetually successful and controversial, well-loved and but loathed composers. When it comes to Lloyd Webber, it is admittedly not easy to help those who passionately disbelieve in Lloyd Webber's work to gain appreciation of this crucially important West End and Broadway composer or those who revere him to discover serious flaws. It should be repeated that, up to this point, the atheists outweigh the faithful and the revisionists. The intention here is to neither praise nor bury Caesar but to try to understand both "the problem of Lloyd Webber" and the pleasure he gives to so many.

Although, as Sternfeld points out, "almost every Lloyd Webber show receives at least a few raves, and most garner mixed reviews rather than outright pans," the criticism of Lloyd Webber and his creative output remains a real problem that I have tried to confront.[56] Perhaps Lloyd Webber has become a symbol, something like Paul Whiteman, a musical figure whose financial success and popularity seem disproportionate to his merits. In the company of music historians I might lead a sheltered life, but I can not think of anyone other than Whiteman or perhaps Kenny G in the jazz field who inspires the kind of antipathy reserved for Lloyd Webber. In any event, as I have tried to show, Andrew Lloyd Webber is a Broadway phenomenon that scholars and historians, if not his idolaters, need to face rather than ignore. His work, although, as I have argued, flawed, has proven lasting and influential as well as popular and merits our attention and respect.

SELECT BIBLIOGRAPHY

Abbott, George. *"Mister Abbott."* New York: Random House, 1963.

Adler, Thomas P. "The Musical Dramas of Stephen Sondheim: Some Critical Approaches." *Journal of Popular Culture* 15 (1978–1979): 513–25.

Alpert, Hollis. *The Life and Times of "Porgy and Bess": The Story of an American Classic.* New York: Knopf, 1990.

Armitage, Merle, ed. *George Gershwin.* New York: Longmans, Green, 1938.

Atkinson, Brooks. *Broadway.* New York: Macmillan, 1970.

Asch, Amy. *The Complete Lyrics of Oscar Hammerstein II.* New York: Knopf, 2008.

Babington, Bruce, and Peter William Evans. *Blue Skies and Silver Linings: Aspects of the Hollywood Musical.* Manchester, England: Manchester University Press, 1985.

Bach, Steven. *Dazzler: The Life and Times of Moss Hart.* New York: 2001.

Banfield, Stephen. *Sondheim's Broadway Musicals.* Ann Arbor: University of Michigan Press, 1993.

———. "Bit by Bit: Five Ways of Looking at Musicals," *Musical Times* 135 (April 1994): 220–23.

———. "Sondheim and the Art that Has No Name." In *Approaches to the American Music*, ed. Robert Lawson-Peebles, 137–60. Exeter: University of Exeter Press, 1996.

———. "Popular Song and Popular Music on Stage and Film." In *The Cambridge History of American Music*, ed. David Nicholls, 309–44. Cambridge: Cambridge University Press, 1998.

———. "Stage and Screen Entertainers in the Twentieth Century." In *The Cambridge Companion to Singing*, ed. John Potter, 63–82. Cambridge: Cambridge University Press, 2000.

———. "Scholarship and the Musical: Reclaiming Jerome Kern," *Proceedings of the British Academy* 125 (2003): 183–210.

Banfield, Stephen. *Jerome Kern*. New Haven: Yale University Press, 2006.

Barrett, Mary Ellin. *Irving Berlin: A Daughter's Memoir*. New York: Simon & Schuster, 1994.

Barrios, Richard. *A Song in the Dark: The Birth of the Musical Film*. New York: Oxford University Press, 1995.

Beckerman, Bernard, and Howard Siegman, eds. *On Stage: Selected Theater Reviews from "The New York Times" 1920–1970*. New York: Arno, 1973.

Berg, A. Scott. *Goldwyn: A Biography*. New York: Knopf, 1989.

Bennett, Robert Russell. *"The Broadway Sound": The Autobiography and Selected Essays of Robert Russell Bennett*, ed. George J. Ferencz. Rochester, New York: University of Rochester Press, 1999.

Bergreen, Laurence. *As Thousands Cheer: The Life of Irving Berlin*. New York: Viking, 1990.

Bernstein, Leonard. "American Musical Comedy." In *The Joy of Music*, 152–79. New York: Simon & Schuster, 1959.

———. *Findings*. New York: Simon & Schuster, 1982.

Blitzstein, Marc. "The Case for Modern Music." *New Masses* 20/3 (July 14, 1936): 27.

———. "The Case for Modern Music, II. Second Generation." *New Masses* 20/4 (July 21, 1936): 28–29.

———. "Author of 'The Cradle' Discusses Broadway Hit." *Daily Worker*, January 3, 1938, 7.

———. "On Writing Music for the Theatre." *Modern Music* 15/2 (January–February 1938): 81–85.

———. *Marc Blitzstein Discusses His Theater Compositions*. Spoken Arts 717 (LP) (1957). Published as "Out of the Cradle," *Opera News* 24/15 (February 13, 1960): 10+; reprinted as "As He Remembered It—The Late Composer's Story of How 'The Cradle' Began Rocking." *New York Times*, April 12, 1964, sec. 2, 13+.

Block, Geoffrey. "Frank Loesser's Sketchbooks for *The Most Happy Fella*." *Musical Quarterly* 73/1 (1989): 60–78.

———. "Gershwin's Buzzard and Other Mythological Creatures." *Opera Quarterly* 7 (Summer 1990): 74–82.

———. "The Broadway Canon from *Show Boat* to *West Side Story* and the European Operatic Ideal." *Journal of Musicology* 11/4 (Fall 1993): 525–44.

———. Review essay, *Sondheim's Broadway Musicals* by Stephen Banfield. *Journal of the Royal Musical Association* 121/1 (1996): 20–27.

———. "Not Only for Cock-Eyed Optimists." *BBC Music Magazine: The Golden Age of Musicals* (Winter 1999): 16–18.

———. *Richard Rodgers*. New Haven: Yale University Press, 2003.

———. Review essay, "'Reading Musicals': Andrew Most's *Making Americans: Jews and the Broadway Musical*." *Journal of Musicology* 21/4 (Fall 2004): 563–84.

———. "The Melody (and the Words) Linger On: Musical Comedies of the 1920s and 1930s." In *The Cambridge Companion to the Musical*. 2nd ed. William A. Everett and Paul R. Laird, 103–23. Cambridge: Cambridge University Press, 2008.

———. "Revisiting the Glorious and Problematic Legacy of the Jazz Age and Depression Musical." *Studies in Musical Theatre* 2/2 (2008): 127–46.

———. "Integration." In *Oxford Handbook of the American Musical*, ed. Raymond Knapp, Mitchell Morris, and Stacy Wolf. New York: Oxford University Press, forthcoming.

Block, Geoffrey, ed. *The Richard Rodgers Reader*. New York: Oxford University Press, 2002.

Bloom, Harold. *Shakespeare: The Invention of the Human*. New York: Riverhead, 1998.

Bordman, Gerald. *American Musical Theatre: A Chronicle*. New York: Oxford University Press, 1978; 2nd ed. New York: Oxford University Press; 3rd ed. New York: Oxford University Press, 2001.

————. *Jerome Kern: His Life and Music.* New York: Oxford University Press, 1980.

————. *American Operetta: from "H. M. S. Pinafore" to "Sweeney Todd."* New York: Oxford University Press, 1981.

————. *American Musical Comedy: From "Adonis" to "Dreamgirls."* New York: Oxford University Press, 1982.

————. *The Oxford Companion to American Theatre.* New York: Oxford University Press, 1984; 2nd ed. New York: Oxford University Press, 1992; 3rd ed. With Thomas S. Hischak. New York: Oxford University Press, 2004.

————. *American Musical Revue: From "The Passing Show" to "Sugar Babies."* New York: Oxford University Press, 1985.

Brecht, Bertolt. "The Modern Theatre Is the Epic Theatre." In *Brecht on Theatre,* ed. and trans. John Willett, 33–42. New York: Hill & Wang, 1964.

————. "On Gestic Music." In *Brecht on Theatre,* ed. and trans. John Willett, 104–6. New York: Hill & Wang, 1964.

————. "On the Use of Music in an Epic Theatre." In *Brecht on Theatre,* ed. and trans. John Willett, 84–90. New York: Hill & Wang, 1964.

Breon, Robin. "*Show Boat*: The Revival, the Racism." *The Drama Review* 39/2 (Summer 1995): 86–105.

Bristow, Eugene K., and J. Kevin Butler. "*Company,* About Face! The Show that Revolutionized the American Musical." *American Music* 5/3 (1987): 241–54.

Brown, Gwynne Kuhner. "Problems of Race and Genre in the Critical Reception of *Porgy and Bess.* Ph.D. dissertation, University of Washington, 2006.

Buchman, Andrew. "Tim Burton's Cinematic *Sweeney Todd* (2007)." Paper presented at the Symposium on the American Musical held at the University of Washington, April 11, 2008.

Burrows, Abe. "The Making of *Guys & Dolls.*" *Atlantic Monthly* (January 1980): 40–47, 50–52.

Burton, Humphrey. *Leonard Bernstein.* New York: Doubleday, 1994.

Butler, J. Kevin (see Bristow).

Bryer, Jackson R., and Richard A. Davison, eds. *The Art of the American Musical: Conversations with the Creators.* New Brunswick, N.J.: Rutgers University Press, 2005.

Carter, Tim. "*Oklahoma!: The Making of an American Musical.* New Haven: Yale University Press, 2007.

Chapin, Ted. *Everything Was Possible: The Birth of the Musical "Follies."* New York: Knopf, 2003.

Citron, Marcia. *Opera on Screen.* New Haven: Yale University Press, 2000.

Citron, Stephen. *Noel & Cole.* New York: Oxford University Press, 1993.

————. *The Wordsmiths: Oscar Hammerstein 2nd and Alan Jay Lerner.* New York: Oxford University Press, 1995.

————. *Sondheim and Lloyd-Webber: The New Musical.* New York: Oxford University Press, 2001.

Clum, John M. *Something for the Boys: Musical Theater and Gay Culture.* New York: St. Martin's Press, 1999.

Costello, Donald P. *The Serpent's Eye: Shaw and the Cinema.* Notre Dame, Ind.: University of Notre Dame Press, 1965.

Crawford, Cheryl. *One Naked Individual.* Indianapolis: Bobbs-Merrill, 1977.

Crawford, Richard. "It Ain't Necessarily Soul: Gershwin's 'Porgy and Bess' as a Symbol." *Yearbook for Inter-American Musical Research* 8 (1972): 17–38.

————. "Gershwin's Reputation: A Note on *Porgy and Bess.*" *Musical Quarterly* 65 (April 1979): 257–64.

————. *The American Musical Landscape.* Berkeley: University of California Press, 1993.

Croce, Arlene. *The Fred Astaire and Ginger Rogers Book.* New York: E. P. Dutton, 1972.

Davis, Lee. *Bolton and Wodehouse and Kern: The Men Who Made Musical Comedy*. New York: James H. Heineman, 1993.

Decker, Todd. "'Do You Want to Hear a Mammy Song:' A Historiography of *Show Boat*. *Contemporary Theatre Review* 19/1 (2009): 8-21.

Denkert, Darcie. *A Fine Romance: Hollywood & Broadway*. New York: Watson-Guptill, 2005.

Dietz, Robert James. "Marc Blitzstein and the 'Agit-Prop' Theatre of the 1930's." *Yearbook for Inter-American Musical Research* 6 (1970): 51–66.

———. "The Operatic Style of Marc Blitzstein in the American 'Agit-Prop' Era." Ph.D. dissertation, University of Iowa, 1970.

Drew, David. "Kurt Weill and His Critics." *Times Literary Supplement*, October 3, 1975, 1142–44; October 10, 1975, 1198–1200.

———. "Weill, Kurt (Julian)." *The New Grove Dictionary of Music and Musicians*. Edited by Stanley Sadie. London: Macmillan, 1980. Vol. 20, 300–310.

———. "Reflections on the Last Years: *Der Kuhhandel* as a Key Work." In *A New Orpheus: Essays on Kurt Weill*, ed. Kim Kowalke, 217–67. New Haven: Yale University Press, 1986.

———. *Kurt Weill: A Handbook*. Berkeley: University of California Press, 1987.

Dudar, Helen. "George Abbott Dusts Off a Broadway Classic." *New York Times*, March 6, 1983, sec. 7, 30.

Edler, Horst (see Kowalke).

Eells, George. *The Life That Late He Led: A Biography of Cole Porter*. New York: G. P. Putnam's Sons, 1967.

Emmet, Linda (see Kimball).

Engel, Lehman. *The American Musical Theater: A Consideration*. New York: Collier, 1967; rev. ed., 1975.

———. *Words with Music: The Broadway Musical Libretto*. New York: Schirmer Books, 1972; Updated and rev. by Howard Kissel as *Words with Music: Creating the Broadway Musical Libretto*. New York: Applause, 2006.

Evans, Peter William (see Babington).

Everett, William A. (see also Prece). *The Musical: A Research and Information Guide*. New York: Routledge, 2004.

———. *Sigmund Romberg*. New Haven: Yale University Press, 2007.

Everett, William A., and Paul R. Laird, eds. *The Cambridge Companion to the Musical*. 2nd ed. Cambridge: Cambridge University Press, 2008.

Ewen, David. "He Passes the Ammunition for Hits." *Theatre Arts* 40/5 (May 1956): 73–75, 90–91.

———. *Richard Rodgers*. New York: Henry Holt, 1957.

———. *George Gershwin: His Journey to Greatness*. New York: Ungar, 1970; 2nd enl. ed., 1986.

———. *New Complete Book of the American Musical Theater*. New York: Holt, Rinehart & Winston, 1970.

Fordin, Hugh. *Getting to Know Him: A Biography of Oscar Hammerstein II*. New York: Ungar, 1977; Da Capo, 1995.

Forte, Allen. *The American Popular Ballad of the Golden Era, 1924–1950*. Princeton: Princeton University Press, 1995.

———. *Listening to Classic American Popular Songs*. New Haven: Yale University Press, 2001.

Freedman, Samuel G. "After 50 Years, 'Porgy' Comes to the Met as a Certified Classic." *New York Times*, February 3, 1985, sec. 2, 1+.

Furia, Philip. *Poets of Tin Pan Alley: A History of America's Great Lyricists*. New York: Oxford University Press, 1990.

——. *Ira Gershwin: The Art of the Lyricist*. New York: Oxford University Press, 1995.

Furia, Philip, with the assistance of Graham Wood. *Irving Berlin: A Life in Song*. New York: Schirmer, 1998.

Gänzl, Kurt. *The Encyclopedia of the Musical Theatre*. 2nd ed., 3 vols. New York: Schirmer, 2000.

Gänzl, Kurt, and Andrew Lamb. *Gänzl's Book of the Musical Theatre*. London: Bodley Head, 1988.

Gates, Henry Louis Jr. "'Authenticity,' or the Lesson of Little Tree." *New York Times Book Review*, November 24, 1991, 1+.

Gershwin, George. "Rhapsody in Catfish Row: Mr. Gershwin Tells the Origin and Scheme for His Music in That New Folk Opera Called 'Porgy and Bess.'" *New York Times*, October 20, 1935, sec. 10, 1–2; reprinted as "Rhapsody in Catfish Row, *George Gershwin*, ed. Merle Armitage, 72–77. New York: Longmans, Green, 1938.

Gershwin, Ira. *Lyrics on Several Occasions*. New York: Knopf, 1959.

Gilbert, Steven E. *The Music of Gershwin*. New Haven: Yale University Press, 1995.

Goldberg, Isaac. *George Gershwin: A Study in American Music*. New York: Simon &Schuster, 1931; reprinted with an extended supplement by Edith Garson. New York: Frederick Ungar, 1958.

Goldman, William. *The Season: A Candid Look at Broadway*. New York: Harcourt, Brace & World, 1969; Limelight, 1984.

Goldstein, Malcolm. *The Political Stage: American Drama and Theater of the Great Depression*. New York: Oxford University Press, 1974.

Goodhart, Sandor, ed. *Reading Stephen Sondheim: A Collection of Critical Essays*. New York: Garland, 2000.

Gordon, Eric A. *Mark the Music: The Life and Work of Marc Blitzstein*. New York: St. Martin's, 1989.

Gordon, Joanne. *Art Isn't Easy: The Theatre of Stephen Sondheim*. New York: Da Capo, 1992.

Gordon, Joanne, ed. *Stephen Sondheim: A Casebook*. New York: Garland, 1997.

Gottfried, Martin. *Broadway Musicals*. New York: Abrams, 1979.

——. *More Broadway Musicals since 1980*. New York: Abrams, 1991.

——. *Sondheim*. New York: Abrams, 1993.

Gottlieb, Jack. "The Music of Leonard Bernstein: A Study of Melodic Manipulations." DMA dissertation, University of Illinois, 1964.

——. *Funny, It Doesn't Sound Jewish: How Yiddish Songs and Synagogue Melodies Influenced Tin Pan Alley, Broadway, and Hollywood*. Albany: State University of New York in association with the Library of Congress, 2004.

Gradenwitz, Peter. *Leonard Bernstein: The Infinite Variety of a Musician*. New York: Berg, 1987.

Grant, Mark. *The Rise and Fall of the Broadway Musical*. Boston: Northeastern University Press, 2004.

Green, Benny, ed. *A Hymn to Him: The Lyrics of Alan Jay Lerner*. New York: Limelight, 1987.

Green, Jesse, "Sondheim Dismembers 'Sweeney.'" *New York Times*, December 16, 2007.

Green, Stanley. *Broadway Musicals of the 30s*. New York: Da Capo, 1971.

——. *Encyclopedia of the Musical Theatre*. New York: Da Capo, 1980.

——. *Rodgers and Hammerstein Fact Book: A Record of Their Works Together and with Other Collaborators*. New York: Lynn Farnol Group, 1980.

——. *The World of Musical Comedy: The Story of the American Musical Stage as Told through the Careers of Its Foremost Composers and Lyricists*. San Diego: A. S. Barnes, 1980; 4th ed., rev. and enl. New York: Da Capo, 1986.

——. *Encyclopedia of the Musical Film*. New York: Oxford University Press, 1981.

Green, Stanley. *Broadway Musicals Show by Show*. Milwaukee, Wisc.: Hal Leonard, 1985.

————. *Hollywood Musicals Year by Year*. Milwaukee, Wisc.: Hal Leonard, 1990.

Green, Stanley, ed. *Rodgers and Hammerstein Fact Book*. New York: Lynn Farnol Group, 1980.

Greenberg, Rodney. *George Gershwin*. London: Phaidon, 1998.

Guernsey, Otis L. Jr. *Curtain Times: The New York Theater 1965–1987*. New York: Applause, 1987.

Guernsey, Otis L. Jr., ed. *Playwrights, Lyricists, Composers, on Theatre*. New York: Dodd, Mead, 1974.

————. *Broadway Song & Story: Playwrights / Lyricists / Composers Discuss Their Hits*. New York: Dodd, Mead, 1985.

Gussow, Mel. "The Phantom's Many Faces over the Years." *New York Times*, January 30, 1988.

————. "'West Side Story': The Beginnings of Something Great." *New York Times*, October 21, 1990, sec. 2, p. 5.

Hamm, Charles. *Yesterdays: Popular Song in America*. New York: W. W. Norton, 1979.

————. *Music in the New World*. New York: W. W. Norton, 1983.

————. "The Theatre Guild Production of *Porgy and Bess*." *Journal of the American Musicological Society* 40 (1987): 495–532.

————. *Putting Popular Music in Its Place*. Cambridge: Cambridge University Press, 1995.

————. *Irving Berlin: Songs from the Melting Pot: The Formative Years, 1907–1914*. New York: Oxford University Press, 1997.

————. "Omnibus Review: Five Recent Books on American Musical Theater." *Kurt Weill Newsletter* 23/2: 9–15.

Hammerstein, Oscar 2nd. "In Re 'Oklahoma!': The Adaptor-Lyricist Describes How the Musical Hit Came into Being." *New York Times*. May 23, 1943, 11.

————. "Turns on a Carousel." *New York Times*, April 15, 1945, sec. 2, 1.

————. "Notes on Lyrics." In *Lyrics*, 3–48. New York: Simon & Schuster, 1949; expanded and ed. by William Hammerstein. Milwaukee, Wisc.: Hal Leonard, 1985.

Harburg, Ernest (see Rosenberg).

Harriman, Margaret Case. *Take Them Up Tenderly: A Collection of Profiles*. New York: Knopf, 1945.

Harrison, Rex. *Rex: An Autobiography*. New York: William Morrow, 1974.

Hart, Dorothy, and Robert Kimball, eds. *The Complete Lyrics of Lorenz Hart*. New York: Knopf, 1986.

Hart, Moss. Preface to *Lady in the Dark*. Vocal score. New York: Chappell Music, 1941.

Hemming, Roy. *The Melody Lingers On: The Great Songwriters and Their Movie Musicals*. New York: Newmarket, 1986.

Hirsch, Foster. *Harold Prince and the American Musical Theatre*. rev. and expanded ed. Cambridge: Cambridge University Press, 1989.

————. "*Porgy and Bess*—The Film." *I.S.A.M. Newsletter* 28/1 (Fall 1998): 12–13.

————. *Kurt Weill on Stage: From Berlin to Broadway*. New York: Knopf, 2002.

Hirschhorn, Clive. *The Hollywood Musical: Every Hollywood Musical from 1927 to the Present Day*. New York: Crown, 1981.

Hirschhorn, Joel (see Kasha).

Hischak, Thomas S. *Boy Loses Girl: Broadway's Librettists*. Lanham, Md.: Scarecrow, 2002.

————. *Through the Screen Door: What Happened to the Broadway Musical When It Went to Hollywood*. Lanham, Md.: Scarecrow, 2004.

Hitchcock, H. Wiley. *Music in the United States*. Englewood Cliffs, N.J.: Prentice Hall, 1969; rev. 3rd ed., 1988.

Holden, Stephen. "A Glimpse of Olden Days, via Cole Porter." *New York Times*, October 18, 1987, sec. 2, 5+.

Horowitz, Mark Eden. *Sondheim on Music: Minor Details and Major Decisions*. Lanham, Md. Scarecrow Press, and Oxford in association with the Library of Congress, 2003.

Horn, David. "From Catfish Row to Granby Street: Contesting Meaning in *Porgy and Bess*." *Popular Music* 13 (1994): 165–74.

Houghton, Norris. "*Romeo and Juliet* and *West Side Story*: An Appreciation." In *Romeo and Juliet/ West Side Story*, 7–14. New York: Dell, 1965.

Houseman, John. *Run-Through*. New York: Simon & Schuster, 1972.

Hubler, Richard G. *The Cole Porter Story* (introduction by Arthur Schwartz). Cleveland: World, 1965.

Hummel, David. *The Collector's Guide to the American Musical Theatre*. 2 vols. Metuchen, N.J.: Scarecrow Press, 1984.

Hunter, John O. "Marc Blitzstein's 'The Cradle Will Rock' as a Document of America, 1937." *American Quarterly* 16 (1964): 227–33.

Hyland, William G. *The Song Is Ended: Songwriters and American Music, 1900–1950*. New York: Oxford University Press, 1995.

———. *Richard Rodgers*. New Haven: Yale University Press, 1998.

Ilson, Carol. *Harold Prince: From "Pajama Game" to "Phantom of the Opera."* Ann Arbor, Michigan: UMI Research Press, 1989.

Jablonski, Edward. *Gershwin: A Biography*. New York: Doubleday, 1987.

———. *Irving Berlin: American Troubadour*. New York: Henry Holt, 1999.

Johnson, Hall. "*Porgy and Bess*—A Folk Opera." *Opportunity* (January 1936): 24–28.

Jones, John Bush. *Our Musicals, Ourselves: A Social History of the American Musical*. Hanover, N.H.: Brandeis University Press, 2003.

Jowitt, Deborah. *Jerome Robbins: His Life, His Theater, His Dance*. New York: Simon & Schuster, 2004.

Kantor, Michael, and Laurence Maslon. *Broadway: The American Musical*, based on the documentary film by Michael Kantor. New York: Bulfinch, 2004.

Kasha, Al, and Joel Hirschhorn. *Conversations with the Great Songwriters*. Chicago: Contemporary, 1985.

Katz, Ephriam. *The Film Encyclopedia: The Most Comprehensive Encyclopedia of World Cinema in a Single Volume*. 2nd ed. New York: HarperPerennial, 1994.

Kawin, Bruce F. (see Mast).

Kennedy, Michael Patrick, and John Muir. *Musicals*. Glasgow: HarperCollins, 1997.

Kerman, Joseph. *Opera as Drama*. New York: Knopf, 1956; new and rev. ed. Berkeley: University of California Press, 1988.

Kimball, Robert., ed. *The Complete Lyrics of Cole Porter*. New York: Vintage Books, 1984.

———. *The Complete Lyrics of Ira Gershwin*. New York: Knopf, 1993.

———. See also D. Hart.

———. See also Krasker.

Kimball, Robert, and Linda Emmet, eds. *The Complete Lyrics of Irving Berlin*. New York: Knopf, 2001.

Kimball, Robert, and Steve Nelson, eds. *The Complete Lyrics of Frank Loesser*. New York: Knopf, 2003.

King, William G. "Music and Musicians. Composer for the Theater—Kurt Weill Talks about 'Practical Music.'" *New York Sun*, February 3, 1940.

Kingman, Daniel. *American Music: A Panorama*. New York: Schirmer, 1979; rev. ed., 1990.

Kirle, Bruce. *Unfinished Business: Broadway Musicals as Works-in-Progress*. Carbondale: Southern Illinois University Press, 2005.

Kivy, Peter. *Osmin's Rage: Philosophical Reflections on Opera, Drama, and Text*. Princeton, N.J.: Princeton University Press, 1988.

Knapp, Raymond. *The American Musical and the Formation of National Identity*. Princeton: Princeton University Press, 2005.

———. *The American Musical and the Performance of Personal Identity*. Princeton: Princeton University Press, 2006.

Kolodin, Irving. "'Porgy and Bess': American Opera in the Theatre." *Theatre Arts Monthly* 19 (1935): 853–65.

Kowalke, Kim H. *Kurt Weill in Europe*. Ann Arbor, Mich.: UMI Research Press, 1979.

———. "*The Threepenny Opera* in America." In *Kurt Weill: "The Threepenny Opera*, ed. Stephen Hinton, 78–120. Cambridge: Cambridge University Press, 1990.

———. "Formerly German: Kurt Weill in America." In *A Stranger Here Myself: Kurt Weill Studien*, ed. Kim H. Kowalke and Horst Edler, 35–57. Hildesheim: Georg Olms Verlag, 1993.

———. "Kurt Weill, Modernism, and Popular Culture: Öffentlichkeit als Stil," *Modernism/Modernity* 2/1 (1995): 27–69.

———. Review essay of *A Chronology of American Musical Theatre* et al. *Journal of the American Musicological Society* 60/3 (Fall 2007): 688–714.

———. See also Symonette.

Kowalke, Kim H., ed. *A New Orpheus: Essays on Kurt Weill*. New Haven: Yale University Press, 1986.

Kowalke, Kim H., and Horst Edler, eds. *A Stranger Here Myself: Kurt Weill Studien*. Hildesheim, Ger.: Georg Olms Verlag, 1993.

Krasker, Tommy, and Robert Kimball. *Catalog of the American Musical: Musicals of Irving Berlin, George and Ira Gershwin, Cole Porter, Richard Rodgers & Lorenz Hart*. Washington, D.C.: National Institute for Opera and Musical Theater, 1988.

Kreuger, Miles. *"Show Boat": The Story of a Classic American Musical*. New York: Oxford University Press, 1977.

———. "Some Words about 'Anything Goes'" and "The Annotated 'Anything Goes.'" Notes to EMI/Angel CDC 7–49848–2 (1989), 9–17 and 133–40.

———. "Some Words about 'Show Boat.'" Notes to EMI/Angel CDS 7–49108–2 (1988), 13–24.

———. See also Morison.

Lahr, John. "Mississippi Mud." *New Yorker*, October 25, 1993, 123–26.

Laird, Paul R. (see also Everett). *Leonard Bernstein: A Guide to Research*. New York: Routledge, 2002.

Laurents, Arthur. *Original Story By: A Memoir of Broadway and Hollywood*. New York: Knopf, 2000.

Lawrence, Greg. *Dance with Demons: The Life of Jerome Robbins*. New York: Berkley, 2001.

Lawson-Peebles., Robert. "Brush Up Your Shakespeare: The Case of *Kiss Me, Kate*." In *Approaches to the American Musical*, ed. Lawson-Peebles, 89–108. Exeter: Exeter Press, 1996.

Lawson-Peebles, Robert, ed. *Approaches to the American Musical*. Exeter: University of Exeter Press, 1996.

Lee, M. Owen. "Recordings." Review of *The Phantom of the Opera* by Andrew Lloyd Webber and *The Complete "Phantom of the Opera"* by George Perry. *Opera Quarterly* 6/1 (Autumn 1988): 147–51.

Lees, Gene. *Inventing Champagne: The Worlds of Lerner and Loewe*. New York: St. Martin's, 1990.

Lenya, Lotte (see Weill).

Lerner, Alan Jay. *The Street Where I Live*. New York: W. W. Norton, 1970.

———. *The Musical Theatre: A Celebration*. London: Collins, 1986.

Leve, James. *John Kander and Fred Ebb*. New Haven: Yale University Press, 2009.

Lieberson, Goddard. "The Ten Musicals Most Worth Preserving." *New York Times Magazine*, August 5, 1956, 26–32.

Litton, Glenn (see Smith).

Loney, Glenn, ed. *Musical Theatre in America: Papers and Proceedings of the Conference on the Musical Theatre in America*. Westport, Conn.: Greenwood, 1984.

Lonoff, Jeffrey. Notes to *A Collector's Sondheim*. CD: RCD3–5480; 3-disc set (1985).

Loesser, Frank. "Some Loesser Thoughts on 'The Most Happy Fella.'" Imperial Theatre program notes, 1956.

———. "Some Notes on a Musical." Imperial Theatre program notes, 1956.

Loesser, Susan. *A Most Remarkable Fella: Frank Loesser and the Guys and Dolls in His Life*. New York: Fine, 1993.

Loney, Glenn, ed. *Musical Theatre in America: Papers and Proceedings of the Conference on the Musical Theatre in America*. Westport, Conn.: Greenwood, 1981.

McBrien, William. *Cole Porter: A Biography*. New York: Knopf, 1998.

mcclung, bruce d. "Psicosi per musica: Re-examining *Lady in the Dark*." *A Stranger Here Myself: Kurt Weill Studien*, Kim H. Kowalke and Horst Edler, eds., 235–65. Hildesheim: Georg Olms Verlag, 1993.

———. "Life after George: The Genesis of *Lady in the Dark*'s Circus Dream." *Kurt Weill Newsletter* 14/2 (Fall 1996): 4–8.

———. *"Lady in the Dark": Biography of a Musical*. New York: Oxford University Press, 2007.

McGlinn, John. "The Original 'Anything Goes'—A Classic Restored." Notes to EMI/Angel CDC 7–49848–2 (1989), 29–34.

———. "Notes on 'Show Boat.'" Notes to EMI/Angel CDS 7–49108–2 (1988), 26–38.

McMillin, Scott. "Paul Robeson, Will Vodery's 'Jubilee Singers,' and the Earliest Script of the Kern-Hammerstein *Show Boat*." *Theater Survey* 41/2 (November 2000): 51–70.

———. *The Musical as Drama: A Study of the Principles and Conventions behind Musical Shows from Kern to Sondheim*. Princeton: Princeton University Press, 2006.

McNally, Terence, Moderator. "West Side Story." In *Playwright, Lyricists, Composers, on Theatre*, ed. Otis Guernsey Jr., 40–54. New York: Dodd, Mead, 1974.

Magee, Jeffrey. "Irving Berlin's 'Blue Skies': Ethnic Affiliations and Musical Transformations," *Musical Quarterly* 84/4 (2000): 537–80.

Mandelbaum, Ken. *"A Chorus Line" and the Musicals of Michael Bennett*. New York: St. Martin's, 1989.

———. *Not Since Carrie: 40 Years of Broadway Musical Flops*. New York: St. Martin's, 1991.

Mann, Martin Arthur. "The Musicals of Frank Loesser." Ph.D. dissertation, City University of New York, 1974.

Maslon, Laurence (see Kantor).

Mast, Gerald. *Can't Help Singin': The American Musical on Stage and Screen*. Woodstock, N.Y.: Overlook Press, 1987.

Mast, Gerald, and Bruce F. Kawin. *The Movies: A Short History*. Rev. and updated. Boston: Allyn and Bacon, 1996.

Mates, Julian. *America's Musical Stage: Two Hundred Years of Musical Theater*. New York: Praeger, 1987.

Mauceri, John. Notes to *On Your Toes*. Polydor 813667–1 Y 1 (1983).

Mellers, Wilfrid. *Music in a New Found Land*. New York: Oxford University Press, 1964; rev. ed., 1987.

Miletich, Leo N. *Broadway's Prize-Winning Musicals: An Annotated Guide for Libraries and Audio Collectors*. New York: Harrington Park Press, 1993.

Miller, Scott. *From "Assassins" to West Side Story: The Director's Guide to Musical Theatre.* Portsmouth, N.H.: Heinemann, 1996.

———. *Destructing Harold Hill: An Insider's Guide to Musical Theatre.* Portsmouth, N.H.: Heinemann, 1996.

———. *Rebels with Applause: Broadway's Groundbreaking Musicals.* Portsmouth, N.H.: Heinemann, 2001.

Mordden, Ethan. *Better Foot Forward: The History of the American Musical Theatre.* New York: Grossman, 1976.

———. *The Hollywood Musical.* New York: St. Martin's, 1981.

———. *Broadway Babies: The People Who Made the American Musical.* New York: Oxford University Press, 1983.

———. "'Show Boat' Crosses Over." *New Yorker,* July 3, 1989, 79–93.

———. *Rodgers & Hammerstein.* New York: Abrams, 1992.

———. *Make Believe: The Broadway Musical in the 1920s.* New York: Oxford University Press, 1997.

———. *Coming Up Roses: The Broadway Musical in the 1950s.* New York: Oxford University Press, 1998.

———. *Beautiful Mornin': The Broadway Musical in the 1940s.* New York: Oxford University Press, 1999.

———. *Open a New Window: The Broadway Musical in the 1960s.* New York: Oxford University Press, 2001.

———. *One More Kiss: The Broadway Musical in the 1970s.* New York: Oxford University Press, 2003.

———. *The Happiest Corpse I've Ever Seen: The Last Twenty-Five Years of the Broadway Musical.* New York: Palgrave Macmillan, 2004.

———. *Sing for Your Supper: The Broadway Musical in the 1930s.* New York: Palgrave Macmillan, 2005.

Morison, Patricia, and Miles Kreuger. "Patricia Morison and Miles Kreuger Discuss the Deleted Songs July 5, 1990." In notes to *Kiss Me, Kate.* EMI/Angel CDS 54033–2, 18–20.

Most, Andrea, *Making Americans: Jews and the Broadway Musical.* Cambridge: Harvard University Press, 2004.

Muir, John (see Kennedy).

Mureller, John. "Fred Astaire and the Integrated Musical." *Cinema Journal* 24/1 (Fall 1984): 28–40.

———. *Astaire Dancing: The Musical Films.* New York: Wings Books, 1985.

Nelson, Steve (see Kimball).

New York Theatre Critics' Reviews. New York: Critics' Theatre Reviews, 1995. [Vols. 1–55, 1940–1994]

Nolan, Frederick. *Lorenz Hart.* New York: Oxford University Press, 1994.

———. *The Sound of Their Music: The Story of Rodgers & Hammerstein.* New York: Applause, 2002.

Norton, Elliot. "Broadway's Cutting Room Floor." *Theatre Arts* 36 (April 1952): 80.

Norton, Richard C. *A Chronology of American Musical Theatre.* 3 vols. New York: Oxford University Press, 2002.

Oja, Carol J. "Marc Blitzstein's *The Cradle Will Rock* and Mass-Song Style of the 1930s." *Musical Quarterly* 73/4 (1989): 445–75.

Osborne, Conrad L. "'Happy Fella' Yields Up Its Operatic Heart." *New York Times,* 1 September 1991, sec. 2, 5, and 17.

Perry, George. *The Complete "Phantom of the Opera."* New York: Holt, 1987.

———. *Andrew Lloyd Webber's "The Phantom of the Opera Companion."* Contains Original Screenplay. London: Pavilion, 2004.

Peyser, Joan. *Leonard Bernstein: A Biography.* New York: William Morrow, 1987.

———. *The Memory of All That: The Life of George Gershwin.* New York: 1993.

Platt, Len. See Walsh.

Pollack, Howard. *George Gershwin: His Life and Work.* Berkeley: University of California Press, 2006.

Portantiere, Michael. *The Theatermania Guide to Musical Theater Recordings.* New York: Back Stage, 2004.

Prece, Paul, and William A. Everett. "The Megamusical: The Creation, Internationalization and Impact of a Genre." In *The Cambridge Companion to the Musical.* 2nd ed. William A. Everett and Paul R. Laird, 103–23. Cambridge: Cambridge University Press, 2008.

Prince, Harold. *Contradictions: Notes on Twenty-six Years in the Theatre.* New York: Dodd, Mead, 1974.

———. See also Sondheim, "Author and Director: Musicals." In Redmond, James, ed. *Themes in Drama.* Vol. 3. Cambridge: Cambridge University Press, 1981.

Reid, Louis R. "Composing While You Wait." *Dramatic Mirror,* June 2, 1917, 5.

Riis, Thomas L. *Frank Loesser.* New Haven: Yale University Press, 2008.

Rich, Frank. *Hot Seat: Theater Criticism for "The New York Times," 1980–1993.* New York: Random House, 1998.

Robbins, Tim. *"Cradle Will Rock": The Movie and the Moment.* New York: Newmarket, 2000.

Robinson, Paul. *Opera & Ideas: From Mozart to Strauss.* Ithaca, N.Y.: Cornell University Press, 1985.

———. "Reading Libretti and Misreading Opera." In *Opera, Sex, and Other Vital Matters,* 30–51. Chicago: University of Chicago Press, 2002.

Rodgers, Richard. *Musical Stages: An Autobiography.* New York: Random House, 1975; repr. with an introduction by Mary Rodgers. New York: Da Capo, 1995, 2000.

Rosenberg, Bernard, and Ernest Harburg. *The Broadway Musical: Collaboration in Commerce and Art.* New York: New York University Press, 1993.

Rosenberg, Deena. *Fascinating Rhythm: The Collaboration of George and Ira Gershwin.* New York: Dutton, 1991.

Salisbury, Mark. *Sweeney Todd: The Demon Barber of Fleet Street.* With Extracts from the Screenplay by John Logan. London: Titan, 2007.

Sanders, Ronald. *The Days Grow Short: The Life and Music of Kurt Weill.* New York: Holt, Rinehart & Winston, 1980.

Savran, David. *A Queer Sort of Materialism: Recontextualizing American Theater.* Ann Arbor: University of Michigan Press, 2003.

Schebera, Jürgen. *Kurt Weill: An Illustrated Life.* New Haven: Yale University Press, 1995.

Schiff, David. "Re-hearing Bernstein." *Atlantic Monthly* (June 1993): 55–76.

Schneider, Wayne, ed. *The Gershwin Style: New Looks at the Music of George Gershwin.* New York: Oxford University Press, 1999.

Schwartz, Charles. *Cole Porter: A Biography.* New York: Dial Press, 1977.

———. *Gershwin: His Life & Music.* New York: Da Capo, 1979.

Scott, Matthew. "Weill in America: The Problem of Revival." In *A New Orpheus,* ed. Kim H. Kowalke, 285–95. New Haven: Yale University Press, 1986.

Secrest, Meryle. *Leonard Bernstein: A Life.* New York: Knopf, 1994.

———. *Stephen Sondheim: A Life.* New York: Knopf, 1998.

Secrest, Meryle. *Somewhere for Me: A Biography of Richard Rodgers*. Knopf, 2001.

Simon, Robert. "Jerome Kern." *Modern Music* 6/2 (January–February 1929): 20–25.

Singer, Barry. *Ever After: The Last Years of Musical Theater and Beyond*. New York: Applause, 2004.

Shirley, Wayne. *"Porgy and Bess."* *Quarterly Journal of the Library of Congress* 31 (1974): 97–107.

———. "Reconciliation on Catfish Row: Bess, Serena, and the Short Score of *Porgy and Bess*." *Quarterly Journal of the Library of Congress* 38 (1981): 144–65.

Shout, John D. "The Musical Theater of Marc Blitzstein." *American Music* 3 (Winter 1985): 413–28.

Siebert, Lynn Laitman. "Cole Porter: An Analysis of Five Musical Comedies and a Thematic Catalogue of the Complete Works." Ph.D. dissertation, City University of New York, 1974.

Simon, Robert. "Jerome Kern." *Modern Music* 6/2 (January–February 1929): 20–25.

Smith, Cecil, and Glenn Litton. *Musical Comedy in America*. New York: Theatre Arts Books, 1950 and 1981.

Smith, June. "Cole Porter in the American Musical Theatre." In *Themes in Drama*, Vol. 3, ed. James Redmond, 47–70. Cambridge: Cambridge University Press, 1981.

Snelson, John. *Andrew Lloyd Webber*. New Haven: Yale University Press, 2004.

Sondheim, Stephen. "Theater Lyrics." In *Playwright, Lyricists, Composers, on Theatre*, ed. Otis Guernsey Jr., 61–97. New York: Dodd, Mead, 1974.

———. "Larger than Life: Reflections on Melodrama and *Sweeney Todd*." In *Melodrama*, ed. Daniel Gerould, 3–14. New York: New York Literary Forum, 1980.

———. "An Anecdote." In *Bernstein on Broadway*, xi–xii. New York and London: Amberson/ G. Schirmer, 1981.

———. "Author and Director: Musicals" (with Harold Prince). In *Broadway Song & Story: Playwrights / Lyricists/ Composers Discuss Their Hits*, ed. Otis Guernsey Jr., 355–70. New York: Dodd, Mead, 1985.

———. "The Musical Theater: A Talk by Stephen Sondheim." In *Broadway Song & Story: Playwrights / Lyricists/ Composers Discuss Their Hits*, ed. Otis Guernsey Jr., 228–50. New York: Dodd, Mead, 1985.

———. "Interview with Stephen Sondheim." In David Savran, *In Their Own Words: Contemporary American Playwrights*, 223–39. New York: Theatre Communications Group, 1988.

———. "Stephen Sondheim in a Q & A Session: Part I." *Dramatists Guild Quarterly* 28/1 (1991): 8–15.

———. "Stephen Sondheim in a Q & A Session: Part II." *Dramatists Guild Quarterly* 28/2 (1991): 10–17.

———. "The Art of the Musical." *Paris Review* 142 (Spring 1997): 259–78.

———. "The Musical Theater." In *Broadway Song & Story: Playwrights / Lyricists/ Composers Discuss Their Hits*, ed. Otis Guernsey Jr., 228–50. New York: Dodd, Mead, 1985.

———. "Interview with Stephen Sondheim." In "2-Disc Special Edition, Special Feature, "Musical Mayhem: Sondheim's *Sweeney Todd*." DreamWorks Pictures 2007.

Sondheim, Steve. " 'Guys and Dolls,' " *Films in Review* 6 (December 1955): 524–25.

Spewack, Bella. "How to Write a Musical Comedy." In *"Kiss Me Kate": A Musical Play*, book by Samuel and Bella Spewack, lyrics by Cole Porter. New York: Knopf, 1953.

Starr, Lawrence. "Gershwin's 'Bess, You Is My Woman Now': The Sophistication and Subtlety of a Great Tune." *Musical Quarterly* 72 (1986): 429–48.

———. "Toward a Reevaluation of Gershwin's *Porgy and Bess*. *American Music* 2 (Summer 1984): 25–37.

———. "The Broadway Musical as a Critique of Modernist Culture, or Sunday in the Park with Sondheim." Paper presented at the Society of American Music (formerly the Sonneck Society), at the 1989 Annual Meeting in Nashville.

———. *George Gershwin*. New Haven: Yale University Press, forthcoming.

Stempel, Larry. "Broadway's Mozartean Moment, or An Amadeus in Amber." In *Sennets & Tuckets: A Bernstein Celebration*, ed. Steven Ledbetter, 39–55. Boston: David R. Godine, 1988.

———. "The Musical Play Expands." *American Music* 10 (1992): 136–69.

———. "*Street Scene* and the Enigma of Broadway Opera." In *A New Orpheus: Essays on Kurt Weill*, ed. Kim H. Kowalke, 321–41. New Haven: Yale University Press, 1986.

Sternfeld, Jessica. *The Megamusical*. Bloomington: Indiana University Press, 2006.

Stewart, John. *Broadway Musicals, 1943–2004*. Jefferson, N.C.: McFarland, 2006.

Steyn, Mark. *Broadway Babies Say Goodnight: Musicals Then and Now*. New York: Routledge, 1997.

Suskin, Steven. *Berlin, Kern, Rodgers, Hart, and Hammerstein: A Complete Song Catalogue*. Jefferson, N.C.: McFarland, 1990.

———. *Opening Night on Broadway: A Critical Quotebook of the Golden Era of the Musical Theatre, "Oklahoma!" (1943) to "Fiddler on the Roof" (1964)*. New York: Schirmer, 1990.

———. *Show Tunes: The Songs, Shows, and Careers of Broadway's Major Composers*, rev. and expanded 3rd ed. New York: Oxford University Press, 1990.

Swain, Joseph P. *The Broadway Musical: A Critical and Musical Survey*. New York: Oxford University Press, 1990; 2nd ed. Lanham, Md.: Scarecrow, 2002.

Swayne, Steven. "Hearing Sondheim's Voices." Ph.D. dissertation, University of California, Berkeley, 1999.

———. *How Sondheim Found His Sound*. Ann Arbor: University of Michigan Press, 2005.

Symonette, Lys, and Kim H. Kowalke, eds. and trans. *Speak Low (When You Speak Love): The Letters of Kurt Weill and Lotte Lenya*. Berkeley: University of California Press, 1996.

Teachout, Terry. " 'Cradle of Lies." *Commentary* (February 2000): 51–55.

Thompson, Era Bell. "Why Negroes Don't Like 'Porgy and Bess.' " *Ebony* 14/12 (October 1959): 51–53.

Thomson, Virgil. "George Gershwin." *Modern Music* 13 (November–December 1935): 13–19; reprinted in *A Virgil Thomson Reader*, 23–27. Boston: Houghton Mifflin, 1981.

———. "In the Theatre." *Modern Music* 15 (January–February 1938): 113.

Walsh, David, and Len Platt. *Musical Theater and American Culture*. Wesport, Conn.: Praeger, 2003.

Walsh, Michael. *Andrew Lloyd Webber: His Life and Works*. New York: Abrams, 1989; rev. and enl. 2nd ed., 1997.

Weill, Kurt. Notes for the original cast recording of *Street Scene*. Columbia OL 4139.

———. "Über den gestischen Charakter der Musik." *Die Musik* 21 (March 1929): 419–23; English version in Kowalke, *Kurt Weill in Europe*, 491–96.

Weill, Kurt, and Lotte Lenya. *Speak Low (When You Speak Love): The Letters of Kurt Weill and Lotte Lenye*, trans. and ed. Lys Symonette and Kim H. Kowalke. Berkeley: University of California Press, 1996.

Welsh, John. "From Play to Musical: Comparative Studies of Ferenc Molnar's 'Liliom' with Richard Rodgers' and Oscar Hammerstein II's 'Carousel'; and Sidney Howard's 'They Knew What They Wanted' with Frank Loesser's 'The Most Happy Fella.' " Ph.D. dissertation, Tulane University, 1967.

Wilder, Alex. *American Popular Song: The Great Innovators 1900–1950*. New York: Oxford University Press, 1972.

Wilk, Max. *They're Playing Our Song.* New York: Zoetrope, 1986.

Williams, Linda. *Playing the Race Card: Melodramas of Black and White from Uncle Tom to O. J. Simpson.* Princeton, N.J.: Princeton University Press, 2001.

Williams, Mary E., ed. *Readings on "West Side Story."* San Diego: Greenhaven, 2001.

Wilson, Alexandra. *The Puccini Problem: Opera, Nationalism, and Modernity.* Cambridge: Cambridge University Press, 2007.

Wolf, Stacy. *A Problem Like Maria: Gender and Sexuality in the American Musical.* Ann Arbor: University of Michigan Press, 2002.

Woll, Allen. *Black Musical Theatre: From "Coontown" to "Dreamgirls."* Baton Rouge: Louisiana State University Press, 1989.

Wood, Graham. "The Development of Song Forms in the Broadway and Hollywood Musicals of Richard Rodgers, 1919–1943." Ph.D. dissertation, University of Minnesota, 2000.

———. "Distant Cousin or Fraternal Twin? Analytical Approaches to the Film Musical." In *The Cambridge Companion to the Musical.* 2nd ed., ed. William A Everett and Paul R.Laird, 305–24. Cambridge: Cambridge University Press, 2008.

Wyatt, Robert, and John Andrew Johnson, eds. *The George Gershwin Reader.* New York: Oxford University Press, 2004.

Zadan, Craig. *Sondheim & Co.* New York: Harper & Row, 1974; 2nd ed. 1986.

INDEX

A Guide to the Index

- The Index includes all names and works in the main text and selective entries for names and works that appear in the online website (Synopses, Discography and Filmography, Appendices, and Notes).
- Titles in **bold** indicate the major shows and films discussed in *Enchanted Evenings*.
- Titles of musicals, films, plays, operas, novels, and miscellaneous other works are placed in *italics*.
- Titles of songs are placed in "quotes."
- Composers and authors are placed in parentheses after the title, and categories of works other than musicals are indicated in [brackets].
- Page numbers in *italics* indicate musical examples.
- Page numbers in **bold** indicate drawings and photographs.
- Numbers preceded by a W indicate pages in the online website.